T0338499

Extracting Knowledge From Opinion Mining

Rashmi Agrawal
Manav Rachna International Institute of Research and Studies, India

Neha Gupta
Manav Rachna International Institute of Research and Studies, India

A volume in the Advances in Data
Mining and Database Management
(ADMDM) Book Series

Published in the United States of America by
    IGI Global
    Engineering Science Reference (an imprint of IGI Global)
    701 E. Chocolate Avenue
    Hershey PA, USA 17033
    Tel: 717-533-8845
    Fax: 717-533-8661
    E-mail: cust@igi-global.com
    Web site: http://www.igi-global.com

Library of Congress Cataloging-in-Publication Data

Names: Agrawal, Rashmi, editor. | Gupta, Neha, editor.
Title: Extracting knowledge from opinion mining / Rashmi Agrawal and Neha
  Gupta, editors.
Description: Hershey PA : Engineering Science Reference, an imprint of IGI
  Global, [2019] | Includes bibliographical references and index.
Identifiers: LCCN 2018001725| ISBN 9781522561170 (hardcover) | ISBN
  9781522561187 (ebook)
Subjects: LCSH: Data mining. | Discourse analysis--Data processing. |
  Language and emotions. | Public opinion.
Classification: LCC QA76.9.D343 E9984 2019 | DDC 006.3/12--dc23 LC record available at
https://lccn.loc.gov/2018001725

This book is published in the IGI Global book series Advances in Data Mining and Database Management (ADMDM) (ISSN: 2327-1981; eISSN: 2327-199X)

British Cataloguing in Publication Data
A Cataloguing in Publication record for this book is available from the British Library.

For electronic access to this publication, please contact: eresources@igi-global.com.

Advances in Data Mining and Database Management (ADMDM) Book Series

ISSN:2327-1981
EISSN:2327-199X

Editor-in-Chief: David Taniar, Monash University, Australia

MISSION

With the large amounts of information available to organizations in today's digital world, there is a need for continual research surrounding emerging methods and tools for collecting, analyzing, and storing data.

The **Advances in Data Mining & Database Management (ADMDM)** series aims to bring together research in information retrieval, data analysis, data warehousing, and related areas in order to become an ideal resource for those working and studying in these fields. IT professionals, software engineers, academicians and upper-level students will find titles within the ADMDM book series particularly useful for staying up-to-date on emerging research, theories, and applications in the fields of data mining and database management.

COVERAGE

- Decision Support Systems
- Data quality
- Association Rule Learning
- Text mining
- Database Testing
- Heterogeneous and Distributed Databases
- Educational Data Mining
- Data Mining
- Neural Networks
- Web Mining

IGI Global is currently accepting manuscripts for publication within this series. To submit a proposal for a volume in this series, please contact our Acquisition Editors at Acquisitions@igi-global.com or visit: http://www.igi-global.com/publish/.

Titles in this Series

For a list of additional titles in this series, please visit:
https://www.igi-global.com/book-series/advances-data-mining-database-management/37146

Optimization Techniques for Problem Solving in Uncertainty
Surafel Luleseged Tilahun (University of Zululand, South Africa) and Jean Medard T. Ngnotchouye (University of KwaZulu-Natal, South Africa)
Engineering Science Reference • ©2018 • 313pp • H/C (ISBN: 9781522550914) • US $195.00

Predictive Analysis on Large Data for Actionable Knowledge Emerging Research and ...
Muhammad Usman (Shaheed Zulfikar Ali Bhutto Institute of Science and Technology, Pakistan) and M. Usman (Pakistan Scientific and Technological Information Center (PASTIC), Pakistan)
Information Science Reference • ©2018 • 177pp • H/C (ISBN: 9781522550297) • US $135.00

Handbook of Research on Big Data Storage and Visualization Techniques
Richard S. Segall (Arkansas State University, USA) and Jeffrey S. Cook (Independent Researcher, USA)
Engineering Science Reference • ©2018 • 917pp • H/C (ISBN: 9781522531425) • US $565.00

Bridging Relational and NoSQL Databases
Drazena Gaspar (University of Mostar, Bosnia and Herzegovina) and Ivica Coric (Hera Software Company, Bosnia and Herzegovina)
Information Science Reference • ©2018 • 338pp • H/C (ISBN: 9781522533856) • US $185.00

Advancements in Applied Metaheuristic Computing
Nilanjan Dey (Techno India College of Technology, India)
Engineering Science Reference • ©2018 • 335pp • H/C (ISBN: 9781522541516) • US $225.00

Applications of Finite Markov Chains and Fuzzy Logic in Learning Contexts Emerging ...
Michael Voskoglou (Graduate Technological Educational Institute of Western Greece, Greece)
Engineering Science Reference • ©2018 • 193pp • H/C (ISBN: 9781522533283) • US $175.00

For an entire list of titles in this series, please visit:
https://www.igi-global.com/book-series/advances-data-mining-database-management/37146

701 East Chocolate Avenue, Hershey, PA 17033, USA
Tel: 717-533-8845 x100 • Fax: 717-533-8661
E-Mail: cust@igi-global.com • www.igi-global.com

Table of Contents

Foreword xvi

Preface xviii

Acknowledgment xxvi

Section 1
Introductory Concepts of Opinion Mining

Chapter 1
Fundamentals of Opinion Mining 1
    Ashish Seth, INHA University, Tashkent, India
    Kirti Seth, INHA University, Tashkent, India

Chapter 2
Feature Based Opinion Mining 20
    Mridula Batra, Manav Rachna International Institute of Research and
        Studies, India
    Vishaw Jyoti, Manav Rachna International Institute of Research and
        Studies, India

Chapter 3
Deep Learning for Opinion Mining 40
    Iman Raeesi Vanani, Allameh Tabataba'i University, Iran
    Morteza Amirhosseini, Allameh Tabataba'i University, Iran

Chapter 4
Opinion Mining: Using Machine Learning Techniques 66
    Vijender Kumar Solanki, CMR Institute of Technology (Autonomous)
        Hyderabad, India
    Nguyen Ha Huy Cuong, Quang Nam University, Vietnam
    Zonghyu (Joan) Lu, University of Huddersfield, UK

Section 2
Ontologies and Their Applications

Chapter 5
Ontology-Based Opinion Mining 84
    Chitra Jalota, Manav Rachna International Institute of Research and
        Studies, India
    Rashmi Agrawal, Manav Rachna International Institute of Research and
        Studies, India

Chapter 6
Ontologies, Repository, and Information Mining in Component-Based
Software Engineering Environment...104
    Rajesh Kumar Bawa, Punjabi University, India
    Iqbaldeep Kaur, Punjabi University, India

Chapter 7
Ontology-Based Opinion Mining for Online Product Reviews 123
    Farheen Siddiqui, Jamia Hamdard, India
    Parul Agarwal, Jamia Hamdard, India

Chapter 8
Applications of Ontology-Based Opinion Mining..149
    Razia Sulthana, SRM Institute of Science and Technology, India
    Subburaj Ramasamy, SRM Institute of Science and Technology, India

Section 3
Tools and Techniques of Opinion Mining

Chapter 9
Tools of Opinion Mining 179
    Neha Gupta, Manav Rachna International Institute of Research and
        Studies, India
    Siddharth Verma, Manav Rachna International Institute of Research
        and Studies, India

Chapter 10
Sentimental Analysis Tools...204
    Sunil M. E., PESITM, India
    Vinay S., PES College of Engineering, India

Chapter 11
Anatomizing Lexicon With Natural Language Tokenizer Toolkit 3 232
 Simran Kaur Jolly, Manav Rachna International Institute of Research
  and Studies, India
 Rashmi Agrawal, Manav Rachna International Institute of Research and
  Studies, India

Section 4
Challenges and Open Issues of Opinion Mining

Chapter 12
Challenges of Text Analytics in Opinion Mining 268
 Vaishali Kalra, Manav Rachna International Institute of Research and
  Studies, India
 Rashmi Agrawal, Manav Rachna International Institute of Research and
  Studies, India

Chapter 13
Open Issues in Opinion Mining 283
 Vishal Vyas, Pondicherry University, India
 V. Uma, Pondicherry University, India

Section 5
Case Study

Chapter 14
Case Study: Efficient Faculty Recruitment Using Genetic Algorithm 299
 Amit Verma, Chandigarh Engineering College, India
 Iqbaldeep Kaur, Chandigarh Engineering College, India
 Dolly Sharma, Chandigarh Group of Colleges, India
 Inderjeet Singh, Chandigarh Group of Colleges, India

Compilation of References 312

About the Contributors 337

Index...344

Detailed Table of Contents

Foreword xvi

Preface xviii

Acknowledgment xxvi

Section 1
Introductory Concepts of Opinion Mining

Chapter 1
Fundamentals of Opinion Mining 1
Ashish Seth, INHA University, Tashkent, India
Kirti Seth, INHA University, Tashkent, India

Mining techniques in computer science have been evolving for the last two decades. Opinion mining is the latest buzzword in this evolution and goes to a deeper level to understand the drive behind people's behavior. Due to the richness of social media opinions, emotions, and sentiments, opinion mining examines that how people feel about a given situation, be it positive or negative. This chapter primarily focuses on explaining the fundamentals of opinion mining along with sentiment analysis. It covers the brief evolution in mining techniques in the last decade. The chapter elaborates on the significance of opinion mining in today's scenario and its features. It also includes a section to discuss the applications, challenges and research scope in opinion mining.

Chapter 2
Feature Based Opinion Mining 20
Mridula Batra, Manav Rachna International Institute of Research and
Studies, India
Vishaw Jyoti, Manav Rachna International Institute of Research and
Studies, India

Opinion mining is the estimated learning of user's beliefs, evaluation and sentiments about units, actions and its features. This method has several features matched with data mining techniques, language processing methods and feature oriented data abstraction. This seems to be extremely difficult to mine opinions from analysis those exist in common human used language. Views are very essentials when one desires to construct a judgment. Data abstraction is an important characteristic for decision making applicable to individuals and organization of different nature. While selecting and purchasing a particular product, it is always beneficial for an individual to collect other views for correct decision making. One association wants to conduct surveys and gather opinions to develop their product excellence. Internet as a source of information, having a number of websites available with the customer reviews as a number of products, it is easy to extract the features from these opinions, sentiments and view, is a task comes under feature-based opinion mining.

Chapter 3

Deep Learning for Opinion Mining 40
Iman Raeesi Vanani, Allameh Tabataba'i University, Iran
Morteza Amirhosseini, Allameh Tabataba'i University, Iran

In this chapter, through introducing the deep learning and relation between deep learning and artificial intelligence, and especially machine learning, the authors discuss machine learning and deep learning techniques, the literature focuses on applied deep learning techniques for extracting opinions. It can be found that opinion mining without using deep learning is not meaningful. In this way, authors mention the history of deep learning and appearance of it and some important and useful deep learning algorithms for opinion mining; learning methods and customized deep learning techniques for opinion mining will also be described to understand how these algorithms and techniques are used as an applicable solution. Future trends of deep learning in opinion mining are introduced through some clues about the applications and future usages of deep learning and opinion mining and how intelligent agents develop automatic deep learning. Finally, authors have summarized different sections of the chapter at conclusion.

Chapter 4

Opinion Mining: Using Machine Learning Techniques 66
Vijender Kumar Solanki, CMR Institute of Technology (Autonomous) Hyderabad, India
Nguyen Ha Huy Cuong, Quang Nam University, Vietnam
Zonghyu (Joan) Lu, University of Huddersfield, UK

The machine learning is the emerging research domain, from which number of emerging trends are available, among them opinion mining is the one technology attraction through which the we could get analysis of the interested domain or we can say about the review from the customer towards any product or we can say any upcoming trending information. These two are the emerging words and we can say it's the buzz word in the information technology. As you will see that its widely use by the corporate sector to uplift the business next level. Before two decade you will not read any words e.g., Opinion mining or Sentiment analysis, but in the last two decade these words have given a new life to information technology domain as well as to the business. The important question which runs in the mind is why use sentiment analysis or opinion mining. The information technology has given number of new programming languages, new innovation and within that the data mining has given this trends to the users. The chapter is covering the three major concept's which comes under the machine learning e.g., Decision tree, Bayesian network and Support vector machine. The chapter is describing the basic inputs, and how it helps in supporting stakeholders by adopting these technologies.

Section 2
Ontologies and Their Applications

Chapter 5
Ontology-Based Opinion Mining 84
    *Chitra Jalota, Manav Rachna International Institute of Research and
        Studies, India*
    *Rashmi Agrawal, Manav Rachna International Institute of Research and
        Studies, India*

E-commerce business is very popular as a large amount of data is available on the internet in the form of unstructured data. To find new market trends and insight, it is very important for an organization to track the customers' opinions/reviews on a regular basis. Reviews available on the internet are very scattered and heterogeneous (i.e., structured as well as unstructured form of data). A good decision is always based on the quality of information within a specified period of time. Ontology is an explicit detailed study of concepts. The word ontology is borrowed from philosophy. It can also be defined as systematic maintenance of information about the things which already exist. In computer science, it could be said that it is a formal representation of knowledge with the help of a fixed set of believed concepts and the relationship between those concepts.

Chapter 6
Ontologies, Repository, and Information Mining in Component-Based
Software Engineering Environment..104
    Rajesh Kumar Bawa, Punjabi University, India
    Iqbaldeep Kaur, Punjabi University, India

This chapter reviews some ontologies, tools, and editors used in building and maintaining the ontology from those reported in the literature, and the main focus is on the interoperability between them. The essential thing while developing an ontology or using an ontology from world web are tools. Through tools, ontology can either be developed or aligned in a manner that the researcher wants and given direction in term of opinion from the source files as meta data. This chapter presents various editors for building the ontology and various tools for matching between the two ontologies and conclusion based on the repository extracted as from the data in term of mining results. Comparison of various ontologies, tools, and editors are also there in order for the ease of user to access a particular ontology tool for selection of data in term of repository or components from the enormous data.

Chapter 7

Ontology-Based Opinion Mining for Online Product Reviews 123
Farheen Siddiqui, Jamia Hamdard, India
Parul Agarwal, Jamia Hamdard, India

In this chapter, the authors work at the feature level opinion mining and make a user-centric selection of each feature. Then they preprocess the data using techniques like sentence splitting, stemming, and many more. Ontology plays an important role in annotating documents with metadata, improving the performance of information extraction and reasoning, and making data interoperable between different applications. In order to build ontology in the method, the authors use (product) domain ontology, ConceptNet, and word net databases. They discuss the current approaches being used for the same by an extensive literature survey. In addition, an approach used for ontology-based mining is proposed and exploited using a product as a case study. This is supported by implementation. The chapter concludes with results and discussion.

Chapter 8

Applications of Ontology-Based Opinion Mining..149
Razia Sulthana, SRM Institute of Science and Technology, India
Subburaj Ramasamy, SRM Institute of Science and Technology, India

Ontology provides a technique to formulate and present queries to databases either stand-alone or web-based. Ontology has been conceived to produce reusable queries to extract rules matching them, and hence, it saves time and effort in creating new ontology-based queries. Ontology can be incorporated in the machine learning process, which hierarchically defines the relationship between concepts, axioms, and terms in the domain. Ontology rule mining has been found to be efficient as compared to other well-known rule mining methods like taxonomy and decision trees. In this chapter, the authors carry out a detailed survey about ontology-related information comprising classification, creation, learning, reuse, and application. The authors also discuss the reusability and the tools used for reusing ontology. Ontology has a life cycle of its own similar to the software development life cycle. The classification-supervised machine learning technique and clustering and the unsupervised machine learning are supported by the ontology. The authors also discuss some of the open issues in creation and application of ontology.

Section 3
Tools and Techniques of Opinion Mining

Chapter 9

Tools of Opinion Mining 179
Neha Gupta, Manav Rachna International Institute of Research and Studies, India
Siddharth Verma, Manav Rachna International Institute of Research and Studies, India

Today's generation express their views and opinions publicly. For any organization or for individuals, this feedback is very crucial to improve their products and services. This huge volume of reviews can be analyzed by opinion mining (also known as semantic analysis). It is an emerging field for researchers that aims to distinguish the emotions expressed within the reviews, classifying them into positive or negative opinions, and summarizing it into a form that is easily understood by users. The idea of opinion mining and sentiment analysis tool is to process a set of search results for a given item based on the quality and features. Research has been conducted to mine opinions in form of document, sentence, and feature level sentiment analysis. This chapter examines how opinion mining is moving to the sentimental reviews of Twitter data, comments used in Facebook on pictures, videos, or Facebook statuses. Thus, this chapter discusses an overview of opinion mining in detail with the techniques and tools.

Chapter 10

Sentimental Analysis Tools...204
Sunil M. E., PESITM, India
Vinay S., PES College of Engineering, India

Opinion mining, also known as sentimental analysis, is the analysis of sentiment (emotion, affection, experience) towards the target object. In the present era, everyone is interested to know the opinions of others before making a decision or performing a task. Hence, it is necessary to collect the information (features) from relatives, friends, or web. These opinions or feedbacks help them to decide their action. With the advent of social media and use of digital technologies, web is a huge resource for data. However, it is time-consuming to read the data collected from the web and analyze it to arrive at informed decisions. This chapter provides complete overview of tools to simplify the operations of opinion mining like data collection, data cleaning, and visualization of predicted sentiment.

Chapter 11
Anatomizing Lexicon With Natural Language Tokenizer Toolkit 3 232
    Simran Kaur Jolly, Manav Rachna International Institute of Research
        and Studies, India
    Rashmi Agrawal, Manav Rachna International Institute of Research and
        Studies, India

NLTK toolkit is an API platform built with Python language to interact with humans through natural language. The very first version of NLTK was released in 2005 (1.4.3), which was compatible with Python 2.4. The latest version was in September 2017 NLTK (3.2.5), which incorporated features like Arabic stemmers, NIST evaluation, MOSES tokenizer, Stanford segmenter, treebank detokenizer, verbnet, and vader, etc. NLTK was created in 2001 as a part of Computational Linguistic Department at the University of Pennsylvania. Since then it has been tested and developed. The important packages of this system are 1) corpus builder, 2) tokenizer, 3) collocation, 4) tagging, 5) parsing, 6) metrics, and 7) probability distribution system. Toolbox NLTK was built to meet four primary requirements: 1) Simplicity: An substantive framework for building blocks; 2) Consistency: Consistent interface; 3) Extensibility: Which can be easily scaled; and 4) Modularity: All modules are independent of each other.

Section 4
Challenges and Open Issues of Opinion Mining

Chapter 12
Challenges of Text Analytics in Opinion Mining 268
    Vaishali Kalra, Manav Rachna International Institute of Research and
        Studies, India
    Rashmi Agrawal, Manav Rachna International Institute of Research and
        Studies, India

Text analysis is the task of knowledge distillation from unstructured text. Due to increase in sharing of information over the web in text format, users required tools and techniques for the analysis of the text. These techniques can be used in two ways: One, this can be used for clustering, classification, and visualization of the data. Two, this can be used for predicting the future aspects, for example, in share market. But all these tasks are not easy to perform, as there are lots of challenges in converting the text into the format onto which various actions can be taken. In this chapter, the authors have discussed the framework of text analysis, followed by the background where they have discussed the steps for transforming the text into the structured form. They have shed light on its industry application along with the technological and non-technological challenges in text analysis.

Chapter 13
Open Issues in Opinion Mining 283
Vishal Vyas, Pondicherry University, India
V. Uma, Pondicherry University, India

Opinions are found everywhere. In web forums like social networking websites, e-commerce sites, etc., rich user-generated content is available in large volume. Web 2.0 has made rich information easily accessible. Manual insight extraction of information from these platforms is a cumbersome task. Deriving insight from such available information is known as opinion mining (OM). Opinion mining is not a single-stage process. Text mining and natural language processing (NLP) is used to obtain information from such data. In NLP, content from the text corpus is pre-processed, opinion word is extracted, and analysis of those words is done to get the opinion. The volume of web content is increasing every day. There is a demand for more ingenious techniques, which remains a challenge in opinion mining. The efficiency of opinion mining systems has not reached the satisfactory level because of the issues in various stages of opinion mining. This chapter will explain the various research issues and challenges present in each stage of opinion mining.

Section 5
Case Study

Chapter 14
Case Study: Efficient Faculty Recruitment Using Genetic Algorithm 299
Amit Verma, Chandigarh Engineering College, India
Iqbaldeep Kaur, Chandigarh Engineering College, India
Dolly Sharma, Chandigarh Group of Colleges, India
Inderjeet Singh, Chandigarh Group of Colleges, India

Recruitment process takes place based on needed data while certain limiting factors are ignored. The objective of the chapter is to recruit best employees while taking care of limiting factors from the cluster for resource management and scheduling. Various parameters of the recruits have been selected to find the maximum score achieved by them. Recruitment process makes a database as cluster in the software environment perform the information retrieval on the database and then perform data mining using genetic algorithm while taking care of the positive values in contrast to limiting values received from the database. A bigger level recruitment process finds required values of a person, so negative points are ignored earlier in the recruitment process because there is no direct way to compare them. Genetic algorithm will create output in the form of chromosomal form. Again, apply information retrieval to get actual output. Major application of this process is that it will improve the selection process of candidates to a higher level of perfection in less time.

Compilation of References 312

About the Contributors 337

Index 344

Foreword

Data mining has become a standard tool helping both the business and scientific worlds. It undergoes a continuous and rapid development; however, while overviewing it we emphasize our own experience. (Fajszi, Cser, & Fehér, 2013)

Data mining has been a promising field of computer science for extracting relevant information from ample amount of data. The amount of data has recently been blowing up in various

application areas of science and technology. Simultaneously, understanding and analyzing these ever growing data sets, the so called Big Data, has become more and more difficult or even impossible using traditional database management and analysis tools. Sentiment analysis and opinion mining is the field of study that analyzes people's opinions, sentiments, evaluations, attitudes, and emotions from written language. It is one of the most active research areas in natural language processing and is also widely studied in data mining, Web mining, and text mining.

Opinion mining/Sentiment analysis is a type of natural language processing for tracking the mood of the public about a particular product. With the explosive growth of social media (e.g., reviews, forum discussions, blogs, micro-blogs, Twitter, comments, and postings in social network sites) on the Web, individuals and organizations are increasingly using the content in these media for decision making. Sentiment analysis systems are applied in almost every business and social domain because opinions are central to almost all human activities and are key influencers of our behaviors. Our beliefs and perceptions of reality, and the choices we make, are largely conditioned on how others see and evaluate the world. For this reason, when we need to make a decision we often seek out the opinions of others. This is true not only for individuals but also for organizations.

The book *Extracting Knowledge From Opinion Mining* edited by Dr. Rashmi Agrawal and Dr. Neha Gupta is a comprehensive book on opinion mining. The authors have put their best efforts to present the concepts and techniques up to every extent. Practical applications of opinion mining are also well presented in some chapters.

I am especially happy to see that the important aspect of user perspective in opinion mining has properly taken into account in the text. I assume that the book at hand is a valuable contribution to the field of opinion mining and sentiment analysis. It gives valuable examples to researchers and scientists as well as to developers of practical applications of opinion mining.

I would like to congratulate the two editors of this book for filling a critical gap. They have brought together some of the most prominent researchers in opinion mining from diverse backgrounds to author a book for researchers and practitioners alike.

Agrawal and Gupta have compiled their knowledge into this comprehensive opinion-mining guide. This book is an important guide for the opinion mining community and should be on the desk of every opinion-mining practitioner.

Babu Ram
Maharishi Dayanand University, India

REFERENCES

Fajszi, B., Cser, L., & Fehér, T. (2013). *Business Value in an Ocean of Data: Data Mining From a User Perspective*. Alinea Press.

Preface

INTRODUCTION

Sentiment analysis and Opinion Mining is the recent study which belongs to human behaviour analysis using computer modeling approach. We can say that it is an active research domain in NLP as well as in Artificial Intelligence. It is also broadly used in data mining, web extraction analysis and text mining. In fact it is interested to note that it not only bound with computer science engineering but also with management house, financial strategist and many other sciences. As the social media is taking more and more lead and millions of users are connected to their links so now it's really interesting to study the opinion mining with machine learning techniques. The sentiment analysis or we can say opinion mining; these two are closely related meaning words, which are used in the computational techniques to help them out about the opinion or sentiment of the users. These two are the emerging words and the buzz word in the information technology. As you will see that it is widely use by the corporate sector to uplift the business next level. Before two decades the words like Opinion mining or Sentiment analysis was not common, but during the last two decade these words have given a new life to information technology domain as well as to the business.

The important question which runs in the mind is why use sentiment analysis or opinion mining. Opinion mining (OM)/Sentiment Analysis (SA) is related to deriving insight through analysis of user's thoughts (reviews, posts, blogs etc.) about entities such as products, movies, people etc. Evaluation of reviews posted by users on e-commerce and social networking is of much use as it contains highly rated information. Calculation of average inclination of opinion towards any entity not only helps business organizations to gain profits but also helps an individual in getting the right opinion about something unfamiliar. With the recent developments in technology, communication among the people is becoming convenient day by day, the major percentage of this communication is happening through internet via various channels such as email, Facebook, Twitter, LinkedIn, Telegram, Whatsapp, etc. This huge data generated over internet communications will be a potential gold mine for discovering the hidden information into them.

The research in the field of sentiments and opinions has been going since a long back, but the term sentiment analysis and opinion mining were first introduced by Nasukawa and Dave in the year 2003. But after the year 2000, the research in the field of opinion mining has grown rapidly. The major reason behind this explosive growth is the expansion of World Wide Web. In addition to this, following factors also contributes to make it more demanding

1.   Recent innovations of machine learning techniques in information retrieval and language processing.
2.   Due to the expansion of World Wide Web and drastic growth of social network, trained datasets for machine learning algorithms are easily available.

OBJECTIVE OF THE BOOK

The main objective of this book is to cover the fundamental concepts of opinion mining and sentiment analysis. It also includes various real time/ offline applications and case studies in the field of engineering, computer science, information security, cloud computing with modern tools & technologies used.

The impact of this edited book is focused on in depth information about data mining, opinion mining methods, recent tools and technologies used, along with, technical approach in solving real time/offline applications and practical solutions through case studies in opinion mining. Companies may get different ways to monitor data coming from various sources and modify their processes accordingly to prevent it from catastrophic events through case studies. Retailers may provide different offers to customers to manage data in real time to market their products and increase sell. This book also provides guidelines on various applications and use of tools and technologies for the same.

The target audience and potential uses include:

1.   The researchers, academician and engineers who gets more insights on opinion mining.
2.   Readers who may discover new things for marketing and at the same time they learn how to protect data from risk and fraud.
3.   Audience who can use various technologies provided in this book to develop their applications.
4.   The students of various universities studying computer science and engineering and information technology, master of computer applications and management.

5. This book will provide correct information to business.
6. Audience can contribute in businesses by providing IT services.

ORGANIZATION OF THE BOOK

This book consists of five sections distributed in 14 chapters. Section 1, "Introductory Concepts of Opinion Mining," contains four chapters which describes the fundamentals of opinion mining and sentiment analysis. Section 2, "Ontologies and Their Applications," contains four chapters which describes the ontology and their applications in opinion mining. Section 3, "Tools and Techniques of Opinion Mining," contains three chapters which describe various tools of sentiment analysis and opinion mining. Section 4 is "Challenges and Open Issues in Opinion Mining," which is described in two chapters. The last section of this book is a case study on "Efficient Faculty Recruitment Using Genetic Algorithm."

A brief introduction of each chapter is given as follows.

Table 1. Organization of the book

Section 1: Introductory Concepts of Opinion Mining			
Chapter 1 Fundamentals of Opinion Mining	**Chapter 2** Feature-Based Opinion Mining	**Chapter 3** Deep Learning for Opinion Mining	**Chapter 4** Opinion Mining: Using Machine Learning Technique
Section 2: Ontologies and Their Applications			
Chapter 5 Ontology-Based Opinion Mining	**Chapter 6** Ontologies, Repository, and Information Mining in Component-Based Software Engineering Environment	**Chapter 7** Ontology-BASED Opinion Mining for Online Product Reviews	**Chapter 8** Applications of Ontology-Based Opinion Mining
Section 3: Tools and Techniques of Opinion Mining			
Chapter 9 Tools of Opinion Mining	**Chapter 10** Sentimental Analysis Tools		**Chapter 11** Anatomizing Lexicon With Natural Language Tokenizer Toolkit 3
Section 4: Challenges and Open Issues of Opinion Mining			
Chapter 12 Challenges of Text Analytics in Opinion Mining		**Chapter 13** Open Issues in Opinion Mining	
Section 5: Case Study			
Chapter 14 Case Study: Efficient Faculty Recruitment Using Genetic Algorithm			

Section 1: Introductory Concepts of Opinion Mining

Chapter 1, "Fundamentals of Opinion Mining," deals with the basics of opinion mining. Authors have put their efforts to describe the fundamentals of opinion mining in the best possible manner. Importance of opinion mining, applications of opinion mining, challenges of opinion mining has been covered well in the chapter. Authors have given a detailed literature review on opinion mining in the chapter. The chapter ends with a brief on some tools or sources used for performing opinion mining.

Chapter 2 on "Feature-Based Opinion Mining" discusses the feature-based opinion mining. Feature based opinion mining is the process of extracting the relevant information regarding the product and the services e.g., website of Trivago does the feature-based opinion mining; they collect the reviews of various hotel booking and then extract the relevant hotel list that meets the customer satisfaction. These features can have negative polarity or positive polarity. Positive polarity features are valuable to increase product sale and to improve the market competition among the producers. Feature extraction opinion mining can be used in some number applications ranges from product production to marketing and sales. This technique is also an area of research for researchers to further improve the web mining contents.

In Chapter 3, authors have described deep learning and some of the different approaches used in the opinion mining. First part considers an ensemble of machine learning techniques using Artificial intelligence algorithms that several sentiment classifiers trained with kinds of features, and an ensemble of features, where the combination has made at the feature level. After this, deep learning in opinion mining models has been discussed. A framework on deep learning technique has been presented. The framework is a useful conceptual model for new kind of deep learning techniques in opinion mining.

In Chapter 4 we discuss three famous machine learning techniques, e.g., Naïve Bayes Classifiers, Decision Tree and Support vector machine. In the chapter, first the basics of the techniques, their applications and then challenges in this technology implementation have been implemented. We feel that this chapter will be helpful to the learners, who are willing to dive in depth of machine learning. We also feel that it will help them to get a impression on what type of problem can be taken in the machine learning field and what will be the expected output in case any of one technique is opted for the problem study. The Section 1 is covering the general Introduction to machine learning techniques and opinion mining, Section 2 covers the three machine learning technology and its applications, and Section 3 covers the challenges of the technology. Section 4 is about the conclusion and scope of the machine learning technique.

Section 2: Ontologies and Their Applications

Ontology is an explicit detailed study of concepts. It can also be defined as systematic maintenance of information about the things which already exist. In Computer Science, it could be said that it is a formal representation of knowledge with the help of a fixed set of believed concepts and the relationship between those concepts. Chapter 5 titled "Ontology-Based Opinion Mining" covers the concepts of ontology and its usage in opinion mining. In Computer Science, "Ontology-Based Opinion Mining" is a formal representation of knowledge with the help of a fixed set of believed concepts and the relationship between those concepts. It could have the reasons about the domain's properties and with the help of that property a domain can be described easily. So, it is a formal explicit description of the basic/core concepts of domain. It also provides a shared word stock/lexicon. Ontologies are used in many areas like Artificial Intelligence, Library Science and Information Science.

Chapter 6 is based on Ontologies and is divided into five sections. In section 1 the emphasis is given on the comparison between various Ontologies. Section 2 explains the basic concept used in ontology. What is semantic web, what is ontology, how ontology is linked to semantic web, and the process of building an ontology. Section 3 explains various types of ontologies and comparison of Ontologies by stating their pros and cons. Section 4 describes the various types of editor tools used in ontology. Section 5 compares the results and at the end we wind up with the conclusion.

Chapter 7 contains ontology based opining mining for online product reviews. First and foremost, it describes preprocessing, which is necessary as presence of irrelevant and incorrect data cannot be ruled out. Several methods like stemming, sentence splitting, and tokenization shall be explored. The next step would be to construct ontology to extract product features in the reviews and thus generate a feature based summary. In order to construct this, ConceptNet is used.

Chapter 8 on starts with the ontology classification. Rule ontology, ontology learning, and ontology creations have been explained well in the chapter. The interesting feature of ontology is its extensibility and reusability. The authors have also provided a list of ontology tools along with the purpose. The authors have detailed out ontology in various applications by focusing on ontology-based clustering and ontology-based classification. Various performance measures for result valuation are also discussed. The chapter is concluded with a number of open issues.

Section 3: Tools and Techniques of Opinion Mining

The idea of Opinion mining and Sentiment Analysis tool is to process a set of search results for a given item based on the quality and features. In Chapter 9, "Tools of Opinion Mining," authors have discussed two opinion mining tools, NLTK and WEKA to classify and analyze the opinion of the datasets. Concepts of these tools have been discussed with all the possible screen shots. User can use any other data set and can implement the opinion mining tool to classify and analyze the data for better decision making. This chapter plays an important role to the readers from the point of application of opinion mining using various tools.

Chapter 10, "Sentimental Analysis Tools," provides a complete overview of tools to simplify the operations of opinion mining like data collection, data cleaning and visualization of predicted sentiment. This chapter provides the insights on sentimental analysis and the activities involved in sentimental analysis. It also explains the various tools available for sentimental analysis. There are plenty of open source and licensed tools available in market for sentimental analysis. Each tool has its own key features and advantages. The usage of a tool depends on the specific needs of an application.

The prime objective of Chapter 11 is to familiarize the authors with the NLTK toolkit which is primarily used in natural language processing. Natural language processing has a strong relation with Natural Language Processing. The chapters complete basics of NLTK. Important modules of the NLTK have been explained well in the chapter. The authors have given the examples, wherever required. Concept of Lemmatization and stemming and its use in NLTK has been covered.

Section 4: Challenges and Open Issues of Opinion Mining

Text analysis is the task of knowledge distillation from the unstructured text. Due to increase in sharing of information over the web in text format, users required tools and techniques for the analysis of the text. These techniques can be used in two ways: One, this can be used for clustering, classification, and visualization of the data. Second, this can be used for predicting the future aspects for example in share market. But all these tasks are not easy to perform, as there are lots of challenges in converting the text into the format onto which various actions can be taken. In Chapter 12, the authors have discussed the framework of text analysis, followed by the background where they have discussed the steps for transforming the text into the structured form. They have shed light on its industry application along with the technological and non-technological challenges in text analysis.

Various research issues and challenges restrict efficiency of opinion mining system, because of which there isn't any satisfactory opinion mining system. The essence of opinion mining is to help people in decision making. The unstructured text, different writing styles, usage of sarcasm etc., in social media, e-commerce assigns a high percentage of difficulty in deriving opinion. E-commerce is not just selling and buying online. Utilizing opinion mining in e-commerce helps in recommending products to customers which will increase the efficiency of organizations and help in competing with other giants in the market. Thus, the necessity of opinion mining is increasing gradually. Hence, the Chapter 13, "Issues of Opinion Mining," discusses the various issues and research challenges involved in opinion mining. The data extracted from the web is unstructured and data cleaning is required at this pre-processing step. The chapter discussed the issues involved in data cleaning such as dealing with missing data and noise.

Section 5: Case Study

Chapter 14 is a case study on "Efficient Faculty Recruitment Using Genetic Algorithm." Recruitment process takes place based on needed data while certain limiting factor ignored. Objective of chapter is to recruit best employees while taking care of limiting factor from the cluster for resource management and Scheduling. Various parameters of the recruits have been selected to find the maximum score achieved by them. Recruitment process makes a database as cluster in the software environment, perform the information retrieval on the database and then perform data mining using genetic algorithm while taking care of the positive values in contrast to limiting values received from the database. A bigger level recruitment process finds required values of a person, so negative points are ignored earlier in the recruitment process because there is no direct way to compare them. Genetic algorithm will create output in the form of chromosomal form. Again, apply information retrieval to get actual output. Major application of this process is that it will improve the selection process of candidates to a higher level of perfection in a less time.

This book is expected to assist researchers, academicians and science and engineering students in contributing their businesses by providing IT services. It addresses innovative conceptual framework for various applications and insights on opinion mining. The book is expected to serve as a reference for the post-graduate students as it offers the essential knowledge for understanding in depth information about opinion mining tools and technologies used. It also discovers new things for marketing and at the same time they learn how to protect data from risk and fraud.

This book is based on research studies carried out by experienced academicians and is expected to shed new insights for researchers, academicians, students and improves understanding of opinion mining concepts by technologies provided in this book to develop their applications.

Rashmi Agrawal
Manav Rachna International Institute of Research and Studies, India

Neha Gupta
Manav Rachna International Institute of Research and Studies, India

Acknowledgment

First of all, we would like to thank the Almighty god, our parents for endless support, guidance and love through all our life stages. We are thankful to our beloved family members for standing beside us throughout our career, move our career forward through editing this book.

Acknowledgement when honestly given is a reward without price. We are thankful to the publishing team at IGI Global accepting to publish this edited book. We thank Marianne Caesar, development editor, for helping us in bringing this project to a successful end. We would also thank Jan Travers, Kayla Wolfe, Meghan Lamb, and Jacqueline Sternberg of IGI Global team for their various supports.

Writing this part is probably the most difficult task. Although the list of people to thank heartily is long, making this list is not the hard part. The difficult part is to search the words that convey the sincerity and magnitude of our gratitude and love.

We would like to acknowledge the help of all the people involved in collation and review process of the book, more specifically, to the authors and reviewers that took part in the review process. Without their support, this book would not have become a reality.

First, we would like to thank each one of the authors for their contributions. Our sincere gratitude goes to the chapter's authors who contributed their time and expertise to this book.

Second, we wish to acknowledge the valuable contributions of the reviewers regarding the improvement of quality, coherence, and content presentation of chapters.

Acknowledgment

In closing, we wish to thank all of the authors for their insights and excellent contributions to this handbook.

Rashmi Agrawal
Manav Rachna International Institute of Research and Studies, India

Neha Gupta
Manav Rachna International Institute of Research and Studies, India

Section 1
Introductory Concepts of Opinion Mining

Chapter 1
Fundamentals of Opinion Mining

Ashish Seth
INHA University, Tashkent, India

Kirti Seth
INHA University, Tashkent, India

ABSTRACT

Mining techniques in computer science have been evolving for the last two decades. Opinion mining is the latest buzzword in this evolution and goes to a deeper level to understand the drive behind people's behavior. Due to the richness of social media opinions, emotions, and sentiments, opinion mining examines that how people feel about a given situation, be it positive or negative. This chapter primarily focuses on explaining the fundamentals of opinion mining along with sentiment analysis. It covers the brief evolution in mining techniques in the last decade. The chapter elaborates on the significance of opinion mining in today's scenario and its features. It also includes a section to discuss the applications, challenges and research scope in opinion mining.

INTRODUCTION

The research in the field of sentiments and opinions has been going since a long back, but the term sentiment analysis and opinion mining were first introduced by Nasukawa and Dave in the year 2003. But after the year 2000, the research in the field of opinion mining has grown rapidly. The major reason behind this explosive growth is the expansion of World Wide Web. In addition to this, following factors also contributes to make it more demanding

DOI: 10.4018/978-1-5225-6117-0.ch001

- Recent innovations of machine learning techniques in information retrieval and language processing.
- Due to the expansion of World Wide Web and drastic growth of social network, trained datasets for machine learning algorithms are easily available (Mukherjee & Liu, 2012).

With the recent developments in technology, communication among the people is becoming convenient day by day, the major percentage of this communication is happening through internet via various channels such as email, Facebook, Twitter, LinkedIn, Telegram, WhatsApp, etc. This huge data generated over internet communications will be a potential gold mine for discovering the hidden information into them.

In computer science both the terms "opinion mining" and "sentiment analysis" are often used interchangeably. Let us first look at the English definition of two key terms "opinion" and "sentiment".

What Is Opinion?

Opinions play very important role in making decisions. To make any decisions, these opinions are key factors to conclude our decision. Opinion in general is a subjective statement not an objective statement. Subjective statement describes what a person thinks or believes about something. Opinion is defined as "a belief or judgment that fall short of absolute conviction, certainty, or positive knowledge; it is a conclusion that certain facts, ideas etc. are probably true or likely to provide so". Alternatively, "it is an estimation of the quality or worth of someone or something" (Pang & Lee, 2008).

What Is Sentiment?

Sentiments are central to almost all human activities and act as key influencers of our behaviors. An individual makes any opinion based on the sentiments he had with the object in context. Sentiment is defined as "an attitude toward something; refined or tender emotion; manifestation of the higher or more refined feelings". It is a thought influenced by a proceeding from feeling or emotion. Sentiments are generally be classified in two ways i.e. Supervised Learning and Unsupervised learning

- *Classification Using Supervised Learning*: It is implemented by building a classifier; two sets of documents are required in this set which are known as training set and test set. This approach is popularly known as Machine Learning based technique. Frequently used algorithms based in these techniques are

2

support vector machines (SVM), Naive Bayes classifier and Maximum entropy. The basic task for this classification is choosing the appropriate set of features for classification. The most commonly used features include presence of term and their frequency, phrases, parts of speech, negations and opinion words.

- *Classification Using Unsupervised Learning*: In this approach, text is classified by comparing it against the word lexicons or sentiment lexicons. The value of these sentiment lexicons is determined prior to the sentiment analysis. Sentiment lexicons are defined by the expressions and collection of words that are used to express views, opinions and people's feelings. The words in text are identified as positive or negative word lexicon. The document is scanned for the presence of these positive and negative word lexicons. Based on the presence of each type of word lexicons in the document it is considered as positive or negative document.

Opinion Mining or sentiment analysis is the computational study of opinions, sentiments and emotions expressed in text. It deals with rational models of emotions, rumors and trends within user communities and with the word-of-mouth inside specific domains. Opinion Mining is attracting an increasing interest from last few years.

Though the data present on the social media is huge and reflect people's opinion, it is highly unstructured, unclean and filtering the meaningful information out of them is tedious task. Typically, each site contains a large volume of opinion data which is not always easily deciphered in long blogs and forum postings. The average human reader will have difficulty identifying relevant sites and extracting and summarizing the opinions in them. Automated sentiment analysis systems are therefore needed.

The technique of transforming the noisy data by a series of sentiment analysis termed as opinion mining. Alternatively, the challenge of analyzing the huge data has created a new scope in computer science which is referred as opinion mining. In the broadest terms, opinion mining is the science of using text analysis to understand the drivers behind public sentiment.

Task of Opinion Mining

An ocean of unstructured data is flowing across the internet; this unstructured, noisy data can be a source of useful information if mined in a scientific way to predict the behavior or mood of public in general. Such data is growing exponentially with time; it keeps on adding when people talk about their likes and dislikes on internet or any social media on the web. Being free to express views people do share their experience in an honest and unsolicited manner, without fear of being an answerable, they mostly share our true feelings towards a politician, a product, brand, or a global event.

Opinion mining aims to deduce some useful information out of this unstructured data by identifying and categorizing the entire text into various elements which are commonly known as opinion representative (see Figure 1)

Representation of Opinion

Opinions are expressed through two representations, basic and detailed representation.

- **Basic Representation:** This help us to make a basic conclusion out of the statement under consideration. It consists of three main components (see figure 2).
  - ○ **Opinion Holder:** Person who expresses his view, this can be a person or organization which holds a particular opinion about something (e.g. person, place, product, event, organization).
  - ○ **Opinion Target:** Object (thing or person) on which opinion is expressed.
  - ○ **Opinion Content:** Statement of expression.
- **Detailed Representation:** This helps us to give a better or detailed conclusion out of the statement under consideration. It consists of two main components.
  - ○ **Opinion Context:** Under what situation was the opinion expressed (e.g. place, duration)?
  - ○ **Opinion Sentiment:** What does the opinion tell us about the opinion holder feelings (i.e. favoring or opposing the person, positive or negative comments, satisfaction or dissatisfaction etc.).

Figure 1. Task of opinion mining

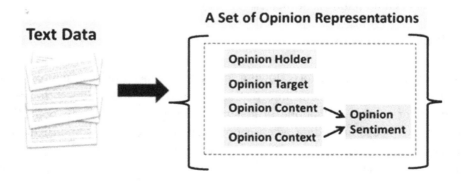

Figure 2. Components of opinion representation

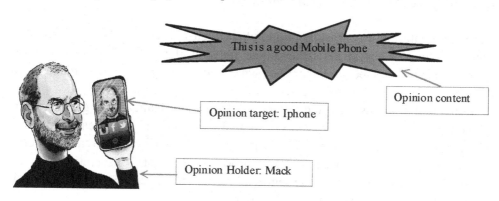

These components of opinion are also expressed in different perspective. In context of above example, components can also be expressed as follows (see figure 3)

- **Opinion Holder:** INC society (expressed by group of people rather than individual)
- **Opinion Target:** Hotel service (may represent one entity, group of entity, etc.).
- **Opinion CONTENT:** A paragraph (or detailed article on the object).
- **Opinion Context:** Year 1938, Tashkent (reflect the place as well as year, may also include more attribute).
- **Opinion Sentiment:** May reflect positive, happy, negative or favorable sentiments.

Figure 3. Representation of opinion components in a text

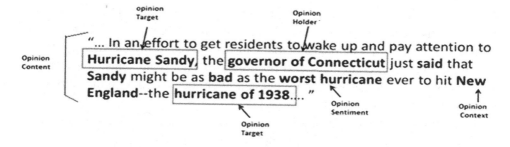

IMPORTANCE OF OPINION MINING

Human by nature always make opinion about their experience about a particular object or thing or any incident they come across in their life. This is because of the presence of very special feature he own called 'intelligence' which makes him different from all other live existences in nature.

Individual opinions are often reflective of a broader reality. A single customer who takes issue with a new product's design on social media likely speaks for many others. The same goes for a member of the public who takes to a political campaigner's web page to praise or criticize the policies proposed. By careful observation one can identify the driving sources of the sentiment, it can then be used to expose critical areas of strength and weakness by using opinion mining.

Public opinions may help the company to make effective plan to hit the target, strategies needed to reinvigorate profitability or reclaim slipping market share. Within the public sector this same data can be used to build strategies and campaigns that resonate with the electorate and react to voters' changing needs. By analyzing conversations for both sentiment and the topics driving that sentiment, a retail bank might discover that of customers' criticisms, queue length and waiting times. A fast food chain might be interested to know that relative to their closest competitor, many consider their portion size too small, though their friendly customer service is a plus. This information of customer service could be further broken down into the sub-categories of turnaround time, order correctness and delivery time.

Opinion mining is not new, in the past, when an individual needed opinion, he/she asked friends and family, currently it fetches more interest to larger organizations and businesses due to technological innovations and moving the people toward more social networks (Bollen et al., 2011).

APPLICATIONS

With the explosive growth of social media and the advancement in technology, organizations are increasingly using the social media contents for decision making. With the presence of social media in many forms such as forum discussions, blogs, micro blogs, twitter, comments, and postings a person is no longer restricted to opinions of one's friends and family but can refer social media on the web to get reviews about the product.

Acquiring public and consumer opinions has long been a huge business itself for marketing, public relations, and political campaign companies. Underlying the importance of opinion to sales of product, organizations or a business, earlier commercials bodies are regularly conducts surveys, opinion polls, and focus groups.

With the increasing presence of social media on the web, for an organization, it may no longer be necessary to conduct surveys, opinion polls, and focus groups in order to gather public opinions because there is an abundance of such information publicly available.

In recent years, companies start focusing on data available on web. Sentiment analysis applications have been widely used in every possible domain, from consumer products, services, healthcare, and financial services to social events and political elections. Many big corporations like Microsoft, Google, Hewlett-Packard, SAP, and SAS have built their own in-house sentiment analytics center to mine these public opinion data available on the web.

Practical applications and industrial interests have provided strong motivations for research in sentiment analysis. Below are some of the application areas which show as application of opinion mining.

- *Shopping (E-Commerce):* Online Shopping is emerging day to day and widely used nowadays. In today's hectic and busy schedule these options provide convenience shopping at home itself. Generally, to get an overall idea of the product, customers frequently visit the feedback page of the concerned product. This page provides number of feedbacks mentioned by existing users of the product. These feedbacks reflect the existing user opinion about the product and help the current customer to make his buying decision. Popular shopping sites like Flipkart, Amazon etc. have provision to compare products with all desired description and feedback of customers, it also displays the opinion result to the user in a "Graphical formats" for quick and easy understanding about the quality/features and services of product. An opinion mining and sentiment analysis tool helps users to select the product to purchase.
- *Entertainment:* Beforehand review of any kind of popular event, program or current release of any movie can be helpful in providing more information about the event. These reviews are based on people feedback. Internet movie database can help the online users to view feedback for movies and other programs. These online reviews provide great help to the customers to decide when there are lots of options available to choose from. Opinion mining can be used for movie or show or TV programs to promote or conclude the users' response to analyse it.
- *Business:* Businesses and large organizations in the real world always spend considerable amount of budget to understand people opinions about their products and services. At the same time consumers or customers also look for the opinions of other users of a product to look for their queries related to a particular product. People opinion for a product proves a great help to

make their decision of purchasing it or continuing their search. As people are more and more connected with the social media, companies want to utilize this to analysis their own performance in terms of the services provided and customer satisfaction about the released product. For this companies ask their customer to provide feedback on their portals. This approach makes saving on a marketing budget. Customer feedback on a company's portal helps them to raise their issue in case of dissatisfaction or appreciate if they found the product justified to its worth. This way companies can be able to analysis the customer mood or sentiment through the feedback and can incorporate the suggestions to enhance the product sale.

- *R&D (Research and Development):* Online customer feedback plays an important role to understand public opinion about the product. Feedbacks at any online shopping portal are increasingly used by industry to improve the quality of the products. Online sites can even invite customers to not only comment on existing product but can describe their expectation and ask the customers to provide their own design views in order to customize new product as per customer requirements. For example, customer not only comment about the battery life but can add more information like time required to charge, its weight etc. these inputs from customer help the industry to improve in the design of the product.

- *Politics:* Nowadays twitter is proved to be an excellent medium to know the political view of public in general. Political parties can extract these views to predict their win or loss in an election, they can also use them to declare a candidate based on his or her popularity in public. These data on internet help these political parties to have an overall knowledge about public opinion which helps them to focus on weakness and strength. In a political election, opinions about political candidates not only help individuals to cast their vote but one can get feedback of popularity of candidates, as these opinions help to generate candidate impression to normal public.

- *Academics:* The demand of Massive online interactive courses (MOOC) are continuously increasing, student opinion plays most important role to ensure about the effectiveness of such programs. In MOOC courses, student's sentiments can be used to design the program. Student's feedback may help to understand and analysis the requirements to make it better for future student's Opinion Mining will help organizations running online courses to be aware of their problems (weakness) and best(strength) within them through student opinion given in the form of feedback and comments.

- *Health:* Online health care will be going to dominate in the near future. The patient report can be shared and consulted by several doctors sitting at home. Users or patients can share prescriptions or treatment, which may help to cure them while they suffer from any illness like headache, fever, digestion, high blood pressure, and diabetes. People are sharing online about their gym experience which suggest which particular exercise is good for a particular part of body, it also contains their opinions to control blood pressure, back pain, migraine etc. which helps all to get rid of problems in their life. Based on these huge data of views and suggestion, users also share their feedback and comment. These comments can be mined in a systematic way to conclude which of the particular remedies are working while others who didn't succeed.

- *Travel & Transportation:* With the evolution of technology and dominance of social media increasing on internet, touring business has been improved in recent years. Users prefer to make their touring plans through online. It has been observed that a person before going to any place for touring or business purpose would collect opinion of other people about the place, people, food, weather, etc. on internet. Transportation like tour and travel, logistic, cab service which is very helpful to people to choose best services mentioned in the feedback and comments from past experience shared by the users. For trading, transportation has been very crucial and important factor; transportation can be any movable items from one place to another as per the requirement. There are many transport modes for example road, air, rail, etc. People share their transport experience on the internet about their business which can be carefully mined and analyzed to budget the expenses incurred for transport

Apart from real-life applications, many application-oriented research papers have also been published. Table 1 summarizes some of the important work done on opinion mining.

Challenges of Opinion Mining

To classifying a text written in a natural language into a positive or negative feeling is sometimes a very complicated task that even different human annotators disagree on the classification to be assigned to a given text. Interpretation of the text by an individual may be different from others; this is because of difference in cultural factors and each person's experience. Secondly, shorter the text, and worse written, the more difficult the task becomes, as in the case of messages on social networks like Twitter or Facebook. It is a hard challenge for language technologies to parse such kind of data to interpret some useful information from it (Bolanle et al., 2012).

Table 1. Literature review on opinion mining

S. no	Year	Researchers	Work Done
1	2012	Kamal et al.	implemented a rule-based system to mine product features, opinions and their reliability scores.
2	2011	Bollen et al.	used the twitter moods to predict the stock markets.
3	2011	Miller et al.	sentiment flow in social media was investigated
4	2011	Mohammad and Yang	mail sentiments were used to determine how genders differed on emotional axes
5	2011	Mohammad	emotions in novels and fairy tales were tracked
6	2011	Bollen et al.	twitter moods were used to predict the stock market
7	2011	In Bar-Haim et al. (2011) and Feldman et al. (2011)	expert investors in microblogs were identified to perform sentiment analysis of stocks.
8	2011	Groh and Hauffa	sentiment analysis was used to characterize social relations.
9	2010	Zhang and Skiena	blog and news sentiment was used to predict trading strategies
10	2010	McGlohon et al.	based on reviews various products and merchants were ranked
11	2010	Hong and Skiena	relationships between the NFL betting line and public opinions in blogs and twitter were identified
12	2010	O'Connor et al.	twitter sentiment was linked with public opinion polls
13	2010	Tumasjan et al.	twitter sentiment used to predict election results
14	2010	Chen et al.	the authors studied political standpoints
15	2010	Yano and Smith	method proposed for predicting comment volumes of political blogs
16	2009, 2010	Asur and Huberman (2010), Joshi et al. (2010) Sadikov et al. (2009)	Twitter data, movie reviews, and blogs were used to predict box-office revenues for movies
17	2010	Ding and Liu	used the supervised learning approach to present the problem of object and attribute co-reference.
18	2010	Paul et al.	suggested a comparative LexRank approach to summarize contrastive viewpoints in opinionated text.
19	2010	Tumasjan et al.	used twitter sentiments to predict election results.
20			
21	2009	Sakunkoo and Sakunkoo	social influences in online book reviews.
22	2008	Chen and Xie	define online customer views as a new element in the marketing communication mix. They studied the role of customer reviews in marketing.
23	2008	Ding et al.	proposed a holistic approach to infer the semantic orientation of an opinion word based on review context and combine multiple opinions words in same sentence.

continued on following page

Table 1. Continued

S. no	Year	Researchers	Work Done
24	2008	Murthy and Bing Liu	proposed a method which study sentiments in comparative sentences and also deals with context-based sentiments by exploiting external information available on the web
25	2007	Liu et al.	model was proposed to predict sales performance.
26	2007	Ghose et al.	uses econometrics to identify the economic value of text showing that user feedback affects the pricing power of merchants.
27	2007	Park et al.	examines the involvement of the online customer reviews in affecting the purchasing intentions.
28	2007	Archak et al.	uses product demand as the objective function and derive a context aware interpretation of opinions showing how the opinions affects the user's choice.
29	2004	Hu and Liu	worked on feature level opinion mining and determined the polarity of the object features without considering the strength of the opinions
30	2003	Dave et al.	trained a classifier using reviews from major websites.
31	2003	Turney and Littman	find out the semantic orientation of a text by calculating its statistical association with a set of positive and negative words
32	2002	Pang et al.	perform document level sentiment classification using standard machine learning techniques
33	2002	Morinaga et al.	presented a framework for mining product reputation on internet.
34	2000	Tatemura	Perform collaborative exploration of movie reviews from various viewpoints based on browsing of virtual reviewers
35	1997	Hatzivassiloglou and McKeown	to find the semantic orientation of the adjectives and predicted whether two conjoined adjectives are of same polarity
36	1997	Terveen et al.	proposed PHOAKS (people helping one another know stuff), to help users locate information on the web. The system uses a collaborative filtering approach to recognize and reuse recommendations
37	1994	Wiebe	study the naturally occurring narratives and regularities in the writings of authors and presents an algorithm that tracks the point of view on the basis of these regularities.

In recent years, postings in social media have helped reshape businesses, and sway public sentiments and emotions. Since opinion mining is a relatively new filed, thus there are several challenges to be faced. Basic challenges that always threats to the correctness of results originated from public opinion is related to the authenticity of the extracted data and the methods used in it.

Challenges of opinion mining are as follows:

Existence of Multilanguage

Globally, there exist many languages and a particular product is used globally by different language speaking people. There feedback or comment on the product can be in different languages which make it complex task to drive a public opinion from the feedback. Moreover, customer are free to express their experience about the product in their own way, this further add more complexity to the mining process as the feedback data will tend towards unstructured shape which is always hard to analyze (Turney, 2002). Even if we assume that all the feedback should be provided in any structured format, still feedback given in different languages will be a challenge.

For example, if the same feedback is provided in five different languages will be treated as five different set of statement by any miner application.

- **In English:** The product is very light weight
- **In French:** Le produit est très léger
- **In Hindi:** उत्पाद बहुत हल्का वजन है
- **In German:** Das Produkt ist sehr leicht
- **In Russian:** Продукт очень легкий

Therefore, even they are saying the same thing in the uniform format, it is still a challenge to understand each language and deduce the same meaning out of it.

Grammar

Noun words are also be said as featured words but verbs and adjective can also be used as feature words which are challenging to judge.

Consider some user feedback on earphone are as follows:

Arohi gave a feedback: "I like the sound quality "
and Ketan's feedback is: "The sound is awesome"
Similarly Raj feebback is: "The sound is superb"

Here Arohi, Ketan and Raj are speaking about the same quality of the product but in different manner. The words which are similar/opposite in their meaning are also difficult task to group together

For Example: "Camera size of mobile phone is small".

Here adjective "small" used in positive manner but if user makes the statement like:

"The battery time is also small"

here the word "small" represent negative meaning for the phone battery. To identify such adjective words which define different meaning in same situation is a difficult to handle it.

Use of Short Words

Users are allowed to feedback in any format, they are free to write in any manner. Users can use symbols, abbreviation, capital letter or small letter, shortcut and regional language in their feedbacks (Figure 4)
Ex.

camera as cam,
pictures as pix,
fine as fi9,
goods as guds
great as gr8
etc.

It is difficult to handle such kind of data, requires careful mining to conclude users point of view. Many users have different point of view using same kind words in their feedback which is challenging to sort out the positive, negative or neutral meaning out of the text.

Presence of Spam and Fake Reviews

The contents on the web can be both authentic as well as spam. For an effective sentiment analysis, this spam content should be detected and removed before

Figure 4. Use of short words in comment, feedback and communications

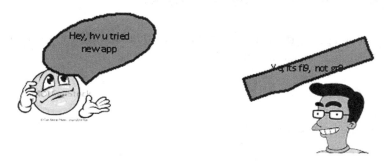

processing. This can be achieved by detecting outliers, identifying duplicates, and by considering reviewer reputation.

Limitation of Filtering

Classification filtering has certain limitation while determining concept or most popular thought, this limitation should be reduced to improve sentiment classification results. These limitations may rise to the risk of creating irrelevant opinion sets and it results false summarization of sentiment.

Limited Availability of Opinion Mining Tools

The tools required for opinion mining is not freely available. They are very expensive and currently affordable only to large organizations and government bodies. It is not available to common people for their research and data analysis. This restricted availability is also a challenge to analyses to data in an effective way. Mining software should be accessible to all people to make task of opinion mining simple.

Integration of Opinion Words With Implicit and Behavior Data

For an effective sentiment analysis, the implicit data and opinion words should be integrated; it will help to determine the actual behavior of sentiment words within the implicit data.

Domain-Independence

Domain dependent nature of sentiment words is one big challenge for opinion mining and sentiment analysis. One features set may give very good performance in one domain, at the same time it perform very poor in some other domain (Dmitry et al., 2010).

Overheads in Natural Language Processing

The natural language overhead like ambiguity, co-reference, Implicitness, inference etc. create hindrance in sentiment analysis.

Research Areas

The major scope in this area is as follows:

1. Identification of Spam data and handling.
2. Mining short sentences like abbreviations.
3. Improving sentiment word identification algorithm.
4. Designing automatic analyzing tool.
5. Effective Analysis of policy opinionated content.
6. Treating and handling bi polar sentiments.
7. Generation of highly content lexicon database.

TOOLS AND SOURCES

Here are some tools or sources used for performing opinion mining **WordNet** (source: https://wordnet.princeton.edu/)

WordNet is a huge database of English words that are connected together by their semantic relationships. It is a collection of words (lexical database) that has been frequently used by major search engines and IR research projects. The database can be accessed through Princeton University's website (https://wordnet.princeton.edu/) and can be downloaded for non-commercial use for use on Linux/Unix/Mac systems. Alternatively, it is considered as a supercharged dictionary or thesaurus with a defined structure.

The Wordnet Hierarchy

Nouns, verbs, adjectives and adverbs are grouped into sets of cognitive synonyms (synsets), each expressing a distinct concept (Morinaga et al., 2002). Synsets are interlinked by means of conceptual-semantic and lexical relations.

A synset, therefore, corresponds to an abstract concept. It forms relations with other synsets to form a hierarchy of concepts. For a given synset, some basic terminology used are as follows:

- **Hypernyms:** Are the synsets that are more general.
- **Hyponyms:** Are the synsets that are more specific.

Hyponyms have an "is-a" relationship to their hypernyms. Along with "is-a" relationships, we can explore "is-made-of" and "comprises" relationships. For a given synset, we can therefore see the following relationships:

- **Holonyms:** Are things that the item is contained in.
- **Meronyms:** Are components or substances that make up the item.

These different forms can be understood in the following example (see Figure 5)

Figure 5. Representation of word phrase in various forms

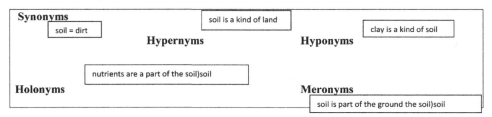

TreeTagger

(source: http://www.ims.unistuttgart.de/forschung/ressourcen/werkzeuge/treetagger.en.html)

The TreeTagger is a tool for annotating text with part-of-speech and lemma information. It was developed by Helmut Schmid in the TC project at the Institute for Computational Linguistics of the University of Stuttgart. This software is freely available for research, education and evaluation.

REFERENCES

Bollen, J., Mao, H., & Zeng, X.-J. (2011). Twitter mood predicts the stock market. *Journal of Computational Science, 2*(1), 1–8. doi:10.1016/j.jocs.2010.12.007

Davidov, D., Tsur, O., & Rappoport, A. (2010). Semi-supervised recognition of sarcastic sentences in twitter and amazon. In *Proceedings of the fourteenth conference on Computational Natural Language Learning*, Uppsala, Sweden (pp. 107-116).

Morinaga, S., Yamanishi, K., Tateishi, K., & Fukushima, T. (2002). Mining product reputations on the web. In Proceedings of the eighth ACM SIGKDD international conference on Knowledge discovery and data mining, Edmonton, Canada (pp. 341-349). ACM.

Mukherjee, A., & Liu, B. (2012, August). Mining contentions from discussions and debates. In *Proceedings of the 18th ACM SIGKDD international conference on Knowledge discovery and data mining* (pp. 841-849). ACM.

Ojokoh, B. A., & Kayode, O. (2012). A feature-opinion extraction approach to opinion mining. *Journal of Web Engineering, 11*(1), 51–63.

Pang, B., & Lee, L. (2008). Opinion mining and sentiment analysis. *Foundations and Trends in Information Retrieval*, 2(1-2), 1–135. doi:10.1561/1500000011

Turney, P. D. (2002). Thumbs up or thumbs down? Semantic orientation applied to unsupervised classification of reviews. In *Proceedings of the Association for Computational Linguistics (ACL)* (pp. 417–424).

ADDITIONAL READING

Brandseye. (2017). What is opinion mining? Retrieved from https://www.brandseye.com/news/what-is-opinion-mining-next-level-sentiment-analytics/

Brandseye. (2017). What is really driving sentiment. Retrieved from https://www.brandseye.com/news/what-drives-sentiment-topic-analysis/

Chen, Y., & Xie, J. (2008). Online Consumer Review: Word-of-Mouth as a New Element of Marketing Communication Mix. *Management Science*, 54(3), 477–491.

Coursera. (n.d.). 5.5 Opinion Mining and Sentiment Analysis: Motivation [video tutorial]. Retrieved from https://ru.coursera.org/learn/text-mining/lecture/o93Yl/5-5-opinion-mining-and-sentiment-analysis-motivation

Das, S., & Chen, M. (2001). Yahoo! for Amazon: Extracting market sentiment from stock message boards. In *Proceedings of the Asia Pacific finance association annual conference (APFA)* (Vol. 35, p. 43).

Dellarocas, C., Zhang, X. M., & Awad, N. F. (2007). Exploring the value of online product reviews in forecasting sales: The case of motion pictures. *Journal of Interactive Marketing*, 21(4), 23–45. doi:10.1002/dir.20087

Dictionary. (n.d.). Opinion. Retrieved from http://www.dictionary.com/browse/opinion

Ding, X., & Liu, B. (2010). Resolving object and attribute coreference in opinion mining. In *Proceedings of 23rd international conference on computational linguistics (Coling 2010)* (pp. 268-276).

Ding, X., Liu, B., & Yu, P. S. (2008, February). A holistic lexicon-based approach to opinion mining. In *Proceedings of the 2008 international conference on web search and data mining* (pp. 231-240). ACM.

Do-Hyung, P., Lee, J., & Han, I. (2007). The effect of on-line consumer reviews on consumer purchasing intention: The moderating role of involvement. *International Journal of Electronic Commerce, 11*(4), 125–148. doi:10.2753/JEC1086-4415110405

Encyclopedia Britannica. (n.d.). Public opinion. Retrieved from https://www.britannica.com/topic/public-opinion

Ganapathibhotla, M., & Liu, B. (2008, August). Mining opinions in comparative sentences. In *Proceedings of the 22nd International Conference on Computational Linguistics* (Vol. 1, pp. 241-248). Association for Computational Linguistics.

Hatzivassiloglou, V., & McKeown, K. R. (1997). Predicting the semantic orientation of adjectives. *Proceedings of Annual Meeting of the Association for Computational Linguistics* (ACL-1997).

Hearst, M. (1992). Direction-based text interpretation as an information access refinement in Text-Based Intelligent Systems. In *Text-based intelligent systems: Current research and practice in information extraction and retrieval* (pp. 257–274). Hillsdale, NJ: L. Erlbaum Associates Inc.

Hu, N., Pavlou, P. A., & Zhang, J. (2006, June). Can online reviews reveal a product's true quality?: empirical findings and analytical modeling of Online word-of-mouth communication. In *Proceedings of the 7th ACM conference on Electronic commerce* (pp. 324-330). ACM.

Jotheeswaran, J., & Koteeswaran, S. (n.d.). Sentiment analysis: A survey of current research and techniques. Research & Reviews. Retrieved from http://www.rroij.com/open-access/sentiment-analysis-a-survey-of-current-researchand-techniques.php?aid=56063

Kim, W. Y., Ryu, J. S., Kim, K. I., & Kim, U. M. (2009, November). A method for opinion mining of product reviews using association rules. In *Proceedings of the 2nd International Conference on Interaction Sciences: Information Technology, Culture and Human* (pp. 270-274). ACM.

Liu, Y., Huang, X., An, A., & Yu, X. (2007). ARSA: A sentiment - aware model for predicting sales performance using blogs. In *Proceedings of ACM SIGIR Conf. on Research and Development in Information Retrieval (SIGIR-2007)*. 10.1145/1277741.1277845

Medhat, W., Hassan, A., & Korashy, H. (2014). Sentiment analysis algorithms and applications: A survey. *Ain Shams Engineering Journal, 5*(4), 1093-1113. Retrieved from https://www.sciencedirect.com/science/article/pii/S2090447914000550

Michael, J. Paul, ChengXiang Zhai and Roxana Girju (2010). Summarizing contrastive viewpoints in opinionated text. In *Proceedings of the 2010 conference on the empirical methods in natural language processing*, MIT Massachusetts (pp. 66-76).

Peter, D. (2003). Turney and Michael L Littman. (2003). Measuring Praise and criticism: inference of semantic orientation from association. *ACM Transactions on Information Systems, TOIS, 21*(4), 315–346.

Princeton University. (n.d.). Retrieved from https://wordnet.princeton.edu/

Roberto, G. Ibanez, Smaranda Muresan and Nina Wacholder.(2011). Identifying Sarcasm in Twitter: A Closer Look. In *Proceedings of the 49th Annual Meeting of the Association for Computational Linguistics*, Portland, OR, June 19-24 (pp. 581-586).

Sentiment analysis symposium. (n.d.). Pre-symposium tutorial, May 7. Retrieved from http://2012.sentimentsymposium.com/tutorial.html

Tumasjan, A., Sprenger, T. O., Sandner, P. G., & Welpe, I. M. (2010). Predicting elections with twitter: What 140 characters reveal about political sentiment. In *Proceedings of the International Conference on Weblogs and Social Media* (ICWSM-2010).

Wikipedia. (n.d.). Sentiment analysis. Retrieved from https://en.wikipedia.org/wiki/Sentiment_analysis

Wikivisually. (n.d.). Sentiment analysis. Retrieved from https://wikivisually.com/wiki/Sentiment_analysis

Chapter 2
Feature Based Opinion Mining

Mridula Batra
Manav Rachna International Institute of Research and Studies, India

Vishaw Jyoti
Manav Rachna International Institute of Research and Studies, India

ABSTRACT

Opinion mining is the estimated learning of user's beliefs, evaluation and sentiments about units, actions and its features. This method has several features matched with data mining techniques, language processing methods and feature oriented data abstraction. This seems to be extremely difficult to mine opinions from analysis those exist in common human used language. Views are very essentials when one desires to construct a judgment. Data abstraction is an important characteristic for decision making applicable to individuals and organization of different nature. While selecting and purchasing a particular product, it is always beneficial for an individual to collect other views for correct decision making. One association wants to conduct surveys and gather opinions to develop their product excellence. Internet as a source of information, having a number of websites available with the customer reviews as a number of products, it is easy to extract the features from these opinions, sentiments and view, is a task comes under feature-based opinion mining.

INTRODUCTION

Web is playing an important role in advertising information regarding products. Web sites are also used by the consumers to express their views related to a product. Customer can say what they think (positive/negative) about the product. It is a good medium to collect consumer feedback, reviews and comments. These costumer

DOI: 10.4018/978-1-5225-6117-0.ch002

responses in the form of reviews and comments are very useful as information that can be further utilized as a base for future analysis of product sales and revenue. The common example is hotel booking, an online customer can check the reviews for setting his sentiments regarding the preference of the hotel likely to be booked.

Therefore customer is utilizing large number of information available on the net (in form of reviews and comments) to improve their decision making process for example in their hotel booking. This is also called as Sentiment analysis. The various web application works on client opinion. Generally, it is seen that a web application approach to the customer is according to its area of interest. This is mined on the basis of customer reviews blogs and search on the internet.This help to analyze customer's inclination on a particular product choice.

Opinion mining process has three basic components

1. **Customer or Opinion Holder:** The customer is the person who has his own view related to a particular object and has the power to communicate those views and opinions.
2. **Product:** An object like goods and services about which views can be formed.
3. **Opinion:** These are views or thoughts or sentiments on an object given by the customer.

For marketing view point, selling the product on the internet with the help of the websites are largely influenced by the sentiments of the customer expressed in the form of reviews. Generally sentiments are related to less cost of the product and good opinion given the other customers on the same products because it is human behavior that people always try to know other people's thoughts and opinions before drawing any conclusion. It is often seen that most of the businesses try to collect and analyze customer reviews regarding their goods and services and try to enhance or modify them as per the customer need e.g. In restaurants individual's reviews in relation to food quality taste and services are collected to enhance the performance . Consumer opinions about the object can be either positive or negative which is referred as the sentiment orientation or the polarity of the sentiment. The internet is utilized for large amount of review collection and to develop the review database. These reviews act as a foundation for decision making.

Feature based opinion mining is the process of extracting the relevant information regarding the product and the services e.g., website of Trivago does the feature based opinion mining; they collect the reviews of various hotel booking and then extract the relevant hotel list that meets the customer satisfaction. There are two basic methods of opinion mining

1. **Direct Opinion:** This method has no comparison value. The subjective opinions on the products are given by the customers and these opinions are evaluated to check the worth of the product.
2. **Comparison Opinion:** This method is largely used in advertising industry. Here the objective opinions are taken related to the product and compared for relative analysis and then these opinions are used for the further promotion of the product.

The expensive utilization of opinion mining is in online sales of products, goods and services. This single platform can provide customers with a large variety of products having reasonable prices and interesting offers and discounts. But with the passage of time competition with the websites are increased due to almost having same kind of product and services. Now the opinion of individual customers is valuable for promotion and sales. As no professional staff assistance is provided for appropriate selection, this sentimental analysis plays a vital role. Every online sale has a platform for customer reviews and rating that will help future customers for buying. The challenge is that the most of the reviews are opaque and it is hard to be believed by the customer. So, the best methods to evaluate these reviews are feature based opinion mining or sentiment analysis.

The process can be initiated as follows:

1. Find the feature of the product depends upon its nature for e.g. for clothes the feature will be type of fabric, style, length etc. The feature should be written correctively in word phrases. It should be not expressed in sentence form.
2. Collect the reviews of the customer on the product. Reviews expressed can be subjective or objective
3. For feature extra.ction, from the customer reviews extract the feature word for negative and positive opinion.
4. Next step is to find the polarity of the feature. The feature can be positively inclined related to opinion or it can be negatively inclined.
5. The formation of feature opinion pairing will be done.
6. Then feature based clustering is used for handling the customer's sentiments for sales of the product.

Hence feature based opinion mining method would be used to mine the customer's knowledge by evaluating their reviews on products and then focusing on making opinion profiles for each products, that can be used for product evaluation and comparison with similar products . This leads to ultimate increase in the brand value of the product.

Extract of the information from the opinions is the key issue because from the subjective opinions key feature of the product is extracted. Product feature extraction is an important task of review mining and summarization. Generally, these kinds of tasks are carried out with the help of text feature extraction.

Applications of Feature Based Opinion Mining

1. **Customer Reviews:** Sentiment analyses analyze the user's opinion data, this analysis is based on one of the three levels: (a) Document Level, (b) Sentence Level, and (c) Attribute Level:

   a. **Document Level:** At this level, customer's review can be positive or negative. The problem of this level is that the complete review is based on a single topic. At this level single review is not considered on multiple topics. This level focuses on opinion sentence polarity identification. This method forecasts the direction of an opinion sentence. For example: "This is not good phone" This sentence holds opinion word 'good' which communicates positive opinion. But sentence communicates negative opinion since there is negation word 'not'. So when opinion word polarity identification is found, it is essential to locate polarity of opinion sentence. For opinion sentence polarity identification a list of negation words such as 'no', 'not' etc. can be set and negation policy can be created.

   b. **Sentence Level:** At this level, customer's review can be positive, negative or neutral. In neutral review no opinion and unrelated words are considered. The categorization of chore at this level can be subjective or objective. Objective sentences describe accurate information while subjective sentences describe slanted opinions. This level focuses on opinion word polarity identification method. In this method significant direction of each opinion word is identified, which means it has to be identified whether opinion word is describing positive, negative of neutral opinion.

   c. **Attribute Level:** The above two levels do not represent the exact linking of the people. It describes the fact that user can express his or her opinion on a particular feature. This level focuses on product feature extraction method of customer review. In feature extraction method, product features are taken out from every sentence. These are basically nouns that are why every noun is taken out from sentence. In review, features can be referred unambiguously or absolutely by the reviewer. Features which are referred in a sentence directly are called as explicit features and features which are referred indirectly are called implicit features. For example, "Battery Life of a phone is less" In this sentence reviewer has pointed out battery life directly so it is explicit feature. It is easy to extract such features. Now consider following sentence, "This phone needs to charge many times in a day" In sentence reviewer is talking about battery of phone but it is not mentioned directly in the sentence. So here battery is implicit feature. It is difficult to understand and extract such features from sentence (Mishra & Jha, 2012). Product feature extraction method has two approaches: Supervised and Unsupervised. The Supervised product feature extraction approach needs a set of preannotated review sentences as training examples (Mishra & Jha, 2012). A supervised learning approach is useful to create an extraction model, which is able to identify product features from new consumer reviews. The supervised approach is practically useful in organizing training examples but this approach is time consuming. The Unsupervised approach repeatedly pulls outs product featured from consumer reviewers without concerning training examples.

2. **Shopping:** Feature based opinion mining is also applied in online shopping. With the fast growth of e-commerce platform, online shopping on the products has improved. Many online shopping websites gives permission to users to react or give their opinion on products. A customer can see the analysis of the product and judge against its features. If the review is mined and result is available in pictorial representation so there will be an ease for the customer to compare its features. Towards the huge variety of products and suitable shopping practice with smart offers, these podiums have become admired for customers and manufacturers but it is very difficult for the customers to acquire the help from the specialized sales personnel to purchase the product. One approach is used to overcome this problem is that merchant provides meta data for products which are sold online. Merchants have prepared a forum which assists the customers to find out the reviews of the product and expresses their opinions about the product, but there are hundred reviews are available for a particular product, so it is difficult to find out to read every customer's review and take the decision on purchasing the product and if customer reads only some reviews and take the decision on those reviews then it will be biased.

3. **Entertainment:** This opinion mining technique is also applied in entertainment. A database named Internet Movie Database which provides the review about movies or television show. This is an online database; this site facilitates registered users to offer new objects and edits to existing opening. However, most of the data is checked, especially if it is submitted by new users, there may be errors in the system. Users with a confirmed track record of submitting realistic data are given immediate sanction for slight add-ons. Users can also give rating to any film on a scale of 1 to 10, and the totals are changed into a weighted mean-rating that is displayed next to each title.

4. **Government:** Government can also take the opinions or reviews of public on their public policies. Public policies are mined online and the online feedback of the general public can be taken against the existing of new policies. Discussions about the bang of public opinion on public policy are planned about what should be there and what is there. Each and everyone have the same point of view that in a democracy public policy should be sturdily exaggerated by public opinion.

5. **Research and Development:** Customers also give their reviews on the features of product which is beneficial for the manufacturer and research and development department, so that R & D department can improve the features of their product.

6. **Education:** Now a day's tutorials or study materials are available on line, known as e-learning. This is very popular amongst students and they use it very frequently. Students also give their opinions or reviews about that study material which is very helpful to improve that service.

7. **Business and Organization:** In the current scenario, businesses spend a large amount of funds to find out consumer's sentiments and reviews. They hire consultants and take the surveys of a particular group of people to find out the opinion of their product so that they can improve their products. This is known as product and service benchmarking and market intelligence. Opinion mining tools permit businesses to take customer's reactions on large scale.

8. **Individuals:** An individual opinion's matters a lot in every field whether it is purchasing a product or using a service of any company and it is also considered on political issues.

9. **Ads Placement:** An advertisement of a product is placed in user-generated content to take the review or opinion of the feature of the product. An advertisement is also placed online when one customer admires or appreciates the product and if a competitor criticizes the product then also advertisement is formed, with fast expansion of user-generated content on the internet symbolized by blogs; Wikipedia's etc. opinion mining tools examine the web data.

Model/Architecture of Feature Based Opinion Mining

Our motivation is to build a model for feature based opinion mining. In this model customer's reviews will be gathered and the features from these reviews will be extracted and refined in another level of the model these features will be classified and ranked for their polarity. Figure 1 represents the proposed model.

The various parts of this model are:

Figure 1. Architecture of feature based opinion mining

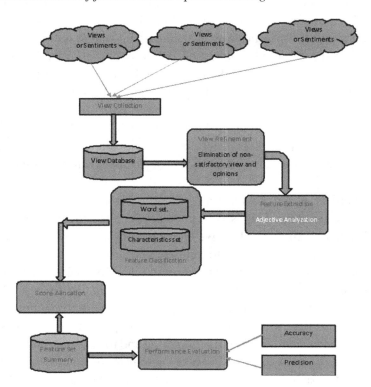

1.   **View Collection:** Various opinions from customers are both subjective and objective in nature. Subjective opinions and views are generated from feedbacks, opinions and emotional statements. Objective views are fact based. They provide the concise information regarding object. A systematic method will be used to classify subjective and objective opinions. The opinion first required to be divided into tokens and these tokens can be analyzed for classification. Data base is prepared from these views.

2.   **View Refinement:** Opinion can be wanted or unwanted, so opinions are refined for the next level. During data refining process unwanted and non-satisfactory statements or phrases will be eliminated. The preprocessing of the opinions will help to recover the accurate and the relevant opinions.

3.   **Feature and Opinion Extraction:** During this phase each opinion is analyzed for finding a feature in the view. Generally, Noun and Noun phrases of opinions are used to find the valuable feature. Each feature has valuable information given by the customer for the product.

4. **Feature Classification:** After the feature extraction process a list of features are prepared. these features are further classified as characteristic set and word set for rating these features. These features list are further passed from a parser to categories them into positive feature and negative feature.

5. **Score Allocation:** For each negative and positive feature quantitative value is assigned to calculate the orientation or the inclination of the opinion. A priority score is assigned to each positive feature to polarize an opinion for future decision making.

6. **Summary of Feature Set:** At the final stage of this model a list of finalized opinion words with their score and polarity will be generated.

7. **Performance Evaluation:** The performance of these opinions will then have evaluated. These reviews are required to be interpreted for their negative and positive polarity with the help of certain parameters. These parameters are accuracy and precision. Accuracy is the degree to which opinion will be helpful in decision making. Precision is the correctness of the opinion. Sometimes an opinion can be defined with negative polarity where it can be used for positive polarity. The change in the polarity can affect decision making. The rating mechanism will help to quantize feature polarity. The correctness of opinion is required for feature based opinion mining.

Mining Classifications of Feature Based Opinion Mining

Feature based Opinion mining trails the outlook, thoughts or review of the community about a specific matter, goods or service. The all kind of information available in the whole world of internet can be divided into two categories of reviews and numerical figures that can represent factual data.

The numerical and statistical data are used to represent real world entities and their characteristics where, reviews are textual data and this terminology is used to represent people's or consumer's reviews, sentiments for the different characteristics of real world objects. According to the latest scenario, it is assumed through the engines that the statistical data are accurate and can be combined with key features or key adjectives whereas while searching data with the help of search engines opinions are not a good choice because depending on opinions with key features make the searchers complicated, so their ranking approaches are not correct or opinion reclamation. Currently the web has drastically altered its mode on public comments and their reviews on goods and services. Consumers use websites and other mechanisms of internet like blogs and forums to give their views and sentiments about goods and services provided by the producer. This opinion database generated by user holds useful information that helps in decision making. Such website remarks are not partial but these are prolonged on worldwide level. Now a day, if the consumer needs the opinion of a specific product then his/ her circle is not limited as he/she can receive the view of that product on the internet throughout assorted assessment or remarks. Feature based opinion mining has many reasons for someone else to react angrily or emotionally. The number one issue required to cater is, in some cases reviews are treated in favor while in another case it is treated as negative. The second issue is that people do not affirm the opinions in a similar mode for all time. The assessment of opinion can be made in two ways:

1. **Direct Opinion:** It provides positive or negative view about the product directly. For example, "The speed of 2G is slow", articulates a direct opinion.
2. **Comparison:** It compares the product with some other alike product. For example, "The speed of 4 G is better than 2 G and 3 G", this describes a comparison.

Feature based opinion mining can be classified on various mining techniques:

1. **Text review and Fact Review Analyzing:** A customer can give both subjective and objective reviews. Prejudiced stuffs characterize customer's view, feelings, reactions etc. and objective contents reveals realistic information. So, the aim of subjectivity/objectivity categorization is to limit needless objective transcript from further processing. For that reason, every assessed text statement is symbolized into noun and noun phrases, after dividing text statements a process is applied to extract the adjective words from these statements and sentences in order to classify between subjective opinions and objective opinions. To set up the effectiveness of the known features for subjectivity purpose, a variety of important classifiers are defined such as Naive Bayes etc.
2. **Feature and Opinion Learning Techniques:** This component is developing of a variety of perspectives for information module (includes feature, modifier, and view) pulling out from subjective analysis sentences pulled out in the preceding pace. For one perspective, the feature mining procedures are instigated through the help of a numerical parser and progressed by a predefined rules mechanism to recognize applicant information modules in supplementary investigation. Additionally, a variety of opinions information are missing because of non availability of noun and noun phrases pairs at sentence level. So, for one more perspective, a review mechanism has offered in order to recognize words that are already referred in previous text which are applicable precursor which subsists in earlier sentences to requisite feature-opinion pairs. Both the perspectives are standard and are implemented on analysis phrases which affects to other goods and services field and there is no earlier information is not required to recognize the product features and customer's opinions articulated over them.

3. **Sentimental Analyzing:** In accumulation to the mining of feature-opinion pairs from assessment credentials, one further vital chore linked with the growth of a relevant feature extracting system in order to categorize emotion that may be in support, against or having no emotions in the reviews. Opinion based databases acts as source of information. A sentimental parser is prepared having predefined rules that is capable of classifying positive and negative reviews from the sentence phrases by the customers. This classification is useful to establish the emotions of prejudiced words maintained after viability investigation.

4. **Feasibility Analyzing:** Throughout information module pulling out phase, various nouns, verbs and adjectives are taken out which are not pertinent product features, modifiers, and opinions. Also, anaphora antecedent binding caused noisy feature-opinion pairs extractions that are not relevant for feature-opinion binding task. In line with Agrawal and Batra (2013), feasibility analysis technique is applied to eliminate noisy feature-opinion pairs based on reliability scores generated through a customized version HITS algorithm, which molds feature-opinion pairs and evaluate article as a bipartite graph which considers feature opinion pairs as core and appraisal credentials as establishment. A superior score value of a pair reproduces a stretched veracity of the two modules in a pair. This score decides the amount of consistency of an opinion uttered over a product feature.

The responsibility of estimation withdrawal is in the direction of discovering the view of an entity that may be in favor or no favor and the characteristics it portrays, characteristics are appreciated etc. The mechanism of an opinion is:

*   **Opinion Holder:** Opinion holder is a person who provides a precise view on an entity.
*   **Object:** Object is article, by an opinion is articulated by consumer
*   **Opinion:** This is a vision, emotion, or assessment of an entity done by consumer.

Pictorial Representation of Mining Techniques

The mining at different levels have different features to be evaluated and summary is generated for future references and help in decision making. All these mining techniques can be combined to form a process to refine the feature set and further enhance the decision-making process.

Figure 2. Pictorial representations of mining techniques

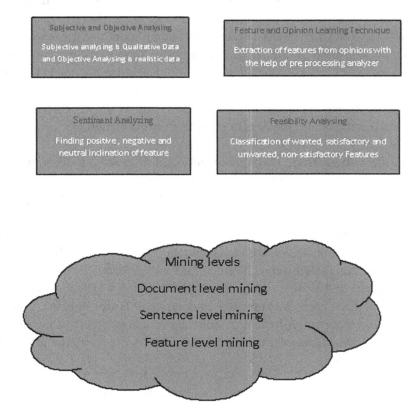

Responsibilities of Opinion Mining at Manuscript Stage

This estimation withdrawal categorizes on whole estimation obtainable via creators in complete manuscript since in favor, no favor or having no views regarding definite entity. Statement in use at manuscript stage be to facilitate every manuscript states about solitary entity and holds the estimation of a single estimation owner. Some author states vocation support on remoteness assess of characteristics originated in entire manuscript which recognized the division that is outstanding or poor. The author gives the description of algorithm having three stages i.e. First stage describes that characteristics are taken out by the side of an expression that presents suitable information. Another stage describes that, the literal meaning direction be confined via calculating remoteness as of expressions of recognized division. The last stage, the pseudo code calculates the regular literal course of every expression which organizes an appraisal since suggested or not.

Responsibilities of Opinion Mining at Ruling Stage

This stage of estimation withdrawal is having two responsibilities. The very first responsibility investigates about the existing task whether it is subjective or objective. The second task discovers view of dogmatic verdict may be in favor, no favor or having no review. Supposition can be considered at ruling stage be so as to verdict holds merely single view e.g., "The speed of 2G is slow."

Responsibilities of Opinion Mining at Characteristic Stage

The task of opinion mining at feature level is to extract the features of the observation object and thereafter conclude the opinion of the object, it can be positive or negative and then cluster the feature synonyms and creates the outline description. To recognize the direction of opinion the lexicon based approach is used. This loom utilizes opinion words and phrase in a sentence to decide the view. The working of lexicon based approach is explained in following steps

- Identification of opinion words
- Role of Negation words
- But –clauses (Mishra & Jha, 2012)

Algorithm of Feature Based Opinion Mining

The Algorithm for feature based opinion mining is divided in to two phases:

- **Phase 1**: This phase will identify the important reviews. The algorithm is called as High Noun and Noun Phrase Count Algorithm (HNNPC). In this phase the algorithm will check the noun and noun phrase associated with it. If any noun has a noun phrase then its adjective is collected and the count of feature will be increased by one. High count features will be passed in to phase two for priority assignment. The steps of algorithm are:
  - **Step 1:** Start
  - **Step 2:** Read Review
  - **Step 3:** Set Score _count to zero.
  - **Step 4:** For complete sentence of review do
    - Scan Noun and Noun Phrase.
    - If Noun and Noun Phrase pair is found
    - Then increase Score _count by 1.
  - **Step 5:** For Each objective review do

Table 1. Responsibilities of opinion mining at various stages

Categorization of Opinion mining at various stages	Hypothesis of Opinion mining at various stages	Responsibilities at various stages
Opinion Mining at Ruling Stage	A verdict holds just single view placed via one estimation owner; that may not be accurate in some situations. The ruling edge is clear in the certain manuscript.	Responsibility 1: recognize the particular verdict as prejudiced or intolerant module: objective and Intolerant. Responsibility 2: View categorization of the specified verdict. module: optimistic Unconstructive and unbiased.
Opinion Mining at Manuscript stage	Every manuscript has a focal point on a solitary entity and holds view placed by a solitary view owner. This is not appropriate for discussion position because there may be several views of numerous substances of these basis.	Responsibility 1: view categorization of evaluation module: optimistic Unconstructive and unbiased.
Opinion Mining at Characteristic stage	The facts have a focal point on characteristics of a sole entity placed by a solitary view owner. This is not appropriate for discussion position because there may be several views of numerous substances of these basis.	Responsibility 1: Recognize and pull out entity characteristics which have been remarked via a view owner. Responsibility 2: module: optimistic Unconstructive and unbiased. Responsibility 3: Cluster characteristic synonyms. create a feature-based opinion synopsis of several evaluations.

(Mishra & Jha, 2012)

- Scan a factual value associated with objective.
- If numeric value is found then increase Score _count by 1.
  ○ **Step 6:** Save the Score _count and pass it to phase two.
- **Phase 2:** This phase is used to allocate the priority of the feature. This algorithm is called as Priority Allocation algorithm. The score _count value from the phase one is received and then further priority is assigned. For each feature word assign a priority between values of -5 to +5. A negative priority indicates Negative view, zero priority indicates neural opinion and a positive priority indicates positive view that can be further used as valuable source for decision making. The steps of this algorithm are:

- ○ **Step 1:** Receive score _count from phase 1.
- ○ **Step 2:** Receive the feature list.
- ○ **Step 3:** If score _count is less than thresh hold values than allocate a negative priority to the feature word and go to step 6.
- ○ **Step 4:** If score _count is zero then feature is neutral and no priority will be assigned to the feature word and go to step 6.
- ○ **Step 5:** If score _count is more than thresh hold values than allocate a positive priority to the feature word and go to step 6.
- ○ **Step 6:** Repeat step 3 to 5 until feature list is empty.
- ○ **Step 7:** Receive refined feature list for decision making.
- ○ **Step 8:** Stop.

This algorithm is future evaluated on a number of parameters for feature evaluation. These parameters are precision and accuracy. The main difference between feature extraction algorithm and simple word count algorithm is that a weight is assigned to each feature word to as priority for further analysis and evaluation.

Applications of Opinion Mining in Web Text Mining

Estimation withdrawal engages content withdrawal and verbal communication and content categorization. Content withdrawal conquers the existing insufficiency. Unluckily, natural language processing come across a variety of complexity because of complicated personality of individual speech. in addition, the region of estimation withdrawal includes trouble of content categorization, that is entirely dissimilar to the standard content withdrawal. Standard content categorization recognizes subject, while in estimation withdrawal, reaction categorization is made that has the focal point of reviewing author's emotions in the direction of the subject matter. Sentiments are not adequately examined with keyword based techniques. Text mining procedures shapeless information, it takes out significant numeric indices from the text, and constructs the information enclosed in the text available to a variety of data mining algorithms. Information can be taken out from the recapitulated terms of the credentials, so the terms can be investigated and also the resemblance between terms and credentials can be determined. On the whole, text mining translates text into statistics that can be incorporated in other study like predictive data mining projects, clustering etc. Text mining is also recognized as text data mining, which submits the procedure of developing superiority information from text. Superiority information is consequent during the statistical pattern learning. Text mining involves the procedure of organizing the input text like parsing and other successive insertion into a database. It derives patterns within the structured data, calculates them and lastly creates the output. It takes explanation of text classification, text clustering, sentiment analysis, document summarization, and entity relation modeling. Text mining is a procedure that utilizes a set of algorithms for adapting unstructured text into structured data objects and the quantitative methods used to analyze these data objects.

Applications of Text Mining

There are a variety of applications of Text mining like default dispensation of messages and emails. For example, it is probable to "clean" out automatically "junk email" on the basis affirms conditions; those messages are repeatedly removed. These default schemes for organizing electronic messages can too be helpful in applications when messages are required to be running automatically to the most suitable section.

Analyzing warranty or insurance claims, diagnostic interviews. In some business domains, the major information is composed in textual form. For example, guarantee asserts or preliminary medical (patient) discussions can be sum up in concise narratives needs to be fixed responses. Ever more, such comments are composed electronically; therefore, such kinds of narratives are voluntarily accessible for input into text mining algorithms.

Analyzing open-ended survey responses. Survey feedback form holds two categories of questions: open -ended and closed-ended. Closed-ended questions describe a distinct set of reactions from which to choose. Such kinds of reactions are simply measured and evaluated but open -ended questions permits the respondent to answer a question in his own words. These kinds of unstructured responses frequently offer comfortable and appreciated information than closed-ended questions.

Web Mining

Now a day, huge amount of data is accessible on web so, WWW is known as usual region for data mining. This study is having the turning point of study from numerous research societies like database, information retrieval, and Artificial Intelligence.

As web acquaintance is sprinkled and because of absence of any standardized format, web mining is a not an easy job to engage any issues.

This is the procedure of pertaining data mining methodologies for finding out prototypes from the Web. Web mining is alienated into three diverse types, these are Web usage mining, Web content mining and Web structure mining.

1. **Web Usage Mining:** This is the procedure of determining the user's perspective that he needs to observe on the Internet. Several customers are fascinated in textual data but some are interested to explore multimedia data. This is completed by making use of user logs.

2. **Web Structure Mining:** This is the procedure of taking out information from web pages by giving focus on the formation. Web structure mining is alienated into two types:
   a. **Extracting Patterns From Hyperlinks in the Web:** A hyper link is a structural module which attaches the web page to a diverse place.
   b. **Mining the Document Structure:** In this type the tree-like structure of page formation to portray HTML or XML tag custom is evaluated.
3. **Web Content Mining:** This procedure aspires to pull out practical information from contents of the web page. It engages scrutinizing of every content on a web page to discover its significance with the investigated inquiry.

Terminologies

- **Text Mining vs. Data Mining:** In Text Mining, prototypes are taken out from natural language text but in Data Mining prototypes are taken out from databases.
- **Text Mining vs. Web Mining:** In Text Mining, the participation is amorphous text, but in Web Mining web foundations are prearranged. (Rashmi Agrawal and Mridula Batra, 2013)

Figure 3. Web Mining Categories (Seerat, 2012)

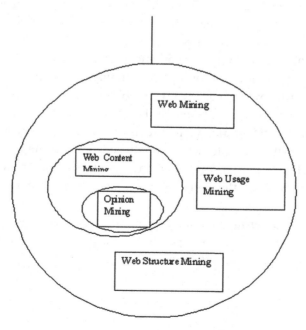

The major applications of Opinion mining and sentiment analysis in web text mining are the following:

1. **Purchasing Product or Service:** When a customer is buying a product, then taking accurate choice is not hard chore. Through this method, users can effortless class other's views and have knowledge about any product or service and too he/she can simply evaluate the rival brands because every data is available on the web and customers give their feedback on the web about the product. So, there is no need for the users to depend on outside advisor. The Opinion mining and pulls out public opinion form the internet and examines it and then offers to them in planned and comprehensible mode.

2. **Quality Improvement in Product or Service:** By this technique of feature-based opinion mining, the producer can gather the opponent's estimation and constructive view about their manufacturing goods and so they can enhance the quality of their product. They can create use online product evaluation from websites such as Amazon and CNet, etc.

3. **Marketing Research:** The outcome of sentiment analysis methods can be employed in marketing research. By this method, the current inclination of customers regarding some product can be studied. Likewise, the current approach of common public towards some new government policy can also be simply studied. So, the entire consequences can be added to combine intellectual study.

4. **Recommendation Systems:** By giving or filling the feedback forms of the product on line the user's view can be found positive or negative about the product, this scheme can easily find out which one ought to be suggested and which one ought not to be suggested.

5. **Detection of "Flame":** The observations of newsgroups, blogs and social media are simply probable by opinion mining. Opinion mining can notice egotistical terms over intense words or abhorrence speech used in emails or tweets on different internet resources by default.

6. **Opinion Spam Detection:** As internet is accessible to everyone, so anybody can place everything on internet, this amplified the opportunity of spam content on the web. People can write down spam content to deceive the public. Opinion mining can categorize the internet content into' spam' content and 'not spam' content.

7. **Policy Making:** During Opinion Mining, strategy creator may take people's point of view regarding some policy and they can use this information in generating new public forthcoming policy.

8. **Decision Making:** User's views and skills are very helpful ingredients in decision making procedure. Opinion mining provides examined people's judgment which can be successfully adopted for decision making. (Rahmath, 2014)

CONCLUSION

Opinion mining is a valuable task now a day. Due to increase in market competition among the producers of goods and services, mining of customer interest can improve in sales and generation of profits. Feature based opinion mining is an efficient tool for extracting customer interest. To extract this information, it is required to mine the customer's reviews on products. From theses reviews the adjective words are mined to find the inclination of the customer towards the product. The websites and internet has played a great role in review generation. In current market maximum product sale is on line and it increases the capture of global market for each individual manufacturer easily. The process starts from collecting the objective and subjective reviews of the customer given for the similar nature of the products. These reviews are classified in to separate list of characteristic set and word set, where characteristic set belongs to objective features and word set is belongs to subjective features. From this word set the adjective words are identified. A score is assigned to each feature. Then theses reviews are pre-processed for feature extraction. These features can have negative polarity or positive polarity. Positive polarity features are valuable to increase product sale and to improve the market competition among the producers. Feature extraction opinion mining can be used in some number applications ranges from product production to marketing and sales. This technique is also an area of research for researchers to further improve the web mining contents.

REFERENCES

Agrawal, R., & Batra, M. (2013). A detailed study on text mining techniques. *International Journal of Soft Computing and Engineering*, 2(6), 118–121.

Mishra, N., & Jha, C. K. (2012). Classification of opinion mining techniques. *International Journal of Computers and Applications*, 56(13).

Rahmath, H. (2014). Opinion mining and sentiment analysis-challenges and applications. *International Journal of Application or Innovation in Engineering & Management*, 3(5).

ADDITIONAL READING

Ding, X., & Liu, B. (2008). A holistic lexicon-based approach to opinion mining. In *Proceedings of the International Conference on Web Search and Web Data Mining, WSDM'08* (pp. 231–240). 10.1145/1341531.1341561

Guo, H., & Zhu, H. (2009). Address standardization with latent semantic association. In *Proceedings of the 15th ACM SIGKDD International Conference on Knowledge Discovery and Data Mining* (pp. 1155–1164). ACM.

Hu, M., & Liu, B. (2004). Mining and summarizing customer reviews. In *Proceedings of the 10th ACM SIGKDD International Conference on Knowledge Discovery and Data Mining, KDD'04.*

Hu, M., & Liu, B. (2004). Mining opinion features in customer reviews. In *Proceedings of the 19th National Conference on Artificial Intelligence AAAI'04* (pp. 755–760).

Kim, S.-M., & Hovy, E. (2004). Determining the sentiment of opinions. In *Proceedings of the 20th International Conference on Computational Linguistics COLING'04.* 10.3115/1220355.1220555

Liu, B., & Cheng, J. (2005), Opinion observer: Analyzing and comparing opinions on the web. In *Proceedings of the 14th International Conference on World Wide Web, WWW'05* (pp. 342–351). 10.1145/1060745.1060797

Meena, A., & Prabhakar, T. V. (2007). Sentence level sentiment analysis in the presence of conjuncts using linguistic analysis. In *Proceedings of the 29th European Conference on IR Research, ECIR'07.* 10.1007/978-3-540-71496-5_53

Miao, Q., & Li, Q. (2008), An integration strategy for mining product features and opinions. In *Proceeding of the 17th ACM Conference on Information and Knowledge Management, CIKM'08* (pp. 1369-1370). 10.1145/1458082.1458284

Mishra, N., & Jha, C. K. (2012). An insight into task of opinion mining. In *Second International Joint Conference on Advances in Signal Processing and Information Technology – SPIT.*

Nasukawa, T., & Yi, J. (2003), Sentiment analysis: Capturing favorability using natural language processing. In *Proceedings of the 2nd International Conference on Knowledge Capture K-CAP'03* (pp. 70-77).

Seerat, B., & Azam, F. (2012). Opinion Mining: Issues and Challenges (A survey). *International Journal of Computers and Applications, 49*(9).

Tian, P., Liu, Y., Liu, M., & Zhu, S. (2009, October). Research of product ranking technology based on opinion mining. In *Second International Conference on Intelligent Computation Technology and Automation ICICTA'09* (Vol. 4, pp. 239-243). IEEE.

Zhai, Z., & Liu, B. (2010). Grouping product features using semi-supervised learning with soft-constraints. In *Proceedings of the 23rd International Conference on Computational Linguistics, COLING'10* (pp. 1272–1280).

Zhang, W., & Yu, C. (2007), Opinion retrieval from blogs. In *Proceedings of the 16th ACM Conference on Conference on Information and Knowledge Management, CIKM'07* (pp. 831–840). 10.1145/1321440.1321555

Chapter 3
Deep Learning for Opinion Mining

Iman Raeesi Vanani
Allameh Tabataba'i University, Iran

Morteza Amirhosseini
Allameh Tabataba'i University, Iran

ABSTRACT

In this chapter, through introducing the deep learning and relation between deep learning and artificial intelligence, and especially machine learning, the authors discuss machine learning and deep learning techniques, the literature focuses on applied deep learning techniques for extracting opinions. It can be found that opinion mining without using deep learning is not meaningful. In this way, authors mention the history of deep learning and appearance of it and some important and useful deep learning algorithms for opinion mining; learning methods and customized deep learning techniques for opinion mining will also be described to understand how these algorithms and techniques are used as an applicable solution. Future trends of deep learning in opinion mining are introduced through some clues about the applications and future usages of deep learning and opinion mining and how intelligent agents develop automatic deep learning. Finally, authors have summarized different sections of the chapter at conclusion.

DOI: 10.4018/978-1-5225-6117-0.ch003

INTRODUCTION

Nowadays, around 4 billion internet users in the world, generate different contents in weblogs, forums, portals, websites and social networks apps in every second and online, these kinds of data have led to potency of social information for figure outing opinions about politics, services, products, news or events, this outburst, has turned opinion mining into a very valuable intangible asset. many surveys, applicable solutions, algorithms and tools such as Bag Of Words (BOW) model, Part Of Speech (POS) tagging, lexicon-based techniques, Natural Language Processing (NLP), Sentiment Analysis (SA), classification algorithm, machine learning and deep learning algorithms have created to handle and mine knowledge from context as an opinion miner.

However, most opinion mining techniques are, based on machine learning which some earlier information about sentiment should use in the analyzing process. On the other hand, an edge over the traditional machine learning algorithms is deep learning techniques, which are to learn automatically new complex features. These overcome the challenges coped by opinion mining and handle the diversities without the expensive demand or manual extraction.

In this chapter, authors want to describe deep learning and some of the different approaches used in the opinion mining. First of all, after some definitions and study on history of deep learning, authors will define deep learning techniques in particular; this part considers an ensemble of machine learning techniques using Artificial intelligence algorithms, that several sentiment classifiers trained with kinds of features, and an ensemble of features, where the combination has made at the feature level.

After this, authors will discuss using deep learning in opinion mining models, because sentiment analysis models have validated by deep learning techniques, in this section, authors focus on applicable and new techniques and explain the important ones. After that, the authors will describe the developed deep learning in opinion mining and applied techniques by describing a sample framework in detail. The framework is a useful conceptual model for new kind of deep learning techniques in opinion mining. Finally, the trend of deep learning techniques in opinion mining will be discussed as the last part of this chapter.

DEEP LEARNING DEFINITION

Before talking about deep learning, relationship with Machine Learning, Artificial Intelligence, and shallow learning is necessary to know. The easiest way to understand this relationship is looking at the diagram in Figure 1.

Figure 1. AI Diagram

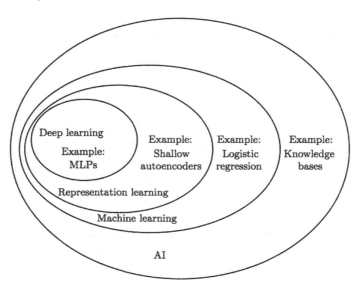

Artificial Intelligence

The term AI emerged in 1956 by John McCarthy, who is also referred as Father of Artificial Intelligence. The idea behind AI is fairly simple yet fascinating, which is to make intelligent machines that can take decisions on its own. You may think it as a science fantasy, but with respect to recent developments in technology and computing power, very idea seems to come closer to reality day by day.

Nowadays, Computers have some intelligence power to all the programs that humans have created and which allow them to "do some intelligence things" that human consider useful. But there are many tasks which humans are able to do rather easily but stay out of reach of computers, at the beginning of the current century. Many of these tasks name under the label of Artificial Intelligence. Researchers believe that we could not create AI for all tasks because we do not know explicitly how to do these tasks, even though our brain can do them. Doing those tasks involve knowledge that is now implicit, but we have information about those tasks through data.

Fuzzy logic, neural networks, machine learning, evolutionary computations, pattern recognition are some of AI algorithms and methods those have been using as a solution for enabling computers to make a decision and allow them for learning.

Machine Learning

Now, that you are familiar with AI, let talk briefly about Machine Learning and understand what it means when researchers say that they are programming machines to learn. Let begin with a very famous definition of Machine Learning:

A computer program is said to learn from experience E with respect to some task T and some performance measure P, if its performance on T, as measured by P, improves with experience E. — Tom Mitchell, Carnegie Mellon University

So, if you want your program to predict, traffic patterns at a busy intersection (task T), you can run it through a machine learning algorithm with data about past traffic patterns (experience E). Now, the accuracy of the prediction (performance measure P) will depend on the fact that whether the program has successfully learned from the data set or not (experience E).

Basically, Machine Learning refers to as a type of artificial intelligence (AI) that provides computers with the ability to learn without being explicitly programmed by exposing them to the vast amount of data. The core principle behind Machine Learning is to learn from data sets and try to minimize error or maximize the likelihood of their predictions being true.

Two main challenges in machine learning are:

- Traditional ML algorithms are not useful while working with high dimensional data that is where we have a large number of inputs and outputs. For example, in case of handwriting recognition, we have a large amount of input where we will have different types of input associated with different type of handwriting.
- The second major challenge is to tell the computer what features it should look for that will play an important role in predicting the outcome as well as to make better accuracy while doing so. This process refers to feature extraction.

Feeding raw data to the algorithm rarely ever works and this is the reason feature extraction is a critical part of the traditional machine learning workflow. Therefore, without feature extraction, the challenge for the programmer increases as the effectiveness of algorithm very much depends on how insightful the programmer is. Hence, it is very difficult to apply these Machine Learning models or algorithms to complex problems like object recognition, handwriting recognition, NLP (Natural Language Processing), etc. (https://www.edureka.co/blog/what-is-deep-learning)

Deep Learning

Deep learning is part of a broader family of machine learning methods based on learning data representations, as opposed to task-specific algorithms. Learning can be supervised, partially supervised or unsupervised. (Bengio et al., 2015)

Deep learning is a class of machine learning algorithms that: (Deng and Yu, 2014)

- Use a cascade of multiple layers of nonlinear processing units for feature extraction and transformation. Each successive layer uses the output from the previous layer as input.
- Learn in supervised (e.g., classification) and/or unsupervised (e.g., pattern analysis) manners.
- Learn multiple levels of representations that correspond to different levels of abstraction; the levels form a hierarchy of concepts.

Deep learning has various closely related definitions or high-level descriptions: (Deng & Yu, 2014)

Definition 1: A class of machine learning techniques that exploit many layers of non-linear information processing for supervised or unsupervised feature extraction and transformation, and for pattern analysis and classification.

Definition 2: A sub-field within machine learning that is based on algorithms for learning multiple levels of representation in order to model complex relationships among data. Higher-level features and concepts are thus defined in terms of lower-level ones, and such a hierarchy of features is called a deep architecture. Most of these models are based on unsupervised learning of representations.

Definition 3: A sub-field of machine learning that is based on learning several levels of representations, corresponding to a hierarchy of features or factors or concepts, where higher-level concepts are defined from lower-level ones, and the same lower-level concepts can help to define many higher-level concepts. Deep learning is part of a broader family of machine learning methods based on learning representations.

Definition 4: Deep learning is a set of algorithms in machine learning that attempt to learn at multiple levels, corresponding to different levels of abstraction. It typically uses artificial neural networks. The levels in these learned statistical models correspond to distinct levels of concepts, where higher-level concepts are defined from lower-level ones, and the same lower-level concepts can help to define many higher-level concepts.

Definition 5: Deep Learning is a new area of Machine Learning research, which has been introduced with the objective of moving Machine Learning closer to one of its original goals: Artificial Intelligence. Deep Learning is about learning multiple levels of representation and abstraction that help to make sense of data such as images, sound, and text.

DEEP LEARNING BACKGROUND

You can find a lot of content as the background of deep learning, authors mention some of them as a timeline and some important events are emphasized. The first general, working learning algorithm for supervised, deep, feed forward, multilayer perceptions were published by Akexey Ivakhnenko and Lapa in 1965. (Ivakhnenko, 1973). The term Deep Learning was introduced to the machine learning community by Rina Dechter in 1986, (Schmidhuber, 2015) and Artificial Neural Networks by Igor Aizenberg and colleagues in 2000, in the context of Boolean threshold neurons.

In 1989, Yann LeCun et al. applied the standard back propagation algorithm, which had been around as the reverse mode of automatic differentiation since 1970, (Griewank and Andreas, 2012) to a deep neural network with the purpose of recognizing handwritten ZIP codes on mail. In 1992, Schmidhuber used unsupervised pre-training for deep hierarchies of data-compressing recurrent neural networks (RNN) and showed its benefits for speeding up supervised learning. (Schmidhuber, 2015)

In 1994, André de Carvalho, together with Fairhurst and Bisset (1994), published experimental results of a multi-layer Boolean neural network, also known as a weightless neural network, composed of a self-organizing feature extraction neural network module followed by a classification neural network module, which was independently trained. (DeCarvalho et al., 1994)

Simpler models that use task-specific handcrafted features such as Gabor filters and support vector machines (SVMs) were a popular choice in the 1990s and 2000s, because of artificial neural networks (ANN) computational cost and a lack of understanding of how the brain wires its biological networks. The impact of deep learning in the industry began in the early 2000s when the convolutional neural network (CNN) already processed an estimated 10% to 20% of all the checks written in the US. (Yann LeCun, 2016)

Since 2006, deep structured learning, or more commonly called deep learning or hierarchical learning, has emerged as a new area of machine learning research. During the past several years, the techniques developed from deep learning research have already been impacting a lot of signal and information processing work within the traditional and the new widened scopes including key aspects of machine learning and artificial intelligence (Deng & Yu, 2014).

Deep learning moving beyond shallow machine learning since 2006

Also, in 2007, hierarchical stacks of RNNs were introduced. They can be trained by hierarchical Connectionist Temporal Classification (CTC). For tasks of sequence labeling, every RNN level predicts a sequence of labels fed to the next level. (Schmidhuber, 2015). Advances in hardware enabled the renewed interest. In 2009, Nvidia was involved in what was called the "big bang" of deep learning, "...as deep-learning neural networks were trained with Nvidia graphics processing units (GPUs)." (Venture Beat, 2016) That year, Google Brain used Nvidia GPUs to create capable deep neural networks (DNNs). While there, Ng determined that GPUs could increase the speed of deep-learning systems by about 100 times.

In recent years and after 2010 till now, several innovations, applied techniques and usages emerge in the world, some usages are in image recognition, natural language processing, drug discovery, customer relationship management, recommendation system, opinion mining, sentimental mining, web mining, text mining, bioinformatics and mobile advertisement.

DEEP LEARNING TECHNIQUES

Recent successes of deep learning techniques in solving many complex tasks by learning from raw data and using various algorithms. The nature of this experience (E) in Deep learning is typically considered for classifying Machine Learning algorithms into the following three categories: supervised, unsupervised, and reinforcement learning: (Carrio et al., 2017)

Today everyone could take some machine learning tools, and start to write code, but without knowing how those algorithms work, is very simple to make huge mistakes. So is very important to understand be basics of learning algorithms and then study deep learning algorithm. One of the first concepts in machine learning is the difference between supervised, unsupervised, reinforcement and deep learning.

In supervised learning, algorithms present with a dataset containing a collection of features. Additionally, labels or target values are provided for each sample. This mapping of features to the label of target values is where the knowledge is encoded. Once it has learned, the algorithm is expected to find the mapping from the features of unseen samples to their correct labels or target values. The purpose of unsupervised learning is to extract meaningful representations and explain key features of the data. No labels or target values are necessary in this case in order to learn from the data. In reinforcement learning algorithms, an AI agent interacts with a real or simulated environment. This interaction provides feedback between the learning system and the interaction experience which is useful to improve performance in the task being learned. Finally, Deep learning (DL) techniques represent a huge step forward for machine learning. DL is based on the way the human brain process information and learns. It consists of a machine learning model composed by several levels of representation, in which every level uses the information from the previous level to learn deeply. Each level corresponds, in this model, to a different area of the cerebral cortex, and every level abstract more the information in the same way of the human brain. Now each of these learning techniques explains to understand.

Supervised Learning Technique

Supervised learning algorithms learn how to associate an input with some output, given a training set of examples of inputs and outputs (Goodfellow et al., 2016). The following paragraphs cover the most relevant algorithms. Nowadays in supervised learning: Feed forward Neural Networks, a popular variation of these called Convolutional Neural Networks (CNNs), Recurrent Neural Networks (RNNs), and a variation of RNNs called Long Short-Term Memory (LSTM) models. Feed forward Neural Networks, also known as Multilayer Perceptions (MLPs), are the most common supervised learning models. Their purpose is to work as function approximations. The approximated function is usually built by stacking together several hidden layers that are activated in the chain to get the desired output. The number of hidden layers is usually called the depth of the model, which explains the origin of the term deep learning: learning using models with several layers Convolutional Neural Networks (CNNs). These models take their name from the mathematical linear operation of convolution which is always present in at least one of the layers of the network. (Carrio et al., 2017)

In contrast to MLPs, Recurrent Neural Networks (RNNs) are models in which the output is a function of not only the current inputs but also of the earlier outputs, which encode into a hidden state. This means that RNNs have a memory of the previous outputs and can encode the information present in the sequence itself, something that MLPs cannot do. As a result, this type of model is very useful to learn from sequential data. RNNs are usually trained using Back Propagation Through Time (BPTT), an extension of back propagation which takes into account temporality to compute the gradients. Using this method with long temporal sequences can lead to several issues. Gradients accumulated over a long sequence can become immeasurably large or extremely small. These problems are referred to an exploding gradient and vanishing gradients, respectively. (Carrio et al., 2017)

Long Short-Term Memory (LSTM) models are a type of RNN architecture proposed by Hochreiter and Schmidhuber (1997) which successfully overcomes the problem of vanishing gradients by maintaining a more constant error with gated cells, which effectively allow for continuous learning over a larger number of time steps.

As it has been already stated, LSTM gated cells in RNN shave internal recurrence, besides the outer recurrence of RNNs. Cells store an internal state, which can be written to and read from them. There are gates controlling how data enter and leave and are deleted from this cell state. Those gates act on the signals they receive, and, similar to a standard neural network, they block or pass on information based on its strength and importance using their own sets of weights. Those weights, as the weights that modulate input and hidden states, are adjusted via the recurrent network's learning process. (Carrio et al., 2017)

Unsupervised Learning Technique

Unsupervised learning aims towards the development of models that are capable of extracting meaningful and high-level representations from high-dimensional sensory unlabeled data. This functionality is inspired by the visual cortex which requires very small amount of labeled data. Deep Generative Models such as Deep Belief Networks (DBNs) (Hinton and Osindero, 2006) allow the learning of several layers of nonlinear features in an unsupervised manner. DBNs are built by stacking several Restricted Boltzmann Machines (RBMs), resulting in a hybrid model in which the top two layers form a RBM and the bottom layers act as a directed graph constituting a Sigmoid Belief Network (SBN). (Carrio et al., 2017).

The learning algorithm proposed in (Hinton and Osindero, 2006) is supposed to be one of the first efficient ways of learning DBNs by introducing greedy layer-by-layer training to get to a deep hierarchical model. In this greedy learning procedure, the hidden activity patterns obtained in the current layer are used as the "visible" data for training the RBM of the next layer.

Once the stacked RBMs have been learned and combined to form a DBN, a fine-tuning procedure using a contrastive version of the wake-sleep algorithm is applied. (Adrian Carrio et al., 2017). Deep neural networks can also be utilized for dimensionality reduction of the input data. For this purpose, deep "auto encoders" (Vincent et al., 2010) have been shown to provide successful results in a wide variety of applications such as document retrieval and image retrieval (Krizhevsky and Hinton, 2011). An auto encoder is an unsupervised neural networking which the target values are set to be equal to the inputs.

Auto encoders are mainly composed of an "encoder" network, which transforms the input data into a low-dimensional code, and a "decoder" network, which reconstructs the data from the code. Training these deep models involves minimizing the error between the original data and its reconstruction. In this process, the weights initialization is critical to avoid reaching a bad local optimum; thus, some authors have proposed a pertained stage based on stacked RBMs and a fine-tuning stage using back propagation (Krizhevsky and Hinton, 2011). In addition, the encoder part of the auto encoder can serve as a good unsupervised nonlinear feature extractor. In this field, the use of Stacked De-noising Auto encoders (SDAE) (Vincent et al., 2010) has been proven to be an effective unsupervised feature extractor in different classification problems. The experiments presented in (Vincent et al., 2010) showed that training de noising auto encoders with higher noise levels forced the model to extract more distinctive and less local features.

Reinforcement Learning Technique

In reinforcement learning, an agent is defined to interact with an environment, seeking to find the best action for each state at any step in time. The agent must balance exploration and exploitation of the state space in order to find the optimal policy that maximizes the accumulated reward from the interaction with the environment. In this context, an agent modifies its behavior or policy with the awareness of the states, actions are taken, and rewards for every time step. Reinforcement learning composes an optimization process throughout the whole state space in order to maximize the accumulated reward. Robotic problems are often task-based with temporal structure. These types of problems are suitable to be solved by means of a reinforcement learning framework. (Kober, 2013)

A general problem in real robotic applications is that the state and action spaces are often continuous spaces. A continuous state and/or action space can make the optimization problem intractable, due to the overwhelming set of different states and/or actions. As a general framework for representation, reinforcement learning methods are enhanced through deep learning to aid the design for feature representation, which is known as deep reinforcement learning. In this review, deep reinforcement learning methods are divided into two main categories: value function and policy search methods.

Value Function Methods allows simplifying more standard actor-critic style algorithms while preserving the benefits of nonlinear value function approximation (GU et al., 2016). NAF is valid for continuous control tasks and takes advantage of trained models to approximate the standard model-free value function. Policy Search Methods is a Policy-based reinforcement learning methods aim towards directly searching for the optimal policy, which provides a feasible framework for continuous control. Deep Deterministic Policy Gradient (DDPG) (Lillirap et al., 2016) is based on the actor-critic paradigm, with two neural networks to approximate a greedy deterministic policy (actor) and function.

Deep Learning Technique

Deep learning techniques are to get the deep neural network to train efficiently. Deep learning is a subfield of machine learning which attempts to learn high-level abstractions in data by utilizing hierarchical architectures. It is an emerging approach and has been widely applied in traditional artificial intelligence domains, such as semantic parsing, transfer learning, natural language processing, computer vision and many more.

Deep learning is a technique for implementing machine learning.

They may also include latent variables organized layer-wise in deep generative models such as the nodes in Deep Belief Networks.

Deep learning architectures such as deep neural networks, deep belief networks and recurrent neural networks have been applied to fields including computer vision, speech recognition, natural language processing, audio recognition, social network filtering, machine translation, bioinformatics, drug design and opinion mining, where they have produced results comparable to and in some cases superior to human experts. (Ghasemi et al., 2017)

In Figure 2, a simple neural network graph and deep one are compared.

Deep learning architectures are often constructed with a greedy layer-by-layer method. Deep learning helps to disentangle these abstractions and pick out which features are useful for improving performance. (Bengio et al., 2013). For supervised learning tasks, deep learning methods obviate feature engineering, by translating the data into compact intermediate representations akin to principal components, and derive layered structures that remove redundancy in representation. (Deng and Yu, 2014). Deep learning algorithms can be applied to unsupervised learning tasks.

Figure 2. Simple neural network and Deep learning neural network

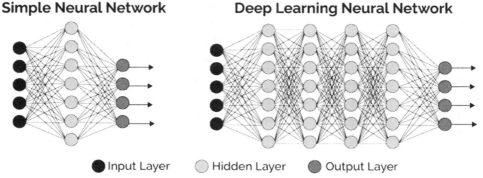

This is an important benefit because unlabeled data are more abundant than labeled data. Examples of deep structures that can be trained in an unsupervised manner are neural history compressors. (Schmidhuber, 2015).

In Figure 3 a schema of an unsupervised deep learning process is shown.

At the end of this part, Authors define the concept of the depth in deep learning as a paragraph. The computations involved in producing an output from an input can be represented by a flow graph: a flow graph is a graph representing a computation, where each node represents an elementary computation and a value (the result of the computation, applied to the values at the children of that node). Consider the set of computations allowed in each node and possible graph structures and this defines a family of functions. Input nodes have no children. Output nodes have no parents.

Traditional feed forward neural networks can be considered to have depth equal to the number of layers (i.e. the number of hidden layers plus 1, for the output layer). Support Vector Machines (SVMs) have depth 2 (one for the kernel outputs or for the feature space, and one for the linear combination producing the output). Depth is important because in some cases insufficient depth can hurt, the brain has a deep architecture and cognitive processes seem deep. (Bengio et al., 2015)

OPINION MINING WITH DEEP LEARNING DEVELOPMENT

Support vector machines (SVMs) have been shown to be highly effective at traditional text categorization, generally outperforming Naive Bayes. They are large-margin, rather than probabilistic, classifiers, in contrast to Naive Bayes and Maximum Entropy. It supports multi-class classification. LIBSVM involves two steps: first, training a data set to obtain a model and second, using the model to predict information of a testing data set. SVM procedure includes Transform data to the format of an SVM package, conduct simple scaling on the data, select model here use linear formula,

Figure 3. An unsupervised Deep Learning process

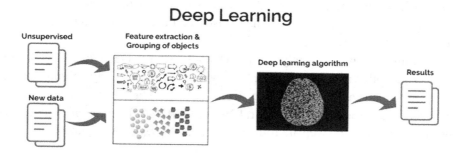

use cross-validation to find the best parameter, use the best parameter to train the whole training set and test. (Khairnar, Kinikar, 2013)

Although the traditional machine learning algorithms like SVM and Naive Bayes Classifier have shown good performance in various NLP tasks for the past few decades, they have some shortcomings and deep learning models have the potential to overcome these limitations to a large extent. The main advantages of deep neural network are the strength of the deep learning models is no demand for carefully optimized hand-crafted features and Deep learning allows good representation learning. (Singhal and Bhattacharyya, 2016)

Deep neural networks provide an alternative approach for text mining tasks and feature extraction. High-level features can be learned automatically, allowing for the removal of human bias in feature engineering and the preservation of more information as the original data can be used for training. As features are learned as part of the training process of a deep neural network, researchers are not required to provide any specialized domain knowledge to the network making this family of approaches language and task-independent. Instead, large volumes (potentially petabytes) of data are leveraged to train through repeated example. Convolutional neural networks (CNN) are a family of neural networks that have been shown to be among the best solutions for training computers in tasks of computer vision. (Prusa and Khoshgoftaar, 2017)

Deep learning includes many networks such as CNN (Convolutional Neural Networks), RNN (Recurrent Neural Networks), Recursive Neural Networks, DBN (Deep Belief Networks) and many more. Neural networks are very beneficial in text generation, vector representation, word representation estimation, sentence classification, sentence modeling and feature presentation. (Ain, Ali, Riaz et al., 2017)

CNNs have been used to perform a variety of natural language processing tasks, including part-of-speech tagging, named entity extraction, identification of semantic roles, and linking semantically similar words. More recently, CNNs have been used for end-to-end discriminative text classification tasks involving the identification of high-level concepts prevalent throughout an entire document. Additionally, a network with a single convolutional layer performed better than any traditional learner, such as Multinomial Naïve Bayes and support vector machine (SVM), on their benchmarking datasets. CNNs have also been used to aid feature extraction from text. (Prusa and Khoshgoftaar, 2017)

Combining Sentiment Analysis and Deep Learning Deep learning is very influential in both unsupervised and supervised learning, many researchers are handling sentiment analysis by using deep learning. The most famous example Socher has used is the Recursive Neural Network (RNN) for the representation of movies reviews from the website rottentomatoes.com. (Ain, Ali, Riaz et al., 2017)

Base steps in text mining, comment mining and opinion mining are doing some advanced actions in Lexicon-based Methods and natural language processing techniques, but in this chapter, we only focus on deep learning algorithms. Most important and basic algorithms are used in opinion mining and sentimental mining are SVM, recurrent neural networks, Recursive neural networks, convolutional neural networks, Word2vec (have been proposed by Google) and deep dense network. Authors discussed SVM, RNN, CNN and some other algorithms in earlier parts, in this section Word2vec is described.

WORD2VEC AVERAGING, NLP AND CONTEXT

The simplest model to apply to the sentiment analysis problem in deep learning platform is to use an average of word vectors trained by a word2vec model. This average can be perceived as a representation of the meaning of a sentence and can be used as an input to a classifier. (Shirani-Mehr, 2016).

However, this approach is not very different from the bag of words approach used in traditional algorithms, since it only concerns about single words and ignores the relations between words in the sentence. The next natural choice is to use a deep dense neural network. As the input, vectors of words in the sentence are fed into the model. Various options like averaging word vectors or padding the sentences were explored, yet none of them achieved satisfactory results. The models either did not converge or over fit to the data with poor performance on the validation set. The intuition for these results is that while these models have too many parameters, they do not effectively represent the structure of the sentence and relations between words. While in theory, they can represent very complex decision boundaries, their extracted features do not generalize well to the validation and test set. This motivates using different classes of neural networks, networks that using their architecture can represent the structure of the sentences in a more elegant way. (Shirani-Mehr, 2016).

Recent approaches using deep CNNs showed significant performance improvement over the state- of-the-art methods on a range of natural language processing (NLP) tasks. Collobert et al. (2011) fed word embedding's into a CNN to solve standard NLP problems such as named entity recognition (NER), part-of-speech (POS) tagging and semantic role labeling. A deep neural network (DNN) can be viewed as a composite of simple, unsupervised models such as restricted Boltzmann machines (RBMs), where each RBM's hidden layer serves as the visible layer for the next RBM. (Soujanya et al., 2016).

In classical natural language processing (NLP) systems, always after language detection, pre-calculation executes and then modeling run on it to prepare the outputs, also in non-traditional solution instead of calculation procedure, a deep learning algorithm execute as a brain to understand the language and with many hidden layers, desire output produce by output units.

The number of hidden layers is the main reason of deep in deep learning. In Figure 4, the main differences between traditional NLP solution and the deep learning-based solution are shown.

An RBM is a bipartite graph comprising of two layers of neurons: a visible and a hidden layer; connections between neurons in the same layer are not allowed. To train such a multi-layer system, one needs to compute the gradient of the total energy function E with respect to weights in all the layers. To learn these weights and maximize the global energy function, the approximate maximum likelihood contrastive divergence approach can be used. This method employs each training sample to initialize the visible layer. Next, it uses the Gibbs sampling algorithm to update the hidden layer and then reconstruct the visible layer consecutively, until convergence occurs. As an example, consider a logistic regression model to learn the binary hidden neurons. (Soujanya et al., 2016)

Figure 4. Classical NLP and Deep learning-based NLP

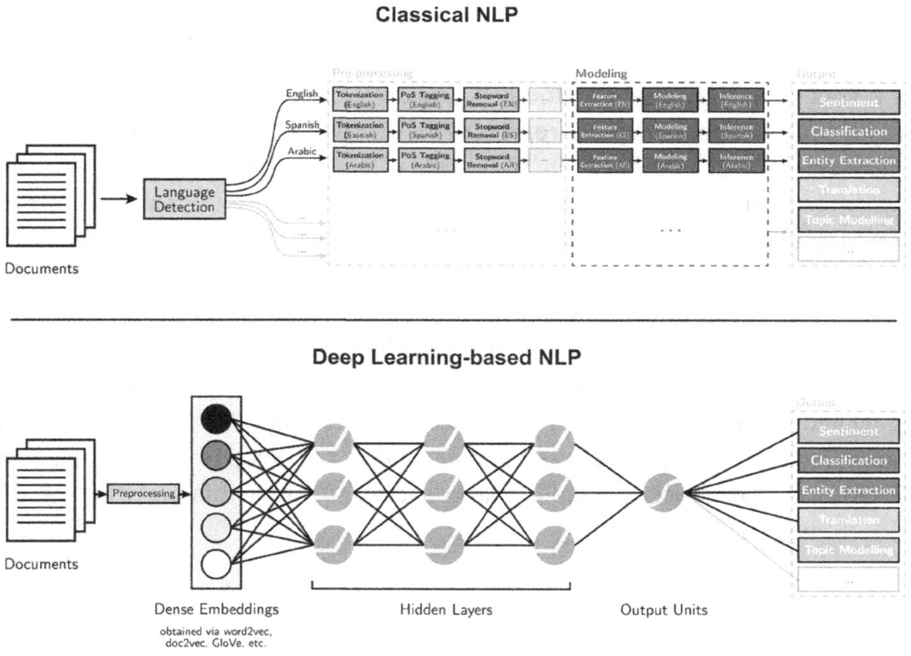

In opinion mining like many text base mining, the context is a very important thing that the designer of deep learning model for opinion mining must consider it.

The common mission is to recognize meaningful relationships between a user action and a certain combination of contexts, which is regarded as a set of condition-action rules. Consequently, they can predict that if a user is under a condition related to the detected contexts, the consequent rule has to be conducted for him. There are many types of contexts. As shown in Figure 5, such contexts are including not only physical contexts (e.g., spatial and temporal contexts) of environments but also conceptual contexts (e.g., preferences, mental states and social affinities) of human users. (Furht, 2010)

More importantly, there are several context models, e.g., stochastic segment model, and ontology-based context model, to represent the contexts. The uncertain and unpredictable factors can be dealt with by several context fusion approaches. These approaches is to integrate as much contexts as possible. Such approach has been applied in many domains such as location-based systems, multiple expert systems, image processing by contextual information and information retrieval systems.

The important assumption behind these approaches is that contexts on user behaviors are interrelated with each other, i.e., constrained by others. Recently, as referring to the work in social network communities, researchers have realized that the context of a certain user strongly depended on those of his acquaintances (e.g., families, colleagues, and friends). It means that a user can make a different decision and take a different action under same environmental and conceptual contexts, depending on whom he is currently staying with. (Furht, 2010)

Figure 5. Physical and conceptual context

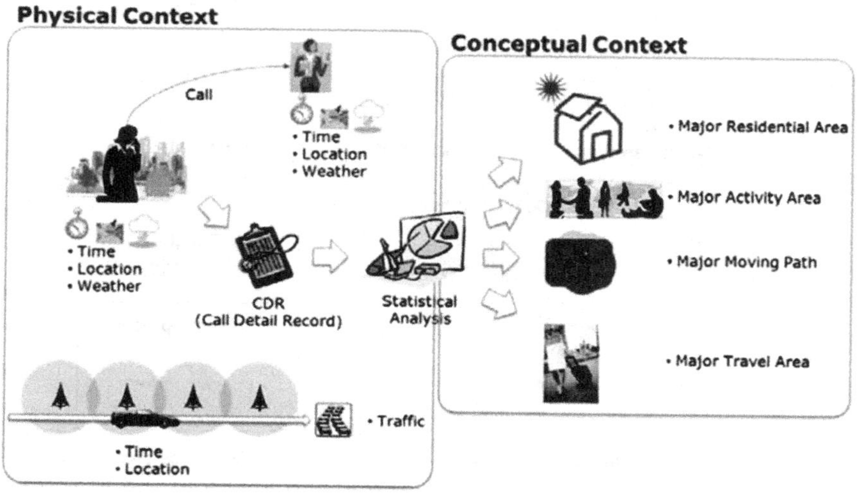

LEARNING METHODS

Some time for validation of deep learning method in text mining and opinion mining, researchers must give some valid data set to learning algorithm for training and optimizing it, figure 6 shows the simple work fellow of this procedure.

Recently, Zhang and LeCun, proposed a novel approach for text learning tasks where they were able to use CNNs to train classifiers by representing text in an image like character-level fashion. Thus enabled them to train a deep convolutional neural network for text classification tasks involving high-level concepts from scratch with no prior feature engineering or extraction. Thy accomplished this by employing 1-of-m embedding, where each character is represented by a vector of size m, where m is the number of characters in their alphabet. Each character in a text instance was represented as a character vector and the instance as a sequence

Figure 6. Training in deep learning work fellow

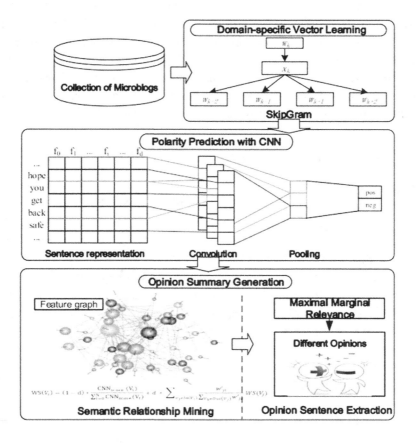

of character vectors. When visualized, a Braille-like output is generated. Using this embedding, they fed their data into a network with six 1D temporal convolutional layers and three fully connected layers. Their results showed training a deep CNN from character-level data outperformed networks trained on data with features generated with bag-of-words, bag-of-centroids and the deep learning approach Word2Vec. (Prusa and Khoshgoftaar, 2017)

In some cases CNN algorithm is the best solution and authors describe it at this part . Convolutional neural networks consist of sparsely connected convolutional layers followed by fully connected dense layers (these dense layers are equivalent to a multilayer perceptron neural network). Convolutional layers are sparsely connected. Neurons in these layers are connected to a small region of the previous layer known as the receptive field, instead of the entire previous layer as is found in a dense layer. The most common receptor field sizes are small, such as 3×3 or 5×5 neurons. By being sparsely connected CNNs view and learn local correlations. The convolutional layers in the network are followed by several densely connected layers with the last layer containing one neuron for each possible classification outcome. Several key hyper parameters control the behavior of the convolutional layers and number of neurons in the fail network including number of filters, stride and padding. (Prusa and Khoshgoftaar, 2017) as mentioned before, deep learning works like a human brain, in human brain millions of neurons are active and work together to understand something and when a human extracts opinion of the text, this system works for it.

Neurons in each layer learn a weight vector to create a feature map. These weights are determined by applying numerous filters, which have a small receptive field size and are convolved across the dimensions of the data to create an activation map of the filter. Multiple filters can be applied so that more features can be extracted by connecting multiple neurons to each region of the previous layer. Stride is the distance between receptive fields on the input volume. Padding refers to adding a border of zeroes around the input volume. Typically, an N*N instance would be reduced in dimension by the application of a convolutional layer when output to the subsequent layer. For example, a 3×3 convolution would reduce an $n \times n$ instance to $(n - 2) \times (n - 2)$. This occurs because the convolution cannot be moved to the extreme edges of the instance as it would have null inputs. Adding padding can eliminate this size reduction as it allows filters to be applied to the edges of the original input volume. Training iterations (epochs) employs gradient decent to learn network parameters. As each convolutional layer is a view of the neurons of the previous layer, stacking layers allows a larger region of the initial input to be viewable by neurons in deeper layers. For example, two 3×3 layers will result in a network that has 5×5 views as each layer transforms 3×3 views to a single output neuron. Convolutional layers are also accompanied by an activation function. The max pooling layer conducts non-linear down sampling by eliminating non maximal values, thus reducing computation for upper layers as many can be discarded. (Prusa and Khoshgoftaar, 2017)

A FRAMEWORK FOR OPINION MINING BY DEEP LEARNING

(Qiudan Li et al., 2016), Figure 7, depicts the proposed framework of automatically generating an opinion summary from a collection of micro blogs related to a hot event. It consists of three stages: data representation, polarity prediction and feature relationship mining and opinion sentence extraction. First, it's necessary y to produce an effective representation for each micro blog. Word2vec is a deep-learning-inspired method that attempts to understand the meaning and semantic relationships among words. It learns vector representations of words using continuous bag-of-words (CBOW) and Skip's gram.

Therefore, at the data representation stage, due to the good performance of capturing syntactic and semantic information, it has used word2vec adoption to learn domain-specific vectors for word and sentence. At the sentiment prediction stage, given the low dimensional representation of sentences or raw sentences without feature engineering, CNN is applied to automatically mine useful features and perform sentiment analysis on the micro blogging system.

The model first uses a convolution operation to produce feature maps. Then the resolution of the feature maps is reduced by a pooling operation, and finally, the obtained useful local features are fed to a fully connected soft max layer to predict the sentiment label of the micro blog. Based on the prediction results, we build positive and negative datasets by selecting the posts and features together with assigned sentiment labels. Making good use of the automatically learned features, the semantic relationships among features are then computed according to a hybrid ranking function. Finally, representative opinion sentences that are semantically related to the features are extracted using the MMR approach.

MINING AND SUMMARIZING REPRESENTATIVE OPINIONS

Learning domain-specific vector representation for word and sentence. It has been demonstrated that lower dimensional vector representation can capture syntactic and semantic information. By mapping word vectors into a vector space, semantically similar words will have similar vector representation. The skip-gram model, which is a state-of-the-art word-embedding method, is used to learn the dense word vector representation.

Figure 7. Opinion mining Framework by Deep learning

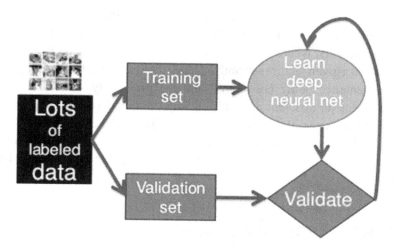

Polarity prediction Borrowing the sentence classification approach for Twitter data using CNN, we automatically learn the important features for identifying the polarity of a micro blog and then perform sentiment analysis on hot events in Chinese micro blogging systems. This consists of convolution operation, pooling operation and label prediction. Convolution operation based on the above vector representation of a sentence, the one-dimensional convolution operation performs dot product between the filter of the convolution. The pooling operation aims to reduce the resolution of feature maps by applying a pooling function to several units in a local region of a size determined by a parameter called pooling size. The pooling operation units will serve as generalizations over the features obtained from convolution

The features produced by the pooling operation form the penultimate layer $U^\wedge = \{c^\wedge 1, c^\wedge 2,.. ., c^\wedge p\}$ (p is the number of filters). Opinion-summary generation, when the sentiment label is assigned to each post, positive and negative datasets are built by selecting the posts and features together with the associated labels. Then, a set of features that best describe each dataset are identified by Semantic Relationship Mining, and finally, representative opinion sentences are selected using the MMR criterion, which strives to reduce redundancy while maintaining semantic relevance to the features.

Semantic relationship mining is the selection of representative features for positive and negative data can provide useful cues for accurate opinion sentence extraction. By performing the max pooling operation on all feature maps, each word in the specific phrase feature receives a vote.

Opinion sentence extraction when a system obtains important features for each sentiment category, system extracts the representative opinion sentences to generate an opinion summary. Sentences are selected according to a combined criterion of relevance and novelty, where the former measures the semantic relevance between the sentence and a given feature set, and the latter measures the dissimilarity between the opinion sentence being considered and the previously selected one. MMR criterion provides an efficient and unified way to consider these two factors and thus is adapted to extract the opinion sentence. (Qiudan Li et al., 2016)

Authors believe that for each opinion mining system, researchers must customize the exist frameworks and should improve the learning methods in deep learning algorithm.

FUTURE RESEARCH DIRECTIONS

Recently, deep learning approaches emerge as powerful computational models that discover intricate semantic representations of texts automatically from data without feature engineering. These approaches have improved the state-of-the-art in many sentiment analysis tasks including sentiment classification of sentences/ documents, sentiment extraction, opinion mining and sentiment lexicon learning. (Duyu Tang et al., 2015)

Deep learning offers a way to harness the large amount of computation and data with little engineering by hand (LeCun et al., 2015). With distributed representation, various deep models have become the new state-of-the-art methods for NLP problems. Researchers expect such trend to continue with more and better model designs. Researchers expect to see more opinion mining applications that employ reinforcement learning and unsupervised learning methods. The former represents a natural way to train NLP systems for the optimization of a particular goal, while the latter promises to learn rich language structure in large unlabeled data. Researchers also expect to see more research on multimodal learning as, in the real world, language is often grounded on (or correlated with) other signals. Finally, we expect to see more deep learning models whose internal memory (bottom-up knowledge learnd from the data) is enriched with an external memory (top-down knowledge inherited from a KB). Coupling symbolic and sub-symbolic AI will be key for stepping forward in the path from NLP to natural language understanding. Relying on machine learning, in fact, is good to make good guesses based on past experience, because sub-symbolic methods encode correlation and their decision-making process is probabilistic. Natural language understanding, however, requires much more than that. (Tom Younga et al., 2016)

Cheap hardware, cheap memory, cheap storage technologies, more processing power, superior deep learning algorithms, and massive data streams will all contribute to the success of opinion mining-powered deep learning applications. This combination will deliver more useful results and emerge more intelligence agent in opinion mining that understands, learn, predict, adapt and potentially operate autonomously, this kind of intelligence agent in opinion mining could be used as a human assistant to mine people's opinion or can use as a full agent service. A human can soon expect to see smart robots around us doing all our jobs – much quicker, much more accurately, and even improving themselves at every step. Will this world need intelligent humans anymore or shall we soon be outclassed by self-thinking robots?

With Big Data making its way back to mainstream business activities, now deep learning algorithms can simply use massive loads of both static and dynamic data to continuously learn and improve enhanced performance in opinion mining.

Deep learning through Cloud technologies, open standards, and algorithm economy will continue. The growing trend of deploying pre-built DL algorithms to enable Self-Service opinion mining and Analytics is a positive step towards democratization of opinion mining.

CONCLUSION

Around 4 billion internet users in the world, generate many different contents, this kind of data can be useful to figure outing opinions about politics, services, products, news or events. Many surveys, applicable solutions, algorithms, and tools are created to handle and extract knowledge from context as opinion miner. Most opinion mining techniques are based on machine learning and specifically deep learning.

Deep learning is part of a broader family of machine learning methods based on learning data representations, as opposed to task-specific algorithms. Learning can be supervised, partially supervised or unsupervised, also deep learning is a technique to implementing machine learning.

Since 2006, deep structured learning, or more commonly called deep learning or hierarchical learning, has emerged as a new area of machine learning research. During the past several years, the techniques developed from deep learning research have already been impacting a wide range of signal and information processing work within the traditional and the new, widened scopes. Supervised learning algorithms learn how to associate an input with some output, given a training set of examples of inputs and outputs and unsupervised learning aims towards the development of models that are capable of extracting meaningful and high-level representations from high-dimensional sensory unlabeled data, also semi-supervised methods are the combination of supervised and unsupervised algorithms.

For opinion mining, some advance actions in Lexicon-based Methods and natural language processing techniques by one of deep learning algorithm are useable. Most important and basic algorithms are used in opinion mining and sentimental mining are SVM, recurrent neural networks, Recursive neural networks (RNN), convolutional neural networks (CNN), Word2vec (have been proposed by Google) and deep dense network (DDN).

Any best practice solution like a framework can help the researcher to get the concept and use it as a basis, of their own solution, for example, the proposed framework of automatically generating an opinion summary from a collection of microblogs related to a hot event with three stages: data representation, polarity prediction and feature relationship mining and opinion sentence extraction.

Deep learning for opinion mining is expected such trend to continue with more and better model designs. Researchers expect to see more opinion mining applications by agent intelligence and as an assistant to human being ones. Researchers also expect to see more research on multimodal learning as, in the real world, language is often grounded on (or correlated with) other signals. Finally, authors expect to see more and more surveys and applications in this topic.

REFERENCES

Ain, Q. T., Ali, M., Riaz, A., Noureen, A., Kamran, M., Hayat, B., & Rehman, A. (2017). Sentiment analysis using deep learning techniques: A review. *Int. J. Adv. Comput. Sci. Appl.*, *8*(6), 424.

Beat, V. (2016, April 5). Nvidia CEO bets big on deep learning and VR. *Machine Learning*, *45*(37).

Bengio, Y., Courville, A., & Vincent, P. (2013). Representation Learning: A Review and New Perspectives. *IEEE Transactions on Pattern Analysis and Machine Intelligence*, *35*(8), 1798–1828. doi:10.1109/TPAMI.2013.50 PMID:23787338

Bengio, Y., LeCun, Y., & Hinton, G. (2015). Deep Learning. *Nature*, *521*(7553), 436–444. doi:10.1038/nature14539 PMID:26017442

Carrio, Sampedro, Rodriguez-Ramos, & Campoy (2017). A Review of Deep Learning Methods and Applications for Unmanned Aerial Vehicles. *Hindawi Journal of Sensors*. .10.1155/2017/3296874

Collobert, R., Weston, J., Bottou, L., Karlen, M., Kavukcuoglu, K., & Kuksa, P. (2011). Natural language processing (almost) from scratch. *Journal of Machine Learning ResearchVolume, 12*(August), 2493–2537.

Cun. (2016). *Slides on Deep Learning Online*. Academic Press.

DeCarvalho, Fairhurst, & Bisset. (1994). An integrated Boolean neural network for pattern classification. *Pattern Recognition Letters, 15*(8), 807–813. doi: 1994-08-0810.1016/0167-8655(94)90009-4

Deng, L., & Yu, D. (2014). Deep Learning: Methods and Applications. *Foundations and Trends in Signal Processing, 7*(3–4), 197–387. doi:10.1561/2000000039

Furht, B. (Ed). (2010). Handbook of Social Network Technologies and Applications. Springer. doi: . doi:10.1007/978-1-4419-7142-5

Ghasemi, F., Mehridehnavi, A. R., Fassihi, A., & Perez-Sanchez, H. (2017). Deep Neural Network in Biological Activity Prediction using Deep Belief Network. *Applied Soft Computing*.

Goodfellow, I., Bengio, Y., & Courville, A. (2016). *Deep Learning*. Cambridge, MA: MIT Press.

Griewank, A. (2012). Who Invented the Reverse Mode of Differentiation? *Document a Matematica*, 389–400.

Gu, S., Lillicrap, T., Sutskever, I., & Levine, S. (2016). Continuous deep q-learning with model-based acceleration. *The 33rd International Conference on International Conference on Machine Learning, 48*, 2829–2838. Retrieved from https://arxiv.org/abs/1603.00748

Guo. (2016, April). Deep learning for visual understanding. *Neurocomputing, 187*(26), 27–48.

Hinton, G. E., Osindero, S., & Teh, Y.-W. (2006). A Fast Learning Algorithm for Deep Belief Nets. *Neural Computation, 18*(7), 1527–1554. doi:10.1162/neco.2006.18.7.1527 PMID:16764513

Hochreiter, S., & Schmidhuber, J. (1996). LSTM can solve hard longtime lag problems. *10th Annual Conference on Neural Information Processing Systems. NIPS, 1996*, 473–479.

Ivakhnenko, A. G. (1973). *Cybernetic Predicting Devices*. CCM Information Corporation.

Khairnar, J., & Kinikar, M. (2013). Machine Learning Algorithms for Opinion Mining and Sentiment Classification. *International Journal of Scientific and Research Publications, 3*(6). Retrieved from www.ijsrp.org

Kober, J., Bagnell, J. A., & Peters, J. (2013). Reinforcement learning in robotics: A survey. *The International Journal of Robotics Research, 32*(11), 1238–1274. doi:10.1177/0278364913495721

Krizhevsky, A., & Hinton, G. E. (2011). *Using very deep auto encoders for content-based image retrieval.* 19th European Symposium on Artificial Neural Networks (ESANN'11), Bruges, Belgium.

LeCun, Y., Bengio, Y., & Hinton, G. (2015). Deep learning. *Nature, 521*(7553), 436–444. doi:10.1038/nature14539 PMID:26017442

Li, Q., Jina, Z., Can, W., & Zenga, D. D. (2016). Mining opinion summarizations using convolutional neural networks in Chinese microblogging systems. *Knowledge-Based Systems, 107*, 289–300. doi:10.1016/j.knosys.2016.06.017

Lillicrap, T. P., Hunt, J. J., & Pritzel, A. (n.d.). *Continuous control with deep reinforcement learning.* Cornel University Library. Retrieved from https://arxiv.org/abs/1509.02971

Poria, S., Cambria, E., & Gelbukh, A. (2016). Aspect extraction for opinion mining with a deep convolutional neural network. *Knowledge-Based Systems, 108*, 42–49. doi:10.1016/j.knosys.2016.06.009

Prusa, J. D., & Khoshgoftaar, T. M. (2017). Improving deep neural network design with new text data representations. *Big Data, 4*(1), 7. doi:10.118640537-017-0065-8

Schmidhuber, J. (2015). Deep Learning. *Scholarpedia, 10*(11), 32832. doi:10.4249cholarpedia.32832 PMID:25462637

Schmidhuber, J. (2015). Deep learning in neural networks: An overview. *Neural Networks, 61*, 85–117. doi:10.1016/j.neunet.2014.09.003 PMID:25462637

Shirani-Mehr, H. (2014). *Applications of deep learning to sentiment analysis of movie reviews. Technical report.* Stanford University.

Singhal & Bhattacharyya. (2016). *Sentiment Analysis and Deep Learning: A Survey.* Dept. of Computer Science and Engineering Indian Institute of Technology, Powai Mumbai, Maharashtra, India.

Tang, D., Qin, B., & Liu, T. (2015). Learning for sentiment analysis: Successful approaches and future challenges. *WIREs Data Mining Knowledge Discovery, 5,* 292–303. doi:10.1002/widm.1171

Vincent, P., Larochelle, H., Lajoie, I., & Manzagol, P. (2010). Stacked de noising auto encoders: Learning useful representations in adeep network with a local de noising criterion. *Journal of Machine Learning Research, 11,* 3371–3408.

Younga, T., Hazarikab, D., Poriac, S., & Cambria, E. (2016). *Recent Trends in Deep Learning Based Natural Language Processing.* Retrieved from https://arxiv.org/pdf/1708.02709.pdf

Chapter 4
Opinion Mining:
Using Machine Learning Techniques

Vijender Kumar Solanki
CMR Institute of Technology (Autonomous) Hyderabad, India

Nguyen Ha Huy Cuong
Quang Nam University, Vietnam

Zonghyu (Joan) Lu
University of Huddersfield, UK

ABSTRACT

The machine learning is the emerging research domain, from which number of emerging trends are available, among them opinion mining is the one technology attraction through which the we could get analysis of the interested domain or we can say about the review from the customer towards any product or we can say any upcoming trending information. These two are the emerging words and we can say it's the buzz word in the information technology. As you will see that its widely use by the corporate sector to uplift the business next level. Before two decade you will not read any words e.g., Opinion mining or Sentiment analysis, but in the last two decade these words have given a new life to information technology domain as well as to the business. The important question which runs in the mind is why use sentiment analysis or opinion mining. The information technology has given number of new programming languages, new innovation and within that the data mining has given this trends to the users. The chapter is covering the three major concept's which comes under the machine learning e.g., Decision tree, Bayesian network and Support vector machine. The chapter is describing the basic inputs, and how it helps in supporting stakeholders by adopting these technologies.

DOI: 10.4018/978-1-5225-6117-0.ch004

1. INTRODUCTION

The information technology has given the number of new programming languages, new innovation and within that, the data mining has given this trend to the users. We would like to say that sentiment analysis has given a tremendous growth to the business sector and that is the reason today almost every growing corporate sector is involving an information technology team who is keeping eyes on opinion mining techniques to bring their business to next level (Rajeev & Rekha, 2016).

Sentiment Analysis or Opinion Mining is the field of information technology, in which the study of the people's mindsets, in term of opinion, attitude, information, and perception is carried out and it helps them, stakeholders, to study about the product, which he is placing in the market for the sale. In early time the feedback is taken as either manual or online or we can say by the point based mechanism. But it has been noticed that the input towards the product, the organization is receiving is not genuine and it seems it's not giving any connection with the real-time statistics. So it has come in the notice that, it's necessary to notice the mood of the users who are giving the opinion about the product. The opinion of users change as their mood change for the same products, this given a new challenge before the business, about the product, that same product is appreciated and depreciated by users in different situations, hence it makes them puzzled to understand who is correct in the term of elevating business (Pang & Lee, 2008).

In this chapter the main focuses have been given on the idea of the three famous machine learning techniques namely,., Naïve Bayes Classifiers, Decision Tree and Support vector machine. In machine learning, though a variety of techniques available, but the authors have taken the basic and foundation based ideas, which are quite popular in the context of machine learning and opinion mining. Please note while preparing the chapter these three parameters have been considered as important, first the basics of the techniques, their applications and lastly the challenges related to these technology implementations have been discussed in this chapter.

According to the authors, this chapter will be helpful to the learners, who are willing to dive in depth of machine learning and it will help them to get an impression on what type of problem can be taken in the machine learning field and what will be the expected outcome in case any of one technique opts for the problem study.

The chapter is divided into the five sections:

- Section I is covering the general Introduction to machine learning techniques and opinion mining.
- Section II will cover the three machine learning technology and its applications and will cover the challenges of the technology, or we cans say that it will basically explore the challenges in implementations and their drawbacks.

- Section III is discussing the conclusion and scope of the machine learning technique.
- Section IV will be the acknowledgment
- Section V is reference section which will be carrying the list of references taken while preparing this chapter, so if they need, it could be referred for the detailed study about the machine learning and opinion minin

2. MACHINE LEARNING TECHNIQUE

Machine Learning is the branch of computer science, in which can design and develops the computational algorithm. Machine learning term was coined in the year 1959, by a computer scientist Arthur Samuel, who was working with pattern recognition and associated algorithms in the IBM Lab. The origin of machine learning comes from the artificial intelligence, as the pattern recognition, NLP is one of an important branch of artificial intelligence (Witten & Frank, 2005). The machine learning basically gives the facility to computers to learn without being explicitly programmed. The machine learning also comes with statistics, as optimization, algorithms' feasibility are basically building with statistics and programming environment. The machine learning is further broadly divided into the Supervised, Unsupervised and reinforcement division. In the supervised regression and classification considered, and their detail approach is covered under them. In the unsupervised regression data-driven like clustering is considered and in the reinforcement algorithms learn to react to environments. The three major domain of the machine learning can be thoroughly detailed up, further to support the various techniques and applications. When we look up the use of the technique in application building, there is the variety of application comes under the banner e.g., Spam filtering, Search engines, Optical character recognition, computer vision, data mining etc (Gamon et al., 2005).

If in general scenario, we say, we do not use machine learning and AI then it's really dishonest sentence, as in today worlds where we are based on internet services for numerous tasks, there are many basic applications which are used by mostly every internet user's, few but very common are given below:

- Spotify
- Lyst
- Uber
- Netflix
- Paypal
- Gmail

- Google Search
- Google map
- Facebook
- Siri & Cortana

The chapter is giving the light on three broad and very important category, used in the variety of application and have their importance (Sharma et al., 2013), So we have explained the three important techniques e.g., Naïve Bayes classifier, Decision trees and support vector machines in the given sections.

Naïve Bayes Classifier

Naïve Bayes is an innovative process for statistics categorization. Although it's considered that neural networks are less difficult to use than this, every so often unsatisfactory results are acquired with that. As far as category assignment is worried it normally involves with education and testing data sets which consist of some records times. Every example within the training set carries one goal values and several attributes. The intention of naïve Bayes is to supply a version which predicts goal value of records times in the checking outset which is given best the attributes class in naïve Bayes is an instance of supervised studying. Regarded labels assist imply whether or not the device is appearing in a proper way or not. This information points to the desired response, validating the accuracy of the device, or be used to help the gadget learn to act effectively. A step in naïve Bayes category involves identification of which can be in detail linked to the known classes (Thomas & Galambos, 2004). This is referred to as features choice or characteristic extraction. Function choice and naïve Bayes categorization together have a use even if the prediction of unknown samples isn't important.

Figure 1. Naïve Bayes categorization

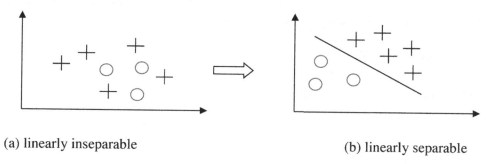

(a) linearly inseparable

(b) linearly separable

Naïve Bayes Categorization Rule

- **Define:** Provided arbitrary variables x, y, z, we are pronouncing x is provisionally unbiased of y given z, if and most effective if opportunity allotment prevailing x is autonomous of the charge of y provided z; this is

$$((Vi;,j,k)P(X = xi|Y = yj, Z = zk) = P(X = xi|Z = zk)$$

For example, keep in mind 3 Boolean arbitrary variables to depict the present day-day weather: rain, thunder, and lightning. We may quite state that thunder is impartial of rain set lightning. Due to the fact we understand lights motives thunder, as soon as we understand whether or no longer or not there can be lightning, no extra statistics approximately thunder is furnished through the rate of rain (Hu & Liu, 2004). Of the route, there may be a smooth dependence of thunder on rain in well-known, though there can be no conditional dependence as brief as we realize the charge of lightning. NBC takings with the resource of the use of supposing that the presence (or absence) of the particular feature of a category is amazing to the absence (or presence) of every specific function. Counting on the unique nature of the opportunity model, we're capable of train NBC very proficiently in a supervised studying the environment. In several realistic practices, parameter estimation for NBC models uses the technique of maximum danger. In spite of in their naïve layout glaringly over-simplified supposition, NBC's have completed in fact nicely in loads of inflexible actual-worldwide situations (Cai et al., 2008).

A top hand of the use of NBC is that it desires some education facts to choose out the parameters essential for the class. As unbiased variables are intended, in the region of calculating whole co-divergence matrix best the divergences of the variables for every beauty want to be evaluated. The naïve Bayes set of rules, a class set of recommendations which follows Bayes guidelines guesses the attributes X1 ...Xn is all conditionally impartial of every considered one of a kind, given y. The significance of this assumption is that it dramatically explicates the example of P(X|Y), the problem of comparing it from the training statistics. Maintain in thoughts the case in which X= hX1, X2i. Here,

$$P(X|Y) = P(X1, X2|Y)$$

$$=P(X1|X2, Y)P(X2|Y)$$

$$= P(X1|Y)P(X2|Y)$$

Here above the 2nd line adopts a general property of probabilities, and the 3rd line adopts conditional independence.

In general, at the same time as x have n attributes which is probably provisionally unbiased of every precise given y, we've were given had been given,

$$P(X_1, \ldots X_n \mid Y) = \prod_{i=1}^{n} P(X_i \mid Y)$$

Examine if Y & Xi are Boolean variables then we need only 2n parameters to describe P(Xi=xik| Y=yj) for the needed i,j,k. This is an remarkable attenuation compared to the 2(2n−1) parameters required to define P(X|Y) if we make no conditional independence hypothesis.

To derive NBC algorithm, let Y is some distinct - valued variable and attributes X1 ...Xn are some real or distinct valued attributes. My aim is to arrange a classifier that will defer probability distribution for each new instance X that we ask for that it categorize over possible values of Y. As per NBC rule, the equation that Y will acquire for the probability on its kth possible value, is

$$P(Y = y_k \mid X_1 \ldots X_n) = \frac{P\left(Y = y_k\right) P(X_1 .. X_n \mid Y = y_k)}{\sum_j P\left(Y = y_j\right) P(X_1 \ldots \ldots X_n \mid Y = y_j)}$$

the sum is occupied over every solo possible values yi of Y. now let us presume, for given Y, Xi is conditionally independent. as a result, we can utilize equation (1) for rewrite this as,

$$P(Y = y_k \mid X_1 \ldots X_n) = \frac{P\left(Y = y_k\right) \prod_i P(X_i \mid Y = y_k)}{\sum_j P\left(Y = y_j\right) \prod_i P(X_i \mid Y = y_j)}$$

For NBC, Equation (2) is the elementary equation. Specified a new instance Xnew = 'X1...Xn', this eq. simplify the way to compute the probability that Y will get on any given value, given the experiential attribute values of Xnew and known the distributions P(Y) and P(Xi|Y) approximated from the training data. If we are concerned barely in the mainly probable value of Y, then we have the NBC rule:

$$Y < -arg \max yk \frac{P\left(Y = y_k\right) \prod_i P(X_i | Y = y_k)}{\sum_j P\left(Y = y_j\right) \prod_i P(X_i | Y = y_j)}$$

It simplify to the subsequent as denominator does not relies on yk.

$$Y < -arg \max yk \, P\left(Y = y_k\right) \prod_i P(X_i | Y = y_k)$$

The Naïve Bayes is the machine learning supervised method, which help

- Multinomial Naïve Bayes
- Binarized Multinomial Naïve Bayes
- The application of Naïve Bayes theorem can be used in sentiment detection, email spam detection and document categorization.

Pros and Cons Associated With Naïve Bayes Classifier

Pros

It is simple and quick to anticipate class of test informational index. It additionally performs well in multi-class forecast At the point when supposition of autonomy holds, Naive Bayes classifier performs better contrast with different models like strategic relapse and you require less preparing information. It performs well if there should be an occurrence of unmitigated info factors contrasted with numerical variable(s). For the numerical variable, typical dissemination is accepted (Sun et al.2009).

Cons:

On the off chance that downright factor has a class (in test informational collection), which was not seen in preparing the informational index, at that point model will allot a 0 (zero) likelihood and will be not able to make an expectation. This is frequently known as "Zero Frequency". To tackle this, we can utilize the smoothing procedure. One of the least difficult smoothing systems is called Laplace estimation.

On the opposite side Naive Bayes is otherwise called a bad estimator, so the likelihood yields from foresee likelihood are not to be considered excessively important.

Another constraint of Naive Bayes is the suspicion of autonomous indicators. In actuality, it is relatively inconceivable that we get an arrangement of indicators which are totally free

Applications

- **Ongoing Prediction:** Naive Bayes is an excited learning classifier and it is certainly quick. Accordingly, it could be utilized for influencing expectations in genuine to time.
- **Multi-Class Prediction:** This calculation is additionally notable for multi-class expectation include. Here we can foresee the likelihood of different classes of the target variable.
- **Content Grouping/Spam Filtering/Sentiment Analysis:** Naive Bayes classifier for the most part utilized as a part of the content order (because of the better outcome in multi-class issues and freedom run) have the higher achievement rate when contrasted with different calculations. Therefore, it is broadly utilized as a part of Spam separating (recognize spam email) and Sentiment Analysis (in online networking examination, to distinguish positive and negative client opinions)
- **Suggestion System:** Naive Bayes Classifier and together forms a Recommendation System that utilizations machine learning and information mining methods to Últer inconspicuous data and predicts whether a client might want a given asset or not

Decision Tree

The tree is an important identity in computational domain, whether its data structure or its database, the role of the tree cannot be ignored. In the machine learning, we use a decision tree to identify the best decisions. We use the tree to represent the family structure, in the organization a tee represents the levels, and if we use the tree, in general, it helps in elevating decisions, step by steps. As the data is growing and getting larger day by day, the data collection, storage optimization for it and to process it further; now becoming a big challenge in case of the automation process . In the machine learning, use of a decision tree to identify the best decision in the pool is one of the best options for the research people.

The decision tree used in object-oriented analysis and data modeling where its effectively used as a tool in generalization, classification, description, and identification of data. The role of decision tree has been widely seen in the number of computational domains, which at present largely seen in the opinion mining as well. We can say that decision tree is based on machine learning technique in which rules are represented as the variety of tree i.e., (hierarchical, sequential or parallel structures) for the data.

If we look towards the decision tree applications, there we find a big opportunity in present as well as for the future. In the medical science, the decision tree can be used like in molecular biology to analyze the amino acid sequence, in the pharmacology it can be used in the drug analysis. Even it can be used in the botany also like in plant to assess the hazards or lifeline of plants. In remote sensing, the decision tree can be used as pattern recognition. In physics it can be used for detection of physical data points, In the power system, it can be used to help in system security assessment. Decision trees have also been used recently for building personal learning assistants

Pros and Cons Associated With Decision Tree

Pros

- Decision trees implicitly perform variable screening or feature selection
- Decision trees require relatively little effort from users for data preparation
- Nonlinear relationships between parameters do not affect tree performance

The best feature of using trees for analytics - easy to interpret and explain to executives!

Support Vector Machines

Support vector machines are the supervised machine learning algorithm which is commonly implemented for regression as well as for classification. Though it works well with classification as well as in regression analysis, it has been noticed that it is majorly used in classification domains. Along with performing linear classification SVM also perform with nonlinear classification.

It also works as the non-probabilistic binary linear classifier. It is named as such because SVM classifies the training pattern into two classes w1 and w2, which are labeled as yi=+1 and yi=-1 and it classifies when the classes are linearly separable.

SVM, which is based on Minimization problem, looks up for a hyper-plane that optimally separates data points of two clusters and no probabilistic approach can be adapted in this case.

The Support vector machine really works very well and it gives the clear margin of separation from the accepted and rejected state. It also gives impressive results in high dimensional spaces. During the training set, the dataset is used, in which we used a subset of training dataset in term of training points called decision function(which we called as support vector) so it helps in memory efficiency also. The best part of Support Vector Machines is it works very efficiently in developing data model even small data sets. The representation of support vector machine is done simply by the coordinates of study individual observation. It basically segregates the two different classes in (hyperplane and line only).

Figure 2.

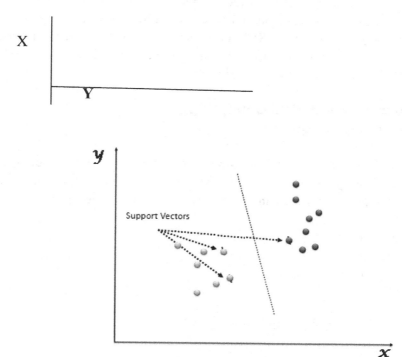

- Before discussing support vector machine we should discuss something about kernel tricks because the reason behind SVM being so smart machine learning algorithm is the kernel trick. Kernel trick has been described by Rasmussen and Williams, in their book entitled as 'Gaussian Processes for Machine Learning,' MIT press, (2006), as "If an algorithm is described solely in terms of inner products in input space then it can be lifted into feature space by replacing occurrences of those inner products by k(x,x'); this is sometimes called the kernel trick (Prabowo & Thelwall, 2009) .

- Applying Kernelization technique on an application creates kernel trick. Kernelization is a technique of designing efficient algorithms which can achieve their efficiency in a preprocessing stage, where inputs to those algorithms are replaced by a smaller input, known as a kernel. Kernelization may be achieved by applying a set of regression rules that reduce the part of instances that are easy to handle. kernel having definite bounds on the size of a kernel (may be described as a function of some parameters related to the problem) may be found in polynomial time. When this is possible, it results in a fixed parameter traceable algorithm, whose total running time is the sum(polynomial time) of the Kernelization step and the time required to solve the kernel(nonpolynomial but bounded by parameter).

- The kernel tricks used by SVM takes the data given by the users as input and transform it and as an output, it returns some unrecognized format of data, which is the beauty of the kernel trick.

How to Implement SVM Using Supportive Programming Language

SVM can be start implementation using python, a library called as scikit-learn is widely used library which we can use to implement machine learning or we can say specially Support vector machine which involve the following stages:

1. Import the library
2. Object Creation
3. Fitting model
4. Prediction

Pros and Cons Associated With SVM

Pros

- It works extremely well with clear edge of partition.
- It is viable in high dimensional spaces.
- It is viable in situations where number of measurements is more prominent than the quantity of tests.
- It utilizes a subset of preparing focuses in the choice capacity (called support vectors), so it is additionally memory proficient.

Cons

- It doesn't perform well when we have the substantial informational collection on the grounds that the required preparing time is higher.
- It likewise doesn't perform extremely well when the informational collection has more clamor i.e. target classes are covering.
- SVM doesn't straightforwardly give likelihood appraises, these are computed utilizing a costly five-crease cross-approval. It is connected SVC strategy for Python sci-unit learn library.

Challenges in Machine Learning Technique

We find the enormous scope for opinion mining as it is giving the fantabulus, support to business.

- **Challenges Using Naives Bayes**
  - ○ Searching Problem
  - ○ Toenisaton and Classification
  - ○ Reliable Content Identification
- **Challenges Using Decision Tree**
  - ○ Opinion words are positive in one scenario and negative in other scenario
  - ○ The style of expression varied by variety of people. Which lead to the ambiguity in same scenarios situations?
- **Challenges Using Support Vector Machine**

Support Vector Machines depend on the idea of the decision planes that characterize choice limits. A choice plane is one that isolates between arrangements of items having diverse class enrollments. A schematic case has appeared in the outline underneath. In this illustration, the items have a place either with class GREEN or RED. The isolating line characterizes a limit on the correct side of which all data points are GREEN and to one side of which all items are RED. Any new protest (white hover) tumbling to the privilege is named, i.e., characterized, as GREEN (or delegated RED should it tumble to one side of the isolating line).

The above is a conventional case of a straight classifier, i.e., a classifier that isolates an arrangement of items into their individual gatherings (GREEN and RED for this situation) with a line. Most characterization undertakings, nonetheless, are not that basic, and frequently more complex structures are required with a specific

Figure 3.

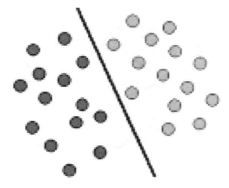

end goal to make an ideal partition, i.e., effectively group new questions (test cases) based on the illustrations that are accessible (prepare cases). This circumstance is portrayed in the below. Contrasted with the past schematic, plainly a full partition of the GREEN and RED items would require a bend. Characterization undertakings in light of attracting isolating lines to recognize objects of various class memberships are known as hyperplane classifiers. Support Vector Machines are especially suited to deal with such undertakings.

The representation underneath demonstrates the fundamental thought behind Support Vector Machines. Here we see the first protests (left half of the schematic) mapped, i.e., revamped, utilizing an arrangement of numerical capacities, known as portions. The way toward improving the items is known as mapping. Note that in this new setting, the mapped objects (right half of the schematic) is straightly distinguishable and, along these lines, rather than developing the intricate bend (left schematic), we should simply to locate an ideal line that can isolate the GREEN and the RED data points.

Support Vector Machine (SVM) is basically a more tasteful technique that performs order assignments by building hyperplanes in a multidimensional space that isolates instances of various class marks. SVM supports both relapse and grouping assignments and can deal with numerous nonstop and all-out factors. For downright factors a spurious variable is made with case esteems as either 0 or 1. In this manner, an unmitigated ward variable comprising of three levels, say (A, B, C), is spoken to by an arrangement of three sham factors:

A: {1 0 0}, B: {0 1 0}, C: {0 0 1}

Figure 4.

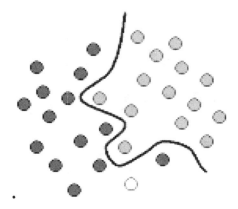

Figure 5.

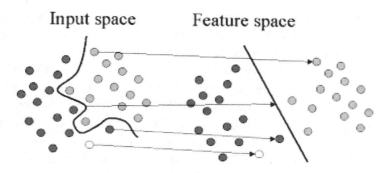

To develop an ideal hyper plane, SVM utilizes an iterative preparing calculation, which is utilized to limit a mistake work. As per the type of the mistake work, SVM models can be ordered into four particular gatherings:

- Classification SVM Type 1
- Classification SVM Type 2
- Regression SVM Type 1
- Regression SVM Type 2

Kernel Functions

The Kernel function speaks to a dot products result of probe data focuses mapped into the higher dimensional element space by the process of transformation

Though support vector machine model is a smart model for analyzing machine learning algorithm and it uses regression as well as linear and non linear classification together, some challenges and issues are still there with SVM model:

- **For Large Datasets SVM Does Not Give Good Performance:** SVM does not give good performance, when you are using large data set, the reason for poor result due to the training time required more in the large data set. SVM usually takes large time for training algorithm due to its choice of kernel, which makes it quite complex for large dataset analysis.SVM tends to be resistant towards over fitting. Even when numbers of attributes are very large, it uses regularization. For large datasets it is a problem. If your datasets are very large and they come in batches, everytime you need to increment your learning model, svm is not a good suggestion for such an incremental machine learning model.

- **Data May Not be Separable While Doing Analysis Using Support Vector Machine:** SVM separates data by classification algorithm using hyper plane. In case of SVM, If data is labelled, SVM can be used to generate multiple separating hyper planes to ensure that the data space is divided into various segments and each segment should contain only one kind of data. This technique is generally useful for such kind of data which has non-regularity that means, data whose distribution is unknown. So sometime the data separation may get hampered. Even in the segregation of data, when in data set we are using large data set, it give more error due to overlapping and noises. SVM is not suitable for highly skewed or imbalanced datasets.

- **Five Stage Cross Validation in SVM Leads to Ambiguity in Probability Estimation:** Cross validation or sometime known as the rotation estimation technique is a model validation technique for the assessment of result of a statistical analysis which will generalize to an independent datasets. It is used in such cases where the goal is decided by using predictive model. One round of cross validation involves partitioning a sample of data into complementary subsets, performing the analysis on one subset, known as training set. The computational complexity as well as the time requirement to perform training using cross validation approach is quite high. Along with this, Cross-validation only gives satisfactory results if the validation set and training set both have been drawn from the same population and only if baseness can be controlled. In case of predictive modelling, the structure being dynamic, i.e, changes over time, is not suitable for cross validation approach.

  The five stage cross validation, seems to be tough and expensive, and it too lead to ambiguity in results and probability estimates get disturbed.

3. FUTURE SCOPE AND CONCLUSION

In the future scope, we would like to state that there is enormous scope for opinion mining as it is giving the fantabulous, support to business. Now the offline as well as online business people react their business according to the opinion mining,

In conclusion, we would like to state that more than million dollar business and across the globe the opinion mining is gaining its reach in the market. Even we can say that the new products are more customers oriented, because before their preparation, the numbers of parameters are kept in the line to ensure that it attracts the user's interest, so the opinion mining using machine learning is going to give a new dimension to the information technology. Also it will give a wide scope to the researcher for identifying and imposing the artificial intelligence techniques

ACKNOWLEDGMENT

Authors are thankful to the book editor for giving opportunity to include our chapter. They are also extending their sincere thanks to the reviewers for their valuable suggestions and remarks, without which it would not be possible to be included in this book as a chapter. We are also thankful to the our institutions' chairpersons CMR Institute of Technology (Autonomous), Hyderabad, India, QuangNam University, Vietnam and Huddersfield University, UK for supporting for this research work morally and for providing the positive atmosphere to contribute to a sound research environment& preparing this research chapter work.

REFERENCES

Cai, K., Spangler, S., Chen, Y., & Zhang, L. (2008). Leveraging Sentiment Analysis for Topic Detection. *IEEE/WIC/ACM International Conference on Web Intelligence and Intelligent Agent Technology, 1*, 265-271. 10.1109/WIIAT.2008.188

Gamon, M., Aue, A., Corston-Oliver, S., & Ringger, E. (2005). Pulse: Mining customer opinions from free text. *Lecture Notes in Computer Science, 36*(6), 121–1324. doi:10.1007/11552253_12

Hu, M., & Liu, B. (2004). Mining and summarizing customer reviews. In *Proceedings of the Tenth ACM SIGKDD International conference on Knowledge discovery and Data mining* (pp. 168-177), ACM.

Pang, B., & Lee, L. (2008). Opinion mining and sentiment analysis. *Foundations and Trends in Information Retrieval, 1*(2), 1–135. doi:10.1561/1500000011

Prabowo, R., & Thelwall, M. (2009). Sentiment Analysis: A Combined Approach. *Journal of Informetrics, 3*(2), 143–157. doi:10.1016/j.joi.2009.01.003

Rajeev, P. V., & Rekha, V. S. (2016). Opinion Mining of User Reviews Using Machine Learning Techniques and Ranking of Products Based on Features. *Advances in Intelligent Systems and Computing., 39*(8), 78–85.

Sharma, R., Nigam, S., & Jain, R. (2013). Supervised Opinion Mining Techniques: A Survey. *International Journal of Information and Computation Technology, 3*(8), 737–742.

Sun, J., Long, C., Zhu X. & Huang M. (2009). Mining Reviews for Product Comparison and Recommendation. *Research Journal on Computer Science and Computer Engineering With Applications, 3*(9), 33- 409.

Thomas, E. H., & Galambos, N. (2004). What Satisfies Students? Mining Student-Opinion Data with Regression and Decision Tree Analysis. *Research in Higher Education*, *45*(3), 251–269. doi:10.1023/B:RIHE.0000019589.79439.6e

Witten, I. H., & Frank, E. (2005). *Data mining: Practical machine learning tools and techniques*. San Francisco: Morgan Kaufmann.

Section 2
Ontologies and Their Applications

Chapter 5
Ontology–Based Opinion Mining

Chitra Jalota
Manav Rachna International Institute of Research and Studies, India

Rashmi Agrawal
Manav Rachna International Institute of Research and Studies, India

ABSTRACT

E-commerce business is very popular as a large amount of data is available on the internet in the form of unstructured data. To find new market trends and insight, it is very important for an organization to track the customers' opinions/reviews on a regular basis. Reviews available on the internet are very scattered and heterogeneous (i.e., structured as well as unstructured form of data). A good decision is always based on the quality of information within a specified period of time. Ontology is an explicit detailed study of concepts. The word ontology is borrowed from philosophy. It can also be defined as systematic maintenance of information about the things which already exist. In computer science, it could be said that it is a formal representation of knowledge with the help of a fixed set of believed concepts and the relationship between those concepts.

INTRODUCTION

Opinion Mining, also known as sentiment analysis, is a process which aims to determine the polarity of a textual corpus i.e document, paragraph or sentence etc., ending towards positive, negative or neutral sense. Economic and Financial modeling could be one of the most promising application of Opinion Mining/Sentiment Analysis.

DOI: 10.4018/978-1-5225-6117-0.ch005

Machine Learning based sentiment classifiers also consist of an opinion mining tool. But the main problem with these classifiers is that they classify opinions of users into classes (+ve, -ve or neutral) which assigns a corresponding score to each of the class as a whole rather than considering that many aspects of the same notion is also there. Machine learning approach always gives a single quantitative (sentiment score) or qualitative result (+ve or –ve). So, there is a requirement of ontology based techniques which is a fine grained version of Opinion Mining/Sentiment Analysis.

Ontology is an explicit detailed study of concepts. The word 'Ontology' is borrowed from philosophy. Ontology can be defined as an "explicit, machine-readable specification of a shared conceptualization'. It is generally considered as a formal specification of conceptualization which consists of concepts and their relations. It can also be defined as systematic maintenance of information about the things which already exist.

In Computer Science, "Ontology Based Opinion Mining" is a formal representation of knowledge with the help of a fixed set of believed concepts and the relationship between those concepts. It could have the reasons about the domain's properties and with the help of that property a domain can be described easily. So, it is a formal explicit description of the basic/core concepts of domain. It also provides a shared word stock/lexicon.

It is an identification and extraction of subjective material from different types of source material or from the unstructured data with the help of natural language processing, computational linguistics and text analytics.

Ontologies are used in many areas like Artificial Intelligence, Library Science and Information Science. Mainly there are 4 categories of ontologies:

1. **Static:** This type of ontology tells us about the existing things, their attributes and relationship between them.
2. **Dynamic:** It describe transition, process and morphisms of various types of things.
3. **Intentional:** It deals with want, prove or disprove and argue about the things as per user's own perception.
4. **Social:** It relates with surrounding environment and its settings.

Ontologies can be used in many ways. Within Computer Science, it is a model for describing world which has a particular set of types, their relationships and properties. It can also be assumed that there is a very thin line of difference between real world and the model features used for ontologies. Text based online reviews by customers for a product is fair and unbiased parameter to quality measure of the product. But the problem is that all these reviews cannot be read by all users. So we have to apply some techniques of opinion mining which can construct a feature specific graphical representation and give us the real picture of relative quality of the product.

The main aim of this is to find out mind set or thought process of a speaker or a writer related to the relevant topic or polarity of the document in terms of context. Mind set could be his/her own judgment or affective state or predefined emotional communication.

As per the form of opinions, they can be classified into three goups:

- **Form 1:** Advantage, Disadvantages and Summary of Opinions.
- **Form 2:** Advantage, Disadvantages of Opinions.
- **Form 3:** Free Form, (No Rules and Regulations for specification of forms).

LITERATURE REVIEW

This section is related to the work carried out in the past on Sentiment Analysis and Opinion Mining. In this chapter, various techniques of Sentiment Analysis and opinion mining will be discussed in detail. Opinions can be extracted with the help of extraction of structured information which could be entities, their attributes and relation among them.

A review encompassing approaches to ensure opinion oriented text data was suggested by Khan et al., (2014). It dealt with sentiment analysis and OM related techniques and challenges focusing on machine learning methods on the basis of their usage as well as significant for OM. Typically utilized classification methods were identified for opinionated documents to assist further research.

Li et al., (2010) proposed an opinion mining system which mines helpful opinion information from camera reviews by utilized Semantic Role Labeling (SRL) as well as polarity calculating techniques. Features lexicon and sentiment lexicon were constructed for mining attributes as well as affective entities. In the end, the contrast between positive as well as negative opinions were presented visually.

Zhuang et al. (2006), Ma et al. (2013), and Agarwal et al. (2015) performed Machine Learning approaches that require largely trained datasets to perform with accuracy. Machine Learning approaches deliver significant results for feature extraction task when the training data sets are manually annotated by a human expert. However, this can be an extremely time-consuming task as the required size of the training dataset should be sufficiently large to bootstrap the learning algorithms.

Two categories are mainly used for Information Extraction i.e.

1.   TBIE (Text Based Information Extraction): It is a key in NLP technology which will automatically extract relevant information from the given text.

2. OBIE (Ontology Based Information Extraction): A process which is used for the identification of relevant concepts, their properties and relation between concepts.

Some IE Approaches Followed by OBIE System

1. **Use-Case Framework:** It is basically used for the conversion of unstructured data/ information into structured information by the use of domain based ontology.
2. **OntoGazetteers and OntoRootGazetteer:** It allows manual mapping between list of gazetteer to classes of ontology. OntoRootGazetteer analyze the already mentioned labels of concept in ontologies with POS taggers or tokenizers.
3. **Hierarchical Learning Approach:** This approach is based on the usage of target ontology which is an urgent requirement of extraction process by including the inter concept relationship.
4. **SOBA (SmartWeb Ontology Based Annotation):** A very important component for OBIE system. It extracts the important information from heterogeneous sources like tables, text images, caption etc.
5. **Distributed Semantic Agent:** Easy tracking of decisions and their explanations to users is possible with this approach.

TEXT MINING APPROACHES FOR OPINION MINING

Opinion Mining focuses on three main tasks:

- Sentiment classification
- Summarization and description of aspect based opinion mining
- Relation mining and comparative analysis

Following is the list of text mining approaches to sentiment analysis:

1. **Word Based Approach:** According to this approach, meaning and sentiment of each and every opinion is carried out by separate words. For this reason, there must be an assigned sentiment to every word in opinion.
2. **Pattern Based Approach:** According to this approach, sentiments can also be identified by human expressions instead of separate words. That's why sentiment is assigned to identify phrases also.

3. **Ontology Based Approach:** According to this approach, ontology is used to present knowledge of specific domain, which is about the subject of opinion. Structure of a product or service is allowed to show to others which has been given ranking/rating in the opinion.

4. **Statistical Learning Approach:** According to this approach, there is a requirement of combination of opinion and sentiments. Based on this, polarity assignment for new opinions is comparatively easy.

As per user's view point, there could be some significant differences between the above mentioned approaches. It is the user, who can find the best approach out of all the approaches as per his/her requirement. Figure given below presents the different types of sentiment analysis and its related text mining approach

Procedure of Opinion Mining

Opinions are base of all human activities and are influence indicators of our behavior. These are very helpful in decision making. In real life scenario, it is almost impossible for a business or an organization to take a decision about its products and services without considering the public opinions. It is also called sentiment analysis which deals and analyze with people's opinions, sentiments, evaluations, appraisals, attitudes and emotions which are related to a particular domain like products, services, organizations, events, topics etc. By calculating positive and negative orientation of information present in the text, it can be considered as a fundamental issue in opinion mining.

Opinion Mining can be done at three levels i.e. document level, sentence level, entity and aspect level. It can also be used for three objectives like Polarity Identification, Subjectivity/Objectivity Identification and feature based analysis. Following are the main tasks of opinion mining:

Figure 1. Different approaches used in particular opinion mining analysis

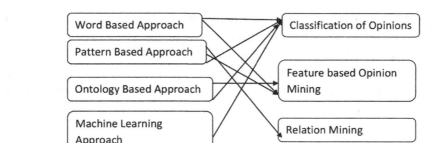

- Entity extraction and categorization
- Aspect extraction and categorization
- Opinion holder extraction and categorization
- Time extraction and standardization
- Aspect sentiment classification
- Outputting the analyzed results in tuples

ONTOLOGY

According to Gruber (1993), it can be defined as a specification of conceptualization, which means, in each ontology there is a combination of objects, classes and entities and their inter relationship belongs to the same domain. There could be three main categories of an ontology model i.e concept or class, property (data property) and relation (object property). There is a wide range of areas in which ontologies can be used like in Philosophy, Artificial Intelligence, Information Technology and Research and Development etc. Ontologies focuses on providing domain specific knowledge understandable to both computers and developers. It plays a very important role in sharing of sources and in identifying future use terms definition such as meta data. It also provides a semantic ground of digital content for better understanding of machines.

Most common language to for ontology formalization is OWL, a proposal of the W3C. Yaakub, Li and Zhang (2013) proposed a feature based ontology which can integrate customer's characteristics by using a multidimensional model. As per this approach, it first identifies the entities and then emotions present in the customer's reviews. But the limitation with this approach is that it is too general and it lacks reasoning ability among multiple products. Ontologies in the community of information system are also known as data models.

Ontology as Vocabulary

Ontology is an unapproachable and dispense definition of every domain as per user's interest. Ontology itself represents wisdom/knowledge as a set of all those ideas which are available within the same domain and association between all those ideas. Ontologies can also have concept/classes in hierarchical manner.

Like Classes, concepts also have different characteristics for the explanation of their properties. Feature based opinion mining can also be improved by introducing the ontologies for feature selection and they also provide a new method for sentiment analysis which is actually based on vector analysis.

For this, we can have four modules:

- *The Natural Language Processing Module (NLP)*
- *The Ontology based feature Identification module*
- *The Polarity Identification Module*
- *The Opinion Mining Module*

The most important feature of ontology based opinion mining is ontologies which are used in many areas like Artificial Intelligence, Library Science and Information Science. Mainly there are 4 categories of ontologies:

1. **Static:** This category of ontology describes only the static aspects of the world i.e it consider only existing things, their attributes and relationship between them. This ontology is ideal for imaginary situations and not applicable for real time systems.
2. **Dynamic:** World is not static. Every moment all aspects are changing. So to consider those changing aspects, we use dynamic ontology. It describe transition, process and morphisms of various and different types of things. Statechart can be defined for the clarity of different states and their respective transition.
3. **Intentional:** This type of ontology constitutes intents, goals, beliefs, prove or disprove and argue about. It also allow reasons and expressions of alternate realities. This type of ontology is required for the situations involving current actions.
4. **Social:** This ontology includes social settings, structure of various organizations and interdependencies. These ontologies are also involved in the area of distributed Artificial Intelligence.

Following are the application areas of Ontologies:

- It shares basic and common understanding of the whole structure of a system among their variety of users.
- It also creates the reusability of domain knowledge.
- Ontology also keeps the Domain Knowledge and Operational Knowledge separately.
- Communication
- Inter-operability
- System Engineering Specification, Reliability and Reusability

DOMAIN KNOWLEDGE ANALYSIS

Most of the ontologies in the community of information systems are also known as data models. As discussed, that ontologies are always concerned with only one domain. For the ontology construction, knowledge of a particular field is required. It is different from domain to domain. No two domains share the same ontology.

It can be seen from Figure 1 that opinions can be classified through ontology based approach and the same is helpful in feature based opinion mining. A single opinion can be used as an instance of ontology.

For the ease conduct of feature based opinion mining, graph-like construction of ontology can be used. The most important characteristics of opinion's subject can be used as an attribute in ontology. After that polarity can be calculated of each feature either for single opinion or for whole set of opinions. Ontology of sentiments/opinions can also be created in ontology based sentiment analysis. It also gives many potential benefits for the knowledge processing and its representation which may also include the gap between domain knowledge and application knowledge. Sharing of common knowledge of more than one subject is also possible between human and computers

CONCEPTNET

It is a semantic network which is freely available and helps the computer to understand the meaning of words used by human being. Crowd sourcing project open mind common sense launched in MIT Media Lab in 1999 gave the idea of Concept Net. It is a knowledgebase of common sense having 2, 50,000 items which are stored in text files but written in Python. Till now, it consist of 1 millions of assertions represented in triplets form i.e. <concept1, relation, concept2> which shows the relation between these two concepts. It can be used by some tools of text mining for understanding the meaning of text and its classification. It is less formal, limited and based on practical aspects of the information usage. It can describe anything which is very obvious, but not always in true sense. This is very useful for our practical everyday word knowledge.

There are 19 binary relations in conceptnet. It maintain and manage the uncertainty of words with the list of its synonyms and its hierarchy which should be "is-a" type. Figure 2 is showing the conceptnet framework in which all relations and their hierarchy are shown.

In the context of natural language search query, it has the potential to find out the meaning of the word which is most likely. It is a very large machine interpretable semantic network which consists of very large number of common-sense concepts.

Figure 2. ConceptNet Framework

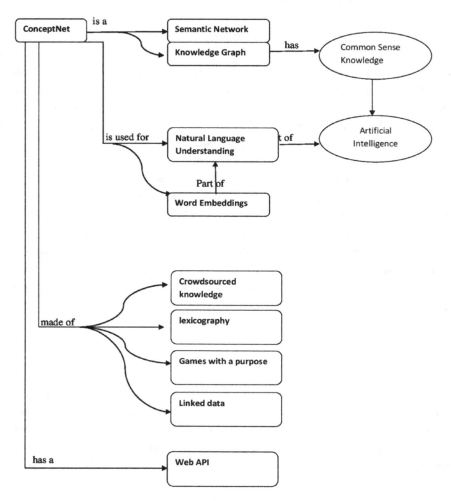

Contribution to knowledgebase of commonsense in ConceptNet is modify by the ordinary people on the Internet. It is the largest publically available common-sense knowledge base which can be used to mine various inferences from the text. It consists of nodes (concepts) connected by edges (relations between concepts). Some of the relationships between concepts in the ConceptNet are IsA, EffectOf, CapableOf, MadeOf, DesireOf, etc. Frequency property represents how often given concepts are used with the given relation, For example, ConceptNet relations, Restaurant UsedFor eat, Restaurant IsA place, and so forth.

ConceptNet vs. WordNet

When we want to give commonsense knowledge to machine, it can be done through ConceptNet. In other words, it can be termed as a tool by which computer can understand daily usage English. It is an open source having Python based SQL toolkit and acquire data from open mind common sense corpus. It was originated in MIT Media Lab and introduced by HugoLiu. Originally, ConceptNet was initiated as ConceptNet2. Then ConceptNet3 was introduced. Now- a- days ConceptNet 5 is available. There are so many applications of ConceptNet like Aommonsense ARIA, GOOSE, makeBelieve etc.

It is a very huge web based resource of knowledge in which a variety of aspects related to our everyday life can be included (e.g. plane could be used in aircraft as well as it could be an unbounded two dimensional shape). ConceptNet is a form of knowledge representation based on the information present in the database of Open Mind Common Sense. It is used in large number of applications like Machine Translation, Speech Recognition System etc. Relations or assertions in conceptnet can be used in the form of triplets i.e. "Concept1, relation, Concept2" which shows the type of relation between two main concepts. It is expressed as a directed graph which has nodes and all nodes stand as concepts and their edges are the assertions or relations between these concepts. Approx. 4,00,000 concepts, as a word or a phrase are included in conceptnet which can be labeled by a unique identifier. It has thirty kinds of relations which are of semantic nature like CapableOf, SubeventOf, MotivationOf etc. It has the tendency of polysemy and synonemy due to which it cannot be used directly for Word Sense Disambiguation purpose.

Like ConceptNet, there are two popular natural language processing toolkit are WordNet and Cyc. WordNet is a lexical database of English words and those all are linked together by semantic relationship. A lexical database is a database of information about words. It forms the grouping of English words into synonyms called synsets which provide short definitions for each word. It can be seen as a combination of thesaurus and dictionary. It is used by humans through a web browser within a synset, if synonyms exist, it is called a lemmas.

SentiWordNet is a lexical resource of opinion mining i.e a database which has one or more dictionaries. To measure the opinion from the text, there is a recent research that shows the "Positive or Negative polarity" related to subjective terms of the text. In SentiWordNet, each synset of WordNet is associated with three types of numerical points i.e. Obj(s), Pos(s), Neg(s).

ConceptNet and WordNet both are very useful in detailed analysis of queries. From the comparative analysis point of view, we consider only three measures i.e. the ability of good judgment, different thought process for same concept and the capability of a machine for producing the same thing again and again. The above two are complementary to each other. There is always a more chance of discrimination ability with WordNet and concept diversity with ConceptNet.

Construction of Domain Specific Ontology From ConceptNet

Ontology can be defined as the connection of different concepts and their semantic relationships. Semantics is the linguistic and philosophical study of meaning. It is concerned with the relationships between signifiers like words, phrases, and symbol. These are very useful in collecting important information from a piece of text. A common sense knowledge based which consists of domain specific concepts and their relations can be considered as constructed ontology. Each ontology is having different purpose. When there is a movement of knowledge from one ontology to another, it requires mapping between those two ontologies. Domain ontologies generally do not cover the kind of common-sense-ontologies. The domain ontology is automatically created from product domain name e.g. camera or telephone which exists as a concept in ConceptNet. The following figure i.e figure 3 is showing the same i.e. how an ontology construction is possible through conceptnet.

ConceptNet Relations

It has a class of 24 primary relations which express connections between various concepts. ConceptNet relations can be categorized into 3 primary categories i.e. hierarchical relations, synonymous relations and functional relations.

- Hierarchical relations represent parent-child relations.

Figure 3. Ontology Construction using ConceptNet

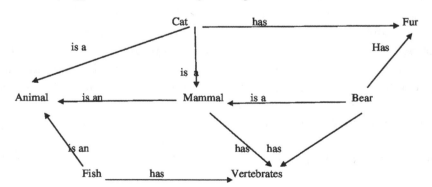

○ It is definitive and used to create the base for ontology tree. In this type of relations, relations are transitive which can be used to construct a tree top-down. It is always preferable during relational conflicts.

Hierarchical relations > Synonymous relations > Functional relations

- Synonymous relations are used to identify related concepts.
  ○ Similar nodes of a tree can be merged during the construction of a tree
- Functional relations are always helpful to checkout the purpose of the concept
  ○ In this relation, relation categorization always helps to give weightage to different relations in a different way

ConceptNet relations can be defined by a set of relations which is applicable to text in any language. Some common relations in ConceptNet are like Related to, FormOf, IsA, PartOf, HasA, CapableOf, MannerOf, HasContext etc.

Figure 4 is used for domain ontology construction of the product (camera) through conceptnet.

A connection of concepts with different kinds of semantic relations can be termed as Ontology. As we all know that semantic relations are useful for getting important information from the whole text. Ontology constructed by user can be taken as a reference for the actual one and at the same time can be considered as a common sense knowledge base which consists the concepts of the related domain and their relations.

In this context, the user can expand the ontology by merging of two ontologies of domain name synonyms for the better explanation of domain specific all features. E.g. ontology for restaurant can be created by merging of ontology of hotels as well as ontology of restaurants with a relation i.e. IsEqualTo.

Table 1. Relation Categorization of ConceptNet

Relation Type	Used for
Hierarchical	HasA, PartOf, MadeOf, IsA
Synonymous	Synonymous or Conceptually RelatedTo
Functional	UsedFor, CapableOf, HasProperty

Figure 4. Camera product-domain ontology construction through conceptnet

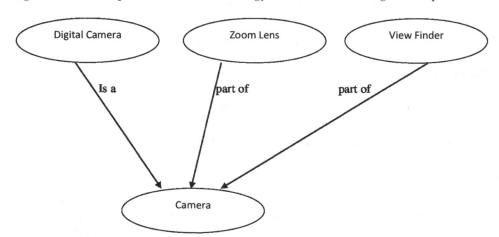

ASPECT EXTRACTION FROM OPINION MINING

A term for which an opinion or a sentiment can be expressed is known as an aspect. e.g. if we are saying that "this is a very nice car", so in this sentence, car is an aspect about which sentiment is expressed. It has been observed that opinion mining can be done at three different levels i.e document level, sentence level and aspect level. Aspect and Entity extractions are two main areas of aspect based opinion mining. Earlier the aspect based opinion mining was started with features based opinion mining. Extraction and summarization of people's opinions on aspects was the prime task of aspect based opinion mining. There are mainly two types of aspects- Explicit Aspects and Implicit Aspects which may depend upon the aspect terms- For aspect knowledge, firstly review POS(part of speech) which is tagged over there and after that all used noun terms are extracted. Now, these all have to be matched with earlier created domain specific ontology so that all unimportant and irrelevant aspects can be eliminated.

Approaches for Aspect Extraction

1. Based on frequently used noun and noun phrases
2. Based on opinion exploitation and target relations. Targets are entities and attributes associated with that entity based on which opinion can be mined.
3. Based on supervised learning
4. Based on topic modeling. Topic Models are good for data exploration. They are useful tool for data analysis as well.

OPINION EXTRACTION (FEATURES SPECIFIC)

Different users may have different opinions related to all features in review of document. For example "Study of this college is very good but infrastructure is very poor". In this sentence, opinion is positive towards study and opinion is negative towards infrastructure. There should always be an association between subject/opinion target (aspect) and the opinion words. There is a need of dependency parsing to find the associations between opinion target and opinion words. They have an important role in algorithm's classification.

Techniques Used for Opinions Extractions

1. Supervised Learning
2. Unsupervised Learning
3. Case Based Reasoning

Opinion Extraction Techniques can be explained in better way by its diagrammatic representation with the help of Figure 5.

AMBIGUOUS, UNAMBIGUOUS AND CONTEXT TERMS

Context dependent words, which change their polarity according to situations/ surroundings, are called ambiguous words. For example "I have a small suggestion that kindly change the direction of your bed". In this sentence, the word "suggestion" is a neutral sentiment. Some words like complaint is in negative sentiment but when it is combined with the word small like "I have a small compliant" then its polarity

Figure 5. Opinion extraction techniques

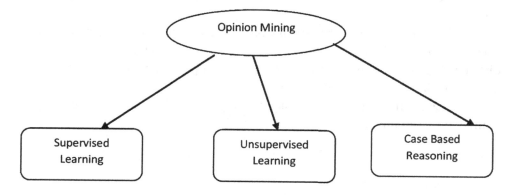

could be changed to neutral. So the words which occur mainly in positive context and occur very less in negative context are known as unambiguous words. But on the other hand, words which have equally weightage of occurrence in positive and negative context are known as ambiguous terms. Context terms always occur with co-occurrence of the ambiguous words that have the power to change the polarity of them as well. Context terms are basically used to calculate the polarity accuracy of the ambiguous words. For this, there should be a context term against each and every ambiguous term. They (context terms) themselves includes all parts of a speech like noun, verb, adverb etc in all those documents which are for review purpose. There should be a separate calculation of probability for positive as well as negative sentiments. If the result of calculation is high for positive class probability, then it is obvious the term is more towards the positive polarity otherwise it may in the favor of negative polarity. To compute the polarity of an ambiguous term, we have to add polarities of all possible context terms.

SENTIMENTS SCORING

Sentiments can always be measured by two ways:

1. **Bag of Words Method:** In this method, we use an algorithm which works on already specified list which includes words or sequences of words associated with either positive or negative polarity, and then find out sentiments scoring index from it.
2. **Statistical Association Method:** This method is useful for the calculation of lexical polarity against external set of variables, not against the predefined list of words.

There are many more sentiment analysis engines which can not only measure positive and negative sentiments but more than that i.e real human emotions and sarcasm.

It is always noted that there is nothing particular with respect to sentiment scores. It is very true that there is no "global sentiment score ". Each and every service is different. E.g. Amazon uses 1 for negative and 5 for positive for customer feedback system, but in many cases, the same is opposite. The most common interface is (0-1) scale starting from negative to positive. Sentiment analysis based on an entity is entirely different topic.

SENTIMENT ANALYSIS VS. OPINION MINING

Sentiment Analysis

Sentiment Analysis is an upcoming and growing field. It is a field related to calculation of opinions of different users, sentiments and text's subjectivity. It is a task related to the field of Natural Language Processing and Information Extraction that focuses on the consumer's opinion either in positive or negative comments by analyzing a large number of documents. The first and the basic step in the data driven approach of sentiment analysis is the conversion of a piece of text to its polarity outcome. Frequency is the most important and considerable issue in the retrieval of information and classification of text. There is 'n' number of opinions of different users on the internet for a particular term or a product and it is very difficult to know the count of positive or negative opinions. For this purpose, a count based approach can be used to compare the different opinions.

For the text's polarity, there is a text classifier which helps different users to know the difference between positive and negative comments and also help users in opinion mining. Unsupervised lexicon technique is the right method for the classification of different kinds of opinions. Sentiment analysis actually evaluates that how different customers can have different viewpoint about the same product (It could be positive or negative).Sentiment analysis always comes before opinion mining.

Challenges in Sentiment Analysis

1. **Consideration of Opinion Word:** Positive in one situation and negative in another situation.
2. **Different Mindset by Different People:** There could be a contradiction by different people in their statements.
3. **Combination of Positive and Negative Comments:** In informal medium like twitter, people combine two or more opinion in the same sentence which is very difficult to parse by a machine.

Sentiment Analysis Tools to Measure User's Sentiments

1. Google Alerts
2. People Browser
3. Google Analytics
4. Hootsuite
5. Facebook Insights

Opinion Mining

It is a natural language processing used to capture the opinion of public in terms of a particular product or a brand from World Wide Web. Its main task is to combine and collect various opinions and categorize them into various sub opinions. This field is much deeper than sentiment analysis and tries to find out the reasons of variations among customers about the same product.

Applications of Opinion Mining

1. Evaluate the success of a new product launch
2. Decision Making
3. Market Analysis
4. Future Directions

Challenges of Opinion Mining

1. Opinion Word Consideration
2. Contradictions of Statements
3. Opinions in different Context

APPLICATION AREAS OF SENTIMENT ANALYSIS AND OPINION MINING

Major application areas of Sentiment Analysis and Opinion Mining are as given below:

1. Right decision for Purchase
2. Quality Checkmark
3. Market Oriented Research
4. Product Recommendation as per market trends
5. Spam Detection
6. Policy and Strategy Formulation
7. Long Term Decision making

RESEARCH CHALLENGES OF SENTIMENT ANALYSIS AND OPINION MINING

1. Public Reviews Authentication

2. Less number of classification filtering
3. Cost pertaining to opinion mining softwares
4. Lack of integrity of implicit and behavior data with opinion
5. Independency of domains
6. Natural language processing hindrances
7. Language Problem i.e. creating building resource for Arabic, German etc.

LIMITATIONS OF SENTIMENT ANALYSIS AND OPINION MINING

Although there is ample amount of research done by researchers in the area of Sentiment Analysis and Opinion Mining, still there are areas where there is a scope of further research in the above mentioned field. Following are the major research areas of Sentiment analysis and opinion mining:

1. Sentiment Analysis for spams.
2. Abbreviation's sentiment analysis.
3. Algorithm for the improvement of sentiment word identification.
4. Development of analyzing tool which is fully automatic.
5. Sentiment Analysis of Policy based contents'.
6. Development of bi polar statements.

CONCLUSION

The above mentioned field i.e. Sentiment Analysis and Opinion Mining is a upcoming field of data mining used to mine the important information i.e. opinion or comments about a specific product or a brand from customer's valuable feedback or comments. Opinion Mining can be done on the basis of document, sentence and feature level sentiment analysis. In the field of Natural Language Processing, Sentiment Analysis and Opinion Mining is a most interesting area of research. More effective techniques need to be discovered so that the current challenges faced by sentiment analysis and opinion mining can be overcome.

REFERENCES

Agarwal, B., Poria, S., Mittal, N., Gelbukh, A., & Hussain, A. (2015). Concept-Level sentiment analysis with dependency-based semantic parsing: A novel approach. *Cognitive Computation*, 7(4), 487–499. doi:10.100712559-014-9316-6

Gruber, T. R. (1993). A Translation Approach to Portable Ontologies. *Knowledge Acquisition*, *5*(2), 199–220. doi:10.1006/knac.1993.1008

Khan, K., Baharudin, B., Khan, A., Ullah, A. (2014). Mining opinion from text documents with the help of Machine learning methods based on Opinion Mining (OM). *Journal of King Saud University-Computer and Information Sciences*, *26*(3), 258-275.

Li, X., Dai, L., & Shi, H. (2010). Opinion mining of camera reviews based on semantic role labeling. *Proceedings of the Seventh International Conference on Fuzzy Systems and Knowledge Discovery*, 5, 2372–2375. 10.1109/FSKD.2010.5569525

Ma, B., Zhang, D., Yan, Z., & Kim, T. (2013). An LDA and synonym lexicon based approach to product feature extraction from online consumer product reviews. *Journal of Electronic Commerce Research*, *14*(4), 304–314.

Yaakub, M.R., Li, Y., & Zhang, Y. (2013). *Integration of Sentiment Analysis into Customer Relational Model: The Importance of Feature Ontology and Synonym*. Academic Press.

Zhuang, L., Jing, F., & Zhu, X.-Y. (2006). Movie review mining and summarization. *Proc. CIKM Conf.*, 43–50.

ADDITIONAL READING

Baccianella, S., Esuli, A., & Sebastiani, F. (2010). SentiWordNet 3.0: An enhance lexical resource for sentiment analysis and opinion mining in proceedings of the seventh conference on international language resources and evaluation (pp.2200–2204). European Language Resources Association.

Balahur, A., & Montoyo, A. (2010). *Semantic approaches to fine and coarse grained feature-based opinion mining in natural language processing and information systems* (pp. 142–153). Berlin, Heidelberg: Springer.

Ghiassi, M., Skinner, J., & Zimbra, D. (2013). Twitter brand sentiment analysis: A hybrid system using n-gram analysis and dynamic artificial neural network Expert Systems with Applications. *International Journal (Toronto, Ont.)*, *40*(16), 6266–6282.

Pang, B., & Lee, L. (2004). A sentiment education: Sentiment analysis using subjectivity summarization based on minimum cuts in proceedings of the ACL (pp. 271–278).

Song, Q., Liu, J., Wang, X., & Wang, J. (2014), A Novel Automatic Ontology Construction Method Based on Web Data in Tenth International Conference on Intelligent Information Hiding and Multimedia Signal Processing. IEEE.

Toutanova, K., Klein, D., Manning, C., & Singer, Y. (2003). Feature-rich part-of Speech tagging with a cyclic dependency network in proceedings of HLT-NAACL 2003(pp. 252–259).

Zhao, L., & Li, C. (2009). Ontology based opinion mining for movie reviews in proceedings of the 3rd international conference on knowledge science, engineering and management (pp. 204–214)

Zhou, L., & Chaovalit, P. (2008). Ontology-supported polarity mining. *Journal of the American Society for Information Science and Technology*, *59*(1), 98–110. doi:10.1002/asi.20735

Chapter 6

Ontologies, Repository, and Information Mining in Component–Based Software Engineering Environment

Rajesh Kumar Bawa
Punjabi University, India

Iqbaldeep Kaur
Punjabi University, India

ABSTRACT

This chapter reviews some ontologies, tools, and editors used in building and maintaining the ontology from those reported in the literature, and the main focus is on the interoperability between them. The essential thing while developing an ontology or using an ontology from world web are tools. Through tools, ontology can either be developed or aligned in a manner that the researcher wants and given direction in term of opinion from the source files as meta data. This chapter presents various editors for building the ontology and various tools for matching between the two ontologies and conclusion based on the repository extracted as from the data in term of mining results. Comparison of various ontologies, tools, and editors are also there in order for the ease of user to access a particular ontology tool for selection of data in term of repository or components from the enormous data.

DOI: 10.4018/978-1-5225-6117-0.ch006

INTRODUCTION

Component based software engineering commences a new field in research area by introducing the term "component". A component is a non trivial, nearly independent and replaceable part of the system that can be plugged with any software and then they are played according to its specification. Component based software engineering helps the component developer to reuse the component rather than building it, by using application developer (XJIN, 2007). Component developer only uses the component which is present in repository. Now a day, searching and retrieving of components are not easy, as repositories have become very large and complex. So, to over-come this problem, well defined repository are required that not only matches the query syntactically but is also related to the query semantically, so that best component is retrieved.

Ontologies play a vital role in retrieval of component as not only does it provides description of the component but also provides the relationship between different components linked together. Ontologies are always misunderstood and there are various misinterpretations for the word ontology. Different authors have different definition regarding ontology. For example, according to author ontology is simply an extension of vocabulary by providing relation and rules to the terms, while as per another author it is explicit specification for conceptualization. But actually ontology in precise term is nothing but the complete overview or jist of the whole scenario by providing hierarchies and taxonomies.

In this chapter the emphasis is given on the comparison between various ontologies. Section 2 explains the basic concept used in ontology. What is semantic web, what is ontology, how ontology is linked to semantic web, and the process of building an ontology. Section 3 explains various types of ontologies and comparison of ontologies by stating their pros and cons. Section 4 describes the various types of editor tools used in ontology. Section 5 compares the results and at the end we wind up with the conclusion.

BASIC TERMINOLGY

In computer science, ontology concerns with systematic arrangement of components that is based on concept and formal specification in such a way that repositories can be extended easily. Ontology is a collection of classes, objects and relationship between these two that provide precise output based on query. Ontology gives brief overview of the entire scenario which user wants to retrieve from the large collection of repositories (Yongpeng, 2009). Therefore the word ontology is illustrated as a combination of various terms that can be represented and is known as concepts (Khan, 2004).

Ontology as defined by FESC should be formal explicit (Broens, 2004), specification of shared conceptualization.(Yadav,2016). There are various components of ontology namely concepts which is represented as nodes in ontology, properties (Dfarias, 2015) which represents the values of particular concepts, relational properties which represent relation between concepts and nodes and many more

Semantic and Web

Semantic web is the expansion of the World Wide Web through W3C which states that semantic web allows a common framework for reusing data across various communities. Semantic web is interpreted as the information that is in machine form. Semantic web is also known as global information mesh (Gsingh, 2014). The difference between semantic web and World Wide Web is that while the semantic web is machine understandable, World Wide Web is machine readable.

Relation Between Ontologies and Semantic Web

Ontologies are viewed as the support of semantic web. Although there is no such definition (Wimalasuriya, 2010) that links semantic web and ontology, but as the semantic web is richer in vocabulary and contains various hierarchies and linking of various terms, it can be considered as a form of ontology, or it's just a collection of uniform resource identifier with its meaning described in it. The architecture and components of semantic web (Table 2) is as follows.

Table 1. Tuples and sets

Tuples	Sets of Tuples
Entities	{ele is a unary predicate }
Hierarchies	Subclassof:
Individuals	{c(i)lc є C^ i is a ground term}
Relationships	{relk(e1/e2) }
Properties	{propk(e1/specification)}
Axioms	{a/a is an assertion}

Table 2. Components and Description

Component	Description
Unicode	Unifying the character set and presents the data in form of triples
URI	Short for Uniform resource identifier that presents data in syntactical form.
RDF	Short for Resource Description Framework that provides information in form of triples.
RDFs	Short for RDF schema extends RDF by making vocabularies for describing properties and classes of RDF based resources.
Ontology	Set of terms describing a particular domain and deriving conclusion from it.
Logic and proof	Different agents makes conclusion by using inference system.
A. Trust	It denotes level of fealty to systems

Semantic and Web

The different phase of building ontology is as follows:

- **Feasibility Study Phase:** This step is used for identifying the problem.
- **Specification Phase:** It is used for identifying the purpose of the ontology. It may includes the structure or values that can be associated with ontology.
- **Reuse Considering Phase:** All those ontologies that can be reused when developing a new one is considered in this phase.
- **Conceptualization Phase:** In this phase, the identification of concepts, instances, relationships that can be used in ontology is considered.
- **Identifying the Terms and Defining the Taxonomies:** In this phase, specification of terms for a specific domain is specified, and determines a range of ontology in a structured list. After specification of domain and range of terms, it is essential to organize in a tree-like fashion.
- **Defining Properties:** After defining a hierarchy, it is essential to organize the properties that link the ontology.
- **Formalize the Ontology:** In this phase a structure is defined for ontology to the acquired knowledge.
- **Integration:** The discovered ontologies are reused with the current ontology.

PREVIOUS CHALLENGES

In Verber (2005), the idea of learning objects is discussed, so that component can be reused rather than redeveloped. An Ontology named ALOCoM was used which was based on Learning Objects. Basically the goal is to automate the learning objects rather than reusing the parts manually. This ontology transforms different tool specific content to ALOCoM ontology flexible content and vice versa. In this model content fragment (CF) which are basically the basic units like text, audio, content objects (CO) which combines content fragments (CF) and add navigation to it and learning objects which is the accumulation of content objects (CO) with the associated learning objective are explained. In Ahmed, (2013), mapping of web service description language (WSDL) component to web ontology language schema (OWL-S) is there. Basically it collects component from WSDL and convert it into OWL-S by database and discovery process. It provides standardized definition adopting the concept of Ontology. An important component that helps in standardized process is contained in this search namely OSSE (Ontology search and standardized engine). For effective retrieval OSSE can not only do statistical ranking, linguistic search but also do structural refining. The proposed algorithm mainly provides WSs to semantic web. In Razmerita (2011),A user behavior model is proposed that is based on the principles of fuzzy classifier system, and the knowledge sharing is defined and implemented through which user classification can be done. These sys-tem are also used by user for personal use in searching and retrieving, because it not only provides user to give feedback to accomplish their short term and long term goals but also facilitate user to have a better access of activities in by making a personal knowledge management possible. In Alnusair (2010), for identifying and retrieving relevant component semantic-based approach is used. For retrieving components there are much ontology that takes part for effective retrieval, namely source code retrieval ontology (SCRO), domain ontology and component ontology. SCRO not only captures the relationship and dependencies between various source code artifacts but also provides automatic generation of semantics instances for concepts and relations. In this searching can be done in various different ways.

In Fu, (2005), a query expansion technique namely SPIRIT is proposed which not only based on domain ontology but also linked to geographic ontology. In this spatially relevant component are retrieved according to user query. This technique is different from another technique in the way that query expansion is done by derivation the footprints of geographical query. By this, a fuzzy spatial relationship can be resolved. The method proposed here dealt with the spatial relationships. In Silva (2014), joining of ontologies are presented using Onto Join that is based on similarity analysis of the terms in ontology that are to be reused. Onto Join is a process of joining two ontologies that are totally different. The final result of this process is the ontology that is composed from reused ones and it is obtained by semantic mapping and joining of the terms in the component sets. Two ontologies namely "sales" and "tourism" are used, and by combining these two ontology the resultant ontology is "turismsales1", an application that not only models the services of tourism but also provides the domain to sell the product. In Ancona, (2012), presented an ontology that not only automatically extract relevant information from the code in libraries but also provides an ontology matching algorithm that pro-vides semantic similarity between various libraries. This approach is fully automated approach through which ontology extraction is possible. In this doclet is implemented in form of ontologies from java libraries. The proposed approach is experimented with four versions of Java API and that the semantic matching or semantic alignment is done by four freely available ontology matchers.

In Chaturvedi (2014), the builder pattern logic and application ontologies are separated, and considered builder pattern as a component. By doing so, retrieving classes or changing classes even at run time becomes easy. The build sequence can be changed anytime while users access that ontology. So, by this the user gets benefit that without knowing coding, it changes the patterns dynamically at runtime. It enhances the flexibility of the pattern and thus the patterns act as a plug and play component where user can add or remove patterns dynamically at runtime. The proposed solution only identifies that pattern which is available in component ontology.

As application logic and pat-tern logic are not combined in an ontology, pattern behaves like a separate component, and by this it becomes a plug and play component. In Khobreh (2013), a framework is provided for establishing links between knowledge skills and abilities and competence required for jobs. This paper developed an ontology named job knowledge (Job-Know) that is based on two domain namely "task" and "knowledge". By using both ontologies the problem of identifying individuals from knowledge domain and occupation form task domain is resolved. .By providing these type of ontologies users are benefitted in many ways like they are benefitted in carrier guidance, for job recruiters for accessing the qualification level of recruiters. For automatic data processing, text mining algorithm may work, particularly when the data is to be searched and retrieved from unstructured data sources. In Gupta (2013), a meta data model and faceted classification for effective storage and retrieval of software component is presented that contains specific information of particular domain. In this recommendation of software components are also there as there is involvement of taxonomies and ontologies(as per Table 3) are there in this. Matching algorithm was also introduced. The drawback of using metadata model is that precision of software component is poor as a result of subjective factor in faceted classification retrieval.

Table 3. Taxonomies and ontologies

Reference Paper	Ontology	Description	Language	API	Future work
(Verber,2005)	ALOCoM	Provides with the idea for developing learning objects, so that component can be reused rather than redeveloped.	Java based	Microsoft net for MS office tools Jena API	Distinguish between content, navigation and presentation in learning material
(Ahmed,2013	OSSE component	Mapping of WSDL to OWL-S. Presents a local repository for retrieval of previously retrieved files using ontologies	C#.net	Yahoo	Discovery mechanism components can be applied.
(Razmerita,2011)	OntobUmf	Ontology based user modeling framework which models users behavior and accordingly classify the user according to its behavior	N/A	N/A	Various semantically enhances resources and ontologies are used in order to improve user support and lifelong learning.
(Alnusair,2010)	CompRE	Ranking of retrieved components are based on the results of previously retrieved component	Java based	Jena framework	Ranking and merging ontologies
(Fu,2005)	SPIRIT	It is Footprint based spatial query expansion technique in which both domain ontology and geography ontology are fully utilized.	Java based	Java Apache SOAP	Resolving spatial relationships.
(Silva,2014)	Ontojoin	Join two ontologies which produces application ontology which is different from the one we used to join.	NA	NA	Integration of ontoJoin with GOADT technique
(Ancona,2012)	Ontlet	presented an ontology that not only automatically extract relevant information from the code in libraries but also provides an ontology matching algorithm that provides semantic similarity between various libraries	Java	Alignment API	Compares different libraries
(Chaturvedi,2014)	Generic Builder ontology	Extracts the pattern logic as a separate components changing the classes becomes easy even at runtime .	Java, php, python,	NA	Identifying the pattern when it is presented in the code.
(Khobreh, 2013)	Job know	Relation between task domains and knowledge domains are discussed	ADONIS	STUDIO systems	Dynamics of job knowledge ontology by considering occupation and educational system.

ONTOLOGY TOOLS AND EDITORS

Ontology Tools

There are various tools that combine two ontologies and produce a third ontology. The tools are:

1. **Alignment API:** Ontology matching or ontology alignment implemented for sharing and expressing knowledge is done by this API. In this the ontologies are expressed in a uniform manner. To express ontologies in this manner, a format is designed, whose objective is to share the available alignment on the web. For accessing the common format the alignment API is used, which is itself a Java description of tools. It describes various interfaces and provides many services such as storing, finding and sharing alignment, manipulating, generating test and comparing alignment.

2. **Jena API:** A framework that can be used to develop semantic web and linked data application, and is free and open source. In this, a narrower concept or the required components of the ontology is not viewed. As this API is basically an RDF platform, this API is restricted to formalize the ontology built on the top of RDF. Varieties of common techniques are supported in jena. Jena is implemented using Java Programming language. It not only provides a procedural environment for resource description framework (RDF), Resource description framework schema (RDFS), Web Ontology Language (OWL), SPARQL but also includes SWRL.

3. **Coma++:** Coma 3.0 is a ontology matching tool. It offers an infrastructure that is complete to enormous real world ontology match problems. As the GUI is very interactive, it allows the user to be attracted towards the match process. It consists of modules such as storage, match execution, mapping process, and user friendly interface. As this is ontology matching tool, it gets input of two ontologies, runs several matching algorithm which is the basis of COMA and outputs the ontology as matching results.

4. Map Onto It aims to discover semantic similarities among various data models such as database schema, conceptual schema and ontologies. Inspired by the clio project, the tool worked in a an interactive and semi-automatic manner. Starting from basic attributes and then analyzing the semantics of data models, Map onto generates a logical formula representing a semantic relationship between two data models. After that user can choose the expected mapping from list.

5. **OLA/OLA2:** Short for Owl Lite Alignment. OLA is dedicated to that alignment that is expressed in owl. OLA is designed as an environment for manipulating environment. In OLA, system offers services as parsing and visualization of ontologies, comparison of alignment, visualization of environment etc.

6. **Potluck:** It is web interface that gives the opportunity to a casual user to combine and re-purpose semantic web data. It lets user merge, navigate, visualize and clean up data all at the same time. This iterative process of integration the data is useful only when the user don't have information regarding the quantity of data to be merged or more precisely when the user is unfamiliar with the data at beginning.

7. **LILY:** It is a system for solving issues related to various diverse ontologies. LILY retrieves semantic subgraph for each entity. Then it utilizes not only lingual information but also semantic graph information is exploited. One can use a successive similarity producing strategy that can produce output as more alignment.

8. **S-Match:** S-Match is a semantic matching framework which provides several semantic matching algorithms to develop new ontologies. It takes any two trees like structure i.e. lightweight ontologies, classification and database schema and gives a output as a set of relation between those nodes, which is semantically related to each other. S-match can be driven by both command line and GUI. Original semantic match (S-match) algorithm is not only customizable and suitable for many applications but also is a general purpose algorithm. In order to support Java API is provided.

9. **Vine:** VINE stands for vocabulary integration environment. The VINE mapping builder allows creation and mapping of concepts and terms in multiple ontologies or controlled vocabulary. Mapping between controlled vocabularies in a given domain is essential for interoperability between different data systems.

10. **ASMOV:** It is an a self activating alignment tool which maps class to class, entity to entity, individual to individual relationships. It was originally designed to facilitate the integration of homogeneous system, but it can also align ontologies in any domain. Full form of ASMOV is automatic semantic mapping of ontologies with verification.

Ontology Editors

There are so many editor tools by which we can either build the ontology or we can extract component or information from ontology. The various editor tools are:

1. **Vitro:** It is the instance editor which is a used to build a wed based ontology and which can be accessed by public easily. It is a web application which is implemented in java and runs on tomcat servlet containers. By using vitro, loading, creating of ontologies in OWL format, and searching ontologies by using Apache solr becomes easy.

2. **The Manager:** IT is used for analyzing and creating SKOS RDF vocabularies. The Manager not only provides management of thesaurus but also provides the management of other types of vocabulary. It is the open source tool for representing knowledge organization systems.

3. **Hozo:** To construct ontology, Hozo environment is used which is developed at Osaka University (Slimani, 2015). Hozo supports to construct only ontologies. One can define the concepts (classes) that can be used for constructing it. The ontologies are managed by server and sheared by all users. The system manages ontologies by project as a unit to manage them.

4. **Lexaurus Editor:** It is a powerful terminology management system. To produce collective editing of information terms, Lexaurus bank can integrate various Lexaurus editors. Lexaurus bank not only retains the background of terms concepts but also retains terminology structure.

5. **SKOS:** It is plug-in in protégé that allows editing the thesauri which is represented in SKOS i.e. simple knowledge organization system. It is under development under protégé. The protégé environment is built on top of OSGI plug-in framework. The advantage of building this on top of protégé is to get the flexible and powerful engine to work on SKOS.

Model Futures OWL Editor

This tool combines simple OWL tools. As the editor is tree based, for accessing classes and relationships navigator is used. It can not only import the XMI (the interchange format for UML) but also export the ontologies to MS Word. The software runs in windows and still undergoes testing.

1. **OBO-Edit:** Short for OBO Biological ontology file format which is developed in Java and can be easily accessible to public as it is open source ontology editor. It is optimized for not only reading but also writing ontologies in this format. Berkeley Bioinformatics developed OBO-Edit which was funded by gene ontology consortium. OBO-Edit Wiki is a central repository for OBO-Edit developer info and technical information.

2. **Pool Party:** It is an environment which is a triple store thesaurus management and which not only utilizes SKOS but also uses text extraction for recommendation of tag. PoolParty is the software platform that is based on semantic knowledge

models to organize enterprise metadata and linked data. This software combines various mapping technologies with knowledge modelling. PoolParty API which is constructed on SPARQL standard, combines various semantic technologies like search engines, wikis etc.

3. **Fluent Editor:** It is a tool for edition, manipulation and querying complex ontologies that are com-posed in Resource Description Framework (RDF), web ontology language (OWL), or SWRL(semantic web rule language).Fluent editor is compatible with almost semantic web like OWL 2,SWrl and has a friendly user interface. Fluent editor has tools that help to manage complex ontologies namely a reviewer window, SPARQL window, XML preview window, a taxonomic tree view and annotation window.

4. **Unilexicon:** It is a visual editor and taxonomy manager for controlled vocabulary with the con-tent tagging extension. An information management software for offering metadata repository and semantic search tools, data integration and record management tools. Visual vocabulary editor is a web based editor that allows a user to construct a con-trolled vocabulary in a hierarchical tree structure. It also provides repositories (as per Table 4) with sophisticated tools for management of vocabularies. A search interface is also provided that makes the searching of concepts easy.

5. **Graffoo:** Short for graphical framework for OWL ontologies is developed by Silvio peroni. It is a new which represents classes, properties, individuals and restrictions using web ontology language (OWL) Ontologies. The advantage of using Graffoo is that it de-scribes the logic relation between elements in ontologies, or a subsection of a ontology, that it can easily be understand by user.

6. **WebOnto:** It is a visualization tool that represents ontology in graphical form. It can support browsing and editing of ontologies while developing and maintain it. Through this tool user can browse and edit knowledge models over the web. In this tool ontology is viewed as a conceptual structure of specific domain and Web Onto presents that ontology in graphical form.

7. **Protégé:** It is a framework for building an intelligent system. Protégé is open source ontology editor and which is freely available on web. It was developed in java. Protégé can not only read ontologies but also save various ontologies in various formats including RDF

Table 4. Ontology and Description

Ontology editor	Description	Programming Language that can be used with the tool	Features
Vitro	An instance editor which is used to make semantic web ontologies.	Java	Create, load and search ontologies in OWL format
ThManager	Managing knowledge organization system	Java	Selection, description, visualization, edition of thesaurus.
Hozo	Only Construct Ontology	Java	Role concept supporting, ontology visualization, dependency management.
Lexaurus Editor	Terminology management system in thesaurus.	NA	Scalable web based repository, synchronization, customizable, multilingual concept interface, translation of data.
SKOSEd	Editor for SKOS(simple knowledge organization system).	Java	Powerful and flexible editor for working with SKOS
Model Futures OWL Editor	Offers tree structure interface and handles large amount of owl files.	-	Can export to MS Word, and can import to express the interchange format of UML to XML files.
OBO-Edit	Reading and writing ontologies in a specific file format	Java	Easy to use editing interface, fast reasoned
PoolParty	Pool party is the editor which is used to build and maintain the linguistic thesaurus by providing a friendly GUI	Java, Javascript	Thesaurus management system and a SKOS editor for semantic web.
Fluent Editor	User friendly GUI that uses OCNL(Ontarian Controlled Natural Language)	R language,	Querying, editing and manipulating complex ontologies
Unilexicon	A visualization editor for controlled vocabularies.	Python, Javascript, Language agnostic	Uses predictive search to explore vocabularies.
Graffoo	Allows the user to create classes, instances relationship between the two and information regarding OWL ontologies are represented.	OWL	Displays the logical relationship among various elements in ontology.
Web Onto	It is the free source ontology customizable software.	Java	Browsing and editing of knowledge models over the web.
Protégé	Visualize and define the ontology using graphical user interface	Java	For validation of models and inserting new information, deductive classifiers are used.

ONTOLOGY BASED COMPONENT RETRIVEVAL PROCESS

To understand the process of component retrieval using ontologies, one should know exactly what the component is how it is retrieved from the ontology and the knowledge of various tools and editor that are used in retrieving component by using ontologies.

In general or real form, a component is nothing but it may be a collection of zip, jar, doc, executable files etc in structured form and that can be retrieved from repository whenever needed. There is a process of retrieving the component from repository, the process is as follows.

- The user query is inputted by using keyword related to the component.
- After that the query is parsed with the editor, so that a query is generated which can easily be understand by computer, so that it can be retrieved easily. For generating queries from keyword SPARQL editor can be used.

After generation of query the semantic entities related to that query are extracted.

Figure 1. Framework for component retrieval using ontology

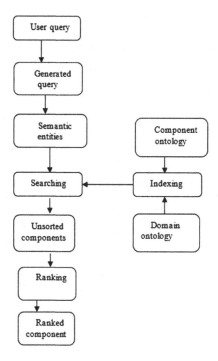

- Then searching of component from various ontology can be done.
- Searching can only be feasible if indexing is done in such a way that includes both component and domain ontology. To join two ontology one should know that both ontology should be different from one another, so that there are no chances of ambiguity of component by this. After searching of the component, the retrieval of components is in unsorted manner.
- Then if ranking algorithm can be applied, then the components are retrieved in order of relevance through ranking. The complete process of component retrieval is shown in figure.

A Step-By-Step Method of Retrieval in Semantic Web Using Algorithm

In the semantic web process, the collection of URI is done. The extraction of URI gives us the component in triple structure (Alobaidi, 2016). The algorithm as per Table 5 is as follows.

After generation of query in form of triple (Table 6), then the algorithm for executing the query is as follows (23).

After that matching of component is done, whether the component matches the query or not. The matching algorithm (Table 7) is as follows (24).

COMPARISON OF RESULTS

In Gupta (2013), an ontology and faceted classification scheme is used to retrieve the component using Meta data repository. Faceted classification and retrieval is very comprehensive, as it requires essential characteristics for single term viewed from various different aspects. A software component can be viewed from various specific angles, so by this a software component may have various facets according

Table 5. Algorithm for parsing of query

```
Triple_Extraction (List URIlist)
{
FOR EACH URI in URIList
{
QueryString (from) Build SPARQL(URI)
QExecute(from) Execute.SPARQL(QueryString)
QExecuteList.add(QExecute)
}
RETURN QExecuteList
}
```

Table 6. Executing the query

```
1) Begin
2) URIList=all URI contained in query Q
3) vActivatedRules=new List
4) vRulesByHeadmap=create a map of rules where the keys are elements in U.
5) If(Tscore>=0)
6) Then
7) Foreach ue U do
8) vRuleList = get the rule list which u is in the rule head from vRulesByHeadMap;
9) Calculate rulescore for all rules in vRulelist
10) decreasingly sort vRulelist
11) aActivatedRulesTemp=new list
12) add to vActivatedRulesTemp the first rules in vRulelist with a rule score is equal or grater than Tscore
13) if vActivatedRulesTemp is empty
14) then
15) add all elements from vRuleList to v Activated Rules
16) else
17) add all elements from vActivatedRulesTemp tovActivationRules
18) end if
19) end for each
20) else
21) add rules from vRules By HeadMap to v Activated rules
22) end if
23) remove rule cycles in vActivatedRules.
24) A=query KBconsidering the rules in v ActivatedRules.
25) Return A
   end
```

to its characteristics. As the method of faceted classification is manual, it leads to low precision. In this paper metadata repository integrates expert knowledge to generalize the concepts used in the domains.

The results of this paper in terms of precision, recall can be seen from the table.

In Geesaman (2013), near miss clone detection is applied for ontology alignment problem and used new "best match" clone detection which achieves similar results from the ontology alignment tool. Best match clone is a new notion that applies filter on the results of previous clone detection algorithm. In this clone detection pairs are accepted and rejected on the basis of its similarity in the target ontology. The results are presented in table in terms of precision, recall and F-Measure and threshold value.

In Yaguinuma (2005), a model that is used for storing and retrieving of component are presented which not only retrieves the component from repository but also recommend interrelated components using ontology that involves the multimedia application domain. For evaluating the results the experiment was performed by two

Table 7. Matching algorithm

```
Match(S,R)
{
R'=register_query(S, R)
R''=register_query(S₀,R')
For all r in R'' do
{
r₁= input_query(r)
if provided(r₁,s₁) then
{
Precise.append(r)}
Else
{
If query_ContextProviders(userID)
Then
{
Precise.append(r)
}
Else{
Approximate.append(r)
}
}
}
P=order_with_contextAttributes(Precise)
A=order_with_contextAttribute(Approximate)
Return result(P,A)
}
```

groups which receive textual information for retrieval of components and consider different ontology. Then a feedback for ease of use and process satisfaction is taken. The results in terms of precision and recall are satisfactory, while search effort (60%) is lower, the groups find that they need more training to use. The results are shown in Table 8.

Table 8. Results

Reference No.	Precision	Recall	F-Measure	Threshold value
(Gupta,2013)	.9566	.9868	NA	NA
(Geesaman, 2013)	.80	.45	.58	0.40
(Yaguinuma,2005)	92	95.83	NA	.60

CONCLUSION

In spite of having many advantages, one should not ignore that ontology now days are not playing an important part while the work on interrelationships of data still goes on. The popularity of ontology is suppressed by different authors and researchers presenting the ontology form in different ways. In this chapter, we have tried to present the meaning of ontology and semantic web, how they are linked, and performed various comparison of tools and editors by which one can easily make decision of selecting tool or editor to be used to built or merge the ontology.

REFERENCES

Ahmed, T., & Farrag, H. (2013). Toward SWSs discovery: Mapping from WSDL to OWL-S based on ontology search and standardization engine. *IEEE Transactions on Knowledge and Data Engineering, 25*(5), 1135–1147. doi:10.1109/TKDE.2012.25

Alnusair, A., & Zhao, T. (2010). Component search and reuse: An ontology-based approach. *IEEE International Conference*, 258-261. 10.1109/IRI.2010.5558931

AlObaidi, M., Mahmood, K., & Sabra, S. (2016). Semantic Enrichment for Local Search Engine using Linked Open Data. *25th International Conference Companion on World Wide Web*, 631-634. 10.1145/2872518.2890481

Ancona, D., Viviana, M., & Ombretta, P. (2012). Ontology-based documentation extraction for semi-automatic migration of Java code. *The 27th Annual ACM Symposium on Applied Computing*, 1137-1143.

Broens, Pokraev, Sinderen, Koolwaaij, & Costa. (2004). Con-text-aware, ontology-based service discovery. *European Symposium on Ambient Intelligence*, 72-83.

Chaturvedi & Prabhakar. (2014). Ontology driven builder pattern: a plug and play component. *29th Annual ACM Symposium on Applied Computing*, 1055-1057.

Farias, D., Mendes, T., Roxin, A., & Nicolle, C. (2015). SWRL rule-selection methodology for on-tology interoperability. *Data & Knowledge Engineering*.

Fu, Jones, & Abdelmoty. (2005). Ontology-based spatial query expansion in information retrieval. *OTM Confederated International Conferences on the Move to Meaningful Internet Systems*, 1466-1482.

Gupta & Kumar. (n.d.). Reusable Software Component Retrieval System. *International Journal of Application or Innovation in Engineering and Management, 2*(1), 187–194.

Jin, X., & Long, Y. (2007). *Research on ontology based representation and retrieval of components. In Software Engineering, Artificial Intelligence, Networking and Parallel/Distributed Computing* (Vol. 1, pp. 494–499). IEEE.

Khan, L., McLeod, D., & Hovy, E. (2004). *Retrieval effectiveness of an ontology-based model for information selection. The VLDB Journal—The International Journal on Very Large Data Bases, 13(1),* 71–85.

Khobreh, Ansari, Fathi, Vas, Mol, Berkers, & Varga. (2013). *An Ontology-based Approach for the Semantic Representation of Job Knowledge.* Academic Press.

Kiwelekar, A. W., & Joshi, R. K. (2014). An ontological framework for architecture model integration. *4th International Workshop on Twin Peaks of Requirements and Architecture*, 24-27.

Peng, Y., Peng, C., Huang, J., & Huang, K. (2009). An Ontology-Driven Paradigm for Component Representation and Retrieval. *IEEE Ninth International Conference on Computer and Information Technology.* 10.1109/CIT.2009.26

Razmerita, L. (2011). An ontology-based framework for modeling user behavior—A case study in knowledge management. *IEEE Transactions on Systems, Man, and Cybernetics. Part A, Systems and Humans*, *41*(4), 772–783. doi:10.1109/TSMCA.2011.2132712

Silva, F., & Girardi, R. (2014). An Approach to Join Ontologies and Their Reuse in the Con-struction of Application Ontologies. *2014 IEEE/WIC/ACM International Joint Conferences, 1*, 424-431.

Singh & Jain. (2014). *Information Retrieval (IR) through Semantic Web (SW): An Over-view.* Academic Press.

Slimani, T. (2015). Ontology development: A comparing study on tools, languages and formal-isms. *Indian Journal of Science and Technology*, *8*(24). doi:10.17485/ijst/2015/v8i1/54249

Verbert, K., Gašević, D., Jovanović, J., & Duval, E. (2005). Ontology-based learning content repurposing. Special interest tracks and posters of the 14th international conference on World Wide Web, 1140-1141.

Wimalasuriya, D. C., & Dou, D. (2010). Components for information extraction: ontology-based information extractors and generic platforms. *19th ACM international conference on Information and knowledge management*, 9-18. 10.1145/1871437.1871444

Yadav, U. (2016). Development and Visual-ization of Domain Specific Ontology using Protégé. *Indian Journal of Science and Technology*, *9*(16). doi:10.17485/ijst/2016/v9i16/88524

Yaguinuma, Marilde, & Vieira. (2005). Ontology-based meta-model for storage and retrieval of software components. *31st VLDB Conference*.

Chapter 7
Ontology–Based Opinion Mining for Online Product Reviews

Farheen Siddiqui
Jamia Hamdard, India

Parul Agarwal
Jamia Hamdard, India

ABSTRACT

In this chapter, the authors work at the feature level opinion mining and make a user-centric selection of each feature. Then they preprocess the data using techniques like sentence splitting, stemming, and many more. Ontology plays an important role in annotating documents with metadata, improving the performance of information extraction and reasoning, and making data interoperable between different applications. In order to build ontology in the method, the authors use (product) domain ontology, ConceptNet, and word net databases. They discuss the current approaches being used for the same by an extensive literature survey. In addition, an approach used for ontology-based mining is proposed and exploited using a product as a case study. This is supported by implementation. The chapter concludes with results and discussion.

DOI: 10.4018/978-1-5225-6117-0.ch007

INTRODUCTION

Opinion mining is also referred as Sentiment Analysis, is a study that comprises of people's emotions, sentiments, behavioral patterns, opinions towards objects like situations, events, products, persons, organizations and similar objects in nature around us. Closely related terms with opinion mining or sentiment analysis but meant for different tasks and purpose are sentiment mining, affect analysis, review mining, opinion extraction, etc. Since, the growth of e-commerce sentiment analysis has become a strong area of research so in this chapter we shall define and discuss the problems associated, along with their solutions by describing the techniques for solving them. Sentiment analysis and opinion mining mainly focuses on opinions which express or imply positive or negative sentiments. The research gained its demand and has become an area of research for the fact that e-commerce gained its popularity. It has kind of binded and shrunk the world. All of us have drifted from the conventional means of buying and shifted to usage of e-commerce. This resulted in proliferation of commercial applications. Secondly, this factor led to a series of challenging research problems one of them being opinion mining. These have led to enormous opinionate data being generated in the Web, more so because of social media influence.

Opinions, which are important influencers of our behaviors, form a focus in all human activities that we perform. Any decision making that we do, we seek the opinions of others. Though, the process of collecting opinions has changed with time. In the past, opinions were collected from friends, family members, surveys, polls and questionnaires. These were useful for businesses like marketing, public relations and even for political campaigns. But today, in e-commerce context and due to the explosive advent of social media, whenever a buying decision has to be made for a product, we are not limited to consulting the above means for opinions; rather the user reviews and discussions on the public forums available on the Web are useful. People make their buying decisions on reviews. The reason is quite obvious, consumer products and services that include movies, clothing, electronic items and hotels are frequently being discussed by the websites in the form of shared opinions (Deshpande & Sarkar, 2010). Famous examples of websites having reviews include www.amazon.com, www.flipkart.com, www.ebay.com and many others. These websites allow the users to express their opinions about the product bought. Thus, when a buying decision has to be made by a new user, he/she reads the reviews and benefits from these reviews. Customer's comment usually covers various issues that are related to different types of products. Some comments are termed as general comments but some focus on certain types of specific technical issues related to any particular product.

Ontology, generally refers to the domain being studied (Gruber, 1993). Its main aim is to provide an insight into the concepts and knowledge which both the developers and the computers can understand. Thus it enumerates the concepts related to domain and explains the relationships that exist between the concepts (Guarino, 1995). Ontology can lead to remarkable improvement in information or feature extraction and reasoning (Pang & Lee, 2008) and also make data interoperable in several applications (Baziz, Boughanem, Aussenac-Gilles, & Chrisment, 2005; Duo, Juan-Zi, & Bin, 2005; Fensel, 2002; Zhou&Chaovalit, 2007). Meersman (2005) suggested that ontologies in context of information also known as data models can be helpful in the construction of a narrow application domain. This paper also highlights that ontologies which include lexicons and thesauri is a useful step for formalization of semantics of information representation. If Lexicon on one hand is language specific ontology, then thesaurus on the other hand is either domain specific or application specific ontology. Ontology theory, manufacturing are domain specific and airlines reservations, Inventory control are a few examples of application specific Ontology.

This chapter shall perform ontology based opining mining for online product reviews. First and foremost, we shall perform preprocessing, which is necessary as presence of irrelevant and incorrect data cannot be ruled out. Several methods like stemming, sentence splitting, and tokenization shall be explored. The next step would be to construct ontology to extract product features in the reviews and thus generate a feature based summary. In order to construct this, we may use ConceptNet (Speer, 2016).

BACKGROUND

The term sentiment analysis was suggested in Nasukawa and Yi, (2003), and opinion mining in Kushal, Lawrence and Pennock, (2003). But related research or concept can be found in Das and Chen (2001); Morinaga et al., (2002); Pang, Lee and Vaithyanathan, (2002); Tong, (2001); Turney, (2002); and Wiebe, (2000). As explained above, some comments may be positive, negative or neutral and have been reported in Yaakub et al., (2011). Since the birth of sentiment analysis can be attributed to social media research so research in opinion mining finds its applications in political sciences, social sciences, economics, management sciences and Natural language processing to name a few. The initial works related to these can be found in Hatzivassiloglou and McKeown, (1997); Hearst, (1992); Wiebe, (1990); Wiebe, (1994); and Wiebe, Bruce and O'Hara, (1999). This chapter shall comprehensively study the related work in this area. In organizations, enormous amount of information is generated by different processes (Sukumaran & Sureka,2006). This enormous information comprises of both structured and unstructured data. Structured data is the numeric data collected typically from transactional data and is useful for capturing quantitative and transactional information (Lahl, 2011). Unstructured data on the other hand, comprises of heterogenous data in form of text found in e-mails, SMS, Customer service surveys, PDF files, comments recorded by call centers and may also include images, vieos and audios represent d in varied formats (Lahl, 2011;Yaakub et al., 2011;Sukumaran & Sureka,2006).But Decision making has to be done on the basis of both structured and unstructured data by using some mining technique (Negash & Grey, 2008). Unstructured data is of heterogenous type and manging such data is a difficult task and can only be manage by using file systems and through document management(Castellanos et al., 2010). In contrast, Structure data has a predefined schema and stored in Data Warehouses or in RDBMS(Relational Database management systems). The main task associated is difficulty in search, retrieval and analysis of unstructured data and its integration with the structured data(Sukumaran & Sureka, 2006).

Further, monitoring and identifying opinion sites and distilling the information is a daunting task as each site contains enormous data in the form of opinion text that is difficult to decipher in long blogs and postings. It is difficult for an average human to identify relevant sites and then extract opinions and further use it for decision making. Many big companies like Microsoft, Google, SAS, SAP, HP and many others have their own in house capabilities. Since Sentiment Analysis has varied applications, so these find its place in various research papers. For ranking products reviews have been used in McGlohon, Glance and Reiter (2010). Twitter sentiments were linked with opinion polls and have been explained in O'Connor et al. (2010). For predicting the election results twitter sentiments have been described in Tumasjan et al. (2010). Twitter data and movie reviews can be used to predict box office revenues in case of movies.This has been explained in Asur and Huberman, (2010); Joshi et al., (2010); Sadikov, Parameswaran and Venetis, (2009). Interesting applications like identifying the gender difference in context of emotional axes on the basis of sentiments in mails are described in Mohammad and Yang (2011). The stock market predictions on the basis of twitter moods have been explained in Bollen, Mao and Zeng, (2011). In Groh and Hauffa, (2011), social relations have been characterized using opinion mining. Social influences for online book reviews have been studied in Sakunkoo and Sakunkoo, (2009). An extensive opinion mining or sentiment analysis system and several case studies have been described in Castellanos et al., (2011). The following subsection describes basic steps for ontology based opinion mining .

Preprocessing Data for Opinion Mining

Preprocessing stage is the important stage at feature level opinion mining classification, It includes sentence splitting, tokenizing strings of words, part of speech (POS) tagging technique and finally applying the suitable term of stemming. The following preprocessing process was used in the present work (Lazhar & Yamina, 2012).

1. Remove irrelevant data: This can be done by removing reviews which do not have any feature.
2. Sentence Splitting: The sentence can be split on the use of delimiters such as ".", ",".
3. Tokenization: The reviews can be broken down into smallest units which we identify as tokens. Thus, each word can be associated as a token.
4. Stemming: This step is an important preprocessing step for input document reviews. Root stemming means to reduce words to their roots.

Construct the Ontology

In ontology based methodology, there is a need to build ontology so as to enable feature selection. Lazhar and Yamina, (2012) focused on domain ontology performing structuring of features, representation of semantic information, extraction the features, and then producing a summary of features. Once, the features have been associated with opinions, these are then classified as positive, negative by using supervised classification techniques. In Yaakub et al., (2011), the authors propose an architecture that uses a multi dimensional model so as to integrate customers' characteristics along with their comments about the products. They first identify the entities, study the reviews for identifying the sentiments and then construct an attribute table by assigning a polarity ranging from -3 to 3. Each polarity denotes negative to positive opinion. For example, if -3 represents poor, then 0 represents neutral opinion and 1 would then represent accept.

Thus, on the basis of customer's comments and reviews for an entity on the basis of its features, a model is the produced based on the dimensions. For example product, customer, time and opinion. The extracted opinions from the reviews in the form of their strength of polarities are included in the opinion table. The opinion polarity was then calculated using their suggested formula. Their study includes short customer comments for extracting sentiments manually. The ontology proposed by the author covers features and its characteristics of mobile phone in general and in other technical terms . We generally write comments in the form of sentences like:

The camera is good, picture clarity excellent, battery life poor, accessories good and so on. These reviews can be collected from websites like www.amazon.com, www.flipkart.com, www.ebay.com.

In Yaakub, Li, Algarni, and Peng (2012) ontology has been constructed for opinion mining of customer reviews for the smart phones. Yaakub developed an ontology to do feature based opinion mining of customer's review on smart phones. The main objective of their work is to transfer reviews to structure table that includes several dimensions, such as, customers, products, time and locations. Polarity of portugese user product reviews based on the the features described in the domain ontology has been reported in Freitas and Vieira (2013).

In Mukherjee and Joshi (2013) ConceptNet database has been exploited for the construction of domain specific ontology for product reviews using lexicons to determine the polarity of opinion words in reviews. Then using the ontological information, the features and its polarity are integrated using the bottom up approach. In Agarwal, Mittal, Bansal, and Garg (2015) they use ConceptNet and WordNet databases for constructing the ontology. They used ontology to determine the domain specific features which in turn produced the domain specific important features. Then, the polarity of the extracted features are determined using more than one lexicons In Cadilhac, Benamara, and Aussenac-Gilles (2010), a hierarchy of features is used which the performance of features based identification systems.But the research papers that are domain ontology based use the ontology as a taxonomy using only "is a" relations between concepts. The opinion words are extracted using rule based approach. In Zhao and Li (2009) the ontology describes the semantics of domain and the concepts with their relation. The features are classified as frequent and infrequent. A random 60-0 positive and negative review was selected for their study and obtained accuracy of 88.30% in positive reviews and 81.7% in negative reviews. In Lau, Lai, Ma, and Li (2009) an automated analysis of the sentiments which can be found in customer's feedbacks was described. They also proposed a model of their Ontology Based Product Review Miner (OBPRM).

Use an Approach for Opinion Mining Classification

Lexicon Based Approach

The lexicon-based approach has concentrated on using adjectives as indicators the polarity of text. First, a list of adjectives and corresponding score values are compiled into a dictionary. Then, for any given text, all adjective words are extracted and annotated with their polarity, using the dictionary scores. The polarity scores are aggregated into a final score for the review.

Wordnet contains words with three scores as given below, that is: 1. Positive score. 2. Negative score. 3. Objective score. For every word, positive, negative and neutral scores are having values between 0.0 and 1.0 and the addition of all the scores, that is, positive score, negative score, and objective score for a word, is 1. The objective score of 1.0 denotes that it is a neutral word and does not express any opinion.

Machine Learning (ML) Approach

Like a human learns from the past experiences, a computer doesn't have experiences, but it learns from data, which represent some past experiences of the application domain. Machine learning defined as "field of study that gives computers the ability to learn without being explicitly programmed." The machine learning approach for opinion mining often relies on supervised classification methods. In this approach, labeled data is used to train classifier. In supervised machine learning, two datasets are used: train and test data. The training data contains a set of training sets. A test data is the unseen data to evaluate classifier accuracy. In classification, the most commonly features used in most methods are the following: Boolean model: Which indicates the presence or absence of a word with Booleans one or zero respectively. Term Frequency: Is the number that the term T occurs in the document D. Term Frequency Inverse Document Frequency (TF-IDF): Is a common weight scheme that is more meaningful, where large weights are assigned to terms that are occurred frequently in relevant documents.

Decision Tree (DT)

The decision tree is supervised machine learning, where it is an active method for make classifiers from data. It is also a flow-chart-like tree structure, where each node denotes a test on an attribute value, each branch represents an outcome of the test and tree leaves represent label classes. In addition, it is used in determining the best course of action, in situations having several possible alternatives with uncertain outcomes. A decision tree classifier is modeled in two stages: tree building and tree pruning. In tree building stage, the decision tree model is built by recursively splitting the training data set and assigning a class label to leaf by the most frequent class. Pruning a sub tree with branches if error is obtained.

Naïve Bayes (NB)

The NB is important for several reasons. It is very easy to construct, and not needing any difficult iterative parameter estimation schemes. This means it may be readily applied to large data sets. It is easy to interpret, understand, it often does surprisingly well and can usually be relied on to be robust and to do quite well. The NB classifier, works as follows

- Let D be training set of tuples and their associated class labels. As usual, each tuple is represented by a n-dimensional attribute vector, $X = (X1, X2,....,Xn)$, n measurements made on the tuple from n attribute, respectively, A1, A2...An.
- Assume that there are m classes, C1, C2...Cm. Given a tuple, X, the classifier will predict that X belongs to the class having the highest probability, conditioned on X. That is, the NB classifier predicts that tuple X belongs to the class Ci if and only if

$(Ci|X) > (Cj|X)$ $1 \leq j \leq m, \neq I$

Thus we maximize P(Ci|X). The class Ci for which P(Ci|X) is the maximized, is called the maximum posteriori hypothesis. By Bayes' theorem

$(Ci|X) = P(X|Ci)P(Ci)$ P(X)

K-Nearest Neighbor (K-NN)

K-nearest neighbor finds a group of k objects in the training set that are closest to the test object, and bases the assignment of a label on the predominance of a particular class in this neighborhood. To classify an unlabeled object, the distance of this object to the labeled objects is computed, its k-nearest neighbors are identified, and the class labels of these nearest neighbors are then used to determine the class label of the object. Once the k-nearest neighbor list is obtained, the test object is classified based on the majority class of its nearest neighbors.

Combined Approach

In combined approach use both lexicon base and machine learning approach. The lexicon based approach uses opinion words and phrases to determine the semantic orientation of the whole document or sentence. Then, using these words to classify the entire sentence in document and then classify the entire document. The next step is to use machine learning approach. The documents that have been classified from the previous step are then used as a training set for the classifier.

USER CENTRIC ONTOLOGY BASED OPINION MINING

Ontology, commonly referred to the concept of a domain aims to provide knowledge and concepts about specific domains that are understandable by both developers and computers. In particular, ontology enumerates domain concepts and relationships among the concepts and provides a sound semantic ground of machine-understandable description of digital content. Ontology is popular in annotating documents with metadata, improving the performance of information extraction and reasoning, and making data interoperable between different applications. Using ontology in opinion mining offers several advantages which are: structuring of the features and extraction of features. In order to build ontologies in our method, we will use domain ontology, ConceptNet and WordNet databases. The main objective of our work is to provide technique that improves the performance of opinion mining classification technique by first using ontology to select features in a user centric way for the review having different features with diverse opinion strengths and then exploit these selected features to determine the proper polarity of the review. The methodology for user centric ontology based opinion mining is:

1. Retrieve customer's reviews for particular product from online social forums.
2. Decide an optimal data preprocessing method for opinion mining.
3. Select a domain ontology tree for the product domain.
4. Determine the user centric features from the review using the ontology selected.
5. Add user specific product features in the product domain ontology.
6. Determine the opinions of the user centric features using public lexicon.
7. Exploit extracted features and opinions to determine the overall polarity of review.
8. Summarization is done to generate feature-based summaries of document reviews.
9. Evaluate the performance using different performance metrics such as accuracy, precision, recall and f-measure.

The significance of this research is in improving the performance of opinion mining at feature level classification and generate complete feature-based summary can be utilized for e-commerce and many businesses' benefit. It can be taken into account in product quality improvement by understand what the customer like and dislike in the product. Also, for the customer who wants to buy a product would like to know the opinions about features in specific product from the existing users. Feature summary can save efforts and time by helping the manufactures to find which features will be improved in the product that customer dislike it.

Challenges

Though opinion mining is deeply researched field, still issues arise for review having dissimilar features with unlike opinion priorities. All opinion mining methodologies consider features recognized from the customer's review to be of equal priority and thus are unable to calculate the correct polarity of the customer's review. Also the opinion summary generation for each feature doesn't consider the user centric features that are present it in the ontology or any additional user specific feature and thus making the feature-based summary is unfinished. In this research, we use ontology structure to determine the important feature in the review and to generate an opinion summary for each feature. Also any feature that is not present in product ontology can be added through the user interactively in the final ontology tree constructed.

In this work, we focus on some of the issues for product opinion mining technique:

1. For analyzing customer's review on a product having different features with diverse opinion strengths most of the techniques considers all features extracted from the reviews to be equally important in failing to determine the proper polarity of the review and makes the review's sentiment classification less accurate.
2. Opinion summary for each feature doesn't consider user centric features that are present it in the ontology.
3. Additional user specific feature can be added dynamically to the ontology for generating polarity of a customer product review.

This research presents a technique using ontology that selects user centric feature from product ontology, assign priority to them and also possibly adds new features to the product ontology to determine polarity of user generated product reviews.

SOLUTIONS AND RECOMMENDATIONS

In this section, we explain our methodology to classify product opinion reviews which we followed in this research. The section organized into six sections. Section discusses about overview of our methodology and short description about each steps document reviews, preprocessing steps that we followed, description of building ontology tree, about determine important additional features, opinion of extracted features, the polarity of opinion word and the overall polarity of review. Also we will discuss performance by comparing proposed method with other supervised and unsupervised techniques.

Methodology Overview

We proposed to use a methodology which is divided into five stages: stage one preparation which contain document reviews and preprocessing steps, stages two ontology construction which contain feature extraction and determine important features, stage three opinion mining which contain determine the opinion of word and overall review, stage four summarization, stage five evaluation

Stage 1: Preparation and Document Reviews

For demonstration of our proposed methodology, we must choose a product domain with features that is available online with English language reviews. Therefore a dataset was selected from domains namely, hotel from review dataset from trip advisor (2016) which contains reviews about hotels and its features such as room,"room service "food"etc. and also pizza dataset from online sources. We collect corpus consists of 2000 reviews. Polarity of the review documents is classified as equal size positive and negative. Table 1 describes the hotel data.

Preprocessing

Preprocessing is a indispensable component for our approach. There always exist few irrelevant missing and incorrect data thus we employ preprocessing methods to reach our goal, the steps employed are:

- Ignore beside the relevant point data: numeric terms and non-english terms are useless for our method. we exclude product reviews not having a few feature.
- Divide sentence on the basis of use of delimiters such as ".", ",".
- Divide the product reviews into tokens. The simplest meaningful token is a term or word that is being used in proposed approach.
- English pos tagger: we used available online tools to produce the part-of-speech tag for each term that can be noun, verb or an adjective

Table 1. Number of positive and negative class with their source

Domain	Positive	Negative
Hotel	1000	1000
Pizza	1000	1000

• Stemming: Stemming at root level implies reducing terms to their roots. In proposed approach root stemming methods are employed to produce effective correspondence of features in the product ontology. Also language sentiment lexicon comprise of words at root level.

Stage 2: Ontology

Constructing Automatic Domain Specific Ontology Tree

In our opinion mining technique, ontology in built in a user centric way by extracting user specific product features in the reviews from the product domain ontology. Also all features are assigned a positive priority value, to denote which selected feature is how much important and to finally create feature guided summary. For the purpose of constructing ontology, ConceptNet (Speer, 2016) as a knowledge resource and domain ontology is used to automatically construct in domain-specific ontology tree for a product. ConceptNet relations consist of inbuilt structures that assist in the construction of an ontology tree from the resource. The sample ontology for "hotel" domain using ConceptNet database demonstrated in Figure 1. In the next step, we expand our ontology by merging with each node in the ontology with synonyms words of English Language using WordNet (Princeton University, 2010) database, the useful of using WordNet to better coverage of domain specific features in english language. Pseudocode was proposed in algorithm described in following section that construct automatic ontology tree. This algorithm is a recursive function used to build automatic ontology tree. It takes the domain name (root) and number of levels of the ontology tree as input parameters. The get_features function using the SQL query to return a list of features from ConceptNet database that subclass of the root name parameter as seen in Table 2. The get_synonyms function also uses a SQL query to return Arabic synonyms words from WordNet database for the feature parameter. Finally, the output of function return ontology tree for specific domain.

Algorithm (4.1): Algorithm for Creation of Ontology Tree

Algorithm: Function Build Ontology Tree Function createOntologyTree (p_rootName, p_levelNo)

```
Input: p_rootName parameter. // name root of ontology.
p_levelNo parameter. // number of ontology tree level.
Output: Ontology tree represents the concepts and their
synonyms.
Root p_rootName //A root node of tree that created recursively.
```

Figure 1.Hotel ontology tree

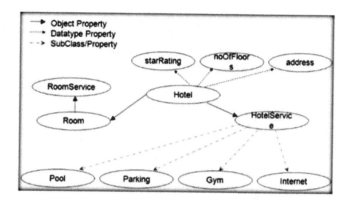

Table 2. Concepts with relations in the ConceptNet database for hotel domain

Start Concept	Relation	End Concept	Weight
Hotel	Used For	Sleep	1
Hotel room	HasA	room service	1
hotel room	part of	Hotel	1

```
No_of_level p_levelNo //The number of levels to deep into
ontology searching for appropriate meaning for the root
concept.
If No_of_level = 0
then
Return root;
List_features=get_features(Root). //return the features that
subclass from root
For each feature ∈ List_features do
Root.Add (feature); // append a node to the root
List_synonyms = Get_synonyms(feature);//return the synonyms for
these feature
For each synonym ∈ List_ synonyms do
Root. addSibling (synonym); // add Sibling a node to the root
Return createOntologyTree (feature, No_of_level-1);
********************************************************
***
Function get_features (root_parameter, ConceptNetDatabase)
```

```
return list
{
Input: root_parameter. // root name or node in the ontology
tree. ConceptNetDatabase parameter. // database have two
concepts with their relation.
Output: return features that sub-class from root feature.
V_list list; // variable list of nodes type;
Select start into V_list from ConceptNetDatabase
where end = root and rel = 'PartOf' and weight = 1
Union
Select end into V_list from ConceptNetDatabase
where start = root and rel = 'hasA';
Union
Select start into V_list from ConceptNetDatabase
where end = root and rel = 'AtLocation' etc.
return V_list;
}
Function get_synonyms (feature, WordNetDatabase)
return list
{
Input: feature parameter. // feature name or node in the
ontology tree.
WordNetDatabase parameter. // database have synonym words for
any word.
Output: return synonyms that related to feature parameter. V_
list list; // variable list of nodes type.
Select Ar_Synonyms into V_list from WordNetDatabase where word
= feature;
return V_list;
}
```

Extract Product Features

In our methodology, constructed ontology from previous step is used to extract product features in a user centric manner interactively. Feature is actually a concept upon which an opinion is submitted by the reviewer of a product. To identify the feature term, all the noun terms are extracted from review. We used the online parser tool to parse each review and to produce the pos tag for each word (whether the word is a noun, verb, adjective, etc.).

Select User Centric Product Features

The main contribution of this research is to determine important features about which any opinion is expressed and identify which features is important than other features on the basis of interactively build user centric ontology. The feature importance is captured by the height or level of a feature node in the ontology tree. For example, in the review:

The hotel is good for staying but I have a remark about its TV. It's kind of an old version and doesn't match with the hotel

Using baseline dictionary, the overall polarity of the review is neutral "but upon checking in the review will see the feature, "staying" is not the same important compared with feature, "television" which means the overall polarity of the review is positive. For this reason, using ontology tree help us to determine the polarity of the review by determine the important features. Two important interactive step takes at this stage. First user select features from ontology and also possibly adds additional features to the ontology. As shown in Figure 2, the level in the hotel ontology presents the important features for example, the feature, "staying" was placed in level 2, but feature "TV" was placed in level 1.

Figure 2. Hotel Ontology depicted with 2 levels from ConceptNet

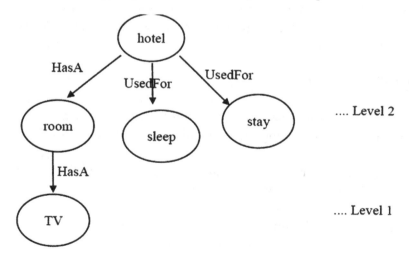

Stage 3: Opinion Mining

Calculate Opinion for Selected Feature

After identifying the features in the review and determine the important features. The next step is to get opinion word related to specific feature. Determine polarity of the feature can get by identify the opinion word related to it's feature. Opinion words may be adjectives, verb and noun, for example"excellent", "love","prefer","excellent", "not good" are considered opinion words.

Determine Polarity of Opinion Words

After opinion words extracted from previous steps, the polarity (positive or negative) of these words must be identified and these opinion words can be used to calculate the overall polarity of the review.

Determine the Overall Polarity (OP) of the Review

After features are extracted from the review document, it is matched in the ontology. The level of ontology where it is located determines the importance of the feature. The features located at higher level near to the root of the ontology are considered to be more important as compared to the lower level features. Finally, the overall polarity of the review is determined by summing up the opinion polarity multiplied by the height of ontology for each feature with respect to c factor that mentioned in previous section. In general, the following formula was proposed to determine the overall polarity of the review:

$$OP = \sum ((P * h) + c) ; 1$$

where summation is from k=1 to fn(number of feature), P is polarity of opinion, h is height of feature in ontology and c if exist, is intensifier factor that effect to opinion polarity.

"The hotel is good for staying but I have a remark about its TV. It's kind of an old version and doesn't match with the hotel"

OP=4*(1) +3*(-1) =1; //Positive with determine important the features.

Stage 4: Feature-Based Opinion Summary

Finally, after the feature and opinion extraction process is done, we are ready to generate the final feature-based summary. Our summary depends on the ontology to identify the opinion summary of each feature in the whole corpus by identifying the opinion of its sub-class terms in the ontology

Stage 5: Evaluate the Performance

In this section we discuss the evaluation of our method. The measures evaluating of the performance of classification are a confusion matrix, which is also called a performance vector that contains information about realistic and predicted classifications (Holte, 1993).

- The number of correct predictions that an instance is positive (TP).
- The number of correct predictions that an instance is negative (TN).
- The number of incorrect predictions that an instance is positive (FP).
- The number of incorrect predictions that an instance is negative (FN).

From the entries in the confusion matrix several concepts have been computed. These include Recall, Precision, F-Measure, and accuracy. Accuracy: Is the proportion of the total number of predictions that were correct. It is determined using this equation (Holte, 1993).

$$Accuracy = TP+FN+FP+TN/(TP+TN) \quad 2$$

Recall: True *positive* rate, Recall, or Sensitivity which is the proportion of Real Positive cases that are correctly predicted positive. This measures the Coverage of the Real Positive cases by the (Predicted Positive) rule. Recall is defined, with its various common appellations, by equation (Holte, 1993).

$$Recall = TP/(TP+FN) \quad 3$$

Precision: True *False Acc*uracy, Precision or Confidence (as it is called in Data Mining) denotes the proportion of Predicted Positive cases that are correctly Real Positives. This is what Machine Learning, Data Mining, and Information Retrieval focus on; Precision is defined, with its various common appellations, by equation (Holte, 1993).

Precision $= TP/(TP+FP)$ 4

F-Measure: F-Measure *or F-Fac*tor is the ratio between recall and precision measurements F-Measure is defined, with its various common appellations, by equation (Holte, 1993)

F $-$ Measure $= 2 *((\text{Precision} * \text{Recall})/ (\text{Precision} + \text{Recall}))$ 5

EXPERIMENTATION

In this section, we describe the conducted experiments to evaluate our approach. We made experiments with ontology considering important feature in the review. In order to compare our result, we used three classifiers which are Decision Tree (DT), Naïve Bayes (NB), and K-Nearest Neighbor (K-NN). We explain the machine environment, and the tools used in our experiment.

Datasets

Our method is performed in two domains corresponding t o hotels and pizza. The two corpora each consists of 2000 reviews of equal number of positive and negative datasets as shown in table 4.1. All the features/words extracted from the review documents are reduced to their root form for better matching of features in the ontology.

Experiments Setup

In this section, a description about the experimental environment, tools used in experiments, measures of performance evaluation of classification methods.

Experimental Environment and Tools

We applied experiments on a machine with properties that is Intel (R) Core (TM) i3- 3110M CPU @ 2.40 GHz, 4.00 GB RAM, 320 GB hard disk drive and Windows 7 operating system installed. To carry out our work (including the experimentation), special tools and programs were used which are:

- Eclipse IDE 3.8: to build and evaluate our method
- Ontology editor protégé 4.3.
- RapidMiner application program (RapidMiner Studio, 2016): used to do supervised classification methods, and extracting the required results that compared with our method.

- MySQL 6.3 (Workbench, 2016): to handle with ConceptNet database and sentiment lexicon database

Ontology Construction

The ontology construction is done using ConceptNet. We extract the concepts/ features from the ConceptNet up to level 4 and domain ontology.The domain ontology for pizza is depicted in Figure 3 We notice from our experiment that some features/concepts don't exist in ConceptNet database, therefore we manually add it in domain ontology as shown in Figure 4. Also in Figure 5 the main novel contribution of interactive user centric ontology construction with feature selection and addition is shown.

Ontology Baseline

In this experimental setting, we extract the features with noun tag from the review documents; further, extracted features are matched in the ontology to select only the product features. Then, get the opinion words corresponding to the features extracted from previous step. Table 3 shows confusion matrix table for pizza domain using ontology with consider important features. Table 4 shows calculated Accuracy, Precision, Recall and F-Measure for pizza domain using ontology baseline.

Subjective Evaluation

Because the result of classification is not enough, we want to know whether the system has extracted the feature correctly. Because that, we need someone have expert

Figure 3. Example of ontology tree in the pizza domain

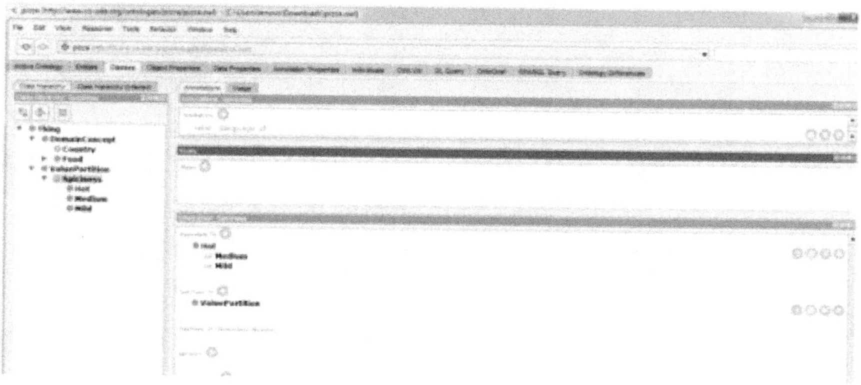

Figure 4. Example of user centric feature selection for pizza domain

Figure 5. Interactive feature addition in ontology

Table 3. Confusion matrix table for pizza domain using ontology which consider important features

Domain	N=2000	Positive	Negative
Pizza	Positive	838	288
	Negative	162	712

Table 4. Accuracy, Precision, Recall and F-Measure for pizza domain using ontology baseline

Domain	Accuracy	Precision	Recall	F-measure
Pizza	78.20%	73.84%	81.00%	77.25%

to evaluate feature and opinion extraction process with it's polarity. We manually evaluate our method using recall and precision formula that shown in section 5.2. We select randomly 100 reviews for each product features in both domains and manual extract tuple (feature, opinion, polarity) for the reviews with the help of someone who has experience. We choose two product features in hotel domain, such as: "room" and "restaurant" and two product feature in pizza domain "toppings"and "base". Table 5 shows the result for pizza ontology.

FUTURE RESEARCH DIRECTIONS

In future, this work can be extended to discover methods to enrich the ontology. Extracting ontology from reviews is also a big task to deal with in future. Also, we want to take more benefit from the ontology by expanding our ontology from more than one ontology to improve the performance. Also, we want to incorporate our method with supervised classification approaches. We need to apply our method

Table 5. Recall, precision and F-measure for feature, opinion and polarity generation for two features in hotel domain.

Features	No. of tuple extracted by Human	No. of system tuple Extracted	Correct system	Recall	Precision	F-Measure
Base	78	70	64	82.05%	91.43%	86.49%
Toppings	76	69	60	78.95	86.96	82.76

in different domains such as mobile, computer and cars etc. We will try to apply the light stemming technique for our datasets and evaluate the performance of our method used large data set. Evaluating the effectiveness of feature and opinion extraction process used more than two features can also be considered.

CONCLUSION

Table 5 shows the recall and precision result for pizza domain in two distinct product features. Column 1, lists of each product features. Column 2, number of tuple generated manually. Column 3, number of tuple generated by our system. Columns 4, number of correct tuple generated by our system. Columns 5 and 6 give the recall and precision of our method generation for each product feature. We notice from the results that our system has good recall and precision in predicting of features with their opinion. The average f-measure of product features in pizza domain is 84.62% . Results show us the effectiveness of our method. Research in opinion mining has been very limited for the user centric feature level classification. In this work, we proposed approach work at feature level opinion mining classification to detect polarity of online product opinion reviews. Furthermore, we combined our approach with ontology information to give better opinion mining classification performance. Using ontology in our method has several advantages, such as extract explicit product features from the review, also to determine the important features from the review. Our approach is very applicable for any product domain that requires a domain name and number of level of the ontology parameter and using ConceptNet and WordNet databases to automatically construct domain specific ontology tree. All the experiments are performed on two review datasets, namely, hotels and pizzas. The data were collected from the websites, obtaining a total of 2000 reviews in both hotel and pizza domain with equal number of positive and negative reviews. We notice from our experiments that our method improves the performance over supervised and unsupervised approaches.

REFERENCES

Agarwal, B., Mittal, P., & Garg, S. (2015). Sentiment Analysis Using Common-Sense and Context Information. *Computational Intelligence and Neuroscience, 2015*, 1–9. doi:10.1155/2015/715730 PMID:25866505

Asur, S., & Bernardo, A. H. (2010). *Predicting the future with social media.* Arxiv preprint arXiv:1003.5699, 2010.

Baziz, M., Boughanem, M., Aussenac-Gilles, N., & Chrisment, C. (2005). Semantic cores for representing documents in IR. *Proceedings of the 2005 ACM symposium on Applied computing*. 10.1145/1066677.1066911

Bollen, J., Mao, H., & Zeng, X.-J. (2011). Twitter mood predicts the stock market. *Journal of Computational Science, 2*(1), 1–8. doi:10.1016/j.jocs.2010.12.007

Castellanos, M., Dayal, U., Wang, S., & Chetan, G. (2010). Information Extraction, Real-Time, Processing and DW2.0 in Operational Business Intelligence, Databases in Networked *Information Systems. Lecture Notes in Computer Science, 5999*, 33–45. doi:10.1007/978-3-642-12038-1_4

Das, S., & Chen, M. (2001). Yahoo! for Amazon: Extracting market sentiment from stock message boards. *Proceedings of APFA-2001*.

Dave, K., Lawrence, S., & Pennock, D. M. (2003). Mining the peanut gallery: Opinion extraction and semantic classification of product reviews. *Proceedings of International Conference on World Wide Web (WWW-2003)*. 10.1145/775152.775226

Duo, Z., Juan-Zi, L., & Bin, X. (2005). *Web service annotation using ontology mapping*. Paper presented at the Service-Oriented System Engineering, SOSE 2005, IEEE International Workshop.

Fensel, D. (2002). Ontology-based knowledge management. *Computer, 35*(11), 56–59. doi:10.1109/MC.2002.1046975

Freitas, L. A., & Vieira, R. (2013). Ontology based feature level opinion mining for portuguese reviews. *Proceedings of the 22nd international conference on World Wide Web companion*. 10.1145/2487788.2487944

Groh, G., & Hauffa, J. (2011). Characterizing Social Relations Via NLP-based Sentiment Analysis. *Proceedings of the Fifth International AAAI Conference on Weblogs and Social Media (ICWSM-2011)*.

Gruber, T. R. (1993). A Translation Approach to Portable Ontology Specifications Acquisition. *Current Issues in Knowledge Modeling, 5*(2), 199-220.

Guarino, N. (1995). Formal ontology, conceptual analysis and knowledge representation. *International Journal of Human-Computer Studies, 43*(5), 1–15.

Lahl, D. (2011). Better Decisions by Analyzing Structured and Unstructured Data Together. *Business Intelligence Journal, 16*(1), 9–1.

Hatzivassiloglou, V., & McKeown, K. R. (1997). Predicting the semantic orientation of adjectives. *Proceedings of Annual Meeting of the Association for Computational Linguistics (ACL-1997)*.

Hearst, M. (1992). Direction-based text interpretation as an information access refinement. In P. Jacobs (Ed.), *Text-Based Intelligent Systems* (pp. 257–274). Lawrence Erlbaum Associates.

Holte, R. C. (1993). Very simple classification rules perform well on most commonly used datasets. *Machine Learning, 11*(1), 1–27. doi:10.1023/A:1022631118932

Joshi, M., Das, D., Gimpel, K., & Smith, N. A. (2010). *Movie reviews and revenues: An experiment in text regression. Proceedings of the North American Chapter of the Association for Computational Linguistics Human Language Technologies Conference (NAACL 2010)*.

Lahl, D. (2011). Better Decisions by Analyzing Structured and Unstructured Data Together. *Business Intelligence Journal, 16*(1), 9–1.

Lau, R. Y., Lai, C. C., Ma, J., & Li, Y. (2009). Automatic domain ontology extraction for context-sensitive opinion mining. *ICIS 2009 Proceedings*, 1-18.

Lazhar, F., & Yamina, T. G. (2012). Identification of Opinions in Arabic Texts using Ontologies. *J Inform Tech Soft Engg, 2*(2), 1–4. doi:10.4172/2165-7866.1000108

Malviya, N., Mishra, N., & Sahu, S. (2011). Developing University Ontology using protégé OWL Tool: Process and Reasoning. *International Journal of Scientific & Engineering Research, 2*(9), 1–8.

McGlohon, M., Natalie, G., & Zach, R. (2010). Star quality: Aggregating reviews to rank products and merchants. *Proceedings of the International Conference on Weblogs and Social Media (ICWSM-2010)*.

Meersman, M. (2005). The use of lexicons and other computer-linguistic tools in semantics, design and cooperation of database systems. *Star Lab Technical Report.* Available at: http://www.starlab.vub.ac.be/website/files/STAR-1999-02_0.pdf

Mohammad, S., & Tony, Y. (2011). Tracking Sentiment in Mail: How Genders Differ on Emotional Axes. *Proceedings of the ACL Workshop on ACL 2011:Workshop on Computational Approaches to Subjectivity and Sentiment Analysis.*

Mukherjee, S., & Joshi, S. (2013). *Sentiment aggregation using conceptnet ontology.* Paper presented at the 6th International Joint Conference on Natural Language Processing.

Nasukawa, T., & Yi, J. (2003). *Sentiment analysis: Capturing favorability using natural language processing. Proceedings of the K-CAP-03, 2nd Intl. Conf. on Knowledge Capture.* 10.1145/945645.945658

Negash, S., & Gray, P. (2008). Business intelligence. In F. Burstein & C. Holsapple (Eds.), Handbook of decision support systems. Springer Link.

O'Connor, B., Balasubramanyan, R., Routledge, B. R., & Smith, N. A. (2010). From Tweets to Polls: Linking Text Sentiment to Public Opinion Time Series. *Proceedings of the International AAAI Conference on Weblogs and Social Media (ICWSM 2010).*

Pang, B., & Lee, L. (2008). Opinion mining and sentiment analysis. *Foundations and Trends in Information Retrieval, 2*(1-2), 1–135. doi:10.1561/1500000011

Pang, B., Lee, L., & Vaithyanathan, S. (2002). Thumbs up? Sentiment Classification Using Machine Learning Techniques. *Proceedings of the conference on Empirical Methods in Natural Language Processing (EMNLP),* 79-86. 10.3115/1118693.1118704

Princeton University. (2010). *WordNet Software.* Retrieved February 1, 2016 from: http://wordnet.princeton.edu/wordnet/license/

Rob Speer, L. F. (2016). *ConceptNet Database.* Retrieved February 1, 2016 from: http://conceptnet5.media.mit.edu/

Sadikov, E., Parameswaran, A., & Venetis, P. (2009). Blogs as predictors of movie success. *Proceedings of the Third International Conference on Weblogs and Social Media (ICWSM-2009).*

Sakunkoo, P., & Sakunkoo, N. (2009). Analysis of Social Influence in Online Book Reviews. *Proceedings of third International AAAI Conference on Weblogs and Social Media (ICWSM-2009).*

Sukumaran, S., & Sureka, A. (2006). Integrating Structured and Unstructured Data Using Text Tagging and Annotation. *Business Intelligence Journal, 11*(2), 8–16.

Tong, R. (2001). An Operational System for Detecting and Tracking Opinions in on-line discussion. *Proceedings of SIGR Workshop on operational Text Classification.*

Tripadvisor. (2016). *Hotel reviews.* Retrieved January 1, 2016 from: https://www.tripadvisor.com/

Tumasjan, A., Sprenger, T. O., Sandner, P. G., & Welpe, I. (2010). Predicting elections with twitter: What 140 characters reveal about political sentiment. *Proceedings of the International Conference on Weblogs and Social Media (ICWSM-2010).*

Turney, P. (2002). Thumbs Up or Thumbs Down? Semantic Orientation Applied to Unsupervised Classification of Reviews. *Proceedings of the 40th Annual Meeting of the Association for Computational Linguistics (ACL)*, 417-424.

Wiebe, J. (1990). Identifying subjective characters in narrative. *Proceedings of the International Conference on Computational Linguistics (COLING-1990)*.

Wiebe, J. (1994). Tracking point of view in narrative. *Computational Linguistics*, *20*, 233–287.

Wiebe, J., Rebecca, F. B., & Thomas, P. O. (1999). Development and use of a gold-standard data set for subjectivity classifications. *Proceedings of the Association for Computational Linguistics (ACL-1999)*. 10.3115/1034678.1034721

Wiebe, J. (2000). Learning subjective adjectives from corpora. In *Proceedings of National Conf. on Artificial Intelligence* (pp. 735-740). AAAI Press.

Yaakub, Li, & Feng. (2011). Integration of Opinion into Customer Analysis Model. *Proceedings of Eighth IEEE International Conference on e-Business Engineering*, 90-95.

Zhou, L., & Chaovali, P. (2008). Ontology-Supported Polarity Mining. *Journal of the American Society for Information Science and Technology*, *59*(1), 98–110. doi:10.1002/asi.20735

Zhao, W. X., Jing, J., Hongfei, Y., & Xiaoming, L. (2010). Jointly modeling aspects and opinions with a MaxEnt-LDA hybrid. *Proceedings of Conference on Empirical Methods in Natural Language Processing*, 56-65.

Chapter 8
Applications of Ontology– Based Opinion Mining

Razia Sulthana
SRM Institute of Science and Technology, India

Subburaj Ramasamy
SRM Institute of Science and Technology, India

ABSTRACT

Ontology provides a technique to formulate and present queries to databases either stand-alone or web-based. Ontology has been conceived to produce reusable queries to extract rules matching them, and hence, it saves time and effort in creating new ontology-based queries. Ontology can be incorporated in the machine learning process, which hierarchically defines the relationship between concepts, axioms, and terms in the domain. Ontology rule mining has been found to be efficient as compared to other well-known rule mining methods like taxonomy and decision trees. In this chapter, the authors carry out a detailed survey about ontology-related information comprising classification, creation, learning, reuse, and application. The authors also discuss the reusability and the tools used for reusing ontology. Ontology has a life cycle of its own similar to the software development life cycle. The classification-supervised machine learning technique and clustering and the unsupervised machine learning are supported by the ontology. The authors also discuss some of the open issues in creation and application of ontology.

DOI: 10.4018/978-1-5225-6117-0.ch008

8.0 INTRODUCTION

Ontology is widely used in machine learning. It is used for instance, in the following applications:

- Classification of customers' reviews of items such as books, movies or any product or service.
- Sentiment analysis using text retrieved from social media.
- Rule mining in semantic web.

With the advent of Web 2.0, the number of Internet users is growing and thereby contribute data to the common pool of global resources. Social networks are important sources of data which can be gainfully used with the help of machine learning techniques for sentiment analysis, product market analysis, changing opinion of the consumers for products etc. The increasing velocity, variety and volume of the data which is popularly known as big data (Xia, Wang, Berkele & Liu, 2017; Padhy, Mishra & Panigrahi, 2012) has resulted in advanced research in machine learning techniques. Usage of Ontology with big data provides significant savings in efforts, cost and efficiency.

8.1 ONTOLOGY

Ontology is a hierarchical representation system. Ontology finds wide use in genetic algorithms, medical databases and machine learning. Since the early 2000s, ontology is applied in semantic web. In the early 1990s ontology was defined by Gruber as "a formal, explicit specification of a shared conceptualization" (Gruber, 1993). It provides a formal and shared conceptualization of a domain that helps in ensuring communication amongst people and supports interactions among application systems.
Creating ontology for an application enables the following:

- A formal documented vocabulary.
- A formal representation understandable by machine.
- Understanding concepts of application domain such as supermarket application.
- Reusing of concepts.
- Sharing of concepts.

8.1.1 Ontology Classification

Ontology can be classified based on the following:

- Creation methodology adopted
- Application

8.1.1.1 Ontology Classification Based on Creation Methodology

The ontologies can be classified into the following based on the methodology adopted for their creation.

- Supervised
- Unsupervised
- Upper / top ontology
- Domain ontology
- Metadata ontology
- User-defined ontology

The creation of ontology can be manual, semi-automatic or automatic. The reference to the research articles discussing the three types are given in Table 1.

Table 1. Articles classified based on Ontology Creation types.

	Ontology Types	Reference to Articles
1	Automated Ontology	(Park & Kang, 2012; Park & Lee, 2007; Pearl, 1984; Park, Kang, & Kim, 2007; Golbreich, 2004; Lin & Pantel, 2001; Szpektor, Tanev, Dagan, & Coppola, 2004; Velardi, Navigli, Cuchiarelli, & Neri, 2005; Navigli & Velardi, 2004; Weng, Tsai, Liu, & Hsu, 2006; Köhler, Philippi, Specht, & Rüegg, 2006; Ma et al., 2012; Faure & Nédellec, 1998; Stumme & Maedche, 2001; Jiang & Tan, 2005; Du, Li, & King, 2009; Yue, Zuo, Peng, Wang, & Han, 2015; Shi & Setchi, 2012)
2	Semi - Automated Ontology	(Li, Du, & Wang, 2005; Cimiano & Völker, 2005; Maedche, & Staab, 2000; Gacitua, Sawyer, & Rayson, 2008; Bisson, Nédellec, & Canamero, 2000; Gal, Modica, & Jamil, 2004; Fan, Luo, Gao, & Jain, 2007; Chi, Lin, & Hsieh, 2014, Sanchez-Pi, Martí, & Garcia, 2016)
3	Manual Ontology	(Maedche & Staab, 2000)

8.1.1.2 Ontology Classification Based on Application

The ontology is classified into various types based on the application in which it is used (Navigli & Velardi, 2004). The reference to the research articles of the various types of ontology based on its application is given in Table 2.

8.1.2 Ontology in Semantic Web

Semantic web can be visualized as three layer architecture as represented in Figure 1. The top layer is user layer, middle is domain layer and the bottom layer is storage layer. The user layer consists of end users and web service components. The domain layer encompasses a set of tools and languages to support semantic web and ontology uniquely for every service. The storage layer acts as a miniature data warehouse with a collection of structured and unstructured files or documents.

Ontology (Gruber, 1995) plays a major role in knowledge sharing and communications among technologies in the web. Ontologies were also developed based on the domains for which the application is developed, which are listed below.

- Cyc (Lenat & Guha, 1989), and MicroCosmos (Mahesh & Nirenburg, 1996), SUMO (http://ontology.teknowledge.com) are generic ontologies.
- WordNet (Fellbaum, 1998) is a lexical ontology.
- Gene Ontology (Gene Ontology Consortium, 2001) and UMLS (Lindberg, 1990) for life sciences.

Table 2 Articles classified based on Ontology application

	Ontology types based on application	Reference to Articles
1	Domain Ontology	(Park & Kang, 2012; Park & Lee, 2007; Park, Kang, & Kim, 2007; Velardi, Navigli, Cuchiarelli, & Neri, 2005; Navigli & Velardi, 2004; Weng, Tsai, Liu, & Hsu, 2006; Köhler, Philippi, Specht, & Rüegg, 2006; Ma et al., 2012; Faure & Nédellec, 1998; Stumme & Maedche, 2001; Jiang & Tan, 2005; Du, Li, & King, 2009; Yue, Zuo, Peng, Wang, & Han, 2015; Li, Du, & Wang, 2005; Cimiano & Völker, 2005; Maedche, & Staab, 2000; Gacitua, Sawyer, & Rayson, 2008; Gal, Modica, & Jamil, 2004; Chi, Lin, & Hsieh, 2014; Sanchez-Pi, Martí, & Garcia, 2016; Maedche & Staab, 2000)
2	Corpus Based Ontology	(Bisson, Nédellec, & Canamero, 2000)
3	User Ontology	(Shi & Setchi, 2012; Fan, Luo, Gao, & Jain, 2007)

Figure 1. Ontology in Web

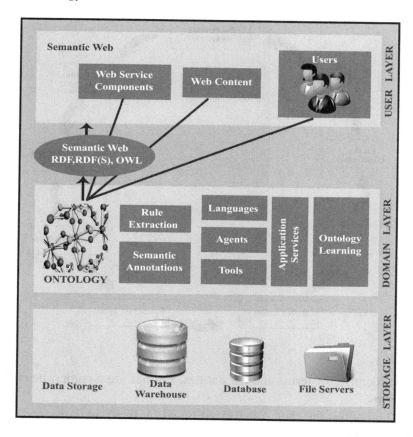

8.1.3 Ontology Development Process

Ontology has been developed for each domain of the application and Ontology Development (Li, Martínez, & Rubio, 2016) process is an iterative process. Ontology development process is represented in Figure 2.

Ontology development process is a continuous life cycle, and it involves the following steps:

Step 1: Initially, the requirement to design the ontology is gathered. E.g. Domain, Application: Real-time or static.

Step 2: Identify the scope and domain of the application for which ontology is created.

Step 3: Identify the candidate relationship between the entities.

Step 4: To ensure ontology reuse in future, the components are made independent of the underlying software.

Figure 2. Ontology development process

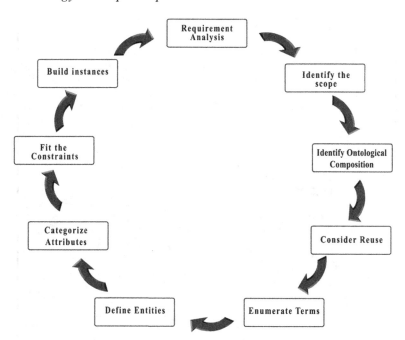

Step 5, 6: Identify the terms and the entities. Entities are a composite collection of terms.

Step 7: The entities are then categorized based on their similarity and grouped under a domain.

Step 8: The entire process starts with a set of rules as a constraint. These constraints restrict the number of terms and entities to pick. It restricts them to be under a common domain.

Step 9: The instances of the ontology are now built, and each hierarchical flow is checked before deployment. This ensures an increase in process accuracy.

This survey has grouped the information under different types of ontology, approaches, applications and the ontology languages supporting them. Section 3 discusses the classical usage of ontology as rules: Rule ontology. Section 4 addresses the state-of-the-art of ontology learning listing the types and algorithms used. Section 5 discusses the role of ontology in the extraction process. Section 6 briefs the usage of ontology in clustering, classification, data analytics. Section 7 lists the performance measures used in validating the ontology system. Section 8 discusses the open issues. Conclusions are in Section 9.

8.2 RULE ONTOLOGY

Rule ontology (Park & Kang, 2012) automatically extracts rules from web sites based on the similar rules extracted from other sites using Breadth First Search (BFS) algorithm. There are different ways of extracting rules from textual information in the semantic web. The rules extracted may be inference rules or entailment rules based on the application. Entailment rules represent the directional information between the components. Inference rules represent the logical relationship between components.

A semi-automatic ontology (SOAM) (Li, Du, & Wang, 2005) extracts rule from a relational database. It extracts the necessary data from the database and then builds an ontology structure. The similar rules are extracted in Park, Kang, and Kim (2007) using ontology based on the semantic similarity measure. An automatic rule acquisition method: OntoRule encapsulates rule components and its structure. It first identifies the rule, and in the second stage, the composition of the rule is determined. A hyponym hierarchy method is used to find the semantic similarity distance. A graph based breadth first search method is used for identifying the relationship in the ontology. A method in Gasse and Haarslev, (2008) uses protégé plugin (Golbreich, 2004) to rewrite the axioms written in Ontology Web Language (OWL) to Description Logics (DL) during rule extraction.

Intelligent search strategies using automated rule extraction and breadth first search method are described in Pearl (1984). Using this method, the nodes in the graph are traversed in layers of depth, and it follows first in first out policy.

Generally, BFS is used for construction of ontology and a set of works are listed below

- Extracts inference rules from similar web sites. Uses OWL to generate RDF graph (Park & Kang, 2012).
- Uses XMRL to identify the rule components (Park & Lee, 2007).
- Enlightens the heuristics method to solve the graph based problems (Pearl, 1984).
- Extracts similar rules from web sites (Park, Kang, & Kim, 2007).
- Extracts rule from the relational database uses OWL (Li, Du, & Wang, 2005).

Extensive research has been carried out in automated ontology development. An automated ontology (Park & Lee, 2007) along with XRML (eXtensible Rule Markup Language) identifies the rule component from texts and tables. It recognizes the variables, classes, and the value of the variable and omitted variables. The similar rules are extracted from the same domain based on simple similarity measure based on synonyms using the bottom-up approach.

8.3 ONTOLOGY LEARNING

Ontology learning (Maedche, 2002) refers to set of data-driven techniques that support ontology engineering. Ontology is widely used in web applications. Ontology learning procedures are classified into four categories (Weng, Tsai, Liu, & Hsu, 2006), they are text clustering, association rules and knowledge based and Formal Conceptual Analysis(FCA).

Ontology can either exist as a separate module or part of web applications. Ontology has evolved from taxonomy (Hakeem & Shah, 2004; Van Rees, 2003; Hoxha, Jiang, & Weng, 2016; Niu & Issa, 2015) providing the advantage of optimally reducing the effort and time taken to carry out an operation in data stores.

Ontology Hierarchy vs. Taxonomical Hierarchy

- Taxonomy is purely hierarchical and is a top-down representation, whereas ontology represents some relationships between the entities. E.g. parent –child relation, sibling relation, child of parent1 can be connected with a grandchild of parent 2.
- Taxonomy contains parent-child relationship, and ontology contains many user-defined varying relationships.

The major advantage of ontology is its reusability. This facilitates creating a repository of ontology which can be dynamically and continuously expanded. Developing ontology can be achieved with the following tools OntoLearn (Navigli & Velardi, 2004), ASIUM system (Faure & Nédellec, 1998), TextToOnto (Maedche, & Staab, 2000), the the Mo'k Workbench (Bisson, Nédellec, & Canamero, 2000), OntoLT (Buitelaar, Olejnik, & Sintek, 2004), DODDLE II (Yamaguchi, 2001), WEB->KB (Craven et al., 2000) which reuse the existing ontology that minimizes the time taken for its construction. Integrating these tools with the application has compatibility issues as these are restricted to otology models, and more importantly, the user interaction is minimal. This can be overcome by use of Text2Onto (Cimiano & Völker, 2005). OntoLT, Text2Onto and DODDLE tools automatically extract the ontology from the web. It works seamlessly with ontology tools.

The tool support for ontology can be grouped into the following categories

- Tools for Ontology Learning.
- Tools for Ontology construction.

KAON (KArlsruhe Ontology and Semantic web infrastructure) is a tool that helps in managing the ontology and its application. TextToOnto (Maedche, &

Staab, 2000) is an ontology learning system applied in KAON. This methodology builds a modeler for an underlying corpus. Many effective algorithms are inbuilt in this system with its own parameters. Ontobuilder (Gal, Modica, & Jamil, 2004) is a tool which extracts ontology from web sources. It encompasses many matching algorithms to identify the structure similarity. More information on ontology learning can be drawn from the ontology learning workshops (ECAI, 2002; K-CAP, 2003; Staab, Maedche, Nedellec, & Wiemer-Hastings, 2000; Maedche, Staab, Hovy, & Nedellec, 2001; ECAI-02, 2002)

The well-known ontology learning tools, the algorithms and the learning methods used by them are given in Table 3.

Ontology learning is the process of understanding existing ontologies. There are two methods for ontology construction. They are listed below:

1.   Modifying an existing ontology.

The existing ontology is learned, the data is extracted and necessary refinement is carried out to suite the new applications. A detailed study about the association among entities has to done to modify an existing ontology. Ontology alignment (Noy & Musen, 1999, 2000) is one of the requirements during the ontology extraction process, and it helps in identifying the association between concepts.

2.   Constructing a new ontology

When a new ontology is created, tools such as protégé are used. Constructing ontology requires deep knowledge about the domain, the entities and the relationship between them.

As a first step, before we consider creating a new ontology it is advisable to learn the existing ontologies. When the user's interest or the rule query changes dramatically, it is better to create a new ontology and when the changes are marginal, then existing ontology can be reused and can be extended to suite the new query.

3.   The developed ontology has to be maintained so as to extract the necessary, timely information from it. An approach to maintaining the developed ontology is noted in Gašević, Zouaq, Torniai, Jovanović, and Hatala (2011) which use collaborative tags for visualization and user interaction. The intuitiveness of the proposed method in relating the folksonomy and taxonomy is measured quantitatively and qualitatively using statistical measures.

Table 3. Ontology learning tools and its construction methods

Paper	Ontology Learning tool and Nomenclature	Principle of operation	Algorithms	Construction Method (Ontology Learning Methods)
(Navigli & Velardi, 2004)	Ontolearn:	Extracts domain ontology from websites and documents hosted by virtual environments.	Structural semantic interconnection: It performs semantic interpretation based on the domain words extracted from the web documents	Knowledge base
(Weng, Tsai, Liu, & Hsu, 2006)	Ontology learning	Builds a map for related ontological concepts that helps the user to search relevant information. Uses FCA and conceptual relationship between term and document for ontology learning	Formal Conceptual Analysis Performs conceptual analysis among ontological concepts	FCA (Formal Concept Analysis)
(Faure & Nédellec, 1998)	ASIUM Ontology Learning	Parses text in natural language, clusters them conceptually developing into generality graph	ASIUM clustering algorithm for learning ontologies. ASIUM follows Bottom-up and best-first method	Corpus-based
(Cimiano & Völker, 2005)	Text 2Onto	Learning from web pages dynamically	Ontology Learning Algorithms Model implemented in Probabilistic Object (POM) It Supports handling RDFS, OWL, F-logic	knowledge base
(Maedche, & Staab, 2000)	TexttoOnto	Determining conceptual structures and engineering ontologies from text	Generalized association rule algorithm: Identity relationship between concepts and determine the appropriate level of abstraction	Association rules
(Bisson, Nédellec, & Canamero, 2000)	Mo'k Workbench:	Develops a workbench that recognizes the clustering method and builds ontology	Uses NLP methods and calculates the similarity distance	Corpus-based text clustering
Gal, Modica, & Jamil, 2004	Ontobuilder:	Learning from web pages and reservation systems.	Word similarity algorithms, String matching algorithms, Value normalization and Value matching	Knowledge base

8.4 ONTOLOGY CREATION

Ontology has been found to be suitable for rule mining, in both in the web and offline applications. The steps in building ontology are given below

- Determine the scope and domain for which ontology is to be constructed.
- Identify the important terms/concepts from the corpus or relational database.
- Determine the class attributes and frame a class hierarchy. A high-quality dynamic ontology can be built if meaningful, correct and minimally redundant class attributes are extracted.
- Identify the relationship between the class attributes i.e. cardinality, intersection, union, complement, etc. which has to be represented in the ontology.
- Filter out the properties of the classes.
- Finally, identify the individual names

The created ontology is stored in the repository and is modified to suit the needs of the application. The co-occurrence frequency of the word is used to detect the non-taxonomic relationship in Concept Relation Concept Tuple-based Ontology Learning (CRCTOL) (Jiang & Tan, 2005) and texttoonto (Maedche, & Staab, 2000). The precision of CRCTOL is 99.7%, and texttoonto is 99.1%. A difference of 0.6% can be seen between them. CRCTOL performs efficiently than texttoonto in multi-word term extraction.

The automatic extraction of ontology from web ensures the quality or continuity of web pages chosen. Most of the web pages on the web are themselves organized in a taxonomical hierarchy or ontological hierarchy. Ontology extraction from web pages that are aligned in ontological hierarchy eases the extraction process. Ontology can be constructed for web sites that have same URL base. Moreover, this makes the navigation process easier. Thus it becomes ontology directed web pages. The specific content from the web pages can be extracted when a thorough study of the web page structure. The ontology can also be created by comparing multiple existing ontologies. A divide and conquer approach (Hu, Qu, & Cheng, 2008) matches two related ontologies from the web by developing a structure based partitioning algorithm and using clustering. The technology governing ontology follows a systematic path comprising of well-defined processes. We call this as ontology life cycle represented in Figure 3. While there may be many variations of Ontology Life cycle (OLC) we portray a simple OLC consisting of 4 phases as explained below:

Figure 3. Ontology Life cycle

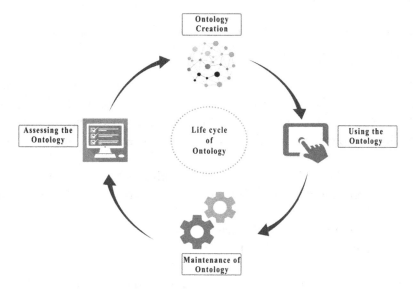

1. **Creation of Ontology:** The creation of ontology can be either from scratch or modify the existing ontology from the same domain. The ontology creation involves the following:
    a. Choosing the ontology type.
    b. Choosing the construction type.
    c. Creation of new ontology versus modifying existing ontology.
2. **Using the Ontology:** The ontology can be applied in various applications by programming in any one of the following languages:
    a. OQL (Ontology query language).
    b. RDF (Resource Description Framework).
    c. RDFS (Resource Description Framework Schema).
3. **Maintenance of Ontology:** The ontology is reusable. The reusability can be achieved by the following:
    a. Automatic update
    b. Semi-automatic update
    c. Manual update
        The ontology structure is designed for reusability
4. **Assessing the Ontology:** Ontology can be called in an application for rule mining to extract knowledge from the data stores. The ontology creation stage has some components and is shown in Figure 4.

Figure 4. Expanded stages of Ontology creation

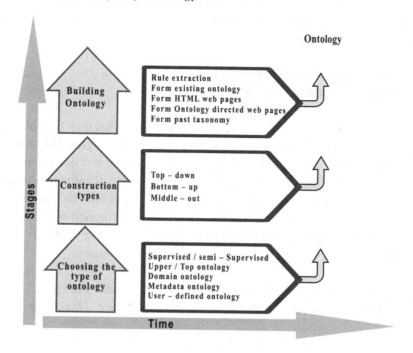

The steps in ontology creation are explained below:

1. **Choosing the Ontology Type:** The foremost step is to choose the type of ontology. The different types of ontology include:
   a. **Domain Ontology:** Developed for a particular application.
   b. **Upper Ontology:** Works in the upper layer and groups all the domain ontologies.
   c. **Metadata Ontology:** Developed with the metadata information of an application. It eases the search process.
   d. **User-Defined:** Developed based on user–defined rules.
2. **Choosing the Construction Type:** Ontology can be constructed in 3 ways:
   a. **Top-Down Ontology:** Built from top to bottom, where the top level entities are identified following which sub-entities are identified.
   b. **Bottom-Up Ontology:** Built from bottom to top, where the low-level entities are identified following which its parents are identified
   c. **Middle-Out Ontology:** Built-in any fashion, where all the entities are identified, and grouped together and linked by finding the relationship between them.

161

3. Creation of new ontology versus modifying existing ontology.
4. The ontology is created using ontology languages or modified by extracting from other ontologies.

8.4.1 Ontology-Based Information Retrieval From Semantic Web

In the past, information from the web pages was extracted using matching algorithms. An improved way for information retrieval is by using ontologies. Ontology-based information retrieval identifies the relationship between the text documents and the contents of the web page in a better way. A scalable mode of information retrieval is proposed in Fernández et al. (2011) for ontology-based information retrieval of web contents. A list of similarity measures used for information retrieval is given below. Similarity measures were used to find the relationship between the query given by the user and the text in the document in a vector space.

- The geometric average of two attributes (Lin & Pantel, 2001).
- Distributional similarity principle (Szpektor, Tanev, Dagan, & Coppola, 2004).
- Rule-based and algebraic methods (Navigli & Velardi, 2004).
- Latent semantic indexing (Ma et al., 2012; Shi & Setchi, 2012).
- Cosine similarity (Yue, Zuo, Peng, Wang, & Han, 2015; Hu, Qu, & Cheng, 2008).
- Lexical similarities based on edit distance (Li, Du, & Wang, 2005).
- The skewed divergence of two attributes (Cimiano & Völker, 2005).
- Log-likelihood (Gacitua, Sawyer, & Rayson, 2008).
- Similarity computation matrix (Bisson, Nédellec, & Canamero, 2000).
- Levenshtein distance (Fernández et al., 2011).
- Dice's coefficient: Identifies the similarity between two strings (Du, Li, & King, 2009).
- Pearson's similarity Measure (Su, Yeh, Philip, & Tseng, 2010).

A set of algorithms used in similarity measure calculation includes Rule-Based Knowledge Similarity Calculation System (RBKSCS) and Conditional Probability Knowledge Similarity Algorithm (CPKSA) (Huang & Cheng, 2008).

8.4.2 Ontology Tools

During the last few decades tools have been developed for creating ontology and ontology learning. These tools provide ease of creation of ontologies. Table 4 lists references to the articles published on the ontology tools used.

8.5 ONTOLOGY IN VARIOUS APPLICATIONS

8.5.1 Ontology-Based Clustering

It is an unsupervised methodology of machine learning approach where the groups are not pre-determined. It is used in information retrieval and exploratory data mining. Ontology is used in clustering approaches (Faure & Nédellec, 1998; Bisson,

Table 4. List of ontology tools and its purpose

Paper	Purpose	Tool
1	Construction of Ontology	1. CODE (Li, Du, & Wang, 2005) 2. Protege tool (Yue, Zuo, Peng, Wang, & Han, 2015; Cimiano & Völker, 2005)
2	Ontology reasoning tools	1. Jena (Reynolds, 2004) 2. F-OWL (Zou, Finin, & Chen, 2004) 3. KAON (Volz, Oberle, Staab, & Motik, 2003) 4. OntoBroker (Decker, Erdmann, Fensel, & Studer, 1999)
3	Miner tool	1. Rule Miner (Park, Kang, & Kim, 2007)
4	Reasoning tools with OWL	1. RACER, Jess (Golbreich, 2004)
5	Ontology learning tools	1. OntoLearn (Navigli & Velardi, 2004) or OntoLT (Buitelaar, Olejnik, & Sintek, 2004) 2. ASIUM system (Faure & Nédellec, 1998) 3. TextToOnto (Maedche, & Staab, 2000) 4. Ontolancs (Gacitua, Sawyer, & Rayson, 2008) 5. Mo'k Workbench (Bisson, Nédellec, & Canamero, 2000) 6. DODDLE II (Yamaguchi, 2001) 7. WEB->KB (Craven et al., 2000)
6	Manual Ontology Tools	1. FCA-Merge (Stumme & Maedche, 2001) 2. SMART (Noy & Musen, 1999) 3. PROMPT (Noy & Musen, 2000) 4. Chimera (McGuinness, Fikes, Rice, & Wilder, 2000)
7	Web based ontology description tools	1. SOAM (Li, Du, & Wang, 2005) → Uses SHOE, RDF(S), DAMN+OIL, OWL

Nédellec, & Canamero, 2000) either to restrict the relevant features or to identify the similarity between the grouping items when they are large in number. Most of the existing clustering algorithms are formulated for handling the English texts where the delimiters can be easily identified. In languages where delimiters or stop words are not cited, clustering methods fail to group them even approximately. Few methods were proposed to cluster documents written in natural language.

An Ontology-based Text Mining (OTMM) approach is used in Ma et al. (2012) for clustering documents written in native Chinese language. The words/concepts and their relationship are stored in ontology repository. It clusters the research proposals together to identify a particular research project. It has also discussed on the challenges faced during clustering, and these are listed below:

- Identifying the features
- Identifying the relationship between the documents
- Minimizing the features selected
- Reducing the dimensionality of data
- Fixing the borderline of the cluster

Few of these challenges in ontology clustering are handled in Yue, Zuo, Peng, Wang, and Han (2015) where a domain specific ontology is constructed for feature selection. The clustering here is done with the help of domain ontology. It has given better clustering results as it reduces the dimensionality of the data by identifying the correlation factor which indicates the dependency between the terms. The domain ontology is then constructed for feature selection. It reduces noise and outliers from the data.

Ontology is used in combination with topic identification to identify the semantic relation between the entities (Shi & Setchi, 2012). The topic identification from the documents is done using OntoSVD and K-Means methods. It identifies the semantic relation by combining the terms and named entities. The named entities are semantic indexes. It compares the topic identification performance of SVD approach and OntoSVD approach and has proven that the OntoSVD has given good performance than SVD. The various clustering methods are given in Table 5.

8.5.2 Ontology-Based Classification

It is a supervised machine learning approach where the grouping is done based on class labels. A classifier is built by testing the classification algorithm with multiple training sets. It is uncertain to predict the performance of classification algorithm, as the behavior of classifier depends on the input data and the chosen class label. In cases, where a document falls under multiple categories with equal probability

Table 5. Different clustering methods using ontology

	Clustering Method	Clustering Objective	Application
1	Self-Organized Mapping (SOM) (Ma et al., 2012)	Neural network algorithm, clusters data based on similarities	It groups the research proposals based on similarity.
2	ASIUM (Faure & Nédellec, 1998)	Conceptual clustering method. This method has restricted forming a maximal of two clusters	It improves the efficiency of syntactic parser
3	Fuzzy Clustering (Yue, Zuo, Peng, Wang, & Han, 2015)	It reduces the dimensionality of the feat are set and improves the clustering result. It outperforms latent semantic analysis and bisection K-means.	It clusters similar documents in food safety supervision domain of government.
4	K-means clustering (Shi & Setchi, 2012)	A semantic information management system that identifies the semantic relationship among stored memories using K-means clustering and singular value decomposition.	Automatic management of stored memories of royal families.
5	Mo'K workbench (Bisson, Nédellec, & Canamero, 2000)	Conceptual clustering method	It supports ontology building process
6	K-means clustering (Trappey, Wang, Hoang, & Trappey, 2013)	A patent clustering method that takes correlation matrix as input and forms clusters applying the k-means algorithm.	Identifies the life span of dental implant patent technologies.
7.	Bisecting *K*-means algorithm (BISK) (Zanjani, Dastjerdi, Asgarian, Shahriyari, & Kharazian, 2015)	Bisection K-Means algorithm	Clustering Persian text using semantic relationship

leading to ambiguous classification, ontology based classification helps in classifying the documents in using a hierarchy. The characteristics or attributes are aligned in a hierarchy in the ontology which eases the classification by allocating it to the nearest parent or relevant child attribute. Table 6 lists the classification methods using ontology.

Ontology assists in classifying both text information and video.

Context based ontology (Fan, Luo, Gao, & Jain, 2007) helps in classification of video using hierarchical boosting classification algorithm.

Ontology-based text classification (Chi, Lin, & Hsieh, 2014) is used to enhance the solution space during development of an application-job hazard analysis. The ontology was used in mapping the unsafe scenarios and safe solutions. A domain dependent text classification using ontology (Sanchez-Pi, Martí, & Garcia, 2016) is used for text classification. It compares ontology classifier and term relevance ontology classifier. Support vector machines (SVM) are supervised learning models that perform non-linear classification of data was introduced in 1995 by Vapnik. It is used in many real-time applications to classify data (Ali, Kwak, Kim, 2016 ; Bi, Zhou, Lu, & Wang, 2007; Zhang, Yoshida, & Tang, 2008).

8.5.3 Ontology in Machine Learning

Machine learning helps in providing knowledge to the computer to learn and understand things on its own. An increasing emphasis on social media application has overwhelmed the growth of machine learning, neural network, fuzzy logics and artificial intelligence.

1.   Ontology using Fuzzy logics

A fuzzy based sentiment analysis (Lau, Li, & Liao, 2014) is implemented on customer reviews for extracting marked intelligence. This system has outperformed the opinion finder (Wilson, 2005) with an overall accuracy of 79.10%. Ontology and Fuzzy sets are used together in knowledge extraction in Huang, Lee, Wang, and Kao (2014); and Liu (2013).

2.   Ontology in handling Big data

Ontology web language (OWL) is modified in García, García-Nieto, and Aldana-Montes (2016) for consolidating the tracked data in web source. A series of analysis were made with data from Google Analytics and Piwik digital foot prints. The data were converted into a standard format and stored in the RDF repository. The data from multiple sources were sorted, and ontology helps in fusing the data in RDF (Resource Description Framework).

Table 6. Classification methods using ontology

	Classification Methods	**Application**
1	Hierarchical boosting (Fan, Luo, Gao, & Jain, 2007)	Video classification
2	Principal component analysis and document vectorization (Chi, Lin, & Hsieh, 2014)	Job hazard analysis
3	Term relevance ontology classifier algorithm (Sanchez-Pi, Martí, & Garcia, 2016)	Occupational health and security application
4	Support vector machines (Ali, Kwak, Kim, 2016 ; Bi, Zhou, Lu, & Wang, 2007; Zhang, Yoshida, & Tang, 2008).	Online review classification, Gene ontology, Text classification

8.5.4 Ontology-Driven Knowledge Maintenance

Ontology is used in knowledge discovery and data mining (KDD facilitating the task of mining data. The ontology also contributes to the evaluation of a system.

- In the traditional method of data mining, the keywords given by the user were used for KDD, and a revised model is proposed in Hilario, Nguyen, Do, Woznica, and Kalousis, (2011) which rely on both data and algorithm.
- The automated process of data mining and KDD (Bernstein, Hill, & Provost, 2002) uses Intelligent Discovery Assistants (IDA) which works effectively in validating the state change using ontology.
- Ontology validates the knowledge discovery workflow in Záková, Kremen, Zelezny, and Lavrac, (2011). It is done by mapping the input to the expected output using ontology workflow.

Ontology development (López, Gómez-Pérez, Sierra, & Sierra, 1999; Suárez-Figueroa et al., 2008) describes the different methods of constructing the ontology for applications. Table 7 lists a couple of ontology used on other domain.

8.6 PERFORMANCE MEASURES FOR RESULT VALUATION

In the field of information retrieval and machine learning, a set of performance measures is used to assess the quality of the system. The articles which use the performance measures are listed in Table 8.

- **Precision:** Or positive predicted value is the fragment of retrieved instances that are relevant. Precision defines "How valuable the results are?" and signifies the quality of the system.

Table 7. Ontology in other domains

	Methodologies for building ontologies	Scope and Focus	Ontology Representation
1	METHONTOLOGY – (López, Gómez-Pérez, Sierra, & Sierra, 1999)	Chemical Ontology	Uses ODE(ontology design environment) to generate code in into lingua
2	NeON - (Suárez-Figueroa et al, 2008)	Distributed network	OWL-DL

- **Recall:** Or true positive rate is the fragment of relevant instances that are retrieved. Recall defines "How complete the results are?" and quantifies the system.
- **F-Measure:** Is the harmonic mean of precision and recall
- **Accuracy:** Is the measure of precision and recall weighted by bias and prevalence.
- **TF-IDF:** (Term Frequency – Inverse Document Frequency) Defines "How informative is a word in a corpus inclosing many documents?"
- **Entropy** is an attribute selection measure which measures the homogeneity of the sample.

Table 8. Articles and the performance measures

	Performance Measures	Papers
1	Precision	(Lin & Pantel, 2001; Szpektor, Tanev, Dagan, & Coppola, 2004; Velardi, Navigli, Cuchiarelli, & Neri, 2005; Navigli & Velardi, 2004; Weng, Tsai, Liu, & Hsu, 2006; Köhler, Philippi, Specht, & Rüegg, 2006; Ma et al., 2012; Jiang & Tan, 2005; Du, Li, & King, 2009; Yue, Zuo, Peng, Wang, & Han, 2015; Shi & Setchi, 2012; Cimiano & Völker, 2005; Gacitua, Sawyer, & Rayson, 2008; Bisson, Nédellec, & Canamero, 2000; Fan, Luo, Gao, & Jain, 2007; Chi, Lin, & Hsieh, 2014, Sanchez-Pi, Martí, & Garcia, 2016; Maedche & Staab, 2000; Ali, Kwak, Kim, 2016; Lau, Li, & Liao, 2014; Kuptabut & Netisopakul, 2016; Guo, Tang, & Kao, 2014; Sulthana & Subburaj, 2016; Sulthana & Ramasamy, 2017)
2	Recall	(Velardi, Navigli, Cuchiarelli, & Neri, 2005; Navigli & Velardi, 2004; Weng, Tsai, Liu, & Hsu, 2006; Köhler, Philippi, Specht, & Rüegg, 2006; Ma et al., 2012; Jiang & Tan, 2005; Du, Li, & King, 2009; Shi & Setchi, 2012; Cimiano & Völker, 2005; Gacitua, Sawyer, & Rayson, 2008; Fan, Luo, Gao, & Jain, 2007; Chi, Lin, & Hsieh, 2014; Sanchez-Pi, Martí, & Garcia, 2016; Maedche & Staab, 2000; Ali, Kwak, Kim, 2016; Lau, Li, & Liao, 2014; Kuptabut & Netisopakul, 2016; Guo, Tang, & Kao, 2014; Sulthana & Subburaj, 2016; Sulthana & Ramasamy, 2017)
3	F-measure	Ma et al., 2012; Faure & Nédellec, 1998; Jiang & Tan, 2005; Sanchez-Pi, Martí, & Garcia, 2016; Zhang, Yoshida, & Tang, 2008; Zhang, Yoshida, & Tang, 2008; Kuptabut & Netisopakul, 2016; Guo, Tang, & Kao, 2014; Sulthana & Subburaj, 2016; Sulthana & Ramasamy, 2017)
4	TF-IDF	(Weng, Tsai, Liu, & Hsu, 2006; Cimiano & Völker, 2005; Maedche, & Staab, 2000)
5	Entropy	(Yue, Zuo, Peng, Wang, & Han, 2015; Shi & Setchi, 2012; Cimiano & Völker, 2005)

8.7 OPEN ISSUES

Furthermore, after an elaborate study on state of the art of the system, it is observed that certain issues still exist in this domain which is depicted below:

- **Making System Understands:** The information collected from various sources is highly unstructured. The system has to validate the information before processing them. Ontologies are used in knowledge sharing and reuse between human and computer. Ontology plays a major role in assisting the computers in speeding up the access and to reduce the waiting time of the user.
- **Implement Machine Learning:** Design the project/ontology to understand the system by executing the training set multiple times. Making the system understand what the user wants, by mitigating the biases and inconsistencies made by human
- **Ontology Representation:** The representation of ontology is designed so as to include the quantified concepts/ attributes, which minimizes the time to access.
- **Ontology Maintenance:** An incremental update to evolve ontology over time has to be done periodically.
- **Identifying the Relations:** The relationships between the concepts are identified using ontology. The identified concepts are inter-connected through the discovered relations. Candidates that represent the domain are identified and are sorted according to the strength of the relations. Co-occurrence patterns of the concepts are studied to identify the n-ary relations.
- **Big data and Ontology:** The senses of ontology have to be fine-tuned to handle the V's of big data.
- **Valuation Yardstick:** The performance benchmark of ontology has to be identified to know its quality.

8.8 CONCLUSION

Ontology is emerging as a powerful technique and is used in semantic web, knowledge discovery and machine learning. In this chapter, we have given an overview of ontology types, ontology application, and ontology in the web, rule ontology, etc. The interesting feature of ontology is its extensibility and reusability. We discuss the same and also the ontology learning tools and the creation of ontology. Ontology-based classification and clustering are also discussed in this paper. We carry out measures so as to compare its efficiency and accuracy. We have listed the performance measures and their references used in conjunction with ontology. This chapter although not comprehensive but extensive.

REFERENCES

Ali, F., Kwak, K. S., & Kim, Y. G. (2016). Opinion mining based on fuzzy domain ontology and Support Vector Machine: A proposal to automate online review classification. *Applied Soft Computing*, *47*, 235–250. doi:10.1016/j.asoc.2016.06.003

Bernstein, A., Hill, S., & Provost, F. (2002). *Intelligent assistance for the data mining process: An ontology-based approach*. Academic Press.

Bi, R., Zhou, Y., Lu, F., & Wang, W. (2007). Predicting Gene Ontology functions based on support vector machines and statistical significance estimation. *Neurocomputing*, *70*(4-6), 718–725. doi:10.1016/j.neucom.2006.10.006

Bisson, G., Nédellec, C., & Canamero, D. (2000, August). Designing Clustering Methods for Ontology Building-The Mo'K Workbench. In ECAI workshop on ontology learning (Vol. 31). Academic Press.

Buitelaar, P., Olejnik, D., & Sintek, M. (2004, May). A protégé plug-in for ontology extraction from text based on linguistic analysis. In *European Semantic Web Symposium* (pp. 31-44). Springer. 10.1007/978-3-540-25956-5_3

Chi, N. W., Lin, K. Y., & Hsieh, S. H. (2014). Using ontology-based text classification to assist Job Hazard Analysis. *Advanced Engineering Informatics*, *28*(4), 381–394. doi:10.1016/j.aei.2014.05.001

Cimiano, P., & Völker, J. (2005, June). text2onto. In *International conference on application of natural language to information systems* (pp. 227-238). Springer.

Consortium, T. G. O. (2001). Creating the gene ontology resource: Design and implementation. *Genome Research*, *11*(8), 1425–1433. doi:10.1101/gr.180801 PMID:11483584

Craven, M., DiPasquo, D., Freitag, D., McCallum, A., Mitchell, T., Nigam, K., & Slattery, S. (2000). Learning to construct knowledge bases from the World Wide Web. *Artificial Intelligence*, *118*(1-2), 69–113. doi:10.1016/S0004-3702(00)00004-7

Decker, S., Erdmann, M., Fensel, D., & Studer, R. (1999). Ontobroker: Ontology based access to distributed and semi-structured information. In *Database Semantics* (pp. 351–369). Boston, MA: Springer. doi:10.1007/978-0-387-35561-0_20

Du, T. C., Li, F., & King, I. (2009). Managing knowledge on the Web–Extracting ontology from HTML Web. *Decision Support Systems*, *47*(4), 319–331. doi:10.1016/j.dss.2009.02.011

Du, T. C., Li, F., & King, I. (2009). Managing knowledge on the Web–Extracting ontology from HTML Web. *Decision Support Systems*, *47*(4), 319–331. doi:10.1016/j.dss.2009.02.011

ECAI-02. (2002). *Ontology Learning Tools Workshop*. Retrieved from http://www-sop.inria.fr/acacia/WORKSHOPS/ ECAI2002-OLT /accepted-papers.html

ECAI-02. (2002). *Workshop on Machine Learning and Natural Language Processing for Ontology Engineering*. Retrieved from http://www-sop.inria.fr/ acacia/WORKSHOPS/ECAI2002-OLT/

Fan, J., Luo, H., Gao, Y., & Jain, R. (2007). Incorporating concept ontology for hierarchical video classification, annotation, and visualization. *IEEE Transactions on Multimedia*, *9*(5), 939–957. doi:10.1109/TMM.2007.900143

Faure, D., & Nédellec, C. (1998, May). A corpus-based conceptual clustering method for verb frames and ontology acquisition. In LREC workshop on adapting lexical and corpus resources to sublanguages and applications (Vol. 707, No. 728, p. 30). Academic Press.

Fellbaum, C. (1998). *WordNet: An Electronic Lexical Database (Language, Speech, and Communication)*. Academic Press.

Fernández, M., Cantador, I., López, V., Vallet, D., Castells, P., & Motta, E. (2011). Semantically enhanced information retrieval: An ontology-based approach. *Journal of Web Semantics*, *9*(4), 434–452. doi:10.1016/j.websem.2010.11.003

Gacitua, R., Sawyer, P., & Rayson, P. (2008). A flexible framework to experiment with ontology learning techniques. *Knowledge-Based Systems*, *21*(3), 192–199. doi:10.1016/j.knosys.2007.11.009

Gal, A., Modica, G., & Jamil, H. (2004, March). Ontobuilder: Fully automatic extraction and consolidation of ontologies from web sources. In *Data Engineering, 2004. Proceedings. 20th International Conference on* (p. 853). IEEE.

García, M. D. M. R., García-Nieto, J., & Aldana-Montes, J. F. (2016). An ontology-based data integration approach for web analytics in e-commerce. *Expert Systems with Applications*, *63*, 20–34. doi:10.1016/j.eswa.2016.06.034

Gašević, D., Zouaq, A., Torniai, C., Jovanović, J., & Hatala, M. (2011). An approach to folksonomy-based ontology maintenance for learning environments. *IEEE Transactions on Learning Technologies*, *4*(4), 301–314. doi:10.1109/TLT.2011.21

Gasse, F., & Haarslev, V. (2008, April). DLRule: A Rule Editor plug-in for Protege. OWLED (Spring).

Golbreich, C. (2004, November). Combining rule and ontology reasoners for the semantic web. In *International Workshop on Rules and Rule Markup Languages for the Semantic Web* (pp. 6-22). Springer. 10.1007/978-3-540-30504-0_2

Gruber, T. R. (1993). A translation approach to portable ontology specifications. *Knowledge Acquisition*, *5*(2), 199–220. doi:10.1006/knac.1993.1008

Gruber, T. R. (1995). Toward principles for the design of ontologies used for knowledge sharing? *International Journal of Human-Computer Studies*, *43*(5-6), 907–928. doi:10.1006/ijhc.1995.1081

Guo, Y. W., Tang, Y. T., & Kao, H. Y. (2014). Genealogical-Based Method for Multiple Ontology Self-Extension in MeSH. *IEEE Transactions on Nanobioscience*, *13*(2), 124–130. doi:10.1109/TNB.2014.2320413 PMID:24893362

Hakeem, A., & Shah, M. (2004, August). Ontology and taxonomy collaborated framework for meeting classification. In *Pattern Recognition, 2004. ICPR 2004. Proceedings of the 17th International Conference on* (*Vol. 4*, pp. 219-222). IEEE. 10.1109/ICPR.2004.1333743

Hilario, M., Nguyen, P., Do, H., Woznica, A., & Kalousis, A. (2011). Ontology-based meta-mining of knowledge discovery workflows. In *Meta-learning in computational intelligence* (pp. 273–315). Berlin: Springer. doi:10.1007/978-3-642-20980-2_9

Hoxha, J., Jiang, G., & Weng, C. (2016). Automated learning of domain taxonomies from text using background knowledge. *Journal of Biomedical Informatics*, *63*, 295–306. doi:10.1016/j.jbi.2016.09.002 PMID:27597572

Hu, W., Qu, Y., & Cheng, G. (2008). Matching large ontologies: A divide-and-conquer approach. *Data & Knowledge Engineering*, *67*(1), 140–160. doi:10.1016/j.datak.2008.06.003

Huang, C. J., & Cheng, M. Y. (2008). Similarity Measurement of Rule-based Knowledge Using Conditional Probability. *Journal of Information Science and Engineering, 24*(3).

Huang, H. D., Lee, C. S., Wang, M. H., & Kao, H. Y. (2014). IT2FS-based ontology with soft-computing mechanism for malware behavior analysis. *Soft Computing, 18*(2), 267–284. doi:10.100700500-013-1056-0

Jiang, X., & Tan, A. H. (2005, November). Mining ontological knowledge from domain-specific text documents. In *Data Mining, Fifth IEEE International Conference on* (pp. 4-pp). IEEE. 10.1109/ICDM.2005.97

K-CAP. (2003, October 26). *Knowledge mark-up and Semantic Annotation workshop.* Retrieved from http://km.aifb.kit.edu/ws/semannot2003/

Köhler, J., Philippi, S., Specht, M., & Rüegg, A. (2006). Ontology based text indexing and querying for the semantic web. *Knowledge-Based Systems, 19*(8), 744–754. doi:10.1016/j.knosys.2006.04.015

Kuptabut, S., & Netisopakul, P. (2016). Event Extraction using Ontology Directed Semantic Grammar. *Journal of Information Science and Engineering, 32*(1), 79–96.

Lau, R. Y., Li, C., & Liao, S. S. (2014). Social analytics: Learning fuzzy product ontologies for aspect-oriented sentiment analysis. *Decision Support Systems, 65,* 80–94. doi:10.1016/j.dss.2014.05.005

Lenat, D. B., & Guha, R. V. (1989). *Building large knowledge-based systems; representation and inference in the Cyc project.* Academic Press.

Li, M., Du, X., & Wang, S. (2005, October). A semi-automatic ontology acquisition method for the semantic web. In *International Conference on Web-Age Information Management* (pp. 209-220). Springer. 10.1007/11563952_19

Li, X., Martínez, J. F., & Rubio, G. (2016). A new fuzzy ontology development methodology (FODM) proposal. *IEEE Access: Practical Innovations, Open Solutions, 4,* 7111–7124. doi:10.1109/ACCESS.2016.2621756

Lin, D., & Pantel, P. (2001, August). DIRT@ SBT@ discovery of inference rules from text. In *Proceedings of the seventh ACM SIGKDD international conference on Knowledge discovery and data mining* (pp. 323-328). ACM. 10.1145/502512.502559

Lindberg, C. (1990). The Unified Medical Language System (UMLS) of the National Library of Medicine. *Journal of the American Medical Record Association, 61*(5), 40–42. PMID:10104531

Liu, C. H., Lee, C. S., Wang, M. H., Tseng, Y. Y., Kuo, Y. L., & Lin, Y. C. (2013). Apply fuzzy ontology and FML to knowledge extraction for university governance and management. *Journal of Ambient Intelligence and Humanized Computing, 4*(4), 493–513. doi:10.100712652-012-0139-6

López, M. F., Gómez-Pérez, A., Sierra, J. P., & Sierra, A. P. (1999). Building a chemical ontology using methontology and the ontology design environment. *IEEE Intelligent Systems & their Applications, 14*(1), 37–46. doi:10.1109/5254.747904

Ma, J., Xu, W., Sun, Y. H., Turban, E., Wang, S., & Liu, O. (2012). An ontology-based text-mining method to cluster proposals for research project selection. *IEEE Transactions on Systems, Man, and Cybernetics. Part A, Systems and Humans, 42*(3), 784–790. doi:10.1109/TSMCA.2011.2172205

Maedche, A., & Staab, S. (2000, August). The text-to-onto ontology learning environment. In *Software Demonstration at ICCS-2000-Eight International Conference on Conceptual Structures* (Vol. 38). Academic Press.

Maedche, A., & Staab, S. (2000). Mining ontologies from text. *Knowledge Engineering and Knowledge Management Methods, Models, and Tools,* 169-189.

Maedche, A., Staab, S., Hovy, E., & Nedellec, C. (2001). The IJCAI-2001 Workshop on Ontology Learning. *Proceedings of the Second Workshop on Ontology Learning-OL'2001.*

Maedche, A. D. (2002). *Ontology learning for the semantic Web*. Kluwer Academic Publishers.

Mahesh, K., & Nirenburg, S. (1996). Meaning representation for knowledge sharing in practical machine translation. *Proceedings of the FLAIRS Track on Information Interchange.*

McGuinness, D. L., Fikes, R., Rice, J., & Wilder, S. (2000, April). *An environment for merging and testing large ontologies*. Academic Press.

Navigli, R., & Velardi, P. (2004). Learning domain ontologies from document warehouses and dedicated web sites. *Computational Linguistics, 30*(2), 151–179. doi:10.1162/089120104323093276

Niu, J., & Issa, R. R. (2015). Developing taxonomy for the domain ontology of construction contractual semantics: A case study on the AIA A201 document. *Advanced Engineering Informatics, 29*(3), 472–482. doi:10.1016/j.aei.2015.03.009

Noy, N. F., & Musen, M. A. (1999, October). SMART: Automated support for ontology merging and alignment. *Proc. of the 12th Workshop on Knowledge Acquisition, Modelling, and Management (KAW'99)*.

Noy, N. F., & Musen, M. A. (2000, August). Algorithm and tool for automated ontology merging and alignment. *Proceedings of the 17th National Conference on Artificial Intelligence (AAAI-00). Available as SMI technical report SMI-2000-0831*.

Padhy, N., Mishra, D., & Panigrahi, R. (2012). *The survey of data mining applications and feature scope*. arXiv preprint arXiv:1211.5723

Park, S., & Kang, J. (2012). Using rule ontology in repeated rule acquisition from similar web sites. *IEEE Transactions on Knowledge and Data Engineering, 24*(6), 1106–1119. doi:10.1109/TKDE.2011.72

Park, S., Kang, J., & Kim, W. (2007, June). A framework for ontology based rule acquisition from web documents. In *International Conference on Web Reasoning and Rule Systems* (pp. 229-238). Springer. 10.1007/978-3-540-72982-2_17

Park, S., & Lee, J. K. (2007). Rule identification using ontology while acquiring rules from Web pages. *International Journal of Human-Computer Studies, 65*(7), 659–673. doi:10.1016/j.ijhcs.2007.02.004

Pearl, J. (1984). *Heuristics: intelligent search strategies for computer problem solving*. Academic Press.

Reynolds, D. (2004). *Jena 2 inference support*. Retrieved from http://jena.sourceforge.net/inference/index.html

Sanchez-Pi, N., Martí, L., & Garcia, A. C. B. (2016). Improving ontology-based text classification: An occupational health and security application. *Journal of Applied Logic, 17*, 48–58. doi:10.1016/j.jal.2015.09.008

Shi, L., & Setchi, R. (2012). User-oriented ontology-based clustering of stored memories. *Expert Systems with Applications, 39*(10), 9730–9742. doi:10.1016/j.eswa.2012.02.087

Staab, S., Maedche, A., Nedellec, C., & Wiemer-Hastings, P. (2000). ECAI'2000 Workshop on Ontology Learning. *Proceedings of the First Workshop on Ontology Learning-OL'2000*.

Stumme, G., & Maedche, A. (2001, August). FCA-Merge: Bottom-up merging of ontologies. *IJCAI (United States), 1*, 225–230.

Su, J. H., Yeh, H. H., Philip, S. Y., & Tseng, V. S. (2010). Music recommendation using content and context information mining. *IEEE Intelligent Systems*, *25*(1), 16–26. doi:10.1109/MIS.2010.23

Suárez-Figueroa, M. C., de Cea, G. A., Buil, C., Dellschaft, K., Fernández-López, M., Garcia, A., ... Villazon-Terrazas, B. (2008). NeOn methodology for building contextualized ontology networks. *NeOn Deliverable D*, *5*, 4–1.

Sulthana, A. R., & Subburaj, R. (2016). An improvised ontology based K-means clustering approach for classification of customer reviews. *Indian Journal of Science and Technology*, *9*(15).

Sulthana, R., & Ramasamy, S. (2017). Context Based Classification of Reviews Using Association Rule Mining, Fuzzy Logics and Ontology. *Bulletin of Electrical Engineering and Informatics*, *6*(3), 250–255.

Szpektor, I., Tanev, H., Dagan, I., & Coppola, B. (2004). Scaling web-based acquisition of entailment relations. *Proceedings of the 2004 Conference on Empirical Methods in Natural Language Processing*.

Trappey, C. V., Wang, T. M., Hoang, S., & Trappey, A. J. (2013). Constructing a dental implant ontology for domain specific clustering and life span analysis. *Advanced Engineering Informatics*, *27*(3), 346–357. doi:10.1016/j.aei.2013.04.003

Van Rees, R. (2003). Clarity in the usage of the terms ontology, taxonomy and classification. *CIB REPORT*, *284*(432), 1–8.

Velardi, P., Navigli, R., Cuchiarelli, A., & Neri, R. (2005). Evaluation of OntoLearn, a methodology for automatic learning of domain ontologies. *Ontology Learning from Text: Methods, evaluation and applications, 123*(92).

Volz, R., Oberle, D., Staab, S., & Motik, B. (2003, May). KAON SERVER-A Semantic Web Management System. WWW (Alternate Paper Tracks).

Weng, S. S., Tsai, H. J., Liu, S. C., & Hsu, C. H. (2006). Ontology construction for information classification. *Expert Systems with Applications*, *31*(1), 1–12. doi:10.1016/j.eswa.2005.09.007

Wilson, T., Hoffmann, P., Somasundaran, S., Kessler, J., Wiebe, J., Choi, Y., . . . Patwardhan, S. (2005, October). OpinionFinder: A system for subjectivity analysis. In Proceedings of hlt/emnlp on interactive demonstrations (pp. 34-35). Association for Computational Linguistics.

Xia, F., Wang, W., Bekele, T. M., & Liu, H. (2017). Big scholarly data: A survey. *IEEE Transactions on Big Data, 3*(1), 18–35. doi:10.1109/TBDATA.2016.2641460

Yamaguchi, T. (2001, August). Acquiring Conceptual Relationships from Domain-Specific Texts. In *Workshop on Ontology Learning (Vol. 38*, pp. 69-113). Academic Press.

Yue, L., Zuo, W., Peng, T., Wang, Y., & Han, X. (2015). A fuzzy document clustering approach based on domain-specified ontology. *Data & Knowledge Engineering, 100*, 148–166. doi:10.1016/j.datak.2015.04.008

Záková, M., Kremen, P., Zelezny, F., & Lavrac, N. (2011). Automating knowledge discovery workflow composition through ontology-based planning. *IEEE Transactions on Automation Science and Engineering, 8*(2), 253–264. doi:10.1109/TASE.2010.2070838

Zanjani, M., Dastjerdi, A. B., Asgarian, E., Shahriyari, A., & Kharazian, A. A. (2015). Short Paper_. *Journal of Information Science and Engineering, 31*, 315–330.

Zhang, W., Yoshida, T., & Tang, X. (2008). Text classification based on multi-word with support vector machine. *Knowledge-Based Systems, 21*(8), 879–886. doi:10.1016/j.knosys.2008.03.044

Zou, Y., Finin, T., & Chen, H. (2004, April). F-owl: An inference engine for semantic web. In *International Workshop on Formal Approaches to Agent-Based Systems* (pp. 238-248). Springer. 10.1007/978-3-540-30960-4_16

Section 3
Tools and Techniques of Opinion Mining

Chapter 9
Tools of Opinion Mining

Neha Gupta
Manav Rachna International Institute of Research and Studies, India

Siddharth Verma
Manav Rachna International Institute of Research and Studies, India

ABSTRACT

Today's generation express their views and opinions publicly. For any organization or for individuals, this feedback is very crucial to improve their products and services. This huge volume of reviews can be analyzed by opinion mining (also known as semantic analysis). It is an emerging field for researchers that aims to distinguish the emotions expressed within the reviews, classifying them into positive or negative opinions, and summarizing it into a form that is easily understood by users. The idea of opinion mining and sentiment analysis tool is to process a set of search results for a given item based on the quality and features. Research has been conducted to mine opinions in form of document, sentence, and feature level sentiment analysis. This chapter examines how opinion mining is moving to the sentimental reviews of Twitter data, comments used in Facebook on pictures, videos, or Facebook statuses. Thus, this chapter discusses an overview of opinion mining in detail with the techniques and tools.

INTRODUCTION

Social networks have become part of our digital life and have changed the way we communicate significantly. There are 255 million of websites on the internet and therefore a lot of facts and opinions are available for companies and customers. Everybody is able to publish subjective information about products, brands and

DOI: 10.4018/978-1-5225-6117-0.ch009

companies. The exchange of information and opinions of consumers on the Web 2.0 also means that a greater confidence in the products, brands and services are created, which e.g. in the e-commerce -sector leads to a higher purchase probability. Therefore it is very important that companies are able to find, extract and analyze this user generated content, because these contents contain significant "real" market relevant data. Furthermore it is an easy and cheap way to gain a current market overview to generate new strategic, tactical and operational plans and policies as well as creating relevant brand messages.

Opinion Mining deals with scientific methods in order to find, extract, and systematically analyze product, company or brand related views on the internet. The identification of sentiment orientation (positive, neutral and negative) of consumers' Opinions is an essential part of the opinion mining process.

PROCESS MODEL OF OPINION MINING

The following process model describes steps, methods and tools to find, extract and analyze web data with regard to their sentiment orientation:

1. Selection of relevant data source
2. Selection of relevant method and tool to analyze the data
3. Pre-processing and pre-structuring of the contents on basis of the chosen methods
4. Transformation of the text in standard and further processed structure
5. Analyzing the content in relation to its semantic orientation
6. Evaluation of the methods and tools

Table 1 outlines commonly used methods and tools for each process step.

VARIOUS DATA SOURCES AVAILABLE FOR OPINION MINING

There are various data sources available on web, i.e. Blogs, Micro blogs, online posts, News feeds, Forums, review sites etc.

- **Blogs:** Blogs are nothing but the user own space or diary on internet where they can share their views, opinions about topics they want. Example indianbloggers.org, bloggersideas.com, digitaltrends.com

Table 1. Methods and tools for various steps of opinion mining

Step	Method (examples)	Tools (examples)
Selection of relevant data	1. Information retrieval on Web 2. Relevance Index	1. WebCrawler 2. RSS feeds, 3. APIs for gathering data
Preprocessing	Thesaurus, Ontologies, Tokenizer, Stemmer, Screen scrapper	1. RDF-OWL, 2. Alchemy API 3. GATE 4. UIMA 5. GETESS 6. Openthesaurus.de
Transformation	Part of speech tagger, Sentence splitter, Orthographic co-references	1. Tree Tagger 2. Sentence splitter, 3. Orthographic co-references
Analysis	Classification methods based on document or sentence level	1. Opinion Observer 2. Rapid Miner
Evaluation	Manual classification of sentiment orientation and feedback	

- **Online Reviews:** On Internet various review sites are available through that you can check online reviews of any product before purchasing that. Example sitejabber.com, toptenreviews.com, trustedreviews.com, in.pinterest.com
- **Micro Blogging:** Micro blogs allow users to exchange small elements of content such as short sentences, individual images, or video links", which may be the major reason for their popularity. Example twitter.com, jaiku.com, qaiku.com
- **Online Posts:** people share their own ideas, opinions, photos, videos, views, likes, dislikes, comments on specific topics etc. example facebook.com, myspace.com, skype.com, linkedin.com, plus.google.com, whatsapp.com, snapchat.com
- **Forums:** An Internet forum, or message board, is an online discussion site where people can hold conversations in the form of posted messages. Example forums.mysql.com, forums.cnet.com, forum.joomla.org, forums.digitalpoint.com, bookforum.com

VARIOUS TOOLS OF OPINION MINING

A wide variety of tools of opinion mining are available in the market for various purposes like data preprocessing, classification of text, clustering, opinion mining, sentiment analysis etc. List of various tools are:

1. Stanford CoreNLP
2. WEKA
3. NLTK (Python Framework)
4. Apache Open NLP
5. LingPipe
6. Gate
7. Pattern (Python Framework)
8. Opinion Finder

In this book chapter we will be discussing WEKA and NLTK (Python Framework) in detail.

NLTK

NLTK stand for natural language tool kit. It is a leading platform for building Python programs to work with human language data. It provides easy-to-use interfaces to over 50 corpora and lexical resources such as WordNet, along with a suite of text processing libraries for classification, tokenization, stemming, tagging, parsing, and semantic reasoning, wrappers for industrial-strength NLP libraries, and an active discussion forum.

NLTK includes graphical demonstrations and sample data. It is accompanied by a book that explains the underlying concepts behind the language processing tasks supported by the toolkit plus a cookbook. NLTK is intended to support research and teaching in NLP or closely related areas, including empirical linguistics, cognitive science, artificial intelligence, information retrieval, and machine learning. NLTK has been used successfully as a teaching tool, as an individual study tool, and as a platform for prototyping and building research systems. The various steps of NLTK toolkit are:

1. **Tokenization:** A Tokenizer in NLTK follows tokenization approach in natural language understanding by splitting a string into its sub-classes. It provides a lexical scanner that handles all the operators and delimiters.

Eg: A tokenizer tokenizes sentence into its morphological forms as given: "this is a dog" is tokenized to 'this','is','a','dog' which are the individual tokens generated.

2. **Stemming:** The idea of stemming in natural language processing is a sort of normalizing method. A word can vary and have different variations.

Eg: I was studying at night.

I studied at night.
I study.

So verb study has three variations above which can be stemmed to its root or canonical form. Hence studying is brought to its root form study which is shown below in the illustration.

Studying---Study

It can be either prefix stemming or suffix stemming which brings word to its root form. So it is a processing interface that removes suffixes and prefixes from the word and bring it down to its affix form. In NLTK toolkit stem (token) is an interface incorporated in NLTK for stemming

3. **C. Segmentation:** Sentence tokenizer or Sentence disambiguation is also known as sentence breaking or segmentation into its constituent words or tokens.

Eg: "Hello Sam. How are you." is segmented to two sentences: Hello Sam, How are you.

4. **D. Collocation:** Collocations as defined by (Navgli, 2009) are the words that occur commonly in same context and frequently. For example, the top ten bi-gram collocations in Genesis are listed below, as measured using Point-wise Mutual Information.

Collocation or lexical collocation means two or more words co-occur in a sentence more frequently than by chance. A collocation is an expression that forms a specific meaning. It may be noun phrase like large villa, verbal phrase like go down, idioms, or technical terms. Collocations are defined by constricted compositionality, that is, it is difficult to predict the meaning of collocation from the meaning of its parts. For example,

He is known for his **fair** and **square** dealings and everybody trusts his work.

Here **fair** and **square** means honest but if we take the individual words though the word fair gives somewhat closer meaning as it means just the word square confuses us. So instead of taking individual words one should take the collocation fair and square and find meaning. It shows that collocations play a key role in understanding sentences. Collocations are recursive in nature so they may contain more than two words in a sentence.

5. **E. Tagging:** Parts of Speech Tagging as discussed by Jose Camacho et al., (2015) means assigning lexical categories to words whether it is a noun phrase, verb phrase or prepositional phrase.

Eg: Cat chases a rat. Here Cat is assigned NN lexical category (noun); Chases is assigned VB lexical category (verb); NN is assigned lexical category (noun).

6. **E. Parsing:** Parsing as discussed by Huang et al. (2012) or Analyzing the Syntactic Structure of the sentence using Context Free Grammar.

A grammar is said to be recursive in nature only when a lexical category that is present on the left handside of the production rules appear on the right hand side of the production rules.The production Nom -> NP Nom (where Nom is the category of nominals) involves direct recursion on the category Nom, whereas indirect recursion on S arises from the combination of two productions, namely S -> NP DET and DET-> N S.

In this book chapter we will be discussing the NLTK kit using python framework. To work with NLTK kit, first we need to install and configure python as per the NLTK kit. Step by step process with screen shots are explained below:

Step 1: Configuring the Development Environment

Install python 3.5 in windows
Configure python with NLTK kit using the command **pip install nltk** (Figure 1)
Test nltk (Figure 2)
Downloading nltk is not enough as nltk will not work without the accompanying datasets.
So datasets needs to be downloaded separately.
The process of downloading and configuring the dataset in NLTK 3.x is simplified, and can be used as GUI utility.
Enter **import nltk** followed by **nltk.download()** in the python prompt.
Just press the download button in the screen below and wait for the data to be downloaded (Figure 3)

Figure 1. Configuring Python

```
Administrator: Command Prompt                                          —   □   ×
C:\Users\siddh\AppData\Local\Programs\Python\Python35\Scripts>pip install nltk
Collecting nltk
  Downloading nltk-3.2.5.tar.gz (1.2MB)
    100% |################################| 1.2MB 198kB/s
Requirement already satisfied: six in c:\users\siddh\appdata\local\programs\python\python35\lib\site-packages (from nltk

Installing collected packages: nltk
  Running setup.py install for nltk ... done
Successfully installed nltk-3.2.5

C:\Users\siddh\AppData\Local\Programs\Python\Python35\Scripts>
```

Figure 2.

```
Administrator: Command Prompt - python
>>>
>>>
>>> import nltk
>>>
```

Figure 3.

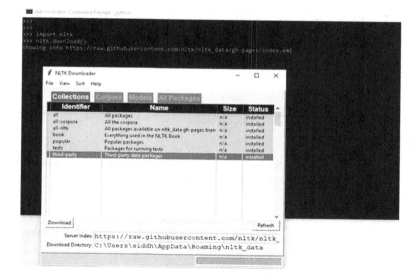

When all the rows turn green and status shows installed in the status column, we are all set to write code.

For development Pycharm IDE will be used, the same can also done on any python IDE or even using the basic prompt. (Pycharm makes coding lot easier)

Step 2: Analyzing and Tokenizing a Text Review

In the following program we will analyze any text review and try to convert the review into a numerical score. This is just a simple demonstration program and it needs optimization before using in a practical scenario (Figure 4)

The above class simply loads the **English. Pickle** dataset from the data corpus we earlier downloaded in NLTK. And then tokenizes the review.

So a text review like this

text = "'"""The food was absolutely wonderful, from preparation to presentation, very pleasing. We especially enjoyed the special bar drinks, the cucumber/ cilantro infused vodka martini and the K&P Aquarium was great (even took photos so we could try to replicate at home)."""**

Will become:

[['The', 'food', 'was', 'absolutely', 'wonderful', ',', 'from', 'preparation', 'to', 'presentation', ',', 'very', 'pleasing', '.'], ['We', 'especially', 'enjoyed', 'the', 'special', 'bar', 'drinks', ',', 'the', 'cucumber/cilantro', 'infused', 'vodka', 'martini', 'and', 'the', 'K', '&', 'P', 'Aquarium', 'was', 'great', '(', 'even', 'took', 'photos', 'so', 'we', 'could', 'try', 'to', 'replicate', 'at', 'home', ')', '.']]

Figure 4.

```
import nltk
class WordExtracter(object):
    def __init__(self):
        self.nltk_splitter = nltk.data.load('tokenizers/punkt/english.pickle')
        self.nltk_tokenizer = nltk.tokenize.TreebankWordTokenizer()

    def split(self, text):
        sentences = self.nltk_splitter.tokenize(text)
        tokenizedData = [self.nltk_tokenizer.tokenize(sent) for sent in sentences]
        return tokenizedData
```

Step 3: Tagging the tokens for Parts of Speech

In this step all the tokens will be tagged for parts of speech using pos_tag function in the nltk package.

"The process of classifying words into their parts of speech and labelling them accordingly is known as part-of-speech tagging, POS-tagging, or simply tagging. Parts of speech are also known as word classes or lexical categories. The collection of tags used for a particular task is known as a tagset." (Figure 5)

Ref--http://www.nltk.org/book/ch05.html

[[('The', 'The', ['DT']), ('food', 'food', ['NN']), ('was', 'was', ['VBD']), ('absolutely', 'absolutely', ['RB']), ('wonderful', 'wonderful', ['JJ']), (',', ',', [',']), ('from', 'from', ['IN']), ('preparation', 'preparation', ['NN']), ('to', 'to', ['TO']), ('presentation', 'presentation', ['NN']), (',', ',', [',']), ('very', 'very', ['RB']), ('pleasing', 'pleasing', ['VBG']), ('.', '.', ['.'])], [('We', 'We', ['PRP']), ('especially', 'especially', ['RB']), ('enjoyed', 'enjoyed', ['VBD']), ('the', 'the', ['DT']), ('special', 'special', ['JJ']), ('bar', 'bar', ['NN']), ('drinks', 'drinks', ['NNS']), (',', ',', [',']), ('the', 'the', ['DT']), ('cucumber/cilantro', 'cucumber/cilantro', ['NN']), ('infused', 'infused', ['VBD']), ('vodka', 'vodka', ['JJ']), ('martini', 'martini', ['NN']), ('and', 'and', ['CC']), ('the', 'the', ['DT']), ('K', 'K', ['NNP']), ('&', '&', ['CC']), ('P', 'P', ['NNP']), ('Aquarium', 'Aquarium', ['NNP']), ('was', 'was', ['VBD']), ('great', 'great', ['JJ']), ('(', '(', ['(']), ('even', 'even', ['RB']), ('took', 'took', ['VBD']), ('photos', 'photos', ['NNS']), ('so', 'so', ['IN']), ('we', 'we', ['PRP']), ('could', 'could', ['MD']), ('try', 'try', ['VB']), ('to', 'to', ['TO']), ('replicate', 'replicate', ['VB']), ('at', 'at', ['IN']), ('home', 'home', ['NN']), (')', ')', [')']), ('.', '.', ['.'])]]

Figure 5.

```
class PartsOfSpeechTagger(object):
    def __init__(self):
        pass

    def pos_tag(self, sentences):
        pos = [nltk.pos_tag(sentence) for sentence in sentences]
        pos = [[(word, word, [postag]) for (word, postag) in sentence] for sentence in pos]
        return pos
```

The POS tagger class uses pre defined tags and tries to match each and every word with a tag.

The POS Tagger uses Tags. The descriptions of all the tags are provided below. (Figure 6)

Figure 6.

Tag	Description
CC	Coordinating conjunction
CD	Cardinal number
DT	Determiner
EX	Existential *there*
FW	Foreign word
IN	Preposition or subordinating conjunction
JJ	Adjective
JJR	Adjective, comparative
JJS	Adjective, superlative
LS	List item marker
MD	Modal
NN	Noun, singular or mass
NNS	Noun, plural
NNP	Proper noun, singular
NNPS	Proper noun, plural
PDT	Pre determiner
POS	Possessive ending
PRP	Personal pronoun
PRP$	Possessive pronoun
RB	Adverb
RBR	Adverb, comparative
RBS	Adverb, superlative
RP	Particle
S	Simple declarative clause, i.e. one that is not introduced by a (possible empty) subordinating conjunction or a wh-word and that does not exhibit subject-verb inversion
SBAR	Clause introduced by a (possibly empty) subordinating conjunction
SBARQ	Direct question introduced by a wh-word or a wh-phrase. Indirect questions and relative clauses should be bracketed as SBAR, not SBARQ
SINV	Inverted declarative sentence, i.e. one in which the subject follows the tensed verb or modal.
SQ	Inverted yes/no question, or main clause of a wh-question, following the wh-phrase in SBARQ.
SYM	Symbol

Step 4: Tag the Words in the Review as Positive and Negative

The next step in the process is to tag the words in the review as positive and negative, for this step we need a pre defined dictionary of negative words for this we will use yaml format. The structure of the file looks like this

ABANDON: [negative]

ABANDONED: [negative]

We have used only 2 files negatives.yml and positives.yml within total of around 2700 words.

Links to these files are provided at the end of the chapter. But for making a proper usable application we will need a few more files like incrementers, decrementers and polarity flippers for handling more complicated reviews and getting better scores.

Also the accuracy of the results will depend on the no of words in the dictionary as well as the quality of the dictionary therefore for making a proper sentiment analysis application we will need a fairly large dictionaries with all kind of negative/ positive words and phrases. (Figures 7 and 8)

Result will be:

Figure 7.

```
y × __init__py × Main.py × positives.yml × DictionaryTagAnalyzer.py × negatives.yml ×

import yaml
class DictionaryTagAnalyzer(object):
    def __init__(self, dictionary_paths):
        files = [open(path, 'r') for path in dictionary_paths]
        dictionaries = [yaml.load(dict_file) for dict_file in files]
        map(lambda x: x.close(), files)
        self.dictionary = {}
        self.max_key_size = 0

        for curr_dict in dictionaries:
            for key in curr_dict:
                #print(key)
                if key in self.dictionary:
                    self.dictionary[key].extend(curr_dict[key])
                else:
                    self.dictionary[key] = curr_dict[key]
                    self.max_key_size = max(self.max_key_size, len(key))

    def tag(self, postagged_sentences):
```

Figure 8.

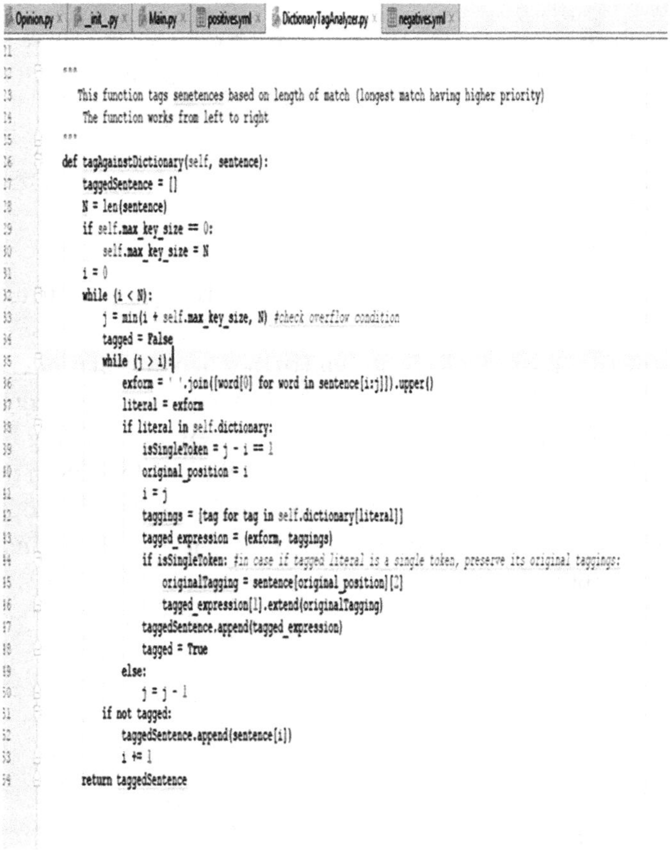

```
Opinion.py    _init_.py    Main.py    positives.yml    DictionaryTagAnalyzer.py    negatives.yml

"""
This function tags senetences based on length of match (longest match having higher priority)
The function works from left to right
"""
def tagAgainstDictionary(self, sentence):
    taggedSentence = []
    N = len(sentence)
    if self.max_key_size == 0:
        self.max_key_size = N
    i = 0
    while (i < N):
        j = min(i + self.max_key_size, N) #check overflow condition
        tagged = False
        while (j > i):
            exform = ' '.join([word[0] for word in sentence[i:j]]).upper()
            literal = exform
            if literal in self.dictionary:
                isSingleToken = j - i == 1
                original_position = i
                i = j
                taggings = [tag for tag in self.dictionary[literal]]
                tagged_expression = (exform, taggings)
                if isSingleToken: #in case if tagged literal is a single token, preserve its original taggings
                    originalTagging = sentence[original_position][2]
                    tagged_expression[1].extend(originalTagging)
                taggedSentence.append(tagged_expression)
                tagged = True
            else:
                j = j - 1
        if not tagged:
            taggedSentence.append(sentence[i])
            i += 1
    return taggedSentence
```

Tagged Statements--------------------->
[[('The', 'The', ['DT']),
('food', 'food', ['NN']),
('was', 'was', ['VBD']),
('absolutely', 'absolutely', ['RB']),
('WONDERFUL', [*'positive', 'JJ'*]),
(',', ',', [',']),
('from', 'from', ['IN']),
('preparation', 'preparation', ['NN']),
('to', 'to', ['TO']),
('presentation', 'presentation', ['NN']),
(',', ',', [',']),

('very', 'very', ['RB']),
('PLEASING', [*'positive', 'VBG'*])*,*
('.', '.', ['.'])],
[('We', 'We', ['PRP']),
('especially', 'especially', ['RB']),
('ENJOYED', [*'positive', 'VBD'*])*,*
('the', 'the', ['DT']),
('special', 'special', ['JJ']),
('bar', 'bar', ['NN']),
('drinks', 'drinks', ['NNS']),
(',', ',', [',']),
('the', 'the', ['DT']),
('cucumber/cilantro', 'cucumber/cilantro', ['NN']),
('infused', 'infused', ['VBD']),
('vodka', 'vodka', ['JJ']),
('martini', 'martini', ['NN']),
('and', 'and', ['CC']),
('the', 'the', ['DT']),
('K', 'K', ['NNP']),
('&', '&', ['CC']),
('P', 'P', ['NNP']),
('Aquarium', 'Aquarium', ['NNP']),
('was', 'was', ['VBD']),
('GREAT', [*'positive', 'JJ'*])*,*
('(', '(', ['(']),
('even', 'even', ['RB']),
('took', 'took', ['VBD']),
('photos', 'photos', ['NNS']),
('so', 'so', ['IN']),
('we', 'we', ['PRP']),
('could', 'could', ['MD']),
('try', 'try', ['VB']),
('to', 'to', ['TO']),
('replicate', 'replicate', ['VB']),
('at', 'at', ['IN']),
('home', 'home', ['NN']),
(')', ')', [')']),
('.', '.', ['.'])]]
Sentiment Score----------------------> 4

After tagging the sentiment score is 4 which means the system has identified 4 words as positive from the dictionary.

Since the dictionary is having very few words so tagging has identified only 4 otherwise the result would have been better.

Similarly we can analyze and summarize any textual data using NLTK with various data sets.

WEKA

WEKA is the product of the University of Waikato (New Zealand) and was first implemented in its modern form in 1997. It uses the GNU General Public License (GPL). The software is written in the Java™ language and contains a GUI for interacting with data files and producing visual results (think tables and curves). It also has a general API, so you can embed WEKA, like any other library, in your own applications to such things as automated server-side data-mining tasks.

Weka is a collection of machine learning algorithms for data mining tasks. The algorithms can either be applied directly to a dataset or called from your own Java code. Weka contains tools for data pre-processing, classification, regression, clustering, association rules, and visualization. It is also well-suited for developing new machine learning schemes.

Weka contains a collection of visualization tools and algorithms for data analysis and predictive modeling, together with graphical user interfaces for easy access to these functions. The original non-Java version of Weka was a Tcl/Tk front-end to (mostly third-party) modeling algorithms implemented in other programming languages, plus data preprocessing utilities in C, and a Makefile-based system for running machine learning experiments. This original version was primarily designed as a tool for analyzing data from agricultural domains, but the more recent fully Java-based version (Weka 3), for which development started in 1997, is now used in many different application areas, in particular for educational purposes and research. Advantages of Weka include:

- Free availability under the GNU General Public License.
- Portability, since it is fully implemented in the Java programming language and thus runs on almost any modern computing platform.
- A comprehensive collection of data preprocessing and modeling techniques.
- Ease of use due to its graphical user interfaces.

Weka supports several standard data mining tasks, more specifically, data preprocessing, clustering, classification, regression, visualization, and feature selection. All of Weka's techniques are predicated on the assumption that the data is available as one flat file or relation, where each data point is described by a fixed number of attributes (normally, numeric or nominal attributes, but some other attribute types are also supported). Weka provides access to SQL databases using Java Database Connectivity and can process the result returned by a database query. Weka provides access to deep learning with Deeplearning4j. It is not capable of multi-relational data mining, but there is separate software for converting a collection of linked database tables into a single table that is suitable for processing using Weka. Another important area that is currently not covered by the algorithms included in the Weka distribution is sequence modeling.

WEKA User interfaces

Weka's main user interface is the Explorer, but essentially the same functionality can be accessed through the component-based Knowledge Flow interface and from the command line. There is also the Experimenter, which allows the systematic comparison of the predictive performance of Weka's machine learning algorithms on a collection of datasets.

The Explorer interface features several panels providing access to the main components of the workbench:

- The Preprocess panel has facilities for importing data from a database, a comma-separated values (CSV) file, etc., and for preprocessing this data using a so-called filtering algorithm. These filters can be used to transform the data (e.g., turning numeric attributes into discrete ones) and make it possible to delete instances and attributes according to specific criteria.
- The Classify panel enables applying classification and regression algorithms (indiscriminately called classifiers in Weka) to the resulting dataset, to estimate the accuracy of the resulting predictive model, and to visualize erroneous predictions, receiver operating characteristic (ROC) curves, etc., or the model itself (if the model is amenable to visualization like, e.g., a decision tree).
- The Associate panel provides access to association rule learners that attempt to identify all important interrelationships between attributes in the data.
- The Cluster panel gives access to the clustering techniques in Weka, e.g., the simple k-means algorithm. There is also an implementation of the expectation maximization algorithm for learning a mixture of normal distributions.
- The Select attributes panel provides algorithms for identifying the most predictive attributes in a dataset.

- The Visualize panel shows a scatter plot matrix, where individual scatter plots can be selected and enlarged, and analyzed further using various selection operators.

Working With WEKA Explorer

In this book chapter we will be discussing Weka as one of the sentiment classification tool of opinion mining on a movie reviews dataset. The goal is to classify a movie review as *positive* or *negative* (for the reviewed movie). The dataset consists of 1200 user-created movie reviews. The reviews are equally partitioned into a positive set and a negative set.

Each review consists of a plain text file (.txt) and a class label representing the overall user opinion. The class attribute has only two values: *pos* (positive) or *neg* (negative).

Below are the steps:

- Open Weka Explorer (Figure 9)
- Click on the open file (Figure 10)
- To perform this experiment we need a dataset of movie reviews, there are a lot of data set available, We are using a dataset of IMDB provided in Cornell university website, link of the data set is given below

http://www.cs.cornell.edu/people/pabo/movie-review-data

To import the reviews dataset in WEKA; WEKA provides a simple import procedure for textual datasets, by means of the *TextDirectoryLoader* component. By using this loader, WEKA automatically creates a relation with 2 attributes: the first one contains the text data, the second is the document class, as determined by the sub-directory containing the file (pos or neg).

- This dataset contains text file having approximately 1200 positive and negative reviews, one for each text file. (Figure 11)
- In the below screen choose the directory where your reviews are saved (Figure 12)
- This dataset contains 692 negative reviews and 694 positive reviews. (Figure 13)
- Click on Edit Button to change the default names (Figure 14)
- Right Click on Attribute name and select (Figure 15)
- Rename both Attributes to ReviewText and ReviewClass Respectively
- For the classification task to be done, a preliminary phase of text preprocessing and feature extraction is essential. We want to transform each text in a vector

Figure 9.

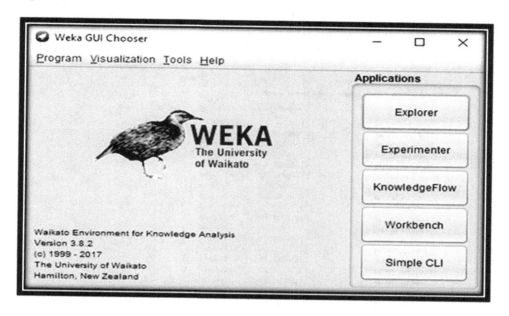

Figure 10.

Figure 11.

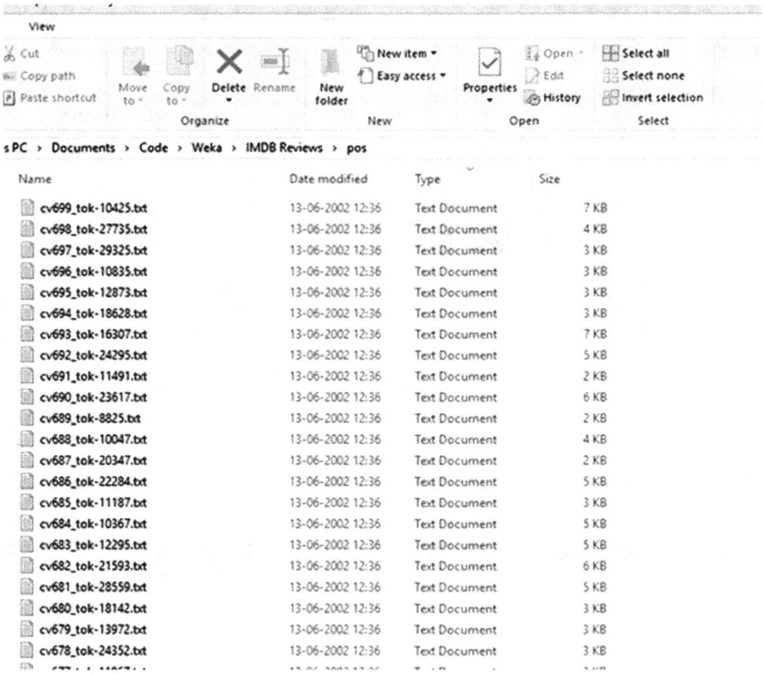

Figure 12.

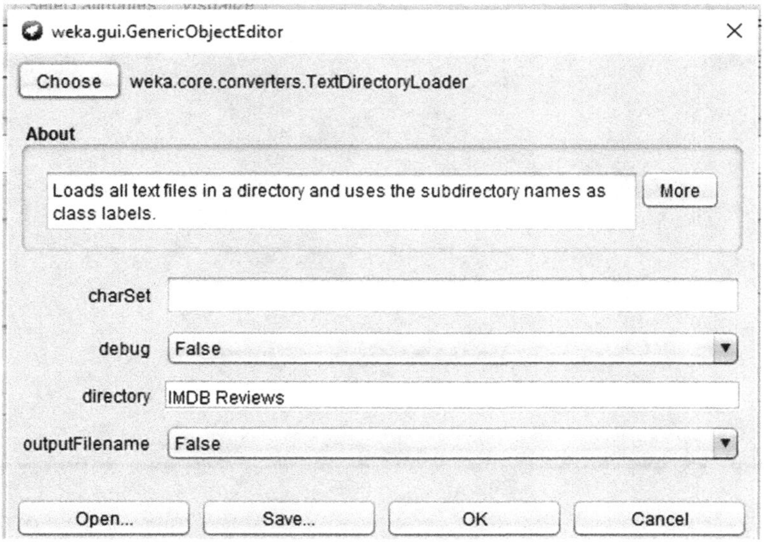

Figure13.

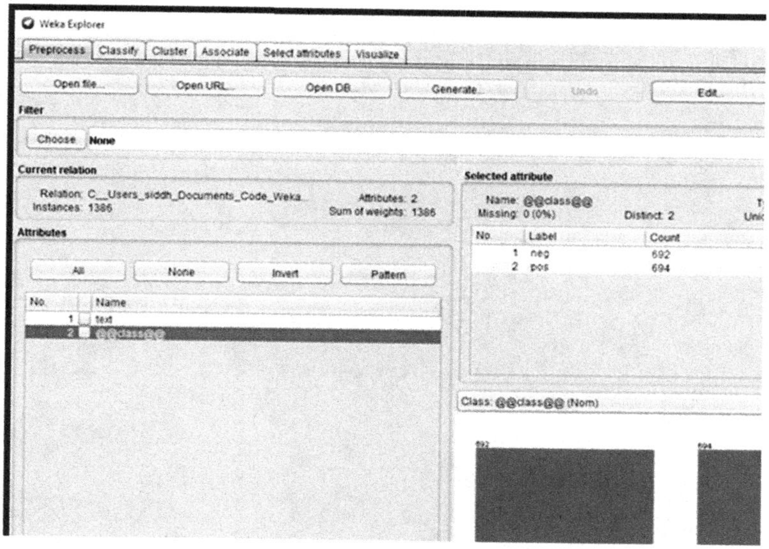

Figure 14.

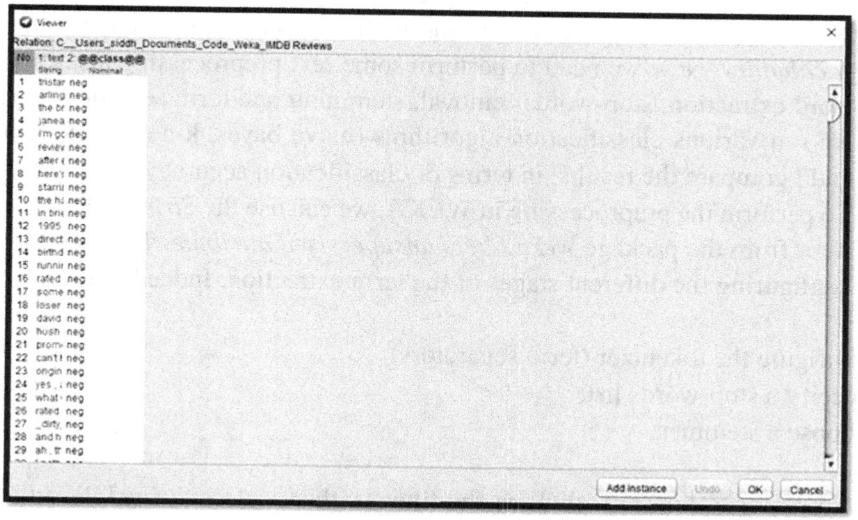

Figure 15.

form, in which each document is represented by the presence (or frequency) of some "important" terms; these terms are the ones contained in the *collection vocabulary*. Now we need to perform some text preprocessing tasks such as word extraction, stop-words removal, stemming and term selection. Finally, we run various classification algorithms (naive bayes, k-nearest neighbors) and I compare the results, in terms of classification accuracy.

- To perform the preprocessing in WEKA, we can use the *StringToWordVector* filter from the package *weka.filters.unsupervised.attribute*. This filter allows configuring the different stages of the term extraction. Indeed, you can:

Configure the tokenizer (term separators);
Specify a stop-words list;
Choose a stemmer.

- To perform this step, click on the filter textbox, select *StringToWordVector* from weka->filters->unsupervised->attribute->StringToWordVector (Figure 16)
- In this form keep other settings as default stop words file in stop words handler. It can be any stop words list. After completing the settings clicks on Ok and then click on apply in front of the filter.

Figure 16.

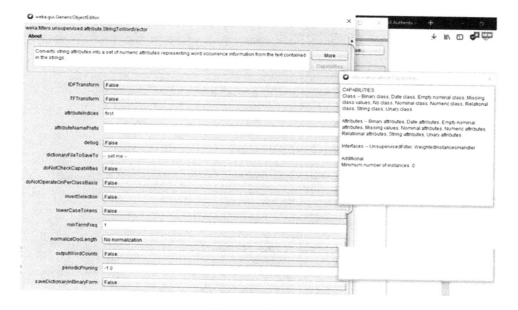

- The default text retrieval model used by the StringToWordVector filter is boolean: each document is represented with an n-dimensional boolean vector, where n is the size of the vocabulary, and each value models the presence or the absence of a vocabulary term in the document. One can also choose to use a frequency-based model such as the TF-IDF weighting model by setting to true the *TFTransform* and *IDFTransform* parameters.
- You can set a stop-words list by clicking on stopwords and setting to true the *useStopList* parameter. In my experiments I used a 630 english stop-words list (whose origin I don't recall) and the Porter's stemmer (for the english language).
- Furthermore, you can set a maximum limit on the number of words to be extracted by changing the *wordsToKeep* parameter (default is 1000 words) and a minimum document frequency for each term by means of the *minTermFreq* parameter (default is 1). The latter parameter makes the filter drop the terms that appear in less than *minTermFreq* documents (Figure 17)
- We get a relation containing 1272 binary attributes. Below is a histogram for the word awful which features mostly in negative reviews (Blue color is for negative reviews) (Figure 18)
- In the final pre-processing step we have to eliminate the poorly characterizing attribute

Figure 17.

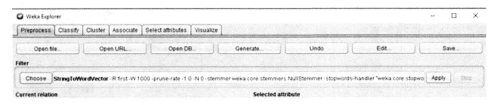

Figure 18.

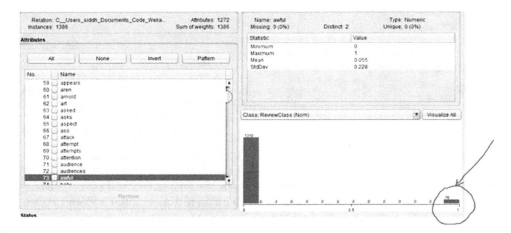

- The last preprocessing operation is the attribute selection. Eliminating the poorly characterizing attributes can be useful to get a better classification accuracy. For this task, WEKA provides the *AttributeSelection* filter from the *weka.filters.supervised.attribute* package. The filter allows choosing an attribute evaluation method and a search strategy The default evaluation method is *CfsSubsetEval (Correlation-based feature subset selection)*. This method works by evaluating the worth of a subset of attributes by considering the individual predictive ability of each feature along with the degree of redundancy between them.
- http://weka.sourceforge.net/doc.stable/weka/attributeSelection/ CfsSubsetEval.htm
- In this step we apply the Filter for this click on the filter textbox, select attribute selection filter from weka->filters->supervised->attribute->attribute selection (Figure 19)

Figure 19.

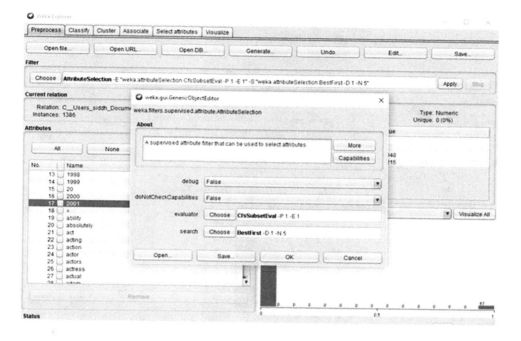

- As a result of applying the Attribute Selection filter we get a more refined result as in the below figure we can see the number of attributes comes down to 41. (Figure 20)
- On the filtered data, classifier will be implemented using various classification techniques. The classification problem is a supervised learning task that consists in assigning a class label to an unclassified tuple according to an already classified instance set that is used as a training set for the algorithm.
- Now we implement supervised learning approach to the filtered data
- For supervised learning, we use Naive Bayes classifier
- And for validation we are using 10-fold Cross validation method
- In WEKA, the Naive Bayes classifier is implemented in the *NaiveBayes* component from the *weka.classifiers.bayes* package. The best result achieved with this classifier has shown a correctness percentage of 79.432%, using a dataset on which only attribute selection was performed. Below are the screen shots. (Figures 21 and 22)
- The correctness percentage is 79.432%

Figure 20.

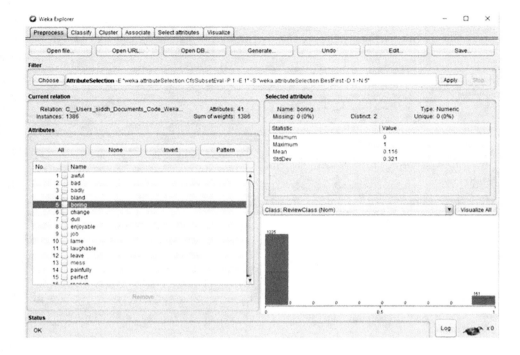

Figure 21.

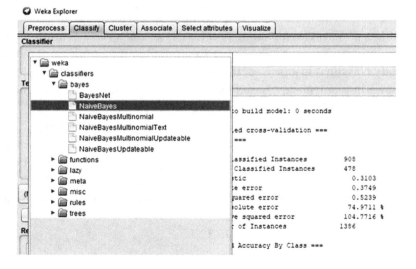

Figure 22.

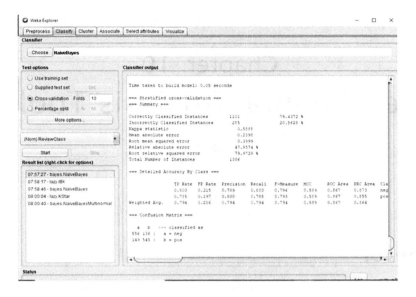

CONCLUSION

The idea of Opinion mining and Sentiment Analysis tool is to process a set of search results for a given item based on the quality and features. In this book chapter we have discussed two opinion mining tools, NLTK and WEKA to classify and analyze the opinion of the datasets. Concepts of these tools have been discussed with all the possible screen shots. User can use any other data set and can implement the opinion mining tool to classify and analyze the data for better decision making.

REFERENCES

Camacho-Collados, J., Pilehvar, M. T., & Navigli, R. (2015). Making sense of word embeddings. A unified multilingual semantic representation of concepts. *Proceedings of the Association for Computational Linguistics*, 741–751.

Huang, E. H., Socher, R., Manning, C. D., & Ng, A. Y. (2012).MaxMax: A Graph-based Soft Clustering Algorithm Applied to Word Sense Induction. *Proceedings of the 14th International Conference on Computational Linguistics and Intelligent Text Processing*, 368–381.

Navigli, R. (2009). Entity linking meets word sense disambiguation: A unified approach. *Transactions of the Association for Computational LinGUIstics*, 2, 231–244.

Chapter 10
Sentimental Analysis Tools

Sunil M. E.
PESITM, India

Vinay S.
PES College of Engineering, India

ABSTRACT

Opinion mining, also known as sentimental analysis, is the analysis of sentiment (emotion, affection, experience) towards the target object. In the present era, everyone is interested to know the opinions of others before making a decision or performing a task. Hence, it is necessary to collect the information (features) from relatives, friends, or web. These opinions or feedbacks help them to decide their action. With the advent of social media and use of digital technologies, web is a huge resource for data. However, it is time-consuming to read the data collected from the web and analyze it to arrive at informed decisions. This chapter provides complete overview of tools to simplify the operations of opinion mining like data collection, data cleaning, and visualization of predicted sentiment.

INTRODUCTION

In recent years sentimental analysis has become a very popular field in the age of web 2.0 with the evolution of social media networks and e-commerce (Song et al., 2011). This has a very diverse effect in the daily life of a common man. Users are keen to know the feedback about products, personalities, movies, ongoing events, etc which is available in social networks. According to Bill Gates, knowledge management plays an important role in searching, organizing, analyzing and optimizing information (Wenyun & Lingyun, 2010). Sentimental analysis is a part of data mining.

DOI: 10.4018/978-1-5225-6117-0.ch010

Merriam-Webster Online Dictionary (n.d.) defines "Opinion is a view, judgment, or appraisal formed in the mind about a particular matter. It is a belief stronger than impression and less strong than positive knowledge". The sentimental analysis tools help to find out people's feelings about event or issue mentioned in the form of text in social networks or in e-commerce websites. Many people also look up to reviews by previous customers for purchasing products in e-commerce websites like Amazon, Flipkart, E-bay, Infibeam. In web, information is widely spread and it is very difficult to read all relevant sources to know the feedback about the target object. This chapter explains how to gather the data, the tools and techniques used to decide the sentiment and how the results are presented using visualization techniques. Figure 1 represents the process of sentimental analysis.

- **Data Collection:** The main component of the sentimental analysis is data collection and it is a very challenging task due to privacy concerns like fear of sharing personal data. Data can be collected from many sources. It can be done through web crawling or by sharing questionnaires on web. The popular tools to create on line survey are Google forms, Survey Monkey, Poll Everywhere and also using social media networks like Facebook, Twitter etc.
- **Preprocessing:** Data collected is generally in structured, semi structured or unstructured formats. Approximately 90% of data is unstructured in nature according to Oracle corporation. So it might be incomplete (some attributes missing, record missing), noisy (duplicate) or inconsistent. It is necessary to perform preprocessing to convert the data to useful format. Hence multiple tools are used in preprocessing like R, weka, RapidMiner, Trifacta Wrangler, python, data preparator.

Figure 1. Opinion mining process

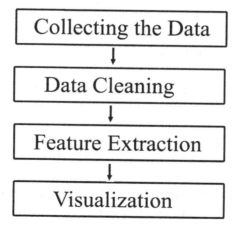

- **Feature Extraction:** Identifying and extracting the feelings or sentiment in a text is called feature extraction. It can be done through MATLAB, WEKA, SciKit-Learn, R, python with NLTK, Orange and KNIME.
- **Visualization:** It is a technique of representing the results of sentimental analysis process in graphical or pictorial formats. Multiple tools used in visualization are SneseNet, Micro_WNop, WEKA, MATLAB, Cognos, Thinkmap etc.

BACKGROUND

All the information generated by user in online can be very helpful for individuals or organizations to make decisions. Positive or negative opinion expressed by users about candidates contesting in elections, views about the policy decisions taken by government, user reviews on a product released by a manufacturing company can help the individual or organization to strategize are some of the examples of making use of information available. This involves determining people's attitudes based on a large amount of natural language documents (Mohandas et al., 2012).

Li et al. (2013) proposed a method Sentiment Classification with Polarity Shifting Detection. In this sentiment classification was done in three steps. First, using polarity-shifted sentences, corpus extracted some detection rules for detecting polarity shifting of sentimental words. Then, polarity-shifted words in the testing data were detected by using detection rules. Third, fully considering those polarity shifted words authors designed a novel term counting-based classifier.

Shein and Nyunt (2010) proposed a method for sentimental classification based on ontology and support vector machine (SVM) classifier. By using this method it is possible to view the strength or weakness of the products or objects in more detailed way. SVM along with formal concept analysis were used for classifying the software reviews as positive, negative or neutral.

Fong et al. (2014) have proposed an innovative analytical model based on event driven neural network system to analyze the public mood from unstructured online messages by implementing cultural moods analyzer using neural networks. Standard words that describe the corresponding moods were trained using Artificial Neural Network (ANN) and these moods are extracted from dictionaries as well as online news websites that supposedly report events in objectively correct moods (unbiased).

Keshtkar (2011) proposed a computational approach to the recognition and generation of emotion in text. Analysis was based on hierarchical emotion and mood classification using machine learning techniques in different levels of the hierarchy. Bootstrapping algorithm, as well as textual and syntactic similarities is used to extract the paraphrases for emotion terms. It also demonstrates that using sentiment orientation features improves the performance of classification. It considered LiveJournal blog corpus as a dataset.

In the thesis titled "In Extracting Opinion Targets from User-Generated Discourse with an Application to Recommendation Systems", Jakoband and Gurevych (n.d.) conducted a comprehensive study to analyze both unsupervised and supervised approaches on the extracted opinions and also addressed the additional challenges as the extraction of anaphoric opinion targets. Best results in the opinion target extraction task were achieved by the approach of Likelihood Ratio Test (LRT).

MAIN FOCUS OF THE CHAPTER

With the advent of social media and access to technology being made easier, people express their opinions largely through text. Thus to understand and analyze the text, sentimental analysis is required. Sentimental analysis makes use of knowledge like Natural Language Processing (NLP), Artificial Intelligence (AI), text mining. The main motto here is to understand the various tools and techniques used to perform sentimental analysis.

Consider a candidate wants to contest in an election. He is keen on knowing citizen's feelings and feedback about himself, his policies and other contesting candidates. He collects the information from various sources which are predominantly web. Analyzing collected information may help him to decide whether he may contest or not, his chances of winning, whether his policies needs tweaking. But to review all these opinions of others is a cumbersome task. Therefore, it requires a method to extract, summarize all the reviews using technology which will help the candidate.

Data Collection

The major component in the sentimental analysis is data. Data can be collected in many ways. Generally for applications data requirement is huge and the content which is available in the web is not structured. Hence it cannot be used for analysis easily. Sometimes data from public records agency (like data.gov.in) are available but the problem is data not in the required format. Other way to collect the data is by writing the code that extracts the raw data but it requires specialization in the field and it is a time consuming process. The best way to collect the data is web scraping. There are plenty of scraping tools available which does not require high degree of programming skills.

Another most commonly used method to collect data is through surveys or questionnaire. These are instruments used for collecting data in survey research. Based on specific topic a set of standardized questions are prepared to collect information about attitudes, behaviors, demographics, or opinions. Google Forms, Survey Monkey, and Poll Everywhere are commonly used websites or programs to create online surveys.

- **Web Scraper Chrome Extension:** Web scraper (n.d.) is a Google chrome extension used for scraping the data from particular website. Sitemap is created as shown in Figure 2 to know how a website should be traversed and what data should be extracted as shown in Figure 3 and extracted data can be exported to CSV file.
  - Install the Web Scraper extension from https://chrome.google.com/webstore/detail/web-scraper/
  - After adding extension to chrome select the website to collect data
  - Go to more tools(Control+Shift+I)
  - Select dock to bottom
  - Web Scraper-->create new site map-->Create sitemap
  - Add the selector to traverse the website
  - Sitemap-->selector graph
  - Sitemap-->Scrape
  - Download the CSV file
- **NetOwl Extractor:** NetOwl Extractor is licensed software used for advanced sentiment analysis, entity extraction, geo tagging and categorization. NetOwl (n.d) has the intelligent natural language processing (NLP) and industry standard entity extraction technologies. So it is more powerful than the traditional sentimental analysis where "positive" or "negative" sentiment is assigned at the document or sentence level. The main drawbacks of such traditional approaches are recognizing multiple and conflicting sentiments present within a single document or in sentence. Traditional approaches also fail to capture the precise object of a sentiment.

The main advantages of NetOwl are entity and aspect based sentimental analysis. It supports sentiment ontology, multilingual and automatically detects the language of a text. High accuracy and throughput can be achieved and it resolves co-referring extracted entities.

- **TWEEPY and Tweet Archivist:** Tweepy is a python library for accessing the Twitter API to collect the data from Twitter and Tweeterarchvist is a powerful tool to capture twitter data. It allows user to monitor the activities in tweets (Batool et al., 2013).

Figure 2. Sitemap creation

Figure 3.

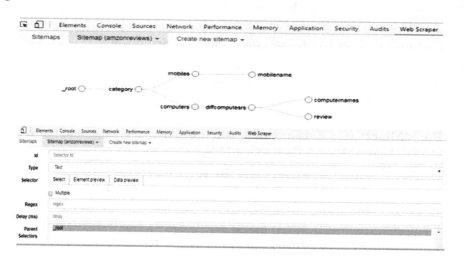

Pre-Processing

Data preprocessing is the process of correcting and repairing the data, since data quality plays an important role in sentimental analysis (Hamad & Jihad, 2011). Preprocessing consists of stop word removal, slang words replace, stemming, tokenization, parts of speech (POS) tagging. It also includes removal of ASCII code, new line, punctuation which are unwanted, extra white spaces, special character etc and conversion from upper to lower letter. Natural Language Tool Kit (NLTK and Python are commonly used to preprocess the dataset.

- **Drake:** Drake(n.d) is an open source project written in Clojure. It is text based data workflow tool that organizes command execution around data and its dependencies. The key features of Drake are simple-to-use, extensible, along with their inputs and outputs data processing steps are defined, Hadoop Distributed File System (HDFS) built-in. It supports multiple inputs and outputs and it can be run and managed by non programmers. It supports for inline Python, Ruby and Clojure. Drake automatically resolves their dependencies and calculates which commands to execute (based on file timestamps) and in what order to execute the commands (based on dependencies).

- **OpenRefine:** It is a powerful tool for working with messy data, formerly known as Google refines (Kusumasari & Fitria, 2014). This is used to cleaning, data format transforming used in web services and external data.

Feature Extraction and Visualization

Feature extraction is heart of sentimental analysis. Sentimental analysis uses the machine learning and statistical based methods to decide the sentiment associated with the target object. This section explains the various tools used in feature extraction and sentimental analysis.

- **RapidMiner:** It is a data mining and predictive analytics solution for the textual content. RapidMiner Studio(Alsaqer & Sasi, 2017) is priced by the number of logical processors and the amount of data used by the model. This can be used for data pre-processing, visualization, statistical modelling, evaluation and deployment. Rapidminer application interface is shown in Figure 4.
  - Install the RapidMiner Studio from https://rapidminer.com

Rapid Miner Panel consists of Repository, Process, Parameters and Operators. For every new project create a repository to have the data and processors. Create the process by adding and connecting operators. Operators are connected via there ports

- **KNIME:** Konstanz Information Miner (KNIME) is an open source platform solution for data-driven innovation, which helps to discover the potential hidden in data, mine for fresh insights, or predict new futures. It is used to

Figure 4. RapidMiner Overview

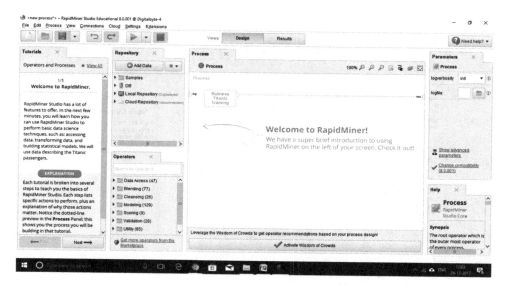

perform extraction, transformation and loading (Minanovic et al., 2014). KNIME is easy to scale, fast to deploy and easy to learn. Figure 5 shows the application interface of KNIME

- ○ Download and Install KNIME from https://www.knime.com/knime-analytics-platform
- ○ It supports XML, JSON, images, documents, and more data types
- ○ Integrations with machine learning libraries such as H2O, Keras for deep learning, Scikit-Learn.

- **WEKA:** Waikato Environment for Knowledge Analysis (WEKA) is open source Machine learning software issued under GNU to solve real world data mining problems developed by Department of Computer Science, University of Waikato, New Zealand. It was built using java and it is platform independent. It has the features like data mining, preprocessing, classification, regression, clustering, association rules, attributes selection, experiments, workflow, and visualization. The key features of WEKA (Kshirsagar & Deshkar, 2015) are approximately 49 data preprocessing tools, 76 classification and regression algorithms, 8 clustering algorithms and many other association and features selection algorithms. WEKA application interface is represented in Figure 6 consisting of three graphical user interfaces Explorer, Experimenter, and KnowledgeFlow.

- **WEKA using Explorer:** It is an environment for exploring data. WEKA explorer is shown in figure 7.

Figure 5. KNIME Overview

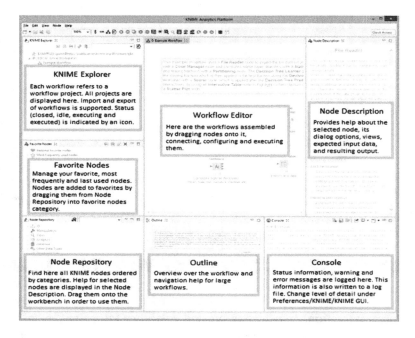

Figure 6. WEKA

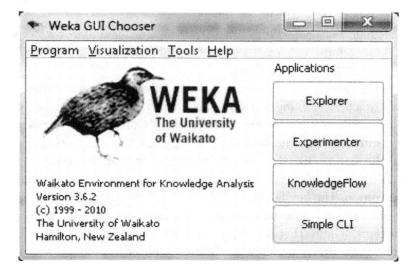

Figure 7. WEKA explorer

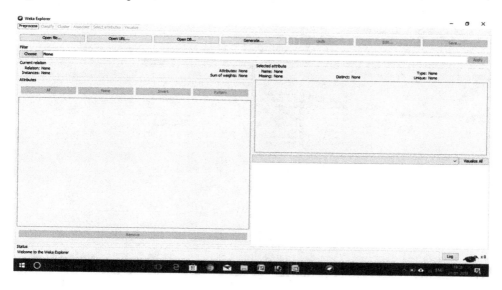

- ○ Download and Install WEKA from
- ○ https://www.cs.waikato.ac.nz/ml/weka/downloading.html
- ○ Loading the data from files in various formats Like ARFF (Attribute-Relation File Format), CSV, C4.5. WEKA uses the appropriate loader based on file type.
- ○ Open a file from local system as shown in figure 8.
- ○ Select the classifier from classifier box as shown in figure 9.
- ○ Set the test options from test box having the modes use training set, supplied test set, cross validation and percentage split.
- ○ Once the classifier, test option and class have been set, learning process is started by clicking start button.
- ○ By pressing shift and alt in classifier, output text area allows to store the output in various formats.
- ○ After training several classifiers, result is produced with several entries.
- ○ After selecting and configuring objects select the cluster schema from cluster box.
- ○ Searching and selecting the attributes for best prediction.
- ○ Finally visualize the results using 2D plots as shown in figure 10.
- • **WEKA using KnowledgeFlow:** KnowledgeFlow is alternative to WEKA explorer as a graphical front end. It provides a data-flow interface to WEKA. User can select the components from a tool bar, place them in layout canvas and connect together to make knowledge flow processing and analyzing the

Figure 8. File Opening

Figure 9. Selecting classifier

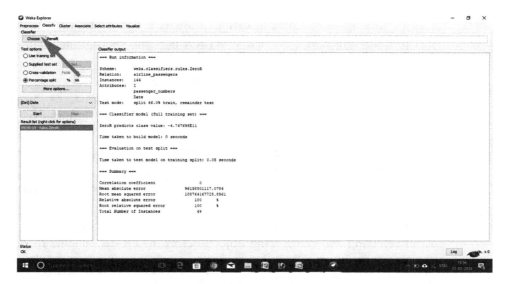

Figure 10. Selecting classifier

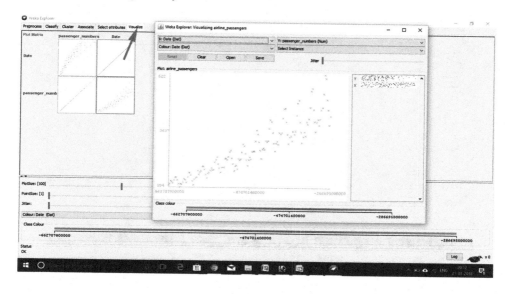

data. Knowledge flow environment is shown in Figure 11, Figure 12 show the components in the Knowledgeflow and complete work flow is shown in Figure 13.

- Load the data using ArffLoader from Data source tab.
- To select the arff file, right click on ArffLoader icon on layout select configure from edit.
- Add the ClassAssigner From Evaluation tab.
- Connect the ArffLoader and ClassAssigner by right clicking on ArffLoader and select the dataset from connections. Move the cursor from ArffLoader to ClassAssigner.
- Drag the CrossValidationFoldMaker from evaluation tab. Connect the ClassAssigner and CrossValidationFoldMaker by right clicking on ClassAssigner, select the dataset from connection.
- Add the Appropriate classification algorithm from Classifier tab.
- Connect the Classifier and CrossValidationFoldMaker twice to set the training data and test data.
- Add the ClassifierPerformanceEvaluator component from Evaluation tab to measure the performance of the algorithm. Connect the Classifier and ClassifierPerformanceEvaluator by right clicking on Classifier and select the batchclassifier.
- Add the appropriate Viewer component from Visualization tab to display the results. Right click on ClassifierPerformanceEvaluator to connect

Figure 11. WEKA KnowledgeFlow

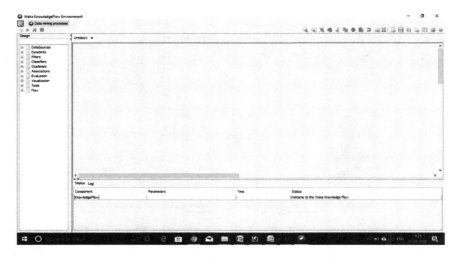

Figure 12. WEKA KnowledgeFlow Components

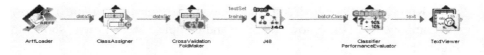

Figure 13. WEKA Workflow

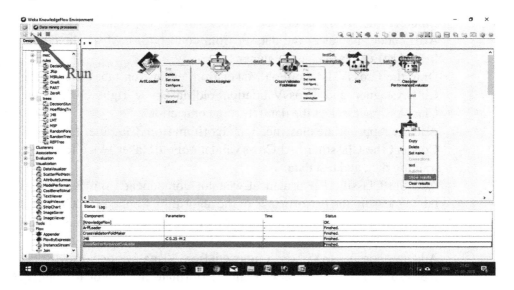

the ClassifierPerformanceEvaluator and TextViewer by selecting the text from ClassifierPerformanceEvaluator.

◦ Start the flow execution by Clicking on run button.

◦ Right click on TextViewer and select the Show results.

- **R-Programming:** It is a free software environment for statistical computing and graphics. Earlier it was developed using C and FORTRAN and now it is developed using the language called R. In recent years most of the data miners and data scientists are using R language (n.d) widely for developing statistical software and data analysis because it is easy to use and has the extensibility. Figure 14 shows the R-studio (n.d) interface.

- **Orange:** It is a python based open source machine learning and data visualization tool with large toolbox for interactive data analysis workflows. It performs simple data analysis and represents the results cleverly by exploring statistical distributions, box plots and scatter plots, or dive deeper with decision trees, hierarchical clustering, heatmaps, MDS and linear projections. Download and install Orange (Demsar et al., 2013) from https:// orange.biolab.si/download/

- **Spring XD:** Spring XD (Sabby et al., 2015) is a unified, distributed, and extensible system for data ingestion, real time analytics, batch processing, and data export. The project's goal is to simplify the development of big data applications.

- **LIWC2015 (Linguistic Inquiry and Word Count):** It is a text analysis module was built in java runs identically on Personal Computer and MAC. LIWC2015 (Pennebaker, 2105) reads a given text and counts the percentage of words that reflect different emotions by comparing each word in the text against a user-defined dictionary. Analyzing text files in two ways are: analyze text feature and analyze text in folder feature.

- **MALLET (Machine Learning for LanguagE Toolkit):** It is an open source Java-based package released under common public license for statistical natural language processing, document classification and clustering. It also supports for topic modeling, information extraction, and other machine learning applications. Download the MALLET (McCallum & Andrew 2002) from http://mallet.cs.umass.edu/download.php

- **Sentiment140:** It is a Twitter sentimental analysis tool used to find the positive or negative about the product or brand. Sentiment140 (n.d) was started as a class project from Stanford University.

- **NLTK and Python:** NLTK provides a pool of language processing tools used everywhere for data mining, machine learning, data scraping, and sentiment analysis and other various language processing tasks (Samal et al., 2017).

Figure 14. RStudio

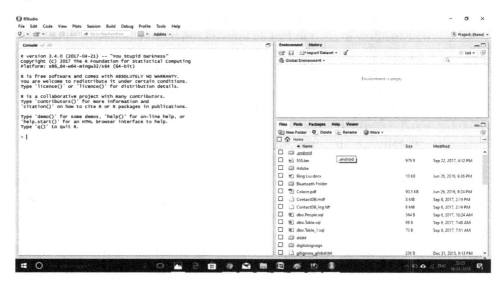

Figure 15. Repustate webpage

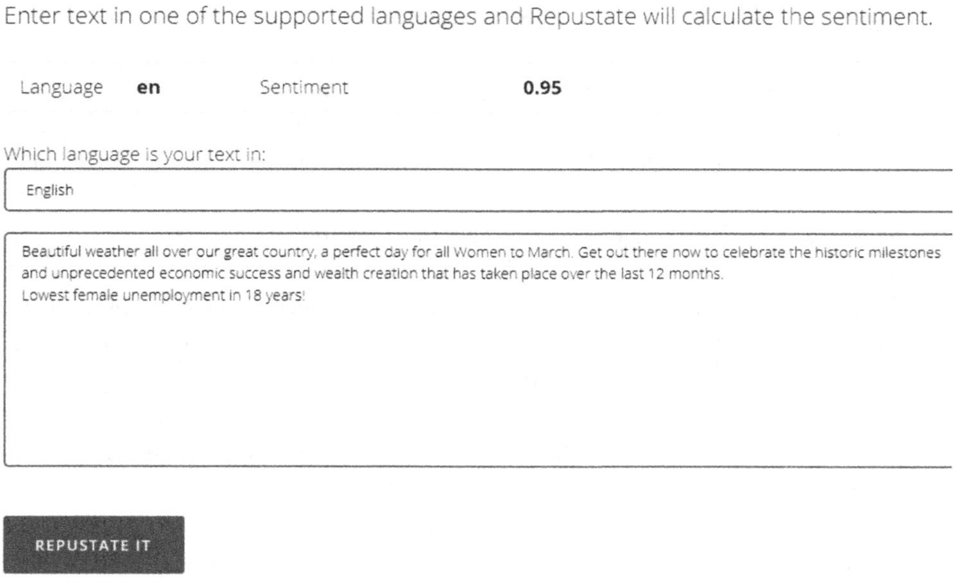

Enter text in one of the supported languages and Repustate will calculate the sentiment.

Language   **en**   Sentiment   **0.95**

Which language is your text in:

English

Beautiful weather all over our great country, a perfect day for all Women to March. Get out there now to celebrate the historic milestones and unprecedented economic success and wealth creation that has taken place over the last 12 months.
Lowest female unemployment in 18 years!

REPUSTATE IT

Python's Natural language toolkit (NLTK) is a suit of libraries for building python programs to work with human language data.

- ○ Tokenizing Text into words and sentences
- ○ Searching those words in WordNet Lexical Dictionary
- ○ Using appropriate techniques like stemming, lemmatization and Enchant spelling dictionary replace and correct the words
- ○ Create the corpora and custom corpus readers
- ○ Use part-of-speech taggers to annotate words
- ○ Extract and transfer chunks know as partial parsing
- ○ Transform text into feature dictionaries using appropriate classifier
- ○ Train the text classifier for sentimental analysis
- ○ Visualize the results

- **GATE (General Architecture for Text Engineering):** It is used for text analysis and General language processing. The advantage of the GATE (Cunningham et al., 2002) is comprehensiveness, scalability, extensibility and reusability. GATE provides an infrastructure for developing and deploying the software component for human language processing. It mainly consists of three components 1) Processing resources (PRs) 2) Language resources (LRs) 3) Visual Resources (VRs). PRs are programs or algorithms used for sort processing of text like tokenizing or dictionary lookup, parsing. LRs consisting of documents, corpora, Ontologies and VRs are used for visualization/.

  - ○ Install the platform specific installer from http://gate.ac.uk/sale/tao/splitch2.html#x5-220002.2.1
  - ○ Load ANNIE(A Nearly New Information Extraction System)
  - ○ Observe Document Reset, ANNIE English Tokeniser, ANNIE Gazetteer, ANNIE Sentence Splitter, ANNIE POS Tagger, ANNIE NE transducers, Orthomatcher, and JAPE PRs are loaded when double click on ANNIE with defaults.
  - ○ Run ANNIE over the document.
  - ○ Select the Language resources
  - ○ Create a Corpus pipeline in GATE
  - ○ Run ANNIE

- **LingPipe:** It is a toolkit for processing text using computational linguistics. LingPipe (Alias-I, 2002) classification framework separates the subjective from the objective sentences and assigns the polarity as positive or negative.

- **Twitter Sentimental Analysis Tools:** Twitter is most famous user generated content social media platform which provides the information about what is happening in the world and what people are talking about right now (n.d). It contains huge amount of textual information which provides useful insights on particular content. Many twitter analysis tools are available freely. But it is unclear how well these tools work. Sentiment polarity classification can be done using commercially and freely available tools like uClassify, ChatterBox, Sentiment140, Repustate etc.

- **Repustate:** It is simple RESTful API used for sentiment analysis in faster, reliable and accurate way. Repustate (Go A et al.,2009) handles the sentiment classification in the following way. Initially parts-of-speech tagging is applied on the given text using Repustate's part of speech tagger. Lemmatization is done to simplify the sentimental analysis. Finding the prior polarity gives the single words that have sentiment associated with them. Applying the negations and amplifiers, calculate the sentiment of entire block of text. Repustate's API allows for scoped sentiment and finally Repustate allows to create sentiment rules that are specific to industry and use case. API endpoint located at https://api.repustate.com/v3 and web interface is shown in figure 15.

  ○ **Example1:** @realDonaldTrump tweet: "Beautiful weather all over our great country, a perfect day for all Women to March. Get out there now to celebrate the historic milestones and unprecedented economic success and wealth creation that has taken place over the last 12 months. Lowest female unemployment in 18 years!." the sentiment found for tweet using repustate is 0.95

  ○ **Example2:** @realDonaldTrump tweet: "Great to see how hard Republicans are fighting for our Military and Safety at the Border. The Dems just want illegal immigrants to pour into our nation unchecked. If stalemate continues, Republicans should go to 51% (Nuclear Option) and vote on real, long term budget, no C.R.'s!." The sentiment found for tweet using repustate is -0.95

- **MeaningCloud:** It provides solution for multilingual sentimental analysis of textual information generated from different sources. It allows user to create own resources dictionary through dictionaries customization engine and customize sentimental analysis for own domain by defining own sentiment model through sentiment models customization engine. Request are submitted using GET or POST data submission to entry point of the API along with parameters like key, output format(of) language(lang), semantic disambiguation grouping(sdg), user dictionary(ud) and sentiment model etc.

- **ML Analyzer:** It is a swiss army knife of NLP and classification API's developed on the mashape platforms (Cieliebak et al., 2013). It includes sentimental analysis, stock symbol extraction and language extraction etc. It uses API keys to allow accesses to the API.

- **Lexalytics:** Lexalytics(2016) technology is one of the most tunable NLP engines in the market. It provides the products salience on-promise and semantria SaaS platforms for social media monitoring. Semantria can be used as cloud API and semantria excel application.

- **uClassify:** It is a free machine learning web service provides JSON and XML APIs which allows user to create and use text classifiers. It includes 3781 classifiers like sentiment, mood, topics language detection, gender analyzer etc. Sentiment classifier detects the sentiment as positive or negative. It works well with long and short texts and trained by 2.8 million documents (twitter data, Amazon product reviews, movie reviews). GenderAnalyzer_V5 this classifier finds the writer gender by analyzing the text. Figure 16 represents the uClassify webpage. Using uClassify, positive sentiment for example1 is 94% and negative sentiment is 6%. For example2 positive sentiment is 71% and negative sentiment is 21%.

- **Sentigem:** It is a sentimental analysis platform for English language. It provides the API service for computing text sentiment via a RESTful interface. Figure 17 represents the sentigem sentiment analysis interface and Figure 18 shows the results of Sentigem. Using sentigem, for example1 sentiment is positive, for exmple2 sentiment is negative.

- **Skyttle:** It is a SaaS system used for text analytics. Skyttle API performs phrase-level sentimental analysis of text in English, German, Russian, and French languages. It is also used for named entity extraction, keyword extraction.

- **SentiStrength:** It is a stand-alone sentiment analysis tool developed as a result of academic research (Thelwal et al., 2010). It assigns the polarity as positive or negative for the text based on sentiment lexicon and it has human level accuracy for short social web texts in English. Figure 19 shows the SentiStrength web application interface.

- **BPEF (Bootstrapping Ensemble Framework):** It is used to build the sentiment series for effective classification of user information as positive or negative. Process is divided into two stages expansion stage and contraction stage. In expansion stage, process is performed on data sets, features, and models components. In contraction stage step-wise, iterative model selection (SIMS) approach was used to select the final subset of parametric models utilized (Hassan et al., 2013).

- **LightSIDE:** It is an open text mining tool mainly used for research studies. It provides GUI for text extraction and classification experiments. It also supports for feature extraction techniques, multi-level modeling techniques and multi-domain learning approaches (Jeri L. Engelking, 1987)

Figure 16. uClassify web Interface

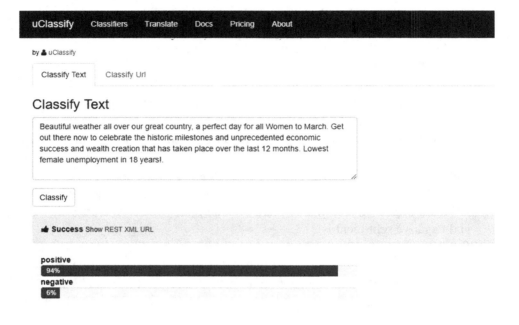

Figure 17. Sentigem web interface

Figure 18. Sentigem Result

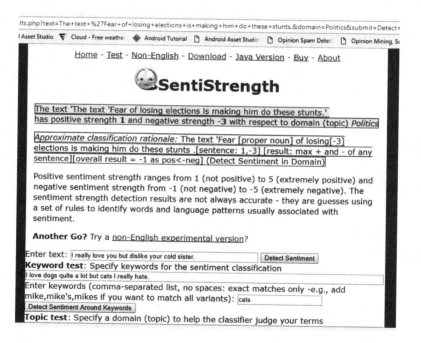

Figure 19. SentiStrength

Figure 20. Sentiment

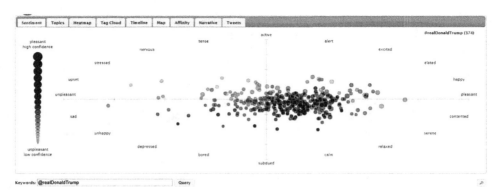

Figure 21. Topics

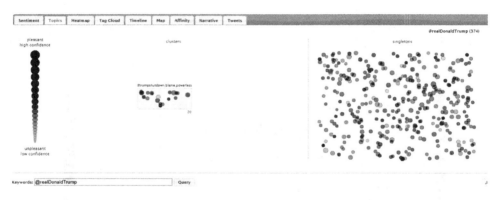

Figure 22. Heatmap

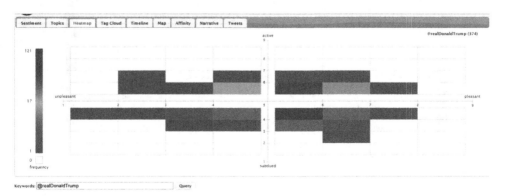

- **Tweet Visualizer:** It is a web app used to determine and visualize sentiment in short text. It was built by Dr. Christopher Healey, Goodnight Distinguished Professor in the Institute of Advanced Analytics at North Carolina State University. It runs on nine-point range scales where as other tools only says positive, negative or neutral. Tweets are visualized in different ways like sentiment, topics, heatmap, tag cloud, time line, map, affinity, narrative and tweet (n.d).

  ○ **Sentiment:** Tweets sentiment is represented by circles. Unpleasant and pleasant tweets are represented by blue and greens circle on right side and sedate, active tweets are represented by dark circle at bottom and brighter circle at top respectively. Figure 20 represents the sentiments generated by the keywords. Enter a keyword in sentiment viz which automatically downloads the recent tweets based on the keywords.

  ○ **Topics:** Topics are grouped into clusters based on the topics generated by keywords is shown in Figure 21.

  ○ **Heatmap:** It represents the number of tweets within different sentiment regions as 8*8 grids. Red and blue regions indicate many and few tweets respectively as shown in Figure 22.

  ○ **Tag Cloud Tab:** It represent frequently occurring tweets in different emotion region as represented in Figure 23.

  ○ **Timeline Tab:** It represents the pleasant and unpleasant tweets, when they are posted using green and blue bars as shown in Figure 24.

  ○ **Maps:** It highlights the location from where tweets were generated as shown in Figure 25.

  ○ **Affinity:** It highlights relationship between the frequent tweets, URLs, peoples and hashtags. Orange circles indicate the peoples, green circles indicate tweets, URLs are indicated by red circles and yellow represents the hash tags as shown in figure 26.

  ○ **Narrative:** It represents the set of tweets or threads conversation about same topic as represented in Figure 27.

  ○ Click the mouse on tweets shows the content of the tweet as shown in Figure 28.

  ○ **Tweet:** It represents the body of the tweet along with date, user, overall pleasure v and arousal a as shown in Figure 29.

Figure 23. Tag Cloud

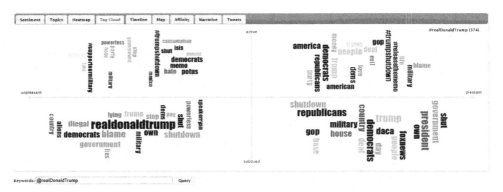

Figure 24. TimeLine

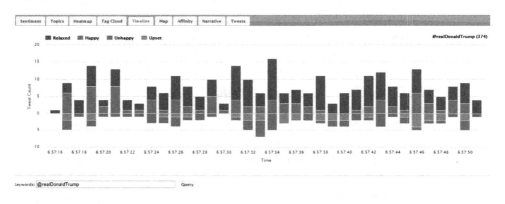

Figure 25. Map

Figure 26. Affinity

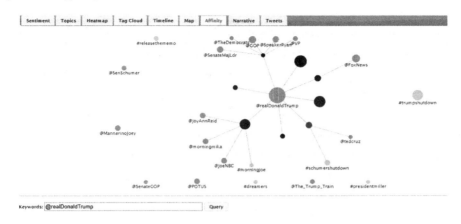

Figure 27. Narrative

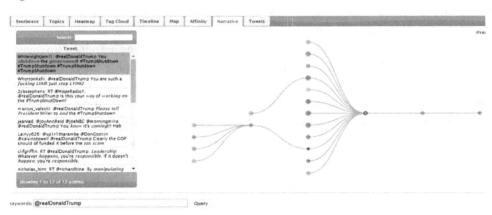

Figure 28. Tweets content with keywords

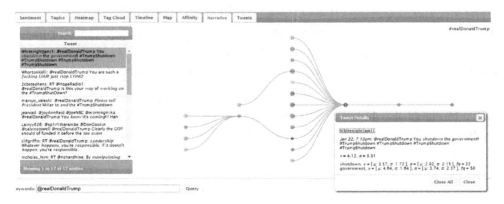

Figure 29. Tweets

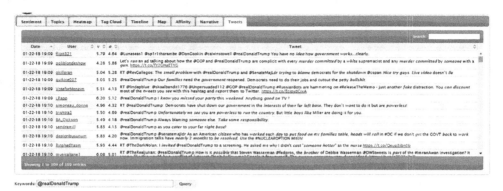

CONCLUSION

Sentimental analysis has become a popular area in the present era due to increasing number of active users, social media, e-commerce and online news channels, etc. This chapter provides the insights on sentimental analysis and the activities involved in sentimental analysis. It also explains the various tools available for sentimental analysis. There are plenty of open source and licensed tools available in market for sentimental analysis. Each tool has its own key features and advantages. The usage of a tool depends on the specific needs of an application. In a world where data is being generated at a huge pace, analyzing them and providing insights to individuals, businesses, and organizations is going to be one of the emerging areas of research in days to come.

REFERENCES

Alias-i. (2008). *LingPipe 4.1.0*. Retrieved from http://alias-i.com/lingpipe

Alsaqer, A. F., & Sasi, S. (2017). Movie review summarization and sentiment analysis using rapidminer. *International Conference on Networks & Advances in Computational Technologies (NetACT)*, 329-335. 10.1109/NETACT.2017.8076790

Anandan, S., Bogoevici, M., Renfro, G., Gopinathan, I., & Peralta, P. (2015). Spring XD: a modular distributed stream and batch processing system. In *Proceedings of the 9th ACM International Conference on Distributed Event Based Systems (DEBS '15)*. ACM. 10.1145/2675743.2771879

Batool, R., Khattak, A. M., Maqbool, J., & Lee, S. (2013). Precise tweet classification and sentiment analysis. *IEEE/ACIS 12th International Conference on Computer and Information Science (ICIS)*, 461-466. 10.1109/ICIS.2013.6607883

Cieliebak, Dürr, & Uzdilli. (2013). Potential and Limitations of Commercial Sentiment Detection Tools. *ESSEM, 1096.*

Cunningham, H. (2002). Article. *Computers and the Humanities, 36*(2), 223–254. doi:10.1023/A:1014348124664

Demsar, J., Curk, T., Erjavec, A., Gorup, C., Hocevar, T., Milutinovic, M., ... Zupan, B. (2013). Orange: Data Mining Toolbox in Python. *Journal of Machine Learning Research, 14*(Aug), 2349–2353.

Drake. (n.d.). *Open Source project*. Retrieved from https://github.com/Factual/drake/wiki

Fong, S., Deb, S., Chan, I. W., & Vijayakumar, P. (2014). An event driven neural network system for evaluating public moods from online users' comments. *Fifth International Conference on the Applications of Digital Information and Web Technologies (ICADIWT)*, 239-243. 10.1109/ICADIWT.2014.6814688

GATE. (n.d.). *GATE User Guide*. Retrieved from http://gate.ac.uk/sale/tao/split.html

Go, A., Bhayani, R., & Huang, L. (2009). Twitter sentiment classification using distant supervision. CS224 Project Report, Stanford.

Hamad, M. M., & Jihad, A. A. (2011). *An Enhanced Technique to Clean Data in the Data Warehouse* (pp. 306–311). Dubai, UAE: Developments in E-systems Engineering. doi:10.1109/DeSE.2011.32

Hassan, A., Abbasi, A., & Zeng, D. (2013). Twitter Sentiment Analysis: A Bootstrap Ensemble Framework. *International Conference on Social Computing*, 357-364. 10.1109/SocialCom.2013.56

HealeyC. (2016). Retrieved from https://www.csc2.ncsu.edu/faculty/healey/tweet_viz/

Jakoband & Gurevych (n.d.). *Extracting Opinion Targets from User-Generated Discourse with an Application to Recommendation Systems* (Doctor of Philosophy). Darmstadt University of Technology, Darmstadt, Germany.

Keshtkar, F. (2011). *A Computational Approach to the Analysis and Generation of Emotion in Text* (Doctor of Philosophy). University of Ottawa, Canada.

Kshirsagar, A. A.., & Deshkar, P. A. (2015). Review analyzer analysis of product reviews on WEKA classifiers. *International Conference on Innovations in Information, Embedded and Communication Systems (ICIIECS)*, 1-5. 10.1109/ICIIECS.2015.7193034

Kusumasari & Fitria. (2016). Data profiling for data quality improvement with OpenRefine. *International Conference on Information Technology Systems and Innovation (ICITSI)*, 1-6. 10.1109/ICITSI.2016.7858197

Lexalytics. (n.d.). Received from https://www.lexalytics.com

Li, S., Wang, Z., Lee, S. Y. M., & Huang, C. R. (2013). Sentiment Classification with Polarity Shifting Detection. *International Conference on Asian Language Processing (IALP)*, 129-132.

LightSIDE. (n.d.). Retrieved from http://www.cs.cmu.edu/~cprose/LightSIDE.html

McCallum. (2002). *MALLET: A Machine Learning for Language Toolkit*. Retrieved from http://mallet.cs.umass.edu

Minanovic, A., Gabelica, H., & Krstić, Ž. (2014). Big data and sentiment analysis using KNIME: Online reviews vs. social media. *37th International Convention on Information and Communication Technology, Electronics and Microelectronics (MIPRO)*, 1464-1468. 10.1109/MIPRO.2014.6859797

Mohandas, N., & Nair, J. P. S. (2012). Domain Specific Sentence Level Mood Extraction from Malayalam Text. *International Conference on Advances in Computing and Communications (ICACC)*, 78-81. 10.1109/ICACC.2012.16

Netowl. (n.d). *Software package*. Retrieved from https://www.netowl.com/

Pennebaker, J. W., Booth, R. J., Boyd, R. L., & Francis, M. E. (2015). Linguistic Inquiry and WorCount. LIWC2015, Austin, TX.

R language. (n.d.). Retrieved from https://www.r-project.org/about.html

Samal, B., Behera, A. K., & Panda, M. (2017). Performance analysis of supervised machine learning techniques for sentiment analysis. *Third International Conference on Sensing, Signal Processing and Security (ICSSS)*, 128-133. 10.1109/SSPS.2017.8071579

Sentiment140. (n.d.). Retrieved from http://help.sentiment140.com/

Shein, K. P. P., & Nyunt, T. T. S. (2010). Sentiment Classification Based on Ontology and SVM Classifier. *Second International Conference on Communication Software and Networks (ICCSN '10)*, 169-172. 10.1109/ICCSN.2010.35

Song, H., Fan, Y., Liu, X., & Tao, D. (2011). Extracting product features from online reviews for sentimental analysis. *6th International Conference on Computer Sciences and Convergence Information Technology (ICCIT)*, 745-750.

R Studio. (n.d.). *Software package*. Retrieved from https://www.rstudio.com/

Thelwall, M., Buckley, K., Paltoglou, G., Cai, D., & Kappas, A. (2010). Sentiment strength detection in short informal text. *Journal of the American Society for Information Science and Technology*, *61*(12), 2544–2558. doi:10.1002/asi.21416

Tweet. (n.d.). Retrieved from https://www.csc2.ncsu.edu/faculty/healey/tweet_viz/

Twitter. (n.d.). Retrieved from https://about.twitter.com/

Web Scraper. (n.d.). *Software package*. Retrieved from http://webscraper.io/

Wen, B., Fan, P., Dai, W., & Ding, L. (2013). Research on analyzing sentiment of texts based on semantic comprehension. *3rd International Conference on Consumer Electronics, Communications and Networks*, 529-532. 10.1109/CECNet.2013.6703386

Wenyun, L., & Lingyun, B. (2010). Application of Web Mining in E-Commerce Enterprises Knowledge Management. *International Conference on E-Business and E-Government*, 1769-1772. 10.1109/ICEE.2010.447

Chapter 11
Anatomizing Lexicon With Natural Language Tokenizer Toolkit 3

Simran Kaur Jolly
Manav Rachna International Institute of Research and Studies, India

Rashmi Agrawal
Manav Rachna International Institute of Research and Studies, India

ABSTRACT

NLTK toolkit is an API platform built with Python language to interact with humans through natural language. The very first version of NLTK was released in 2005 (1.4.3), which was compatible with Python 2.4. The latest version was in September 2017 NLTK (3.2.5), which incorporated features like Arabic stemmers, NIST evaluation, MOSES tokenizer, Stanford segmenter, treebank detokenizer, verbnet, and vader, etc. NLTK was created in 2001 as a part of Computational Linguistic Department at the University of Pennsylvania. Since then it has been tested and developed. The important packages of this system are 1) corpus builder, 2) tokenizer, 3) collocation, 4) tagging, 5) parsing, 6) metrics, and 7) probability distribution system. Toolbox NLTK was built to meet four primary requirements: 1) Simplicity: An substantive framework for building blocks; 2) Consistency: Consistent interface; 3) Extensibility: Which can be easily scaled; and 4) Modularity: All modules are independent of each other.

DOI: 10.4018/978-1-5225-6117-0.ch011

INSTALLING PYTHON AND NLTK

In order to install python 3.4 version go to https://python.org and install the version 3.4. (Figure 1)

After installing python version 3.4 install the NLTK toolkit version 3.0.

1. First we install NLTK(natural language toolkit): pip install nltk.
2. Install Numpy (optional) package if user needs: pip install numpy.
3. While testing the installation of nltk toolkit we can run it on python GUI and write the command:

    >>>import nltk(it will import the whl(wheel files) of nltk and related packages)

There are two existing versions of nlp i.e. python 2.7 and python 3.4 which are very much incompatible with each other. The python 3.y versions are more coherent, more consistent and user friendly GUI is provided. All the instructions written for versions of python 2x may not run in version of python 3y and if they run the output of the code id different in both the versions. Not all the organizations have updated to python 3.y versions and are still relying on python 2.x versions due to the ongoing service and credibility.

INSTALLING PYTHON 3.4 ON WINDOWS SYSTEMS

There are two variants of Python 3.4 for Windows — a 32-bit version and a 64-bit version. Obviously, the 64-bit version requires a 64-bit Windows computer.

Figure 1. Installation of Python 3.4

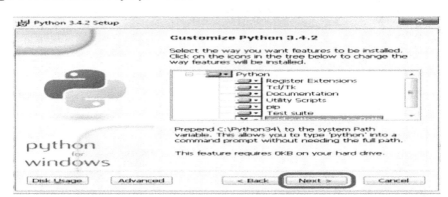

Fortunately, most Windows PCs sold over the past few years are 64-bit. However, the 32-bit version of Python can run on both 64-bit Windows PCs and 32-bit Windows PCs.

For this training user are using 32 bit version of python GUI on windows 8 because of the official release of numerical python i.e. numpy is currently available on 32 bits windows only. course, user must use the 32-bit version of Python on Windows. The reason is that the official release of numpy is currently available for Windows only in 32-bit format.

If the reader wants to install the correct version of python 3.4 then click on the hyperlink given: python-3.4.1.msi— and download the executable file for the setup or reader can browse to http://www.cs.wpi.edu/~cs1004/a14/Resources and download them from there.

Double-click on the file **python-3.4.1.msi** to start the installation. Following dialog box pops up on the screen. (Figure 2)

If subsequently a dialog box resembling below for any version of Python 3, select Remove Python for that version.

Removing Python will take several minutes and may require to confirm in one or more additional dialog boxes.

Figure 2. Python Installation Completed

After having removed the previous version of Python, click Finish and start over. After clicking Next, user should see a dialog box resembling the following:

1. Whether user choose to install "for all users" or just for self is a matter of personal preference. Click Next to bring up the following dialog box.
2. Click Next to select the default directory. If it tells user the directory already exists and asks if user are sure that user want to overwrite existing files, click Yes. In the next dialog box, may customize the installation. Simply click Next without making any changes.
3. The installation should begin and will take several minutes and may require confirmation in additional dialog boxes. When it completes, user sees the final dialog box.

Click Finish to complete the installation of Python 3.4.1.

Testing Your installation on Windows 8

If user is running Windows 8, user may confirm installation by clicking the Start button to bring up the Windows Start menu. Select All Programs and scroll down to Python 3.4. Open this folder to expose the following shortcuts: (Figure 3)

Click on IDLE (Python GUI) to bring up the following window (only the upper part of which is shown here): (Figure 4)

The above shown figure is IDLE, the Python command prompt and graphical user interface, where user shall start all programs and projects in this chapter. For now, simply type any Python statement or expression after the ">>>" prompt. For example, in 4, the expression 2 + 3 + 4 was typed and Python resulted with the value 9.

TESTING INSTALLATION IN WINDOWS 8

Windows 8 does not have a Start button but rather a Start screen that is intended to make the user experience more like the smart phone experience. Unfortunately, when Python is installed as instructed above, its icon does not automatically appear on the Start screen. It also does not appear in the list of apps.

To find it, move the cursor to the upper-right or lower-right corner of the screen to expose the Windows 8 pallet of "charms". Select the Search charm to bring up a Search box. Type the word "Python." This will bring up a list of matching items.

Figure 3. Testing the IDLE

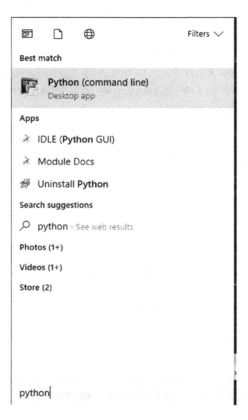

Figure 4: Mathematical Operations in IDLE

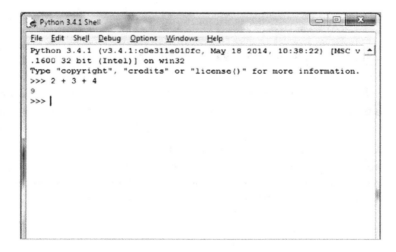

Note that this list is similar to the Python 3.4 folder in the Start Menu in Figure 3. Right-click on the item labeled IDLE (Python GUI). From the menu, select "Pin to Start" to cause an icon to be added to the Start screen. user may also want to pin the item to the Task bar (i.e., the bar of tiny icons at the bottom of the screen). user may also select "Open file location," which will bring up the following window:

From this window, user can copy any or all of the Python links to the desktop.

Installing Matplotlib, Numpy, and Other Packages

One of the many benefits of Python is that user get to install wide variety of third party packages to be installed which are open source and free and may start as follows:

- Matplotlib (a package for creating 2D plots and graphs similar to Matlab),
- Numpy (meaning "Numerical Python," a package for efficient handling of large arrays of numerical data), and
- Graphics.py, a simple tool written in Python 3 and created by the textbook author for making simple drawings.
- NLTK(it is a natural language processing tool kit for carrying out all the tasks.

Installing Graphics.py

To install graphics.py, click on this link — graphics.py — and download the file to the folder where user keep Python programs. Follow the instructions on p.488 of the textbook.

Installing numpy 1.8.1

In either Windows 7 or Windows 8, click on the following link—numpy-1.8.1-win32-superpack-python3.4.exe — to download the numpy installer. Open this to begin the installation. After confirming that user doeskin wants to allow the system to install software, it will start the installation and show the following dialog box (Figure 5).

Click Next. If installation of Python 3.4 is correct, it gives the following dialog:

If instead, it complains that user does not have Python 3.4 installed, ask for help. Such a complaint could arise if Python was not correctly installed or if it has the 64-bit version.

After the installation completes, click Finish.

user can test installation of numpy by opening an IDLE window. Type or paste the following commands into IDLE, one line at a time, exactly as written.

The result should resemble the following Figure 6.

Figure 5. Installing Graphics.py

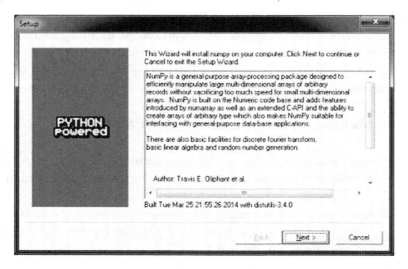

Figure 6. Installing in GUI

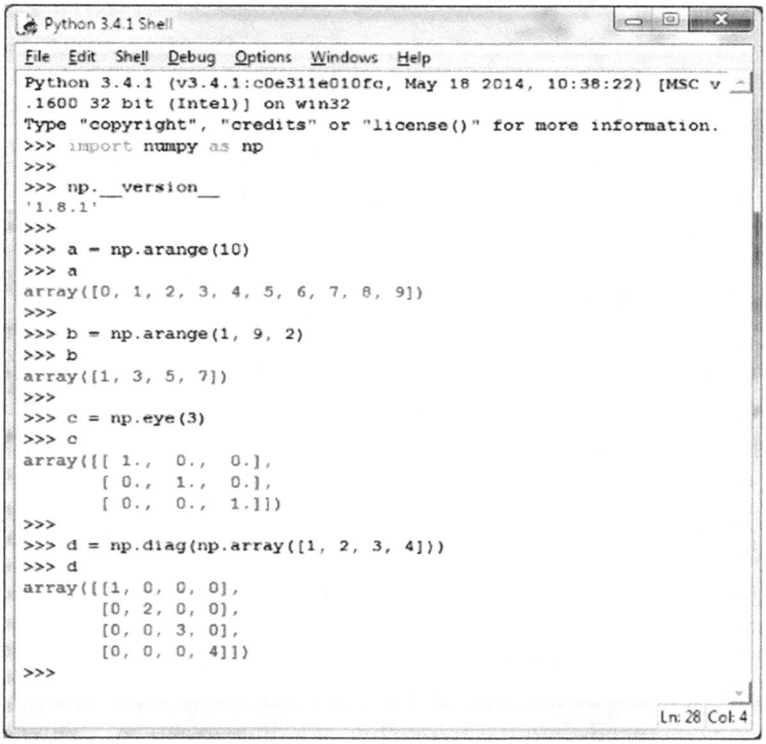

Congratulations! User has now installed a working versions numpy 1.8.1.

Installing Matplotlib on Windows

Installing Matplotlib is not nearly so straightforward. There is no "officially released" installer that captures all of the dependencies. The only installer that the Professor could find at the time of this writing is an "unofficial" one that contains just Matplotlib itself. Therefore, user need to download and manually install each of the packages upon which Matplotlib depends.

Download and open Windows/matplotlib-1.3.1.win32-py3.4.exe. The installer will open two dialog boxes similar to but not identical to Figure 11 and Figure 12. Allow the installation to run to completion.

Next, download and run the installers for each of the following packages:

- Windows/python-dateutil-2.2.win32-py3.4.exe
- Windows/pyparsing-2.0.2.win32-py3.4.exe
- Windows/pytz-2014.4.win32-py3.4.exe
- Windows/six-1.7.3.win32-py3.4.exe

These should all install uneventfully, again with dialog boxes resembling Figure 11 and Figure 12.

To test matplotlib installation, type or paste the following commands into IDLE, one line at a time, exactly as written:

```
Frommatplotlibimportpyplot
pyplot.plot([1,2,3,4],[1,4,9,16])
pyplot.show()
```

The IDLE window should look something like the following (Figure 7).

After user type the **ENTER** key following the last line, the following window should appear:

To close this window, click on the "close" button in the upper right.

Congratulations! user now has a working version of matplotlib installed.

LANGUAGE PROCESSING

Python, is an interactive interpreter that is working on graphical user interface called IDLE where user will be doing various operations of NLP (natural language processing) with python 3.4.

Figure 7. Installing Matplotlib

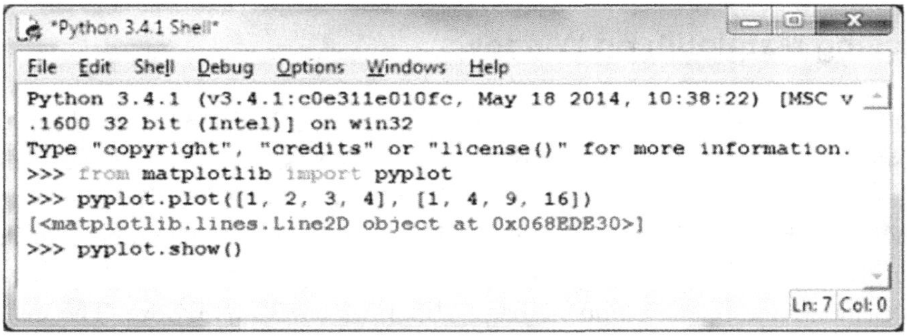

The language processing given by Steve Abney (2008) from the world wide web such as corpus of data is to is from the web such as text collections in corpora where goal is to:

1. Write programs to access text from local files and web
2. Split document into words and symbols, punctuation marks.
3. Produce the formatted output and save it in a file.

While we are installing NLTK on python GUI run the following command in command script:

--Pip install NLTK

This command gives output as follows (Figure 8).

-   **Numpy:** Numpy is core library for performing scientific operations in python. While we install numpy on to the system either user can install it from the internet as it is open source or user can open the command prompt of python package and type the following command (Figure 9):

    --pip install numpy

-   **MATPLOLIB:** Matplotlib is a Python 2D plotting library that assembles quality figures like graphs in various formats like hard copy formats and other interactive environment formats in different platforms. Matplotlib can be used in Python scripts, the Python and IPython shell, the jupyter notebook, web application servers, and four graphical user interface tool-kits.

Figure 8. Installing NLTK

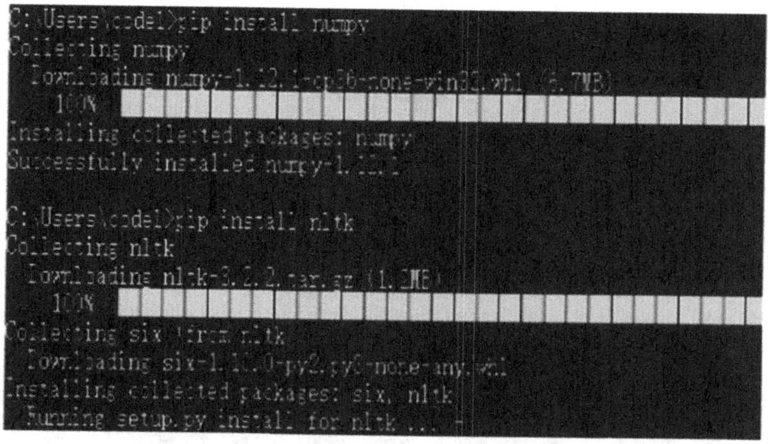

Figure 9. Installing Numpy

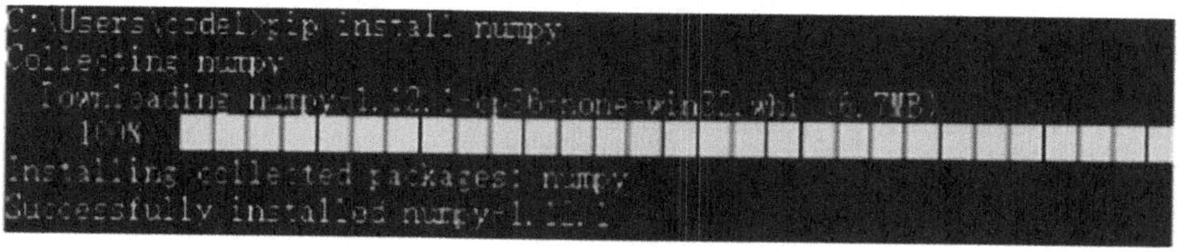

Mat-plot-lib tries to make task easy and probable. A user can generate plots, histograms,error graphs and scatter plots according to its adaptability with easy lines of codes. e.g. For simple plotting the pyplot module provides a MAT-LAB-like interface, particularly when combined with Python. For the power user, user have full control of line styles, font properties, axes properties, etc, via an object oriented interface or via a set of functions which is very much similar to MATLAB users. (Figure 10)

After the installation of all the packages in python IDLE user can now import these packages and data-set related to them using the following commands:

```
>>>import NLTK
>>>import numpy as np
>>>np._version_
    1.13.3'
>>>a = np.arrange(10)
>>>a
```

Figure 10. Installing Matplotlib

```
>>>from matplotlib import pyplot
>>>pyplot.show()
```

IMPORTANT MODULES OF THE SYSTEM

NLP known as Natural Language Processing is a technique of Artificial Intelligence given by Jurafsky et al. (2015) for extracting gist out of the corpus of data and converting words in data.

The important packages of the system are described below in detail:

a.   **Tokenization:** A Tokenizer in NLTK follows tokenization approach in natural language understanding by splitting a string into its sub-classes. It provides a lexical scanner that handles all the operators and delimiters.

Eg: A tokenizer tokenizes sentence into its morphological forms as given: "my name is Simran" is tokenized to 'my','name','is','Simran' which are the individual tokens generated.

•   In NLTK **Twitter Tokenizer** is deployed below to tokenize tweets.

Figure 11. Installing Matplotlib

```
🏂 Python 3.4.1 Shell
File Edit Shell Debug Options Windows Help
Python 3.4.1 (v3.4.1:c0e311e010fc, May 18 2014, 10:38:22) [MSC v.1600 32 bit (Intel)] on win32
Type "copyright", "credits" or "license()" for more information.
>>> import nltk
>>> import numpy as np
>>> np.__version__
1.13.3'
>>> a = np.arange(10)
>>> a
array([0, 1, 2, 3, 4, 5, 6, 7, 8, 9])
>>> b = np.arange(1, 9, 2)
>>> b
array([1, 3, 5, 7])
>>> c = np.eye(3)
>>> c
array([[ 1.,  0.,  0.],
       [ 0.,  1.,  0.],
       [ 0.,  0.,  1.]])
>>> d = np.diag(np.array([1, 2, 3, 4]))
>>> d
array([[1, 0, 0, 0],
       [0, 2, 0, 0],
       [0, 0, 3, 0],
       [0, 0, 0, 4]])
>>> from matplotlib import pyplot
>>> pyplot.plot([1, 2, 3, 4], [1, 4, 9, 16])
<matplotlib.lines.Line2D object at 0x062A94F0>]
>>> pyplot.show()
>>>
```

Figure 12. Dispersion Plot

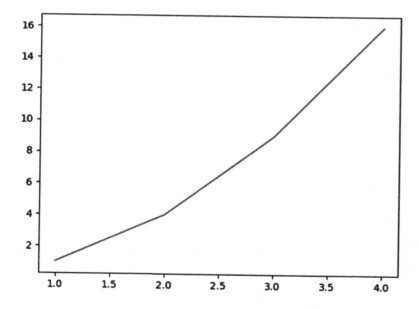

Twitter tokenizer is a very coherent system designed to adapt new domains and tasks.

The sentence string below is tokenized into tokens along with delimiters and punctuation marks.

```
Syntax: import NLTK
        From NLTK.tokenize import TweetTokenizer
        s1 = ""
        Tknzr.tokenize(s1)
```

The above illustration show tokenization of tweets on twitter in NLTK toolkit and conversion of sentence into its morphological forms.

b.   **Stemming:** The idea of stemming in natural language processing is a sort of normalizing method. A word can vary and have different variations.

Eg: I was studying my chapter.

I studied my chapter.
I study.
So verb study has three variations above which can be stemmed to its root or canonical form.
Hence studying is brought to its root form study which is shown below in the illustration.
Studying---Study

Figure 13. Tokenization

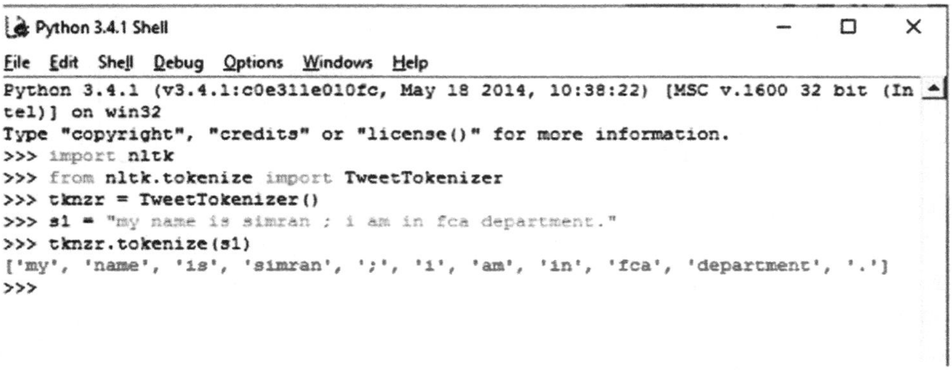

```
Python 3.4.1 Shell                                      —   □   ×
File  Edit  Shell  Debug  Options  Windows  Help
Python 3.4.1 (v3.4.1:c0e311e010fc, May 18 2014, 10:38:22) [MSC v.1600 32 bit (In
tel)] on win32
Type "copyright", "credits" or "license()" for more information.
>>> import nltk
>>> from nltk.tokenize import TweetTokenizer
>>> tknzr = TweetTokenizer()
>>> s1 = "my name is simran ; i am in fca department."
>>> tknzr.tokenize(s1)
['my', 'name', 'is', 'simran', ';', 'i', 'am', 'in', 'fca', 'department', '.']
>>>
```

It can be either prefix stemming or suffix stemming which brings word to its root form.

So it is a processing interface that removes suffixes and prefixes from the word and bring it down to its affix form.

In NLTK toolkit stem(token) is an interface incorporated in NLTK for stemming

There are variations of the stemming algorithm as described below:

a. **Porter Stemmer Algorithm:** This algorithm removes suffixes from the word forms in NLTK.

Eg: studying--study

```
Syntax: from NLTK.stem.porter import PorterStemmer
        Porter_Stemmer = PorterStemmer()
Porter_stemmer.stem('word to be stemmed'')
```

The illustration (Figure 14) shows porter stemming algorithm and stemming of the word to its root form.

b. **Lancaster Stemmer:** A word stemmer that is based on lancaster stemmer algorithm in NLTK.

Eg: maximum--maxim

```
Syntax: from NLTK.stem.lancaster import LancasterStemmer
        st = LancasterStemmer()
        St.stem('word to be stemmmed')
```

Figure 14. Porter Stemmer

```
>>> from nltk.stem import PorterStemmer
>>> from nltk.tokenize import sent_tokenize, word_tokenize
>>> words = ["studying","studied"]
>>> ps = PorterStemmer()
>>> for word in words:
        print(ps.stem(word))


studi
studi
```

Figure 15. Lancaster Stemmer

```
>>> from nltk.stem.lancaster import LancasterStemmer
>>> st = LancasterStemmer()
>>> st.stem('maximum')
'maxim'
>>> st.stem('danced')
'dant'
>>> |
```

Figure 16. Regex Stemmer

```
>>> from nltk.stem import RegexpStemmer
>>> st = RegexpStemmer('ing$|s$|e$|able$', min=4)
>>> st.stem('bars')
'bar'
>>> st.stem('polluted')
'polluted'
>>> |
```

The above illustration shows lancaster stemming algorithm and stemming of the word to its root form.

c. ***Regex Stemmer:*** This word stemmer used regular expressions for converting into morphological affixes.

Eg: bars--bar

```
Syntax: from NLTK.stem import RegexStemmer
        St = RegexStemmer()
        St.stem('')
```

3. **Segmentation:** Sentence tokenizer or Sentence disambiguation is also known as sentence breaking or segmentation into its constituent words or tokens.

Eg: "My name is Simran. I live in India." is segmented to two sentences: My name is Simran, I live in India.

```
Syntax: text = "sentences to be segmented"
        From NLTK.tokenize import sent_tokenize
```

```
Sent_tokenize_list=sent_tokenize(text)
Len(sent_tokenize_list)
Sent_tokenize_list
```

The illustration (Figure 17) shows segmentation of texts into its constituent sentences.

4. **Collocation:** Collocations as defined by (Robert Navgli, 2009) are the words that occur commonly in same context and frequently. For example, the top ten bi-gram collocations in Genesis are listed below, as measured using Point-wise Mutual Information.

Collocation or lexical collocation means two or more words co-occur in a sentence more frequently than by chance. A collocation is an expression that forms a specific meaning. It may be noun phrase like large villa, verbal phrase like go down, idioms, or technical terms. Collocations are defined by constricted compositionality, that is, it is difficult to predict the meaning of collocation from the meaning of its parts. For example,

He is known for his **fair** and **square** dealings and everybody trusts his work.

Here **fair** and **square** means honest but if we take the individual words though the word fair gives somewhat closer meaning as it means just the word square confuses us. So instead of taking individual words one should take the collocation fair and square and find meaning. It shows that collocations play a key role in understanding sentences. Collocations are recursive in nature so they may contain more than two words in a sentence.

```
Syntax:  text = "I do not like salad and rice, I do not like
them . yes I hate them!"
  tokens = NLTK.wordpunct_tokenize(text)
  finder = BigramCollocationFinder.from_words(tokens)
  scored = finder.score_ngrams(bigram_measures.raw_freq)
```

Figure 17. Segmentation

```
>>> text = "i am living in india. this is a beautiful country. it is your turn."
>>> from nltk.tokenize import sent_tokenize
>>> sent_tokenize_list=sent_tokenize(text)
>>> len(sent_tokenize_list)
3
>>> sent_tokenize_list
['i am living in india.', 'this is a beautiful country.', 'it is your turn.']
>>>
```

```
sorted(bigram for bigram, score in scored)  # doctest:
+NORMALIZE_WHITESPACE
```

[(',', 'I'), ('.', 'yes'), ('I', 'do'), ('I', 'hate'), ('and', 'rice'), ('do', 'not'), ('hate', 'them'), ('like', 'salad'), ('like', 'them'), ('not', 'like'), ('rice', ','), ('salad', 'and'), ('them', '!'), ('them', '.'), ('yes', 'I')]

In the above example collocation interface provides collocation finder that considers all n-gram in the text as collocation pairs

In above illustration it extracts 10 words from the corpus genesis that are collocation words I.e. used in same context: cutting and instrument; gray and hairs;most and high;many and colors;living and creature.

5. **Tagging:** Parts of Speech Tagging as discussed by (Robert et al.,2015) means assigning lexical categories to words whether it is a noun phrase, verb phrase or prepositional phrase.

Eg: Cat chases a rat. Here Cat is assigned NN lexical category(noun);Chases is assigned VB lexical category(verb); NN is assigned lexical category(noun).
    The illustration of the sentence is given below:

```
from NLTK.tokenize import word_tokenize//
 text = word_tokenize("cat chases a rat")// tokenize the
sentence
 NLTK.pos_tag(text)// assign them lexical category
[('cat', 'NN'), ('chases', 'VBZ'), ('a', 'DT'), ('rat',
'NN')]// output
```

Figure 18: Collocation Measure

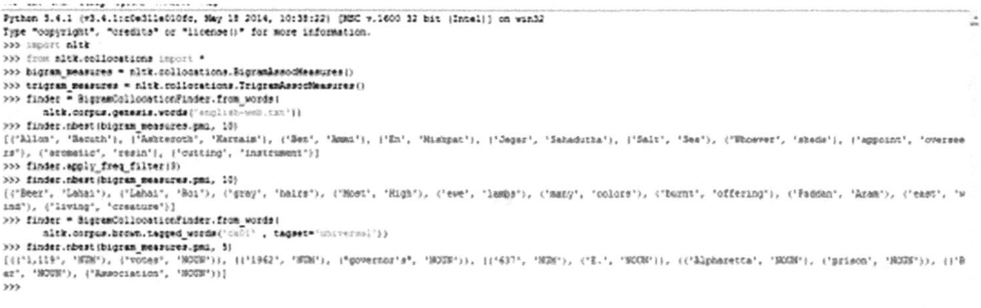

```
Syntax: from NLTK.tokenize import word_tokenize
 text = word_tokenize("They refuse to permit us to obtain the
refuse permit")
```

[('They', 'PRP'), ('refuse', 'VBP'), ('to', 'TO'), ('permit', 'VB'), ('us', 'PRP'), ('to', 'TO'), ('obtain', 'VB'), ('the', 'DT'), ('refuse', 'NN'), ('permit', 'NN')]

In the above illustration the sentence that is tokenized is assigned different lexical headings.

6. **Parsing:** Parsing as discussed by Manning et al. (2012) or Analyzing the Syntactic Structure of the sentence using Context Free Grammar.

A grammar is said to be **recursive in nature only when a lexical category that is present on the left handside of the production rules appear on the right hand side of the production rules.**The production Nom -> NP Nom (where Nom is the category of nominals) involves direct recursion on the category Nom, whereas indirect recursion on S arises from the combination of two productions, namely S -> NP DET and DET-> N S.

```
Syntax: from NLTK import Nonterminal, nonterminals, Production,
CFG
>>> nt1 = Nonterminal('NP')
>>> nt2 = Nonterminal('VP')
>>> nt1.symbol()
'NP'
>>> nt1 == Nonterminal('NP')
True
>>> nt1 == nt2
False
 S, NP, VP, PP = nonterminals('S, NP, VP, PP')
```

Figure 19: Parts of Speech Tagger

```
>>> text = word_tokenize("word sense disambiguation in nlp is a grammatical dilemma that handles ubiquitous ambiguity .")
>>> from nltk.tokenize import word_tokenize
>>> text = word_tokenize("word sense disambiguation in nlp is a grammatical dilemma that handles ubiquitous ambiguity .")
>>> nltk.pos_tag(text)
[('word', 'NN'), ('sense', 'NN'), ('disambiguation', 'NN'), ('in', 'IN'), ('nlp', 'NN'), ('is', 'VBZ'), ('a', 'DT'), ('grammatical', 'JJ'), ('dilemma', 'NN'), ('that', 'WDT'), ('handles', 'VBZ'), ('ubiquitous', 'JJ'), ('ambiguity', 'NN'), ('.', '.')]
>>>
```

```
N, V, P, DT = nonterminals('N, V, P, DT')
prod1 = Production(S, [NP, VP])
prod2 = Production(NP, [DT, NP])
prod1.lhs()
S
prod1.rhs()
(NP, VP)
prod1 == Production(S, [NP, VP])
True
prod1 == prod2
False
grammar = CFG.fromstring("""
    S -> NP VP
    PP -> P NP
    NP -> 'the' N | N PP | 'the' N PP
    VP -> V NP | V PP | V NP PP
    N -> 'cat'
    N -> 'dog'
    N -> 'rug'
    V -> 'chased'
    V -> 'sat'
    P -> 'in'
    P -> 'on'
    """)
from NLTK.parse import RecursiveDescentParser
rd = RecursiveDescentParser(grammar)
sentence1 = 'the cat chased the dog'.split()
sentence2 = 'the cat chased the dog on the rug'.split()
for t in rd.parse(sentence1):
        print(t)
Output:

(S (NP the (N cat)) (VP (V chased) (NP the (N dog))))
for t in rd.parse(sentence2):
    print(t)

(S
  (NP the (N cat))
  (VP (V chased) (NP the (N dog) (PP (P on) (NP the (N
rug))))))
```

```
(S
  (NP the (N cat))
  (VP (V chased) (NP the (N dog)) (PP (P on) (NP the (N
rug)))))
```

In the Figure 20 parsing of the sentence into its tree form is annotated.

In the above illustration recursive descent parser is used that breaks high level goals into lower level subgoals . here goals are sentence on the lhs(left hand side) and noun phrase and verb phrases are on rhs(right hand side). The subgoals are further replaced by other subgoals.

7.   **Word Sense Disambiguation:** (Debeng Lin,1998) discussed prospect of Word Sense Disambiguation in NLP is a grammatical dilemma that handles ubiquitous ambiguity .

Eg: in the sentence:"While hunting in India, I shot a deer in my pajamas. How he got into my pajamas, I don't know."

Here we can see ambiguity in the phrase "shot a deer " that whether the person shot with an gun or camera.

Figure 20. Lexical Parsing

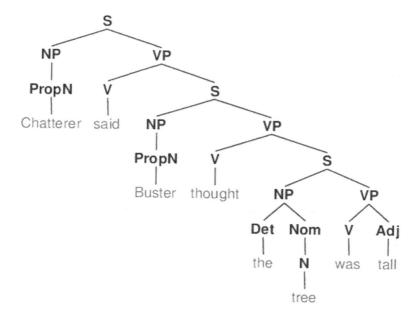

Figure 21. parsing

```
Python 3.4.1 Shell
File  Edit  Shell  Debug  Options  Windows  Help
>>> from nltk import Nonterminal, nonterminals, Production, CFG
>>> nt1 = Nonterminal('NP')
>>> nt2 = Nonterminal('VP')
>>> nt1.symbol()
'NP'
>>> nt1 == Nonterminal('NP')
True
>>> nt1 == nt2
False
>>> S, NP, VP, PP = nonterminals('S, NP, VP, PP')
>>> N, V, P, DT = nonterminals('N, V, P, DT')
>>> prod1 = Production(S, [NP, VP])
>>> prod2 = Production(NP, [DT, NP])
>>> prod1.lhs()
S
>>> prod1.rhs()
(NP, VP)
>>> prod1 == Production(S, [NP, VP])
True
>>> prod1 == prod2
```

Figure 22. Recursive Parsing

```
>>> grammar = CFG.fromstring("""
    S -> NP VP
    PP -> P NP
    NP -> 'the' N | N PP | 'the' N PP
    VP -> V NP | V PP | V NP PP
    N -> 'cat'
    N -> 'dog'
    N -> 'rug'
    V -> 'chased'
    V -> 'sat'
    P -> 'in'
    P -> 'on'
    """)
>>> from nltk.parse import RecursiveDescentParser
>>> rd = RecursiveDescentParser(grammar)
>>> sentence1 = 'the cat chased the dog'.split()
>>> sentence2 = 'the cat chased the dog on the rug'.split()
>>> for t in rd.parse(sentence1):
        print(t)


(S (NP the (N cat)) (VP (V chased) (NP the (N dog))))
>>> for t in rd.parse(sentence2):
        print(t)


(S
  (NP the (N cat))
  (VP (V chased) (NP the (N dog) (PP (P on) (NP the (N rug))))))
(S
  (NP the (N cat))
  (VP (V chased) (NP the (N dog)) (PP (P on) (NP the (N rug)))))
>>>
```

Figure 23. CFG Parsing

```
>>> groucho_grammar = nltk.CFG.fromstring("""
    S -> NP VP
    PP -> P NP
    NP -> Det N | Det N PP | 'I'
    VP -> V NP | VP PP
    Det -> 'an' | 'my'
    N -> 'deer' | 'pajamas'
    V -> 'shot'
    P -> 'in'
    """)
```

Here in above syntax user can see context free grammar generated for the sentence: I shot a deer in my pajamas.

In the above syntax the parse tree for the sentence is generated which signifies whether prepositional phrase point towards shooting with camera or shooting event hence removing ambiguity.

Henceforth all the techniques when are combined together and applied on big data-set or corpus of data for machine translation,speech recognition gives us logjam of fruitful results.

NLP is important in all the field i.e. scientific,educational,medicinal,corporate and cultural fields. NLP is experiencing fast maturation as its belief and method acting are deployed in a variety of new language technologies. For this reason it is important for a wide range of people to have a working cognition of NLP. Within

Figure 24. Word Sense disambiguation

```
>>> for tree in parser.parse(sent):
        print(tree)


(S
  (NP I)
  (VP
    (VP (V shot) (NP (Det an) (N deer)))
    (PP (P in) (NP (Det my) (N pajamas)))))
(S
  (NP I)
  (VP
    (V shot)
    (NP (Det an) (N deer) (PP (P in) (NP (Det my) (N pajamas))))))
```

Figure 25. Word Sense disambiguation

S(sentence)

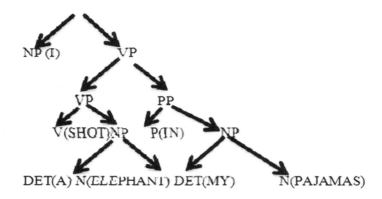

industry, this includes people in human-computer fundamental interaction, business information reasoning, and web software alteration.

So basic goals of NLP are **language analysis and language technology.**

In language analysis data modelling,text mining and knowledge representation techniques are applied while in language technology statistical algorithms are used deploying data structures.

NLTK as described above is a natural language toolkit (Navigli, 2009) designed for symbolic and statistical processing of data sets and language developed by team NLTK.

GETTING READY WITH NLTK

- Here the import command imports all modules of NLTK from the book and download the NLTK data. user can browse the NLTK books using command NLTK.download() .

```
>>>import NLTK
>>>NLTK.download()
```

These both commands basically import grouped sets of data which has 30 compressed files present in the folder book. So once the data is downloaded into the machine user can easily import all the packages of NLTK.

Figure 26: Importing NLTK Toolkit

```
Python 3.4.1 (v3.4.1:c0e311e010fc, May 18 2014, 10:38:22) [MSC v.1600 32 bit (Intel)] on win32
Type "copyright", "credits" or "license()" for more information.
>>> import nltk
>>> nltk.download()
showing info https://raw.githubusercontent.com/nltk/nltk_data/gh-pages/index.xml
|
```

Figure 27: Importing Book Package

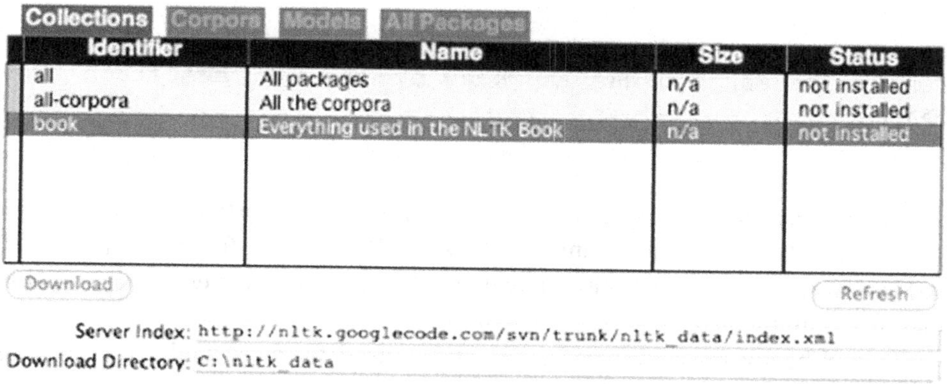

- When the data is downloaded in machine, user can load the data using the interpreter. Here the first command is from NLTK.book import *, Which basically loads all of the data from NLTK book module and load all the items. The book modules prints the welcome message and load all of the text of several books.

```
>>> from NLTK.book import*
```

The command gives following output in the python interpreter:

- After the data is being loaded from the book user can find about particular texts using the following command:

```
>>> text1: this command searches the particular text of a book
```

Figure 28. Importing the Text from Books

```
>>> from nltk.book import*
*** Introductory Examples for the NLTK Book ***
Loading text1, ..., text9 and sent1, ..., sent9
Type the name of the text or sentence to view it.
Type: 'texts()' or 'sents()' to list the materials.
text1: Moby Dick by Herman Melville 1851
text2: Sense and Sensibility by Jane Austen 1811
text3: The Book of Genesis
text4: Inaugural Address Corpus
text5: Chat Corpus
text6: Monty Python and the Holy Grail
text7: Wall Street Journal
text8: Personals Corpus
text9: The Man Who Was Thursday by G . K . Chesterton 1908
>>> |
```

The concordance command shows the occurrence of the particular word together with other texts eg: the word cannibal with *Moby Dick* in text1 followed by a period.

Here in the below illustration it searches for the word flower and cannibal in reference with the text.

Note: Whenever concordance command is used for a particular text it takes time to build the index for subsequent search depending on the occurrence of the frequency of the words.

- In order to find similar words similar command is used as follows:

```
>>> text2.similar("lived")
```

Here in the above figure words similar to lived are returned in text2.

- Lexical dispersion plot determines the location of words that are used in same context beginning from starting of the sentence.

Figure 29. Searching for a Text

```
>>> text1
<Text: Moby Dick by Herman Melville 1851>
>>> |
```

Figure 30. Concordance Command in NLTK

```
>>> text1.concordance("flower")
Displaying 2 of 2 matches:
s ' elephant that so frequented the flower - market , and with low salutations
em on the Line in time for the full flower of the Equatorial feeding season ,
>>> |
```

Figure 31. Concordance Command in NLTK

```
>>> text2.similar("lived")
was said been had came found called were is happened spoke went
expected continued engaged talked promised arrived tried added
>>>
```

Figure 32. Similar function

```
>>> text2.similar("lived")
was said been had came found called were is happened spoke went
expected continued engaged talked promised arrived tried added
>>>
```

```
>>>text4.dispersion_plot(["citizens","democracy","freedom","dut
ies","america"])
```

The output generated by the function dispersion_plot is as follows:

So in the above figure the stripes are the instances of the words and rows are the texts.

BUILDING A CORPUS

Corpus is a large body of text in context of natural language and processing .Their are different corpus existing online but here in the given context user will be using the word-net dictionary discussed by Jurafsky et al., (2015) for building same genres of text and then performing natural language tasks on them to generate similar words and pattern extraction or frequency distribution.

Word-Net is a semantically organized dictionary of English words that is very much, like our traditional thesaurus but with a richer semantic structure. It includes words with 155,287 words and 117,659 synonym sets.

The below given illustration imports the vocabulary from word-net dictionary.

Figure 33. Generating Synsets

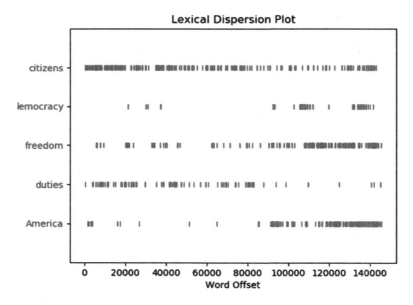

- In order to find synonyms of the word cannibal user can use the following command:

```
>>> wn.synsets('cannibal') # here wn stands for Word-Net
```

The words similar to the lemma is generated below.

- The reader can also define a particular word from the corpus using the function define.

```
>>> wn.synset().definition()
```

- The reader can also generate synonomous names of the word cannibal using the function lemmas().

```
>>> wn.synset('cannibal.n.01').lemmas()
```

As user can see in above figure user can find syn sets for the word cannibal I.e synonyms, synonym sets (words resembling),definition and context in which it is used.

Figure 34. Generating Synsets

```
>>> wn.synsets('cannibal')
[Synset('cannibal.n.01')]
>>> wn.synset('cannibal.n.01').lemma_names()
['cannibal', 'man-eater', 'anthropophagus', 'anthropophagite']
>>> wn.synset('cannibal.n.01').definition()
'a person who eats human flesh'
>>> wn.synset('cannibal.n.01').examples()
[]
>>> wn.synset('cannibal.n.01').lemmas()
[Lemma('cannibal.n.01.cannibal'), Lemma('cannibal.n.01.man-eater'), Lemma('cannibal.n.01.anthropophagus'), Lemma('cannibal.n.01.anthropophagite')]
>>> wn.lemma('cannibal.n.01.man-eater')
```

Figure 35. Lemmatization

```
>>> wn.lemma('cannibal.n.01.man-eater')
Lemma('cannibal.n.01.man-eater')
>>> wn.lemma('car.n.01.automobile').synset()
Synset('car.n.01')
>>> wn.lemma('cannibal.n.01.cannibal').name()
'cannibal'
>>> wn.synsets('tree')
[Synset('tree.n.01'), Synset('tree.n.02'), Synset('tree.n.03'), Synset('corner.v.02'), Synset('tree.v.02'), Synset('tree.v.03'), Synset('tree.v.04')]
>>> for synset in wn.synsets('car'):
        print(synset.lemma_names())


['car', 'auto', 'automobile', 'machine', 'motorcar']
['car', 'railcar', 'railway_car', 'railroad_car']
['car', 'gondola']
['car', 'elevator_car']
['cable_car', 'car']
>>> for synset in wn.synsets('tree'):
        print(synset.lemma_names())


['tree']
['tree', 'tree_diagram']
['Tree', 'Sir_Herbert_Beerbohm_Tree']
['corner', 'tree']
['tree']
['tree']
['tree', 'shoetree']
```

- Lemmatization usually denotes to doing things properly with the use of a lexicon and morphological analysis of words, normally aiming to remove inflectional endings only and to return the base or dictionary form of a word, which is known as the lemma . If faced with the token *saw*, stemming might return just *s*, whereas lemmatization would attempt to return either *see* or *saw* depending on whether the use of the token was as a verb or a noun. The two may also differ in that stemming most ordinarily breaks derivationally related words, whereas lemmatization commonly only collapses the various inflectional forms of a lemma. Linguistic processing for stemming or lemmatization is often done by an additional add-in component to the classification process, and a number of such components exist, both commercially and open-source.

Although the definition of a particular word helps to understand its meaning, words in syn set are often more useful for our programs. To remove ambiguity user identify the above given words ('cannibal.n.01.cannibal'),('cannibal.n.01.man-eater). This pairing of a syn set with word is called a lemma. user can get all the lemmas for a given syn set, look up a particular lemma, get the syn set corresponding o a lemma, and get the "name" of lemma.

BUILDING GRAMMAR USING NLTK

Attribute extraction (Mikolov et al., 2013) is an important aspect of natural language and processing that is relying on expected classifiers for gathering and stating the features of the words as shown below:

```
>>> jim = {'CAT': 'NP', 'ORTH': 'jim', 'REF': 'k'}
>>> chase = {'CAT': 'V', 'ORTH': 'chased', 'REL': 'chase'}
```

The objects here are jim and chase both are sharing similar features like: CAT(grammatical category) and or kim and ORTH (orthography i.e. the semantic meaning).Apart from this it has a linguistically oriented characterstics as well: jim['REF'] is intended to give the referent of kim, while chase['REL'] gives the relation that is depicted by chase. This mechanism of combining different features is known as feature structures.

Attribute structures contain various kinds of information about descriptive lingual objects. This information is thorough in nature and user can further extend these features. Eg: in case of a verb the reader should know what role does the verb plays . in the above mentioned case the subject plays role of agent while object plays role of patient. Here "sbj" stands for subject while "obj" stands for object.

Figure 36.Stemming

```
>>> from nltk.stem.porter import PorterStemmer
>>> porter_stemmer = PorterStemmer()
>>> porter_stemmer.stem('maximum')
'maximum'
```

Figure 37. Stemming

```
>>> porter_stemmer.stem('multiply')
'multipli'
>>> from nltk.stem.lancaster import LancasterStemmer
>>> lancaster_stemmer = LancasterStemmer()
>>> lancaster_stemmer.stem('maximum')
'maxim'
>>> from nltk.stem import SnowballStemmer
```

Figure 38. Stemming

```
>>> snowball_stemmer = SnowballStemmer("english")
>>> snowball_stemmer.stem('maximum')
'maximum'
>>> from nltk.stem import WordNetLemmatizer
>>> wordnet_lemmatizer = WordNetLemmatizer()
```

Figure 39. lemmatization

```
>>> wordnet_lemmatizer.lemmatize('dogs')
'dog'
>>> wordnet_lemmatizer.lemmatize('is', pos='v')
'be'
```

Figure 40. Feature Extraction

```
>>> jim = {'CAT': 'NP', 'ORTH': 'Kim', 'REF': 'k'}
>>> chase = {'CAT': 'V', 'ORTH': 'chased', 'REL': 'chase'}
```

```
>>> chase['AGT'] = 'sbj'
>>> chase['PAT'] = 'obj'
```

When the sentence "jim chased tom" is processed it binds the verb's agent role to patient role to object by making a hypothesis that noun phrases to left hand side of the verb is object and noun phrases to right hand side of the verb is subject.

Here in the output generated reader can clearly sees the orthographic relationship is chase and the agent and the patient.

Figure 41. Subject Object Agreement

```
>>> verb['PAT'] = obj['REF']
>>> for k in ['ORTH', 'REL', 'AGT', 'PAT']:
        print("%-5s => %s" % (k, verb[k]))


ORTH  => chased
REL   => chase
AGT   => sbj
PAT _ => l
```

Figure 42. Orthographic Relationship

```
>>> import nltk
>>> nltk.data.show_cfg('grammars/book_grammars/feat0.fcfg')
% start S
# ####################
# Grammar Productions
# ####################
# S expansion productions
S -> NP[NUM=?n] VP[NUM=?n]
# NP expansion productions
NP[NUM=?n] -> N[NUM=?n]
NP[NUM=?n] -> PropN[NUM=?n]
NP[NUM=?n] -> Det[NUM=?n] N[NUM=?n]
NP[NUM=pl] -> N[NUM=pl]
# VP expansion productions
VP[TENSE=?t, NUM=?n] -> IV[TENSE=?t, NUM=?n]
VP[TENSE=?t, NUM=?n] -> TV[TENSE=?t, NUM=?n] NP
# ####################
# Lexical Productions
# ####################
Det[NUM=sg] -> 'this' | 'every'
Det[NUM=pl] -> 'these' | 'all'
Det -> 'the' | 'some' | 'several'
PropN[NUM=sg]-> 'Kim' | 'Jody'
N[NUM=sg] -> 'dog' | 'girl' | 'car' | 'child'
N[NUM=pl] -> 'dogs' | 'girls' | 'cars' | 'children'
IV[TENSE=pres, NUM=sg] -> 'disappears' | 'walks'
TV[TENSE=pres, NUM=sg] -> 'sees' | 'likes'
IV[TENSE=pres, NUM=pl] -> 'disappear' | 'walk'
TV[TENSE=pres, NUM=pl] -> 'see' | 'like'
IV[TENSE=past] -> 'disappeared' | 'walked'
TV[TENSE=past] -> 'saw' | 'liked'
>>> |
```

REPRESENTING SYNTATIC STRUCTURE OF THE SENTENCE

Sentences have a very interesting property that they can be embedded withing larger sentences. Eg:

1.   Salma broke 100m record.(S)
2.   The indian reporter reported that salma broke 100m record.
3.   Andy said that the indian reporter reported that salma broke 100m record.

So in the above given sentences sentenc a is the embedded sentence, so user can name it as S. henceforth the indian reporter reported that S.(where S is the embedded sentence)

So grammar is explicit construction of utterances intertwined with each another that has enormous collection of grammatical sentences using recursive rules.

s---s and s(where s signifies sentences)

This dog runs: this is grammaticaly correct

These dog runs: this is grammatically incorrect

So to make the sentences grammaticaly correct parsers are incorporated in NLTK .A processing class for deriving trees that represent possible structures for a sequence of tokens. These tree structures are known as "parses". Typically, parsers are used to derive syntax trees for sentences. But parsers can also be used to derive other kinds of tree structure, such as morphological trees and discourse structures.

Grammar() is the subclass of parse().

According to context free grammar these agreement exists:

S -> NP VP
NP -> Det N
VP -> V
SYNTATIC FORM:
Det -> 'this'
N -> 'dog'
V -> 'runs'

Now representing "these dog runs" in context free grammar form:
As user know above sentence is in plural form

NP_SG -> Det_SG N_SG
NP_PL -> Det_PL N_PL
VP_SG -> V_SG
VP_PL -> V_PL
SYNTATIC FORM:
Det_SG -> 'this'
Det_PL -> 'these'
N_SG -> 'dog'
N_PL -> 'dogs'
V_SG -> 'runs'
V_PL -> 'run'

Figure 43. Tree Parser

```
>>> import nltk
>>> nltk.data.show_cfg('grammars/book_grammars/feat0.fcfg')
% start S
# ####################
# Grammar Productions
# ####################
# S expansion productions
S -> NP[NUM=?n] VP[NUM=?n]
# NP expansion productions
NP[NUM=?n] -> N[NUM=?n]
NP[NUM=?n] -> PropN[NUM=?n]
NP[NUM=?n] -> Det[NUM=?n] N[NUM=?n]
NP[NUM=pl] -> N[NUM=pl]
# VP expansion productions
VP[TENSE=?t, NUM=?n] -> IV[TENSE=?t, NUM=?n]
VP[TENSE=?t, NUM=?n] -> TV[TENSE=?t, NUM=?n] NP
# ####################
# Lexical Productions
# ####################
Det[NUM=sg] -> 'this' | 'every'
Det[NUM=pl] -> 'these' | 'all'
Det -> 'the' | 'some' | 'several'
PropN[NUM=sg]-> 'Kim' | 'Jody'
N[NUM=sg] -> 'dog' | 'girl' | 'car' | 'child'
N[NUM=pl] -> 'dogs' | 'girls' | 'cars' | 'children'
IV[TENSE=pres,  NUM=sg] -> 'disappears' | 'walks'
TV[TENSE=pres, NUM=sg] -> 'sees' | 'likes'
IV[TENSE=pres,  NUM=pl] -> 'disappear' | 'walk'
TV[TENSE=pres, NUM=pl] -> 'see' | 'like'
IV[TENSE=past] -> 'disappeared' | 'walked'
TV[TENSE=past] -> 'saw' | 'liked'
>>> |
```

Here det stands for determiner, sg stands for singular, pl stands for plural, np stands for noun phrase, vp stands for verb phrase.

- User can also use attributes and constraints where category N has a grammatical feature called NUM for number p1 for plural

Det[NUM=sg] -> 'this'
Det[NUM=pl] -> 'these'
N[NUM=sg] -> 'dog'
N[NUM=pl] -> 'dogs'
V[NUM=sg] -> 'runs'
V[NUM=pl] -> 'run

In the above illustration sentence form is converted into lexical productions where detailed syntactic analysis of the sentence is done and the dependency of the noun and verb phrases are formed as shown above.

The figure above illustrates the working of a tree parser with a feature-based grammar. After tokenizing the sentences that are fed as the input, load_parser function is imported that has input as grammar and the output as tree parser cp. When the pareser's parse method is called that will produce an iteration over the parse trees.

The trees will be empty if the grammar fails to parse the input and will contain one or more parse trees, depending on whether the input is syntactically ambiguous or not.

CONCLUSION AND FUTURE SCOPE

Hence user finally consider all the classical approaches to natural language processing that are implied in the chapter stepwise with syntax and semantics. These approaches can be further implied practically in deep learning, machine translation and speech synthesis which can be further used in different domains either for information extraction or natural language understanding and generation in an amplified way.

NLP can be deployed in different domains like:

1. **Adding Features to Existing Interfaces:** Spell correction, question answering, information retrieval, machine gradually replace humans
2. Back-end processing of the data into indices
3. Using Hand held devices for recording speech and language converters
4. **Studying Syntactical Structure:** This basically examines non topical features for discriminative models, Cost-efficient rough parsing, Unsupervised or partially supervised learning, Other philosophies besides CFG (dependency grammar)
5. **Machine Interlingual Rendition:** It basically follows analyse,transfer and generate rule.
6. **Linguistics Tasks:** Sentiment analysis, Summarisation, Information extraction, slot-filling, Discourse analysis, Textual deduction
7. **Speech Synthesis:** It is used for langauge modelling i.e. semantic and syntactic analysis, Finer models of acoustics, vocalization, less speaker-specific parameters, to enable fast adaptation to new speakers,more robust remembering, emotional speech, informal conversation, meetings,juvenile/elderly voices, bad audio, background noise
8. Some techniques to solve these are: non-local features, physiologically informed models, spatial property reduction.

Natural language processing throws light on interesting language challenges faced while carrying out the computational tasks, which are examined in the foremostly incorporating tokenization, corpus building, sentence splitting, tagging, classification a, grammar building and semantic discourse. So in broader view NLTK toolkit helped us to gain insight in hands on training of natural language processing to the onlookers.

REFERENCES

Abney, S. (2008). *Semi supervised Learning for Computational Linguistics.* Chapman and Hall.

Agirre, E., & Edmonds, P. (2007). *Word Sense Disambiguation: Algorithms and Applications.* Springer. doi:10.1007/978-1-4020-4809-8

Camacho-Collados, J., & Pilehvar, M. T. (2015). Making sense of word embeddings. A unified multilingual semantic representation of concepts. *Proceedings of the Association for Computational Linguistics*, 741–751.

Croft, B., Metzler, D., & Strohman, T. (2009). Search Engines: Information Retrieval in Practice. Addison Wesley.

Ferraresi, A., Zanchetta, E., Baroni, M., & Bernardini, S. (2008). Introducing and evaluating ukwac, a very large web-derived corpus of english. *Proceedings of the 4th Web as Corpus Workshop (WAC-4).*

Huang, E. H., Socher, R., Manning, C. D., & Ng, A. Y. (2012). MaxMax: A Graph-based Soft Clustering Algorithm Applied to Word Sense Induction. In *Proceedings of the 14th International Conference on Computational Linguistics and Intelligent Text Processing* (pp. 368–381). Samos, Greece: Springer Verlag.

Li, J., & Jurafsky, D. (2015). Improving word representations via global context and multiple word prototypes. *Proceedings of the ACL*, 873– 882.

Mikolov, Chen, Corrado, & Dean. (2013). An information-theoretic definition of similarity. *Proceedings of ICML*, 98, 296–304.

Moro, A., Raganato, A., & Navigli, R. (2014). Efficient estimation of word representations in vector space. *Workshop at International Conference on Learning Representations (ICLR)*, 1310–1318.

Navigli, R. (2009). Entity linking meets word sense disambiguation: a unified approach. *ACM Computing Surveys*, *41*(2), 10.

For a more accurate representation of the figures in this chapter, please see the electronic version.

Section 4
Challenges and Open Issues of Opinion Mining

Chapter 12

Challenges of Text Analytics in Opinion Mining

Vaishali Kalra
Manav Rachna International Institute of Research and Studies, India

Rashmi Agrawal
Manav Rachna International Institute of Research and Studies, India

ABSTRACT

Text analysis is the task of knowledge distillation from unstructured text. Due to increase in sharing of information over the web in text format, users required tools and techniques for the analysis of the text. These techniques can be used in two ways: One, this can be used for clustering, classification, and visualization of the data. Two, this can be used for predicting the future aspects, for example, in share market. But all these tasks are not easy to perform, as there are lots of challenges in converting the text into the format onto which various actions can be taken. In this chapter, the authors have discussed the framework of text analysis, followed by the background where they have discussed the steps for transforming the text into the structured form. They have shed light on its industry application along with the technological and non-technological challenges in text analysis.

INTRODUCTION TO TEXT ANALYTICS

In real world, organization needs to take decision every other minute, in order to ensure organizational success. Such decisions may include but not limited to introduction of new product and its potential demand, profitability, market share, competitor's benchmarking etc. In the past, such decisions were taken by the top

DOI: 10.4018/978-1-5225-6117-0.ch012

management based on their experience only but such decisions may not be always good for the organization, however, with the advent of technology the amount of data has increased massively, so now decision cannot be taken easily and requires analytics technique. Using Analytics techniques businesses can take strategic decision which are more reliable compared to decision taken on judgment of single person.

Text Analytics is one of the methods to analyze the textual data available on web. Text analytics can be defined as a way for computers to analyze the text using natural language processing to derive the certain facts from raw text. Such analysis can be in form of retrieval of customer opinion regarding any product, hotel reviews, movie reviews, categorization of documents based on the given information, can be used in market analysis and prediction and so many other similar tasks (Irfan et al., 2015).

In order to achieve the above purpose, the users need to follow the text mining process. Generally, Text mining and text analytics are alternatively used but there is thin line difference between the two. Text Mining can be understood as the process to retrieve information from data; however, information can be retrieved from data using text analytics techniques (Agrawal & Batra, 2013)

But both cannot be used in isolation as the end objective is same to take informed decision and taking an informed decision is not possible without using both. To further elaborate, Text analytics can be applied to any text data, which can be in any native language like Japanese, Chinese, English, Hindi etc. and same is available on the web. Such web data is not only the textual content always and it can have images, audios, and videos, which make it completely unstructured data. So the task of text analytics is to extract the text from retrieved real-world information from the web and application of text mining to visualize the text data only.

On the above retrieved text in the past, the text analytics only plays with bag of words, the word frequencies and are used for summarization, clustering the documents and classification of document topic wise (Agrawal, 2014). It does not have the capability of knowing the meaning of the text; it has difficulty in handling the problem of polysemy, homonymy, synonyms and deriving the hidden information that is called semantic analysis or qualitative analysis (Hu & Liu, 2012). Textual data comes with additional challenges such as incorrect spellings, incorrect syntax of the sentences and it leads to challenges for the extraction of the correct information out of that and its processing also. Therefore, researchers are focusing more on handling such data because of above issues (Knoblock, Lopresti, Roy, & Subramaniam, 2007). They are investing quality time in handling the complexities and its high dimensionality of the large corpus of data.

Although the researchers are applying statistical methods and techniques like using singular value decomposition and support vector machine for handling the high dimensionality issues, word sense disambiguation for handling synonyms problems, however, the challenges has not completely resolved and work is still in progress.

The intent of this chapter is to study some of the challenges faced by researchers today, let's make a deep dive.

BACKGROUND

Framework of Text Analytics

The text analytics is performed on text documents, so the first step of text analytics should be extraction of text data from the web which is followed by conversion of this text data into an actionable form is shown in Figure 1.

The data source is any repository available for the analysis, for market analysis it can be data available on social media sites like Twitter, Facebook, blogs, etc, it can be the sensors data, academic records, patient history, like this there are various resources are available from where the data can be extracted. Text content available in these repositories is in unstructured format, as there is not only the text data. There are videos, images audio available on the sites. Using text retrieval functions only text content can be retrieved and this text may not be in same formatting styles then this has to be preprocessed (Abbasi, 2008; Roberts, 2000; Lacity, 1994). The pre-processing has various steps from tokenization to removal of stop words, conversion of words into same formatting styles (Kalra, & Agrawal, 2017). Pre-processing requires the support of NLP, which process the raw string and checks for its syntax, semantic and pragmatic structure of sentence (Sun, Luo, & Chen, 2017). In the next section NLP will be discussed in detail. After pre-processing the

Figure 1. Text analytics framework

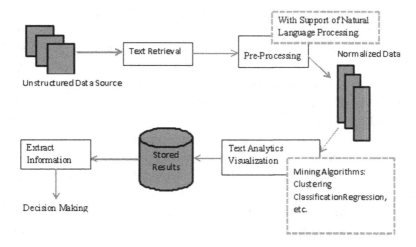

data is normalized, normalization is required to reduce the dimension of the data. Once the data is normalized any mining algorithms can be applied. These mining algorithms can be used to extract information which can further be utilized to take informed decisions.

Natural Language Processing

Natural language processing (NLP) is a backbone of text analytics. Text analytics performed before application of any machine learning algorithm. NLP determines the syntax and semantics of the sentence. The NLP is performed on a raw string, which converts the raw string into two forms:

- Set of characters
- Set of Words

Set of characters is the most common and easiest way of representation of text. But it does not play any important role in text analytics; it has the application in text compression only. Whereas the set of words play an important role in text analytics, with the help them you can do topic characterization, opinion mining, sentiment analysis, you can also describe the entities from these words and can give the relationship between them which may be helpful in information extraction. Identification of set of words is not easier to find in all languages, languages like Chinese and Japanese where no boundary is defined for the word characterization it becomes difficult but with the help of specialized tools, the words can be found for such languages also. So, our focus is on the processing of words. NLP on words can be done at three levels: Lexical analysis, semantic analysis, and syntactic analysis (Sun, S., 2017).

Levels of NLP Analysis

As explained above NLP on words can be performed at three different levels as follow:

1. Lexical Analysis:

This is the first step of text analytics where it breaks the sentence into set of tokens (words). In English language space, comma between the words helps in characterizing the tokens. On these tokens, Part of Speech (POS) Tagger can be used to Tag each word as noun, verb, adjective, determiner, etc. POS helps in determining the right context of the word whether it is an adverb or a noun. For example, in the given sentence: she gives a fire performance on stage, "fire" is an adverb and the

POS tagging can correctly determine it. Another measure use of POS tagging is, it helps in determining the relationship between words or entities, for example A cat is chasing a Rat; here POS tagging determines that chase relationship exist between cat and rat (Vyas, 2014).

POS tagging helps in removing language ambiguities known as word sense disambiguation. It assigns the tag to each word by considering its neighboring words also. For example, if the word appears with determiner in the end than it can be a noun or if the same word appears with a determiner in the mid then it can be an adjective or an adverb. This depends on the neighboring words which can give a different meaning to the same word. In support of this, let's take an example of the word back.

She sits at the back. Where back is a noun

I went back to the church. Here it is an adverb.

So, the same word can behave differently and POS tagging helps in identifying the right context of the word which resolves the various ambiguities occurring in the language.

The POS tagger algorithm takes the raw string as an input and produces the words with relevant tags which appear just immediately after the word in the sentence.

While/IN reading/VBG the/DT board/NN she/PRP generally/RB makes/VBZ mistake/NN because/IN of/IN poor/JJ eyesight/NN syndrome/NN

Here in the above example words are tagged like IN is used for tagging a preposition.

- **VBG:** Used for the verbs like playing, eating etc.
- **DT:** Is a determiner a, an, the comes in this category.
- **NN:** Is a Noun
- **PRP:** Is a pronoun
- **RB:** Is an adverb
- **VBZ:** Used for plural verbs
- **JJ:** Is an adjective

These are the few defined categories for English language. For each language there is a different rule for tagging.

2. *Syntactic Analysis*

Syntactic analysis is the task of identifying the correct grammatical structure of the sentence. After the lexical analysis, you will have the words with tags which determine the correct context of the word in the sentence. Next task is to determine the correct structure of the sentence, and to achieve this chunking is required. Chunking works on tagged words, it starts grouping the tagged words together to create a next higher level of the hierarchy of non-overlapping of tagged words for syntactic check. For example for the English language:

Article + Noun *creates* Noun Phrase Chunk

Verb + Noun Phrase *creates* Verb Phrase Chunk

Now, after creation of the chunks the text parser start parsing these chunks based on the native language grammatical rule, for example:
English Language Grammar Rule states that:
Sentence is made up of Verb Phrase and Noun Phrase, where Verb Phrase should be followed by Noun Phrase.
Let's try to analyze the above grammar rule with the help of below flow diagram shown in Figure 2.

3. Semantic Analysis

Semantic analysis is the task to find out the meaning of the text written by human in their native language. To perform the semantic analysis, the machine required to recognize the tokens correctly in form of context of the complete sentence written by

Figure 2. Text parsing

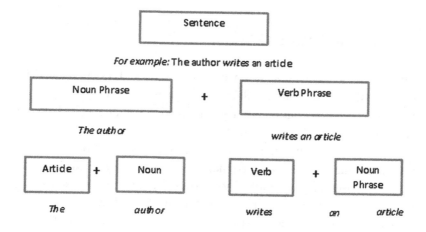

the user in their native language. This can be done with the help of lexical analysis and syntactic analysis. So for semantic analysis, the lexical analysis and syntactic analysis has to be performed first.

The applications of semantic analysis are:

- Helps to remove the semantic ambiguities of text.
- Helps to determine the relationship between words.
- Helps to give the summary of whole document.

To perform the above three tasks of semantic analysis the machine required the support of external dictionaries and statistical approaches. External dictionaries like Wordnet helps in determining the relationship between words. For example, election and politician can have a sense of togetherness. So if in any page the word election appears then it can categorize to the politics text document. The statistical approaches are used to give the whole context of the document, about what the user has stated in his text document. Next is the task how to remove the ambiguities of text. The ambiguities mainly appear due to the words which can infer different meanings. For example bank, the bank has two meanings one is related to a river and another it is a place where we submit our money. The POS tagging determines it as noun in both cases. So here syntactic analysis cannot remove the ambiguity. The semantic analysis can remove it, by going through the whole document to find its correct meaning. The semantic meaning cannot be driven from a single line of the text. For this analysis, the machine has to go through the whole text to find the correct meaning. By keeping in mind the objective of the chapter, The authors have not discussed much about NLP here. This entirely required enough space of discussion otherwise.

APPLICATION IN INDUSTRY

Text analysis has its vast application in industry nowadays, it is used in search engines to give the appropriate results for the query, in banking to make the future planning, movie makers, health care departments, almost at every place it plays an important role (Tated, & Ghonge, 2015).

Several well-known companies are using it, for example, Netflix is making wide use of this technique for the review of their movies and they are trying to do better for their user's, based on their preferences. Bank of England is also using the text analytics, they review tweets and from there they try to find about their clients when they can withdraw their money and based on that, they can make their financial decisions. Similarly in healthcare domain, Memorial Sloan-Kettering Cancer Center is making use of IBM Watson Technology to get the patient case history and use this information for prescribing the medication (Ittoo, Nguyen, & van den Bosch, 2016).

So, let's analyze few applications which are using the text analytics. The next subsequent table explained the use of text analytics in different applications

In Table 1, different broad categories of applications are discussed corresponding to the techniques of text mining. However, all defined applications are somewhere already using these techniques but this also defines scope of improvement in some applications also.

Challenges in Text Analytics

There are several challenges for performing Text Analytics and it is difficult to discuss all of them in detail, however, the challenges can be broadly defined in the following two categories:

- Common Challenges: These should be understood challenges faced all the times while performing text analytics for any data set.
- Specific Challenges: These challenges are domain specific challenges which may or may not appear all the time for all datasets.

Common Challenges and Its Classification

The most commonly faced challenges for Text Analytics can fall into any of the following categories:

- Unstructured and Inappropriate data
- Incomplete data (because of cloud-based data)
- Inconsistent data

1. **Unstructured and Inappropriate Data:** Unstructured and inappropriate data cites biggest challenge for text analytics. The data available on the web and repositories may be full of grammatical errors, may have used short forms of words, misspellings. Such erroneous data is the biggest roadblock in achieving the appropriate results.

2. **Incomplete Data:** The data available on the web does not necessarily have the complete information; some attributes may have missing values. In the real-world scenarios the failure of any node of a sensor device may cause some missing values. Although there are various techniques are available for handling the missing data like the attributes can be ignored if doesn't have much weightage or some other value can be substituted in replace based on

Table 1. Applications corresponding to techniques

	NER	Sentiment Analysis	Opinion Mining	Classification	Clustering
Biomedical	Drugs relationships and genes relationship (Simpson, 2012)			Classification of disease based on the history available in databases and electronic reports	1. Used to develop a system to collect the reports in one repository of similar types. 2. Drugs functioning the same effect can be grouped together
Banking		Banks used sentiment analysis to know their reputation in the market, by getting their clients reviews from social media.	People views shared on Twitter can be helpful for banks in making strategy	Banks can classify their clients based on their investments in bank and their credit can use and can provide benefits accordingly to leverage their customers.	
Search engines	Heavily rely on NER system for giving better search results.			Search Engines used it to automatically classifying the documents into predefined categories for efficient web search, eg: Yahoo	If the predefined category is not given then categories the documents based on their content similarity to improve search results.eg: Google
Q & A System	Helps in finding out the entities relation to give a better match for the asked question.			Classification of documents to the pre-defined category for retrieval of efficient results.	Grouping of documents which are relatively matched with each other for giving the good results of the asked question.
Agriculture		Helps farmer in choosing the fertilizers from the reviews given by the other users and scientists.	Blogs related to the agriculture and climate helps to cultivate the crop to give industry benefit.	Used for classifying the types crops production based on climate behavior, soil type, fertilizers etc.	Used for categorizing various crops production according to the tropical region
Traffic Management			Tweets shared on social media helps in traffic management.		
Product Review		1. Product reviews given by users on e-comers sites helps users for purchasing the product. 2. Helps industries also in production & improvement.			
Education		Reviews of different institutes helps students and parents in choosing the right institute for studies	Students feedback given in natural language required the support of opinion mining can help the management in building a strong system		

some. But in some applications, it causes the measurable difference in results. So handling of incomplete data is a challenge (Grimes, 2010).

3. **Inconsistent Data:** Real-time data is a time-variant data and generally it causes inconsistency in the data as Kaisler, Armour and Espinosa(2013, January) mentioned that the data is increasing at rapid growth and the data is integrated from various sources available at different places. The different sources have the different structured formats which cause the inconsistency in the data.

Next, in the Table 2 various challenges are categorized to the specific type mentioned above.

Specific Challenges of Text Analytics

As explained earlier in this chapter, specific challenges may not appear all the time but can be present in any of data sets, so some domain-specific challenges are explained below:

Table 2. Common challenges of text analysis

S.No.	Challenge	Type
1	**Handling of unstructured data**: Conversion of unstructured data into the structured form required special skills; this handling is a challenge for the analysts.	Unstructured and inappropriate data
2	**Noisy Data**: Data available on web contains lots of information other than the content which needs to be analyzed, the data may have advertisements along with the information and the textual content itself may be inappropriate structure. So conversion and extraction of relevant information is a challenge for the text analysts.	Unstructured and inappropriate data
3	**Multilingual Data:** Data available on the web is not in a single language, it is in multiple languages. Text analytics tools are language dependent, they cannot work independently. Development of support for each language is a challenging task for the analysts. Sharma, Gupta, Motlani, Bansal, Srivastava et al. (2016) have designed a model for the handling of Hindi-English combined usage of language in social media. For handling of this bilingual model, they have first identified the words that with which native language they actually belong. They have categorized into three classes Hindi, English and Rest. After then they have done normalization POS Tagging of words followed by shallow parsing where they have tagged each word	Unstructured and inappropriate data
4	**Heterogeneous Source of Information:** Data is extracted from different sources and collected at one place. Heterogeneous place of information has its own formatting and structure. Conversion of this heterogeneous information into homogeneous task required lots of efforts of analysts.	Incomplete data
5	**Time-Variant Real-Time Data:** The advancement required a lot from the data available on the web, performing analytics on real-world data required lots of efforts in gathering the information and performing the right prediction from the extracted information to leverage its customers(Sun, 2014)	Inconsistent Data
6	**Reliability of Available Data:** Lot of data is available on the web and in repositories but choosing the right data for analysis and making trust in the available data is difficult. The data available is the reliable one or not cannot be assured easily.	Unstructured and Inappropriate data
7	**Lack of Resources of Data:** Technology advancement is on boost and it is benefitting the companies also. But still, some companies hesitate in providing the data, which lacks in giving a good source of information.	Incomplete data
8	**Quality Results:** Inappropriate data always leads to inaccurate results. When the data available on web source is unstructured and noisy, it could not give appropriate results. The industry expects more from this data. So it's the biggest challenge for analysts to derive the accuracy in results.	Unstructured and Inappropriate data

1. **Named-Entity Recognition (NER):** NER is used in various applications like in Information Extraction, Topic analysis, Indexing of full documents, Sentiment Analysis etc. but Marrero, Urbano, & Sánchez-Cuadrado et. al. (2013) have tested this NER results on various tools like MUC-7, AUC-08, CoNLL-03 and they found each tool is having its own boundaries and rules for defining each entity in different categories. For example, MUC defines the date in Time/ Date category and AUC mentioned this into temporal expression. Some tools determine date mentioned in numeric as an entity but if it is mentioned in words then they do not determine it as an entity. So there are different rules and it's not easy to analyze the results as it can give different annotation to the same entity and sometimes they do not classify into any category of annotation. Although lots of research has been done on this, still various categories remain to sort and the main challenge of NER is to categorise the entity based on their semantic behavior. The new tools must be adaptive in nature so that they can be trained on new words time to time.

2. **Sentiment Analysis:** Sentiment Analysis gives a review on a product or on a service in form of positive, negative and neutral. It can be given in form of scores also to help its customers or the market for strategy planning accordingly. But it is difficult to analyze and give a correct opinion about the product or a particular feature. As to collect the sentiments from different places available in different formats and different formats can state differently. There are different yardsticks used by the different site to measure the customer sentiments or service which creates a bigger challenge as data cannot be statically analyzed. For example, some may rate in the format of 4.1 and some may have rated in form of good, very good product. So reviewing the sentiments from heterogeneous sources of information is difficult (Aggarwal & Zhai, 2012).

Pang & Lee(2008) describe another challenge of sentiment analysis the correct set of documents which only targets the sentiment is a difficult task. If one has managed to choose the right set of documents, then also it is difficult to find the opinion regarding a particular attribute. Pang also mentioned that overall opinion is context dependent, the independent sentence cannot describe the correct opinion about the product. However, the positive words have the more frequency in the description of the product, but if the last line describes the negative review then the product review gets the negative polarity.

So the sentiment analysis has the various challenges from a selection of the documents to the prediction of correct contextual sentiment. And if the sentiment is extracted correctly then applying this information in a right manner for market strategy planning is again a challenge. Although one can say it helps user for choosing the right direction for decision making but sometime it may mislead if they are not correctly classified.

3. **Opinion Mining:** Sentiment analysis and opinion mining suffer from the same kind of problems. They both have to tackle multilingual languages used in users reviews and each language requires the separate training for processing, which is time-consuming and required a lot of effort for the creation of training set. Opinion Mining always required the complete contextual information for giving the complete feedback otherwise it may misinterpret the results. For example, if a sentence has maximum good words than it doesn't mean that it is giving a good feedback, it can be said sarcastically also (Maynard, Bontcheva & Rout, 2012). That can be interpreted correctly only by the complete paragraph or a complete document containing the information. Opinion mining also suffers from the problem of selection of target documents on which the task is needed to be performed. It also has the difficulty in selection of evaluation method because both sentiment analysis and the opinion mining are feature dependent and another person cannot determine easily the other's viewpoint.

Opinion mining can be done on the feedback of the users given on twitter also, and it's a challenging task because tweets are in a microscopic format which does not tell much about the context from which you can determine about the opinion of the user. To perform the task efficiently, (Maynard, et. al. 2012) have used the support of machine learning algorithms and retrieval of entities and their relationships so that correct classification can be made on the user's viewpoint.

4. **Classification:** Classification is the task of categorizing the set of documents to the labeled class. Classification is easy to perform on documents which are having high density of content related to a particular topic. But it is not easy to perform on documents which are having less content. This type of classification is named as short text classification. The challenge of short text classification is lesser relevant content related to a particular labeled class. The example of the dataset is web blog data used for classification or the instant messages, and tweets classification etc. Few words specified in messages are not enough to perform classification accurately. This is the problem on which most research is going on (Aggarwal, 2012).

5. **Clustering:** The most common problem of clustering is to specify the number of clusters manually. Which the researchers resolved by using semi-supervised approaches. Using semi-supervised approaches the researchers can determine the value of k. But the other problem which generally faced is overfitting of documents to the specified number of clusters. Sometimes it's not necessary

that all the documents may have the mapping in the available cluster set. But still, clustering will map that document only to specified clusters, which generate the erroneous results (Aggarwal, 2012).

CONCLUSION

The text analysis is an emerged area for the researchers and nowadays it has its vast applications in the market from decision making to prediction, categorization of documents, and sentiment analysis to opinion mining. These all tasks required a dataset, and the source of this dataset is the web. The web information is neither complete nor correct which gives a lot of challenges to the researchers for doing any of the text analytic tasks efficiently. In this chapter we tried to shed light on the basic framework of text analysis, its application and various challenges which occurs due to web information and some domain specific challenges also which occurs while performing the above-defined application.

All the challenges which have been discussed give the future direction for the researchers where more work can be done. What can be concluded from the mentioned challenges that, the task of performing text analytics is not an easy task and this must require the domain knowledge of the application to produce the good results. This domain knowledge is gathered from the expertise and given as input while training the system. This trained system could be able to produce good results.

REFERENCES

Abbasi, A., & Chen, H. (2008). CyberGate: A design framework and system for text analysis of computer-mediated communication. *Management Information Systems Quarterly*, *32*(4), 811–837. doi:10.2307/25148873

Agrawal, R. (2014). K-Nearest Neighbor for Uncertain Data. *International Journal of Computers and Applications*, *105*(11).

Agrawal, R., & Batra, M. (2013). A detailed study on text mining techniques. *International Journal of Soft Computing and Engineering*, *2*(6), 118–121.

Al-Daihani, S. M., & Abrahams, A. (2016). A text mining analysis of academic libraries' tweets. *Journal of Academic Librarianship*, *42*(2), 135–143. doi:10.1016/j. acalib.2015.12.014

Hu, X., & Liu, H. (2012). Text analytics in social media. *Mining text data*, 385-414.

Irfan, R., King, C. K., Grages, D., Ewen, S., Khan, S. U., Madani, S. A., & Tziritas, N. (2015). A survey on text mining in social networks. *The Knowledge Engineering Review*, *30*(2), 157–170. doi:10.1017/S0269888914000277

Ittoo, A., Nguyen, L. M., & van den Bosch, A. (2016). Text analytics in industry: Challenges, desiderata and trends. *Computers in Industry*, *78*, 96–107. doi:10.1016/j.compind.2015.12.001

Kaisler, S., Armour, F., Espinosa, J. A., & Money, W. (2013, January). Big data: Issues and challenges moving forward. In *System Sciences (HICSS), 2013 46th Hawaii International Conference on* (pp. 995-1004). IEEE.

Kalra, V., & Agrawal, R. (2017). Importance of Text Data Preprocessing & its implementation using RapidMiner. Academic Press.

Knoblock, C., Lopresti, D., Roy, S., & Subramaniam, L. V. (2007). Special issue on noisy text analytics. *International Journal on Document Analysis and Recognition*, *10*(3), 127–128. doi:10.100710032-007-0058-9

Lacity, M. C., & Janson, M. A. (1994). Understanding qualitative data: A framework of text analysis methods. *Journal of Management Information Systems*, *11*(2), 137–155. doi:10.1080/07421222.1994.11518043

Marrero, M., Urbano, J., Sánchez-Cuadrado, S., Morato, J., & Gómez-Berbís, J. M. (2013). Named entity recognition: Fallacies, challenges and opportunities. *Computer Standards & Interfaces*, *35*(5), 482–489. doi:10.1016/j.csi.2012.09.004

Maynard, D., Bontcheva, K., & Rout, D. (2012). Challenges in developing opinion mining tools for social media. *Proceedings of the @ NLP can u tag# user-generated content*, 15-22.

Pang, B., & Lee, L. (2008). Opinion mining and sentiment analysis. *Foundations and Trends® in Information Retrieval*, *2*(1–2), 1-135.

Roberts, C. W. (2000). A conceptual framework for quantitative text analysis. *Quality & Quantity*, *34*(3), 259–274. doi:10.1023/A:1004780007748

Seth Grimes. (2010, February 8). *Text Analytics Opportunities and Challenges for 2010, BeyeNETWORK*. Retrieved from http://www.b-eye-network.com/view/12638

Sharma, A., Gupta, S., Motlani, R., Bansal, P., Srivastava, M., Mamidi, R., & Sharma, D. M. (2016). *Shallow Parsing Pipeline for Hindi-English Code-Mixed Social Media Text*. arXiv preprint arXiv:1604.03136

Simpson, M. S., & Demner-Fushman, D. (2012). Biomedical text mining: A survey of recent progress. In Mining text data (pp. 465-517). Springer US.

Sun, S., Luo, C., & Chen, J. (2017). A review of natural language processing techniques for opinion mining systems. *Information Fusion*, *36*, 10–25. doi:10.1016/j.inffus.2016.10.004

Sun, X. (2014). Structure regularization for structured prediction. In Advances in Neural Information Processing Systems (pp. 2402-2410). Academic Press.

Tated, R. R., & Ghonge, M. M. (2015). A survey on text mining-techniques and application. *International Journal of Research in Advent Technology*, *1*, 380–385.

Tated Aggarwal, C. C., & Zhai, C. (Eds.). (2012). *Mining text data*. Springer Science & Business Media. doi:10.1007/978-1-4614-3223-4

Vyas, Y., Gella, S., Sharma, J., Bali, K., & Choudhury, M. (2014, October). *POS Tagging of English-Hindi Code-Mixed Social Media Content* (Vol. 14). EMNLP. doi:10.3115/v1/D14-1105

Chapter 13
Open Issues in Opinion Mining

Vishal Vyas
Pondicherry University, India

V. Uma
Pondicherry University, India

ABSTRACT

Opinions are found everywhere. In web forums like social networking websites, e-commerce sites, etc., rich user-generated content is available in large volume. Web 2.0 has made rich information easily accessible. Manual insight extraction of information from these platforms is a cumbersome task. Deriving insight from such available information is known as opinion mining (OM). Opinion mining is not a single-stage process. Text mining and natural language processing (NLP) is used to obtain information from such data. In NLP, content from the text corpus is pre-processed, opinion word is extracted, and analysis of those words is done to get the opinion. The volume of web content is increasing every day. There is a demand for more ingenious techniques, which remains a challenge in opinion mining. The efficiency of opinion mining systems has not reached the satisfactory level because of the issues in various stages of opinion mining. This chapter will explain the various research issues and challenges present in each stage of opinion mining.

INTRODUCTION

Opinion mining (OM)/Sentiment Analysis (SA) is related to deriving insight through analysis of user's thoughts (reviews, posts, blogs etc.) about entities such as products, movies, people etc. Evaluation of reviews posted by users on e-commerce and social networking is of much use as it contains highly rated information.

DOI: 10.4018/978-1-5225-6117-0.ch013

Calculation of average inclination of opinion towards any entity not only helps business organizations to gain profits but also helps an individual in getting the right opinion about something unfamiliar.

Natural Language Processing (NLP) deals with actual text element processing. The text element is transformed into machine format by NLP. Artificial Intelligence (AI) techniques are applied on information provided by NLP to determine whether text sentence is positive or negative. Text mining can also be used in extracting the opinion. The difference is that, in text mining, data mining techniques are used to identify the opinion.

In both the techniques, content from the text corpus is pre-processed and opinion word extraction is performed before the opinion is derived. The raw text contains unwanted words which have no contribution to the opinion and such words are removed in preprocessing. The clean data is the output of the preprocessing stage. Various issues such as noise removal, missing values etc. are to be dealt in preprocessing stage. Many methods are available for pre-processing of text in opinion mining. The time complexity involved in pre-processing is high as compared to proceeding stages. High usage of abbreviations is normal when it comes to publishing more information using fewer characters. For instance in Twitter, only 280 characters are allowed in single post. Though various acronym dictionaries such as netlingo, urban dictionary are available, to deal with emerging slangs is a difficult task. Real-time updation of such dictionaries is the need of the hour.

Considering the next stage in opinion mining, the objective to create a predictive model for opinion mining can be fulfilled effectively by proper feature selection. Better feature selection not only produces accurate results but it also reduces the time complexity. In-depth knowledge of the problem domain is a prerequisite for feature selection. Filter, wrapper and embedded methods are used for feature selection in text mining. Presently, selection of a feature is a big issue, as the orientation of opinion changes with respect to the domain. Opinion mining is not limited to textual data but extending it to data in different formats such as real-time video, audio etc. is a real challenge.

Analysis being the next stage in OM, with what sentiment the author of the text is giving the opinion is identified through classification of the text. The chapter discusses the following challenges involved in classification of text for opinion mining. Researchers mainly use online reviews on movies and products for opinion mining. It is hard to identify whether the content is authentic or fake. Singh (2018) discussed a model to classify whether the review is authentic or fake. For better opinion mining, the elimination of spam content is necessary. The chapter discusses issues in the application of opinion mining for spam detection. Sentiment detection of the writer is important to get the accurate opinion from content. It ultimately tells the reputation of the writer. Identification of duplicates, sentiment detection of writer/reviewer from outliners by knowing the reputation of the content generator is still a challenging task in opinion mining. In online reviews, most of the times we come across mixed opinions. Consider the sentence, *"The car looks good but its interiors are not up to the mark"*. With aspect-based opinion mining, it is possible to get an opinion on particulars rather than getting an aggregate opinion in case of mixed reviews. There is still an effort required to raise the accuracy score while dealing with mixed reviews.

NLP and text mining play a vital role in OM. The ultimate goal is to the fill the gap how the humans communicate (natural language) and what the computer understands (machine language). User generated online content from social networking websites is easy to access and preferable for opinion mining but there exists social media imposed challenges such as cross-lingual opinion mining, sarcasm, negation handling and relevance. A huge amount of study has been carried out in English language. Hence, a lot of resources such as dictionaries and methods are available in English language for opinion mining. Opinion mining for Non- English languages is still a less explored area. The mapping of available resources in English language to other languages which is cross-lingual analysis is still a challenge in opinion mining. Opinion mining helps political organizations to get a better understanding of their competitors. Political debates, posts and discussions contain sarcastic sentences. An advanced NLP approach to deal with sarcasm detection is still not available. The chapter will briefly cover the issues viz. cross-lingual OM, sarcasm detection, relevance and negation handling which are some of the challenges imposed by social media.

Various research issues and challenges restrict efficiency of opinion mining system, because of which there isn't any satisfactory opinion mining system. The essence of opinion mining is to help people in decision making. The unstructured text, different writing styles, usage of sarcasm etc., in social media, e-commerce assigns a high percentage of difficulty in deriving opinion. E-commerce is not just selling and buying online. Utilizing opinion mining in e-commerce helps in recommending products to customers which will increase the efficiency of organizations and help in competing with other giants in the market. Thus, the necessity of opinion mining is increasing gradually. Hence, this chapter discusses the various issues and research challenges involved in opinion mining.

VARIOUS APPROACHES TO OPINION MINING (OM) /SENTIMENT ANALYSIS (SA)

Sentiment analysis is used to identify the feeling expressed by an individual whereas; opinion mining is used to identify the user's view. The approaches used are mostly common.

There are specific approaches to OM/SA that are important in designing a system that gives an accurate result while deriving opinion. These approaches are Document-level sentiment analysis, Sentence level sentiment analysis, Aspect-Based sentiment analysis and Comparative-Based sentiment analysis.

1. In Document level Sentiment Analysis, whole document is considered as single information unit and classified as positive, negative or neutral sentiment polarity. Supervised learning and unsupervised learning are the main approaches used in solving document level Sentiment Analysis.
2. Sentence level Sentiment Analysis considers each sentence as one information unit. Before real analysis of polarity, each sentence is determined to be Subjective or Objective. Only subjective sentences are further analysed. The sentiment polarity of the whole document is known after examining each sentence.
3. In Aspect-Based Sentiment Analysis, classification of sentiment concerns particular Sentiment Aspect/Entity. Firstly, aspects and their entities are identified. For instance, in the opinion about a car "Mileage of the car is very low but it is equipped with high-end safety features", "Mileage" and "Safety features" are two aspects of entity "Car."
4. In comparative-based Sentiment Analysis, rather than having a direct opinion about a product, text has comparative opinions such as "Most of the features in Audi car are better than BMW." Firstly, comparative sentences are identified in the text and then preferred entities are extracted. Focus on words like "more", "less", "most", "better", "superior" etc. help in identifying comparative sentences.

ISSUES INVOLVED IN PREPROCESSING

Anomalies in the assembled data from different online sources are the biggest issue in achieving accurate opinion. Product reviews and social networks which are a valuable source of data are usually preferred to acquire content for opinion mining. Online text is generally created by humans and it is heterogeneous in nature for e.g. different styles to write the date, name, etc. It is naïve to use unstructured data as it degrades the performance of any technique which is used for opinion mining.

Preprocessing is the first step in the process of opinion mining which aims at refining online content. Preprocessing involves some distinct steps which are (a) Data cleaning. (b) Data Integration. (c) Data Transformation.

Issues in Data Cleaning

Raw data are incomplete and contain noise which steers to irregularities in the dataset for opinion mining. Extraction of useful information (opinion) from online content is only possible when the acquired data is clean. Data cleaning provides consistent data for opinion mining.

Dealing With Missing Data

Ignoring a record with missing values is not a right option as it may affect the accuracy of the model for opinion mining. Manually entering missing values is the most accurate approach but it is time-consuming. The other option one can think of is, inserting predicted values in place of missing data but it may inject bias in the data. The said method is beneficial for validating results procured by snubbing records with missing values. Missing data account for inaccurate opinion mining system. Data extracted for opinion mining is human input. Different mindset or limit of words such as 280 words in Twitter are some of the reasons which leave a possibility of small, incorrect words etc. that give nil or wrong opinion. It is necessary to deal with missing values to get an accurate opinion mining system.

Dealing With Noisy Data

The content extracted for opinion mining is generally a manual entry by people of different mindset. Lexical accuracy in online content (Reviews, Blogs, and Posts etc.) remains an issue when it comes to getting an automated opinion. Challenges arise while data is extracted from social media websites as it is erroneous, unstructured and of dynamic nature. Online data contains abbreviations which an author of the text furnishes it according to its requirement of his/her mindset. Using slangs and transliterating etc. usually incorporate inconvenience to the opinion mining system. Such kind of content increases the difficulty level to mine the opinion and it is still a challenging task for researchers to deal with noisy data.

Various approaches namely binning methods, clustering and machine learning are being used for data smoothing. JHam et al. (2006) have described these approaches of data preprocessing. There is still a need for better data smoothing technique to get accurate insight from the data during opinion mining.

Issues in Data Integration

Data cleaning and data integration are important steps to get a reliable data set. Data is extracted from different sources and combining heterogeneous data sources is still an open issue. A data warehouse is used where extract, transform and load (ETL) process is repeated continuously to synchronize the data. Sometimes, the problem occurs when there is no access to full data and query is triggered. The different data formats to address similar items in various data sources are a big issue. For example, in a sentence which discusses a mobile phone "my phone" and "her phone" may occur. To deal with such kind of issues, NLP techniques such as parsing, word sense disambiguation and co-reference are being used. These are classic problems in NLP but there is still no accurate solution present to deal with the issue of data integration.

Issues in Data Transformation

The raw data extracted for analysis is not suitable for analysis. It is to be transformed into a format that is best suitable to derive opinion. The difference between the source (raw) data and the final (required) data tells the complexity of data transformation. The steps which are being applied to transform the data are (a) Data discovery (b) Data mapping (c) Code generation (d) Code execution and (e) Data review. Each step is equally important based on the complexity of the transformation required. The other possible option to get the data in user format is by applying normalization, aggregation and generalization. With the increase in the data, there is a need for advanced techniques to deal with data transformation, which is still a research challenge in the field of opinion mining.

ISSUES INVOLVED IN FEATURE EXTRACTION

While dealing with reviews of products, the text contains information about different characteristics of the reviewing entity. For example, *"Considering the mileage, Maruti's car is above all but it lacks in safety features"*. In above example "Mileage" and "Safety" are the two different characteristics/feature of an entity "Maruti car". Till now, noun-based approach is used to get the features from product reviews. Frequently used nouns are extracted and are identified as features of the entity. Liu (2011) discussed an approach that can identify nouns that imply the opinion. Identification of verb is a complex task but it can also be the characteristic/feature. Identification of contributing feature always remains a challenging task.

ISSUES INVOLVED IN CLASSIFICATION

Online content is rich and contains hidden information. It is necessary to derive opinion from such content. Classification is a form of data analysis that is used to extract models to describe data classes. Classification is a machine learning approach used to predict group membership (positive/negative in-case of OM/SA) for data instances.

Different Writing Style

Mining opinion from online content which includes web forums, posts and reviews etc. is a challenging task. The content we get online is usually a manual entry from people of a different mindset. Expression of opinion differs from person to person. The difference in the text comes when people use abbreviations, negative/positive words as per their ease. Sometimes the word is identified as an abbreviation which is in original a half-written word. Anna Stavrianou and Jean-Hugues Chauchat. (2008) have discussed the opinion mining issues in the online forum and Christopher (2008) addressed the issue of mining consumer opinion from the online web using linguistic and NLP techniques. However, it is found that these techniques are not suitable for user-generated text in online forums. Class association rules are suggested for getting insight from the online text and through and their result showed that content mining approach is better than NLP approach. Research focus is required to address this issue.

Requirement of World Knowledge

World knowledge requires being integrated into the opinion mining system. Consider the following example:

He is living with a Frankenstein without any awareness.

The sentence derives negative opinion but one has to have the knowledge of "Frankenstein". There is a need for a lexicon of words with their usage. The lexicon can incorporate the Knowledge required to derive opinion from the sentences where it becomes difficult to get the insight.

Synonym Grouping

The issue which occurs while dealing with product reviews to get an opinion is the usage of dissimilar words that are used to refer to same features of different products. Synonyms are to be identified and grouped together. The issue of synonym grouping requires serious attention as it is not well addressed in the past. Zhai et al. (2010, 2011) addressed the issue of synonym grouping using semi-Supervised and constrained LDA (Latent Dirichlet Allocation) respectively. Pham et al. (2011) discussed the issue and gave a solution to group Vietnamese synonym feature words in product reviews.

Spam Detection

False positive opinions to mislead users are normal these days. Bogus opinions are given to online users either to promote some product or to damage the reputation of any entity. Spams are mainly intended to confuse people between true positive and false negative opinions. Detecting these spams is a tedious but an important task. Jindal and Liu (2007, 2008) discussed review spam detection and opinion spam detection. Indurkhya et al. (2010) broadly classified spams into Email spam and Web spams. An email spam refers to unsought commercial emails which are intended to sell, promote or advertise something. Web spam refers to the use of illicit means to increase the search rank position of web pages. By exploiting the weakness of current search ranking algorithms some businesses are helping other by improving their page ranking. Such businesses are known as "search engine optimization" (SEO). Detecting fake reviews is a research challenge in opinion mining. Singh et al. (2018) discussed a model to detect fake or spam reviews.

CHALLENGES IMPOSED BY SOCIAL MEDIA

In addition to the research challenges discussed earlier, Social media imposes various issues on opinion mining. The text element (reviews, blogs etc.) can be analysed using NLP and text mining. It is still not possible to have a generalized opinion mining system for any kind of text. The text extracted from social media is a human input and therefore, it has a lot of ambiguity. Some of the issues which are imposed by social media are discussed here.

Cross-Lingual Opinion Mining

Much of the literature on opinion mining is focused on English text. Hence, most of the resources developed are in English language. Existing resources are utilized for opinion mining of content source language. Exploiting the present resources for

Table 1. Theoretical and technical challenges in opinion mining/ sentiment analysis

Reference	Theoretical/Technical	Opinion Mining / Sentiment Analysis Challenge	Technique Used
Bas et al. (2011)	Theoretical	Negation	Parts of speech (POS)
Yulan et al. (2011)	Theoretical	Domain dependence	Naïve Bayes and Support vector machine
Maral (2011)	Theoretical	Negation	Bag of words (BOWs) term frequencies
Svetlana et al. (2014)	Theoretical	Domain dependence	SemEval-2013
Alexandra et al. (2013)	Theoretical	Domain dependence	WordNet- lexicon based
Lucie et al. (2015)	Technical	Bi-polar words	n-grams
Emitza and Walid (2014)	Technical	Feature and keyword extraction	POS tagging with fine-grained app
Qingxi and Ming (2014)	Theoretical	Spam and fake reviews	Combine lexicon and use shallow dependency parser
Mohammad et al. (2014)	Theoretical & Technical	Domain dependence and NLP overheads	Lexicon-based method depends on POS tagging
Doaa et al. (2015)	Theoretical & Technical	Lexicon, feature extraction, negation and world knowledge	Enhanced BOW model
Jiang and Min (2011)	Theoretical	Domain dependence	n-grams
Walter and Mihalea (2011)	Theoretical & Technical	Extracting features and domain dependence	Character n-grams instead of terms
Myle et al. (2011)	Theoretical	Spam and fake reviews	POS tagging similarities and n-gram algorithm
Ning Luo et al(2018)	Theoretical	Fake reviews	Multi-aspect Feature based Neural Network Model
Shehnepoor et al. (2017)	Theoretical	Spam detection	NetSpam Framework

other languages is domain adaptation. Deshmukh and Tripathi (2018) discussed entropy based classifier for cross domain opinion mining. Lo et al. (2017) discussed challenges in multilingual sentiment analysis and provided a framework to deal with scarce resource languages.

Relevance

Identification of relevant pages is not always correct. Comment threads in social media usually diverge into un-associated topics. In the forum of a topic, there remains a possibility of comments on other topics too. On Twitter, people talk about diverse fields. It is difficult to have a single lexical model of "interesting tweets" as it differs from person to person. Mynard et al. (2012) discussed the challenges in having opinion mining tool for social media.

Dealing With Sarcasm and Irony

In the presence of sarcasm and irony, opinion mining gives erroneous results. The senses of positive and negative words do not remain the same as in normal sentences. Firstly, sarcastic and ironical sentences are needed to be identified. Identification of a sentence with sarcasm is a challenging task in opinion mining. Gonzalez-Ibanez (2011) addressed sarcasm in microblog website, Twitter. Filatova (2012) conceived a corpus to handle irony and sarcasm using crowdsourcing, Reyes(2013) addressed irony in Twitter using a multidimensional approach and Bharti et al. (2016) streamed tweets in real time and detected sarcastic sentiments. Following example shows how a sentence can have a positive/negative opinion without bearing an opinion word.

How can anyone travel on this bus?

The above sentence is not carrying any negative word but it is a sentence of negative opinion. It shows opinion mining is not only achieved by syntax detection but identification of semantics is the need of the hour.

Negation Handling

Negation changes the truth value of the premise. Words such as "not" and "never" are used to express negation which changes the opinion in its scope. In opinion mining, negation handling is a challenging task. Farooq (2017) discussed negation handling at the sentence level. The approach which is usually applied to handle negation is reversing the polarity of the words that
appear after negative word. In the example, *"I do not like the camera which I received as a gift"*, *"Like"* has appeared after a negative word "not". Using the classic approach it would *become "Like not"* but this approach does not work. In case of *"I do not like the camera which I received as a gift, but it has got nice features"*. Here it is required to consider the scope of the negative word which extend till the

conjunction the word but. The issue does not stop here. In the example sentence, *"Not only did I like the car but I loved its features"* there is no need to change the polarity of the word appearing after the negative word. There is a need for a generalized algorithm, as manually it is very difficult to consider all the different cases.

MATHEMATICAL APPROACHES USED IN ADDRESSING THE ISSUES

In E-commerce, it is usually seen that for the same product or its feature, customer express their feeling with different word or phrases. Opinion from such unstructured online reviews is usually derived by clustering product features and applying supervised and unsupervised methods. Jiajia et al. (2016) proposed a constrained orthogonal non-negative matrix factorization (CONMT) model to categorize features. Here, three assumptions are exploited to build feature-opinion namely relation matrix, cannot-link constrain matrix and must-link matrix. These three matrices are incorporated into CONMT model. The model outperformed several baseline methods. Irrespective of applying machine learning algorithm to assess sentiment in micro-blogging messages, Chan et al. (2013) provides an efficient tool utilizing the rough set theory by Pawlak (1982) for deriving new perspectives of sentiment analysis from micro-blogging messages. More specifically, they introduced the use of rough set theory to formulate sentimental approximation spaces based on keywords for assessing sentiment of micro-blogging messages. Various other researches are being carried out worldwide in addressing the issues.

CONCLUSION

With the advancements in Web 2.0, web content is increasing every day. There is a demand for more ingenious techniques and it is a challenge in opinion mining. With the advancement in internet related applications, opinion mining has become an interesting research area in NLP community. Opinion mining is beneficial for a business organization, as they analyse social media and get insight from ongoing activities. Merely, with their online presence, they can get overall performance utilizing the opinions mined. Popular individuals can benefit by knowing the audience attitude and this is possible through opinion mining. This chapter discusses the open issues in opinion mining. The data extracted from the web is unstructured and data cleaning is required at this preprocessing step. The chapter discussed the issues involved in data cleanings such as dealing with missing data and noise.

The cleaned data is not a final input for opinion mining system hence the issues data integration and data transformation are briefly explained in the chapter. Various issues involved in opinion mining such as different writing style, world knowledge, synonym grouping and spam detection are elaborated in the chapter. The data for opinion mining is usually extracted from social media hence there is also an explanation about the challenges imposed by the source of data extraction. This chapter has given an overall idea about the challenges that exist in opinion mining. The development of a novel approach to achieve a satisfactory opinion mining system is still an open challenge.

REFERENCES

Al-Kabi, M. N., Gigieh, A. H., Alsmadi, I. M., Wahsheh, H. A., & Haidar, M. M. (2014). Opinion mining and analysis for Arabic language. *International Journal of Advanced Computer Science and Applications*, *5*(5), 181–195.

Alexandra, B., Ralf, S., Mijail, K., Vanni, Z., Erik, V. D. G., Matina, H., ... Jenya, B. (2013). Sentiment analysis in the news. *Proceedings of the Seventh International Conference on Language Resources and Evaluation (LREC'10)*.

Bharti, S. K., Vachha, B., Pradhan, R. K., Babu, K. S., & Jena, S. K. (2016). Sarcastic sentiment detection in tweets streamed in real time: A big data approach. *Digital Communications and Networks*, *2*(3), 108–121. doi:10.1016/j.dcan.2016.06.002

Chan, C. C., & Liszka, K. J. (2013). Application of rough set theory to sentiment analysis of microblog data. In *Rough Sets and Intelligent Systems-Professor Zdzisław Pawlak in Memoriam* (pp. 185–202). Berlin: Springer. doi:10.1007/978-3-642-30341-8_10

Dadvar, M., Hauff, C., & de Jong, F. M. (2011, February). Scope of negation detection in sentiment analysis. In *Proceedings of the Dutch-Belgian Information Retrieval Workshop, DIR 2011*. University of Amsterdam.

Deshmukh, J. S., & Tripathy, A. K. (2018). Entropy based classifier for cross-domain opinion mining. *Applied Computing and Informatics*, *14*(1), 55–64. doi:10.1016/j.aci.2017.03.001

El-Din, D. M., Mokhtar, H. M., & Ismael, O. (2015). Online paper review analysis. *International Journal of Advanced Computer Science and Applications*, *6*(9).

Farooq, U., Mansoor, H., Nongaillard, A., Ouzrout, Y., & Qadir, M. A. (2017). Negation Handling in Sentiment Analysis at Sentence Level. *JCP*, *12*(5), 470–478. PMID:28097676

Filatova, E. (2012, May). Irony and Sarcasm: Corpus Generation and Analysis Using Crowdsourcing. In LREC (pp. 392-398). Academic Press.

Flekova, L., Preoţiuc-Pietro, D., & Ruppert, E. (2015). Analysing domain suitability of a sentiment lexicon by identifying distributionally bipolar words. In *Proceedings of the 6th Workshop on Computational Approaches to Subjectivity, Sentiment and Social Media Analysis* (pp. 77-84). Academic Press. 10.18653/v1/W15-2911

González-Ibánez, R., Muresan, S., & Wacholder, N. (2011, June). Identifying sarcasm in Twitter: a closer look. In *Proceedings of the 49th Annual Meeting of the Association for Computational Linguistics: Human Language Technologies: Short Papers-Volume 2* (pp. 581-586). Association for Computational Linguistics.

Guzman, E., & Maalej, W. (2014, August). How do users like this feature? a fine grained sentiment analysis of app reviews. In *Requirements Engineering Conference (RE), 2014 IEEE 22nd International* (pp. 153-162). IEEE. 10.1109/RE.2014.6912257

Han, J., Kamber, M., & Pei, J. (2006). *Data preprocessing. Data mining: concepts and techniques* (pp. 47–97). San Francisco: Morgan Kaufmann.

He, Y., Chenghua, L., & Harith, A. (2011). Automatically extracting polarity-bearing topics for cross-domain sentiment classification. *Proceedings of the Annual Meeting of the Association for Computational Linguistics*.

Heerschop, B., van Iterson, P., Hogenboom, A., Frasincar, F., & Kaymak, U. (2011). Accounting for negation in sentiment analysis. In *11th Dutch-Belgian Information Retrieval Workshop (DIR 2011)* (pp. 38-39). Academic Press.

Indurkhya, N., & Damerau, F. J. (Eds.). (2010). *Handbook of natural language processing* (Vol. 2). CRC Press.

Jiajia, W., Yezheng, L., Yuanchun, J., Chunhua, S., Jianshan, S., & Yanan, D. (2016, June). Clustering Product Features of Online Reviews Based on Nonnegative Matrix Tri-factorizations. In *Data Science in Cyberspace (DSC), IEEE International Conference on* (pp. 199-208). IEEE. 10.1109/DSC.2016.32

Jindal, N., & Liu, B. (2007, May). Review spam detection. In *Proceedings of the 16th international conference on World Wide Web* (pp. 1189-1190). ACM. 10.1145/1242572.1242759

Jindal, N., & Liu, B. (2008, February). Opinion spam and analysis. In *Proceedings of the 2008 International Conference on Web Search and Data Mining* (pp. 219-230). ACM.

Kasper, W., & Vela, M. (2011, October). Sentiment analysis for hotel reviews. In Computational linguistics-applications conference (Vol. 231527, pp. 45-52). Academic Press.

Kiritchenko, S., Zhu, X., & Mohammad, S. M. (2014). Sentiment analysis of short informal texts. *Journal of Artificial Intelligence Research, 50,* 723–762.

Lau, R. Y., Li, C., & Liao, S. S. (2014). Social analytics: Learning fuzzy product ontologies for aspect-oriented sentiment analysis. *Decision Support Systems, 65,* 80–94. doi:10.1016/j.dss.2014.05.005

Liu, B. (2012). Sentiment analysis and opinion mining. *Synthesis Lectures on Human Language Technologies, 5*(1), 1-167.

Lo, S. L., Cambria, E., Chiong, R., & Cornforth, D. (2017). Multilingual sentiment analysis: From formal to informal and scarce resource languages. *Artificial Intelligence Review, 48*(4), 499–527. doi:10.100710462-016-9508-4

Luo, N., Deng, H., Zhao, L., Liu, Y., Wang, X., & Tan, Z. (2017, July). Multi-aspect Feature based Neural Network Model in Detecting Fake Reviews. In *2017 4th International Conference on Information Science and Control Engineering (ICISCE)* (pp. 475-479). IEEE. 10.1109/ICISCE.2017.106

Maynard, D., Bontcheva, K., & Rout, D. (2012). Challenges in developing opinion mining tools for social media. *Proceedings of the@ NLP can u tag# usergeneratedcontent,* 15-22.

Ott, M., Choi, Y., Cardie, C., & Hancock, J. T. (2011, June). Finding deceptive opinion spam by any stretch of the imagination. In *Proceedings of the 49th Annual Meeting of the Association for Computational Linguistics: Human Language Technologies-Volume 1* (pp. 309-319). Association for Computational Linguistics.

Pawlak, Z. (1982). Rough sets. *International Journal of Computer & Information Sciences, 11*(5), 341-356.

Penalver-Martinez, I., Garcia-Sanchez, F., Valencia-Garcia, R., Rodriguez-Garcia, M. A., Moreno, V., Fraga, A., & Sanchez-Cervantes, J. L. (2014). Feature-based opinion mining through ontologies. *Expert Systems with Applications, 41*(13), 5995-6008.

Peng, Q., & Zhong, M. (2014). Detecting Spam Review through Sentiment Analysis. *JSW, 9*(8), 2065–2072. doi:10.4304/jsw.9.8.2065-2072

Pham, H. T., Vu, T. T., Tran, M. V., & Ha, Q. T. (2011, December). A solution for grouping Vietnamese synonym feature words in product reviews. In *Services Computing Conference (APSCC), 2011 IEEE Asia-Pacific* (pp. 503-508). IEEE. 10.1109/APSCC.2011.48

Reyes, A., Rosso, P., & Veale, T. (2013). A multidimensional approach for detecting irony in Twitter. *Language Resources and Evaluation, 47*(1), 239–268. doi:10.100710579-012-9196-x

Shehnepoor, S., Salehi, M., Farahbakhsh, R., & Crespi, N. (2017). NetSpam: A network-based spam detection framework for reviews in online social media. *IEEE Transactions on Information Forensics and Security, 12*(7), 1585–1595. doi:10.1109/TIFS.2017.2675361

Singh, M., Kumar, L., & Sinha, S. (2018). Model for Detecting Fake or Spam Reviews. In *ICT Based Innovations* (pp. 213–217). Singapore: Springer. doi:10.1007/978-981-10-6602-3_21

Stavrianou & Chauchat.(2008). *Opinion Mining Issues and Agreement Identification in Forum Texts*. Academic Press.

Yang, C. C., & Wong, Y. C. (2008, May). Mining Consumer Opinions from the Web. In WEBSITE (2) (pp. 187-192). Academic Press.

Yang, J., & Hou, M. (2010). Using Topic Sentiment Sentences to Recognize Sentiment Polarity in Chinese Reviews. *CIPS-SIGHAN Joint Conference on Chinese Language Processing*.

Zhai, Z., Liu, B., Xu, H., & Jia, P. (2010, August). Grouping product features using semi-supervised learning with soft-constraints. In *Proceedings of the 23rd International Conference on Computational Linguistics* (pp. 1272-1280). Association for Computational Linguistics.

Zhang, L., & Liu, B. (2011, June). Identifying noun product features that imply opinions. In *Proceedings of the 49th Annual Meeting of the Association for Computational Linguistics: Human Language Technologies: short papers-Volume 2* (pp. 575-580). Association for Computational Linguistics.

Section 5
Case Study

Chapter 14
Case Study:
Efficient Faculty Recruitment Using Genetic Algorithm

Amit Verma
Chandigarh Engineering College, India

Iqbaldeep Kaur
Chandigarh Engineering College, India

Dolly Sharma
Chandigarh Group of Colleges, India

Inderjeet Singh
Chandigarh Group of Colleges, India

ABSTRACT

Recruitment process takes place based on needed data while certain limiting factors are ignored. The objective of the chapter is to recruit best employees while taking care of limiting factors from the cluster for resource management and scheduling. Various parameters of the recruits have been selected to find the maximum score achieved by them. Recruitment process makes a database as cluster in the software environment perform the information retrieval on the database and then perform data mining using genetic algorithm while taking care of the positive values in contrast to limiting values received from the database. A bigger level recruitment process finds required values of a person, so negative points are ignored earlier in the recruitment process because there is no direct way to compare them. Genetic algorithm will create output in the form of chromosomal form. Again, apply information retrieval to get actual output. Major application of this process is that it will improve the selection process of candidates to a higher level of perfection in less time.

DOI: 10.4018/978-1-5225-6117-0.ch014

INTRODUCTION

US7, 930,197 B2, titled "Personal data mining" defines how data mining helps in business operations. Personal data mining is identified as mechanism/methods those are employed to find relevant information extraction that otherwise remains undiscovered for many operations. The user gives input as personal data that is further analyzed in association with data related with a plurality of distinct users to provide meaningful information that can evolve in various business operations and hence quality of life. The data assumed as personal can be extracted alone or in association with 3rd party data to specify correlations amongst the data and associated users.

Data is a set of information, which can be present in the form of written document, graphs, tables, images or coded in the digital form. Data is mainly stored so that important information can be collected for keeping record or to process later.

Information retrieval is collection of certain information from a database. Data mining refers to collecting the data from a database and using certain rules (such as classification, clustering, etc.) on data and the collected data is further evaluated to extract meaningful information out of it (Sarin et al., 1978; Stafylopatis & Likas, 1992; Wives & Loh, 1998).

Recruitment process was done based on scores collected. They could be collected based on different parameters according the different institutions. Institutions collected scores but there was no method to compare the limiting factors. To get accurate output limiting factors must be taken into consideration.

Work done will include adding the limiting factors along with older factors. Genetic Algorithm will be used to perform data mining and information retrieval on the given dataset (Chung, 2002). Genetic algorithm has been used in computer science as it mimics the natural process of selection (Jun-shan et al., 2009). Other hybrid models may be studied (Karpov, 2015; Kaur & Budwal, 2014; Dalai et al., 2014; Drias et al., 2009; Balasubramaniam, 2005; Ahmad & Ansari, 2012; Remi & Varghese, 2015; Takenouchi & Tokumaru, 2015). Related tools have also been proposed by researchers (Borg et al., 2012; Al-Odan & Al-Daraiseh, 2015; Sklyarov et al., 2015).

In natural genetic process, chromosomes of parents are utilized to form children with traits of parents. Each chromosome has a set of genes. Each gene is responsible for a particular trait. Parents with higher traits have been selected. In nature, selection mostly takes place in the form of 'survival of the fittest'. It takes place when genes of one parent crossovers with the genes of another parent, it result in mixture of two forms of a particular trait to form a better trait. There can also be a certain change in genes because of mutation, which can result in a completely different trait from those of the parents. In computer science, various traits of multiple objects can be crossed over, and it can be tested for a certain number of iterations (generations) to gain certain traits in the children. In this research work, genetic algorithm has been used in the faculty recruitment process.

METHOD APPLIED

Simple process that has been applied in work has been shown in Figure 1.

First of all recruitment process would create a database calculating overall scores and salary demand.

- **Chromosome:** Each parent acts as a chromosome in case of genetic algorithm. A chromosome can have two values, i.e. 0 or 1. When the value is 1 it means parent is accepted, while a parent with chromosome 0 is rejected. At the initial stage value of each parent's chromosome is 1. Method used for proposed work has been shown in figure 2 below.
- **Fitness Function:** A fitness function is a formula which will be used to implement the actual required process while using genetic algorithm. Fitness function performs the actual evaluation on the available dataset. A dataset contains parents and the value of their certain attributes which is to be measured.
- **Initial Generation:** Initial generation contains the list of parents which are to be crossed over using genetic algorithm to get the required output. In our case initial generation is in the form of candidates. It contains the names of the candidates. Initial generation (or population) has been taken from the available database. Figure 2 show the method applied to perform the proposed work.

Figure 1. Basic process applied for proposed work.

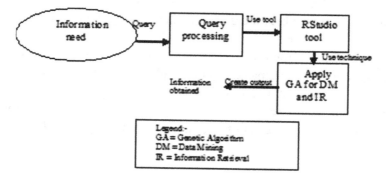

- **Evaluate Fitness:** When all the above data is available then evaluate the fitness of the population using 'fitness function'.
- **Selection:** While the evaluation process is taking place, first of all there is selection of the parents. Each possible combination of two parents is selected in the first generation.
- **Crossover:** After selection, crossover takes place between the selected parents. Crossover measures their attributes in pairs. How parents crossover until they are found unfit for this process in Figure 3.
- **Mutation:** There is a very rare chance of mutation in the process. It is possible that some new trait comes into existence after crossover which is not expected. It could suddenly increase the certain trait to minimum or maximum level. Mainly the chance of mutation of mutation is only 0.01%.
- **Elite Candidates:** It happens that when two parents selected fail to crossover because of some reason. Then there is selection of some other parent from the 'initial generation', this new parent is known as elite candidate.
- **Next Generation:** When the crossover results in a successful output, within the limit, it adds the two parents and the values of their attributes are added. It results in the formation of a single child. Child has added attributes of both the parents. Then a new parent is selected from the database which crossovers with the newly formed child using 'fitness function'. If the sum of attributes is within the limit provided, then there is success in this crossover. And a new child is formed from it. This process continues until the whole 'initial population' took part in selection process. There are chances that adding attributes of certain parents result in maximization of one attribute and minimization of the other attribute or within a limit, so this results in crossover of certain parents while the crossover of other parents fail. Each generation try combination of different parents to get the best output. If the outputs are within given condition, crossover process keep find best parents for this process. As soon as the limit to an attribute reaches, it results in stopping of genetic algorithm. Output comes in the form of 0 and 1. The parents providing the best output within the provided limits are shown as 1 while the parents which are unfit for selection are shown as 0 in the output, in the serial manner.
- **Stop Condition:** Stop condition is the limit after which the crossover can't take place in any more parents. This results in selection of all those parents which are giving best output within the provided limit.
- **Information Retrieval:** Perform information retrieval on available list of chromosomes to get the list of candidates who are fit to be selected.

Figure 2. Method to perform faculty recruitment using Genetic algorithm

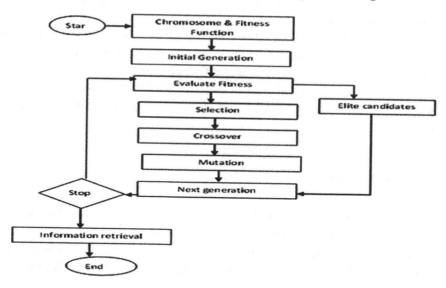

Figure 3. Crossover to create next generation

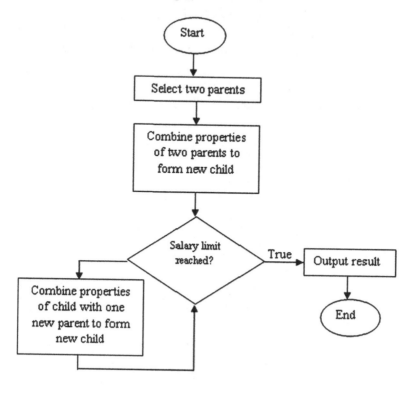

US 5,255,345 A, titled "Genetic algorithm" defines how genetic algorithm finds best solution. In one scenario, an optimization technique provides the most optimum solution to the problem for which a margin of space of solution exists ; in the said technique, trial solutions those are in synchronization with scheme (between token and trial solution) take on values by an iterative process, the value of the token is the key parameter that changed to explore more good solutions and further solutions analyzed and the last iteration is modified without interrupting the succession of iterations.

ALGORITHM APPLIED

US 7,801,836 B2, titled "Automated predictive data mining model selection using a genetic algorithm" defines that genetic algorithm can be used to predict results for the purpose of data mining. A predictive data mining model can be selected based on how well the model meets an objective function (Kweon, 2006). In certain implementations genetic algorithms can be used to search a space of predictive data mining model building parameters to determine an optimal predictive data mining model based on a score function corresponding to, for example, the accuracy of the selected predictive data mining model (Hao & Zhang, 2010; Yao, & Yao, 2003; Pereira & Baeza-Yates, 2005).

Genetic algorithm to find the candidates has been shown below:

```
Input: Recruits= t[t1, t2, t3, t4, t5, t6, t7]
Recruit_skill = tskl[st1, st2, st3, st4, st5, st6, st7];
Recruit_salary_demand = tsal[tsal1, tsal2, tsal3, tsal4, tsal5,
tsal6, tsal7];
Salary_limit = sal limit;
        Number of iterations iter;
Output: limited number of best recruits within a minimum salary
limit
begin
        do   {
initialize iter = 1;
            Select t and tsal;
            Perform CrsOvr t to t+1;
//CrsOvr = Crossover
            Perform Mtn = 0.01;
//Mtn = Mutation
   if(tsal<sal limit)
```

```
{

Calculate tskl;
                  Add tskl to tskl+1;
While elt = true;        // elt= Elitism
                }
}
until itr = 100;
        Return list of best candidates;
end;
```

It shows that first of all recruit names, their overall score (or skill score) and their salary demand must be present in the database. Then a salary limit of the institution which it is willing to pay or it can afford can be entered. Number of candidates providing maximum skill within that overall salary limit can be found. If the recruits are performing better than expectations then we can decrease the institution's payment limit to recruit required number of best faculty. Above algorithm shows that process takes place by performing various iterations. During this process, crossover takes place. One of the best iteration chooses the result.

EXPERIMENTAL SETUP OF PROBLEM USING SIMPLE EXAMPLE

First there is need of a dataset in required format. Average score of candidates has been calculated based on multiple parameters. It could be different for different institution's need such as multiple interview marks, written test marks, papers published, experience, etc., out of 50. Their salary demand must be known. Then apply above algorithm on the available database in Table 1.

Table 1. Initial dataset

S. No.	Candidate	Score	Salary Demand
1	Candidate1	30	90000
2	Candidate2	34	75000
3	Candidate3	15	50000
4	Candidate4	14	40000
5	Candidate5	30	70000
6	Candidate6	36	80000

Above dataset contains seven objects of 3 variables, Maximum salary limit of institution ready to pay is set to 2, 50,000 rupees. When the evaluation function applied on above dataset, certain conditions have been taken care of. Population size is set to 200, number of generations is set 100, and elitism is set true, while the mutation chance is 0.01.

RESULT AND DISCUSSION

Based on above data when evaluation function applied, following result has been obtained, which is in chromosomal form.

Best solution 0 1 0 1 0 1 1

Now, perform the information retrieval using the found chromosome, to find the required output. Output has been shown in Table 2.

From the above found result, it has been found that when salary limit set to Rs. 2, 50,000 it provides best Candidate candidates, who have maximum score, within that salary limit. We can see from Table 1 and Table 3 that Candidate1 had high skill of 30 and high salary demand of 90,000, Candidate3 has low skill of 15 and low salary demand of 50,000, both of these are not selected because genetic algorithm finds that in available salary limit, some other candidates can give maximum skill. If institute select these candidates, then it will be at loss of money and skill. It has been shown in calculations below,

Result total score $= 34 + 14 + 36 + 20 = 104$

Result total salary demand $= 75,000 + 40,000 + 80,000 + 50,000 = 2, 45,000$

From above we can see that total skill of 104 coming in company at best fit price of 2, 45,000 rupees, which is below 2, 50,000 rupees.

Table 2. Result obtained after applying genetic algorithm to select four candidates

S. No.	Candidate	Score	Salary Demand
2	Candidate2	34	75,000
4	Candidate4	14	40,000
6	Candidate6	36	80,000
7	Candidate7	20	50,000

If we want to choose 3 best candidates, put maximum salary limit of 2, 40, 000, genetic algorithm will give following solution in chromosomal form,
Best solution 0 1 0 0 1 1 0
This result has been retrieved in Table 3.

Candidate2+Candidate5+Candidate6 score $= 34 + 30 + 36 = 100$

Candidate2+Candidate5+Candidate6 salary demand $= 75,000 + 70,000 + 80,000 = 2, 25,000$

No other candidates' combination can give the maximum skill within the salary demand which the institution can afford. We can decrease or increase the 'salary limit' of institute to get lesser or more best candidates. It will help the institution to gain maximum skill at price of maximum benefit. When thousands of candidates apply online and give online tests, and then the best can be found out of them quickly through the technique explained above.

For information retrieval process, visit other database related to this database and which contains name, address, contact number, email address, etc. related to the selected candidate. It will give the final result.

CONCLUSION

Every institution has been made for benefits in various forms so efficient recruitment is very important in any institution. This chapter proposes a new technique using genetic algorithm. This technique is important during recruitment process for maximum monetary benefit to an institute and to gain maximum skill in an institute. Results have been shown theoretically and experimentally discussed with the help of an example. It has been observed that this method of selection of candidates is efficient and beneficial than the normal recruitment process. In case of smaller

Table 3. Result obtained after applying genetic algorithm to select three candidates.

S. No.	Candidate	Score	Salary Demand
2	Candidate2	34	75,000
5	Candidate5	30	70,000
6	Candidate6	36	80,000

database, genetic algorithm gives only one best result. In case of larger databases genetic algorithm can give different combination of results to select, for maximum benefit with a minor variation in them. So we can select other combination of candidates in case one combination fails to work. It is a benefit. Future work would include selecting that one combination, in a shorter span of time, which would give the best result out of all best combinations which have slight differences in them, in case of a larger database.

REFERENCES

Ahmad, M. W., & Ansari, M. A. (2012, June). A Survey: Soft Computing in Intelligent Information Retrieval Systems. In *Computational Science and Its Applications (ICCSA), 2012 12th International Conference on* (pp. 26-34). IEEE.

Al-Odan, H. A., & Al-Daraiseh, A. A. (2015, March). Open Source Data Mining tools. In *Electrical and Information Technologies (ICEIT), 2015 International Conference on* (pp. 369-374). IEEE. 10.1109/EITech.2015.7162956

Balasubramaniam, K. (2015). Hybrid Fuzzy-ontology Design Using FCA Based Clustering for Information Retrieval in Semantic Web. *Procedia Computer Science*, *50*, 135–142. doi:10.1016/j.procs.2015.04.075

Borg, M., Runeson, P., & Brodén, L. (2012, May). Evaluation of traceability recovery in context: A taxonomy for information retrieval tools. In *Evaluation & Assessment in Software Engineering (EASE 2012), 16th International Conference on* (pp. 111-120). IET. 10.1049/ic.2012.0014

Chung, H. M., Gey, F., & Piramuthu, S. (2002, January). Data Mining and Information Retrieval. In *System Sciences, 2002. HICSS. Proceedings of the 35th Annual Hawaii International Conference on* (pp. 841-842). IEEE.

Dalai, J., Hasan, S. Z., Sarkar, B., & Mukherjee, D. (2014, March). Adaptive operator switching and solution space probability structure based genetic algorithm for information retrieval through pattern recognition. In *Circuit, Power and Computing Technologies (ICCPCT), 2014 International Conference on* (pp. 1624-1629). IEEE. 10.1109/ICCPCT.2014.7054823

Drias, H., Khennak, I., & Boukhedra, A. (2009, November). A hybrid genetic algorithm for large scale information retrieval. In *Intelligent Computing and Intelligent Systems, 2009. ICIS 2009. IEEE International Conference on* (Vol. 1, pp. 842-846). IEEE. 10.1109/ICICISYS.2009.5358038

Hao, Y., & Zhang, Y. F. (2010, October). Research on knowledge retrieval by leveraging data mining techniques. In *Future Information Technology and Management Engineering (FITME), 2010 International Conference on* (Vol. 1, pp. 479-484). IEEE.

Jun-shan, T., Wei, H., & Yan, Q. (2009, March). Application of genetic algorithm in data mining. In *Education Technology and Computer Science, 2009. ETCS'09. First International Workshop on* (Vol. 2, pp. 353-356). IEEE. 10.1109/ETCS.2009.340

Karpov, A. V., Sysoev, A. A., Poteshin, S. S., Chernyshev, D. M., & Sysoev, A. A. (2015). Genetic algorithm for voltage optimization of gridless ion mirror. *Physics Procedia, 72*, 236–240. doi:10.1016/j.phpro.2015.09.070

Kaur, N., & Budwal, J. S. (2014, May). Intelligent Web search optimization with reference to mutation operator of Genetic and Cultural Algorithms framework. In *Advanced Communication Control and Computing Technologies (ICACCCT), 2014 International Conference on* (pp. 619-623). IEEE. 10.1109/ICACCCT.2014.7019162

Kweon, S. C., Sawng, Y. W., & Kim, S. H. (2006, May). An Integrated Approach Using Data Mining & Genetic Algorithm in Customer Credit Risk Prediction of Installment Purchase Financing. In *Collaborative Technologies and Systems, 2006. CTS 2006. International Symposium on* (pp. 125-131). IEEE.

Ozzie, R. E., Gates, W. H., III, Flake, G. W., Bergstraesser, T. F., Blinn, A. N., Brumme, C. W., . . . Glasser, D. S. (2011). *U.S. Patent No. 7,930,197*. Washington, DC: U.S. Patent and Trademark Office.

Pereira, Á. R., & Baeza-Yates, R. (2005, August). Applications of a web information mining model to data mining and information retrieval tasks. In *Database and Expert Systems Applications, 2005. Proceedings. Sixteenth International Workshop on* (pp. 1031-1035). IEEE.

Remi, S., & Varghese, S. C. (2015). Domain Ontology Driven Fuzzy Semantic Information Retrieval. *Procedia Computer Science, 46*, 676–681. doi:10.1016/j.procs.2015.02.122

Sarin, R. K., Sicherman, A., & Nair, K. (1978). Evaluating proposals using decision analysis. IEEE Transaction on Systems, Man, and Cybernetic, 8(2), 128-131.

Shaefer, C. G. (1993). *U.S. Patent No. 5,255,345*. Washington, DC: U.S. Patent and Trademark Office.

Sklyarov, V., Skliarova, I., Silva, J., Sudnitson, A., & Rjabov, A. (2015, May). Hardware accelerators for information retrieval and data mining. In *Information and Communication Technology Research (ICTRC), 2015 International Conference on* (pp. 202-205). IEEE.

Stafylopatis, A., & Likas, A. (1992). Pictorial information retrieval using the random neural network. Software Engineering. *Transfer: European Review of Labour and Research*, *18*(7), 590–600.

Sureka, A. (2010). *U.S. Patent No. 7,801,836*. Washington, DC: U.S. Patent and Trademark Office.

Takenouchi, H., & Tokumaru, M. (2015, September). Applying a hybrid IGA-SimE algorithm to a multimedia retrieval system. In *Awareness Science and Technology (iCAST), 2015 IEEE 7th International Conference on* (pp. 60-65). IEEE.

Wives, L. K., & Loh, S. (1998, September). Hyperdictionary: a knowledge discovery tool to help information retrieval. In *String Processing and Information Retrieval: A South American Symposium, 1998. Proceedings* (pp. 103-109). IEEE.

Yao, J. T., & Yao, Y. Y. (2003, October). Web-based information retrieval support systems: building research tools for scientists in the new information age. In *Web Intelligence, 2003. WI 2003. Proceedings. IEEE/WIC International Conference on* (pp. 570-573). IEEE.

ADDITIONAL READING

Adda, M. (2013). A formal model of information retrieval based on user sensitivities. *Procedia Computer Science*, *19*, 428–436. doi:10.1016/j.procs.2013.06.058

Chithra, S., Sinith, M. S., & Gayathri, A. (2015). Music Information Retrieval for Polyphonic Signals Using Hidden Markov Model. *Procedia Computer Science*, *46*, 381–387. doi:10.1016/j.procs.2015.02.034

Dankar, F. K., El Emam, K., & Matwin, S. (2014). Efficient Private Information Retrieval for Geographical Aggregation. *Procedia Computer Science*, *37*, 497–502. doi:10.1016/j.procs.2014.08.074

Farhadi, F., Sorkhi, M., Hashemi, S., & Hamzeh, A. (2011, December). An effective expert team formation in social networks based on skill grading. In Data Mining Workshops (ICDMW), 2011 IEEE 11th International Conference on (pp. 366-372). IEEE. 10.1109/ICDMW.2011.28

Garimella, R. M., Gabbouj, M., & Ahmad, I. (2015). Image Retrieval: Information and Rough Set Theories. *Procedia Computer Science*, *54*, 631–637. doi:10.1016/j.procs.2015.06.073

Marlin Delminger and William F. Marsden. (1963). Development of an Information retrieval system System for an Electronics R&D Laboratory. Transaction on Engineering writing and Speech on 6(1), on (10-19) IEEE.

Menzies, T., Chen, Z., Hihn, J., & Lum, K. (1901). *Best Practices in Software Effort Estimation. Transactions on Software Engineering, 1(1), on* (pp. 883–895). IEEE.

Mooers, C. (1954). Choice and coding in Information retrieval system systems. *Transactions of the IRE Professional Group on Information Theory*, *4*(4), 112-118. 10.1109/TIT.1954.1057470

Rao, B., Mitra, A., & Mondal, J. (2015). Algorithm for retrieval of sub-community graph from a compressed community graph using graph mining techniques. *Procedia Computer Science*, *57*, 678–685. doi:10.1016/j.procs.2015.07.444

Thakare, A. D., & Dhote, C. A. (2013, August). An improved matching functions for information retrieval using Genetic Algorithm. In Advances in Computing, Communications and Informatics (ICACCI), 2013 International Conference on(pp. 770-774). IEEE. 10.1109/ICACCI.2013.6637271

Compilation of References

Abbasi, A., & Chen, H. (2008). CyberGate: A design framework and system for text analysis of computer-mediated communication. *Management Information Systems Quarterly, 32*(4), 811–837. doi:10.2307/25148873

Abney, S. (2008). *Semi supervised Learning for Computational Linguistics*. Chapman and Hall.

Agarwal, B., Mittal, P., & Garg, S. (2015). Sentiment Analysis Using Common-Sense and Context Information. *Computational Intelligence and Neuroscience, 2015*, 1–9. doi:10.1155/2015/715730 PMID:25866505

Agarwal, B., Poria, S., Mittal, N., Gelbukh, A., & Hussain, A. (2015). Concept-Level sentiment analysis with dependency-based semantic parsing: A novel approach. *Cognitive Computation, 7*(4), 487–499. doi:10.100712559-014-9316-6

Agirre, E., & Edmonds, P. (2007). *Word Sense Disambiguation: Algorithms and Applications*. Springer. doi:10.1007/978-1-4020-4809-8

Agrawal, R. (2014). K-Nearest Neighbor for Uncertain Data. *International Journal of Computers and Applications, 105*(11).

Agrawal, R., & Batra, M. (2013). A detailed study on text mining techniques. *International Journal of Soft Computing and Engineering, 2*(6), 118–121.

Ahmad, M. W., & Ansari, M. A. (2012, June). A Survey: Soft Computing in Intelligent Information Retrieval Systems. In *Computational Science and Its Applications (ICCSA), 2012 12th International Conference on* (pp. 26-34). IEEE.

Ahmed, T., & Farrag, H. (2013). Toward SWSs discovery: Mapping from WSDL to OWL-S based on ontology search and standardization engine. *IEEE Transactions on Knowledge and Data Engineering, 25*(5), 1135–1147. doi:10.1109/TKDE.2012.25

Ain, Q. T., Ali, M., Riaz, A., Noureen, A., Kamran, M., Hayat, B., & Rehman, A. (2017). Sentiment analysis using deep learning techniques: A review. *Int. J. Adv. Comput. Sci. Appl., 8*(6), 424.

Al-Daihani, S. M., & Abrahams, A. (2016). A text mining analysis of academic libraries' tweets. *Journal of Academic Librarianship, 42*(2), 135–143. doi:10.1016/j.acalib.2015.12.014

Alexandra, B., Ralf, S., Mijail, K., Vanni, Z., Erik, V. D. G., Matina, H., ... Jenya, B. (2013). Sentiment analysis in the news. *Proceedings of the Seventh International Conference on Language Resources and Evaluation (LREC'10).*

Alias-i. (2008). *LingPipe 4.1.0.* Retrieved from http://alias-i.com/lingpipe

Ali, F., Kwak, K. S., & Kim, Y. G. (2016). Opinion mining based on fuzzy domain ontology and Support Vector Machine: A proposal to automate online review classification. *Applied Soft Computing, 47,* 235–250. doi:10.1016/j.asoc.2016.06.003

Al-Kabi, M. N., Gigieh, A. H., Alsmadi, I. M., Wahsheh, H. A., & Haidar, M. M. (2014). Opinion mining and analysis for Arabic language. *International Journal of Advanced Computer Science and Applications, 5*(5), 181–195.

Alnusair, A., & Zhao, T. (2010). Component search and reuse: An ontology-based approach. *IEEE International Conference,* 258-261. 10.1109/IRI.2010.5558931

AlObaidi, M., Mahmood, K., & Sabra, S. (2016). Semantic Enrichment for Local Search Engine using Linked Open Data. *25th International Conference Companion on World Wide Web,* 631-634. 10.1145/2872518.2890481

Al-Odan, H. A., & Al-Daraiseh, A. A. (2015, March). Open Source Data Mining tools. In *Electrical and Information Technologies (ICEIT), 2015 International Conference on* (pp. 369-374). IEEE. 10.1109/EITech.2015.7162956

Alsaqer, A. F., & Sasi, S. (2017). Movie review summarization and sentiment analysis using rapidminer. *International Conference on Networks & Advances in Computational Technologies (NetACT),* 329-335. 10.1109/NETACT.2017.8076790

Anandan, S., Bogoevici, M., Renfro, G., Gopinathan, I., & Peralta, P. (2015). Spring XD: a modular distributed stream and batch processing system. In *Proceedings of the 9th ACM International Conference on Distributed Event Based Systems (DEBS '15).* ACM. 10.1145/2675743.2771879

Ancona, D., Viviana, M., & Ombretta, P. (2012). Ontology-based documentation extraction for semi-automatic migration of Java code. *The 27th Annual ACM Symposium on Applied Computing,* 1137-1143.

Asur, S., & Bernardo, A. H. (2010). *Predicting the future with social media.* Arxiv preprint arXiv:1003.5699, 2010.

Balasubramaniam, K. (2015). Hybrid Fuzzy-ontology Design Using FCA Based Clustering for Information Retrieval in Semantic Web. *Procedia Computer Science, 50,* 135–142. doi:10.1016/j.procs.2015.04.075

Batool, R., Khattak, A. M., Maqbool, J., & Lee, S. (2013). Precise tweet classification and sentiment analysis. *IEEE/ACIS 12th International Conference on Computer and Information Science (ICIS),* 461-466. 10.1109/ICIS.2013.6607883

Baziz, M., Boughanem, M., Aussenac-Gilles, N., & Chrisment, C. (2005). Semantic cores for representing documents in IR. *Proceedings of the 2005 ACM symposium on Applied computing.* 10.1145/1066677.1066911

Beat, V. (2016, April 5). Nvidia CEO bets big on deep learning and VR. *Machine Learning, 45*(37).

Bengio, Y., Courville, A., & Vincent, P. (2013). Representation Learning: A Review and New Perspectives. *IEEE Transactions on Pattern Analysis and Machine Intelligence, 35*(8), 1798–1828. doi:10.1109/TPAMI.2013.50 PMID:23787338

Bengio, Y., LeCun, Y., & Hinton, G. (2015). Deep Learning. *Nature, 521*(7553), 436–444. doi:10.1038/nature14539 PMID:26017442

Bernstein, A., Hill, S., & Provost, F. (2002). *Intelligent assistance for the data mining process: An ontology-based approach.* Academic Press.

Bharti, S. K., Vachha, B., Pradhan, R. K., Babu, K. S., & Jena, S. K. (2016). Sarcastic sentiment detection in tweets streamed in real time: A big data approach. *Digital Communications and Networks, 2*(3), 108–121. doi:10.1016/j.dcan.2016.06.002

Bi, R., Zhou, Y., Lu, F., & Wang, W. (2007). Predicting Gene Ontology functions based on support vector machines and statistical significance estimation. *Neurocomputing, 70*(4-6), 718–725. doi:10.1016/j.neucom.2006.10.006

Bisson, G., Nédellec, C., & Canamero, D. (2000, August). Designing Clustering Methods for Ontology Building-The Mo'K Workbench. In ECAI workshop on ontology learning (Vol. 31). Academic Press.

Bollen, J., Mao, H., & Zeng, X.-J. (2011). Twitter mood predicts the stock market. *Journal of Computational Science, 2*(1), 1–8. doi:10.1016/j.jocs.2010.12.007

Borg, M., Runeson, P., & Brodén, L. (2012, May). Evaluation of traceability recovery in context: A taxonomy for information retrieval tools. In *Evaluation & Assessment in Software Engineering (EASE 2012), 16th International Conference on* (pp. 111-120). IET. 10.1049/ic.2012.0014

Broens, Pokraev, Sinderen, Koolwaaij, & Costa. (2004). Con-text-aware, ontology-based service discovery. *European Symposium on Ambient Intelligence*, 72-83.

Buitelaar, P., Olejnik, D., & Sintek, M. (2004, May). A protégé plug-in for ontology extraction from text based on linguistic analysis. In *European Semantic Web Symposium* (pp. 31-44). Springer. 10.1007/978-3-540-25956-5_3

Cai, K., Spangler, S., Chen, Y., & Zhang, L. (2008). Leveraging Sentiment Analysis for Topic Detection. *IEEE/WIC/ACM International Conference on Web Intelligence and Intelligent Agent Technology, 1*, 265-271. 10.1109/WIIAT.2008.188

Camacho-Collados, J., & Pilehvar, M. T. (2015). Making sense of word embeddings. A unified multilingual semantic representation of concepts. *Proceedings of the Association for Computational Linguistics*, 741–751.

Camacho-Collados, J., Pilehvar, M. T., & Navigli, R. (2015). Making sense of word embeddings. A unified multilingual semantic representation of concepts. *Proceedings of the Association for Computational Linguistics*, 741–751.

Carrio, Sampedro, Rodriguez-Ramos, & Campoy (2017). A Review of Deep Learning Methods and Applications for Unmanned Aerial Vehicles. *Hindawi Journal of Sensors.* .10.1155/2017/3296874

Castellanos, M., Dayal, U., Wang, S., & Chetan, G. (2010). Information Extraction, Real-Time, Processing and DW2.0 in Operational Business Intelligence, Databases in Networked *Information Systems*. *Lecture Notes in Computer Science*, *5999*, 33–45. doi:10.1007/978-3-642-12038-1_4

Chan, C. C., & Liszka, K. J. (2013). Application of rough set theory to sentiment analysis of microblog data. In *Rough Sets and Intelligent Systems-Professor Zdzisław Pawlak in Memoriam* (pp. 185–202). Berlin: Springer. doi:10.1007/978-3-642-30341-8_10

Chaturvedi & Prabhakar. (2014). Ontology driven builder pattern: a plug and play component. *29th Annual ACM Symposium on Applied Computing*, 1055-1057.

Chi, N. W., Lin, K. Y., & Hsieh, S. H. (2014). Using ontology-based text classification to assist Job Hazard Analysis. *Advanced Engineering Informatics*, *28*(4), 381–394. doi:10.1016/j.aei.2014.05.001

Chung, H. M., Gey, F., & Piramuthu, S. (2002, January). Data Mining and Information Retrieval. In *System Sciences, 2002. HICSS. Proceedings of the 35th Annual Hawaii International Conference on* (pp. 841-842). IEEE.

Cieliebak, Dürr, & Uzdilli. (2013). Potential and Limitations of Commercial Sentiment Detection Tools. *ESSEM, 1096.*

Cimiano, P., & Völker, J. (2005, June). text2onto. In *International conference on application of natural language to information systems* (pp. 227-238). Springer.

Collobert, R., Weston, J., Bottou, L., Karlen, M., Kavukcuoglu, K., & Kuksa, P. (2011). Natural language processing (almost) from scratch. *Journal of Machine Learning ResearchVolume*, *12*(August), 2493–2537.

Consortium, T. G. O. (2001). Creating the gene ontology resource: Design and implementation. *Genome Research*, *11*(8), 1425–1433. doi:10.1101/gr.180801 PMID:11483584

Craven, M., DiPasquo, D., Freitag, D., McCallum, A., Mitchell, T., Nigam, K., & Slattery, S. (2000). Learning to construct knowledge bases from the World Wide Web. *Artificial Intelligence*, *118*(1-2), 69–113. doi:10.1016/S0004-3702(00)00004-7

Croft, B., Metzler, D., & Strohman, T. (2009). Search Engines: Information Retrieval in Practice. Addison Wesley.

Cun. (2016). *Slides on Deep Learning Online*. Academic Press.

Cunningham, H. (2002). Article. *Computers and the Humanities*, *36*(2), 223–254. doi:10.1023/A:1014348124664

Dadvar, M., Hauff, C., & de Jong, F. M. (2011, February). Scope of negation detection in sentiment analysis. In *Proceedings of the Dutch-Belgian Information Retrieval Workshop, DIR 2011*. University of Amsterdam.

Dalai, J., Hasan, S. Z., Sarkar, B., & Mukherjee, D. (2014, March). Adaptive operator switching and solution space probability structure based genetic algorithm for information retrieval through pattern recognition. In *Circuit, Power and Computing Technologies (ICCPCT), 2014 International Conference on* (pp. 1624-1629). IEEE. 10.1109/ICCPCT.2014.7054823

Das, S., & Chen, M. (2001). Yahoo! for Amazon: Extracting market sentiment from stock message boards. *Proceedings of APFA-2001*.

Dave, K., Lawrence, S., & Pennock, D. M. (2003). Mining the peanut gallery: Opinion extraction and semantic classification of product reviews. *Proceedings of International Conference on World Wide Web (WWW-2003)*. 10.1145/775152.775226

Davidov, D., Tsur, O., & Rappoport, A. (2010). Semi-supervised recognition of sarcastic sentences in twitter and amazon. In *Proceedings of the fourteenth conference on Computational Natural Language Learning*, Uppsala, Sweden (pp. 107-116).

DeCarvalho, Fairhurst, & Bisset. (1994). An integrated Boolean neural network for pattern classification. *Pattern Recognition Letters, 15*(8), 807–813. doi: 1994-08-0810.1016/0167-8655(94)90009-4

Decker, S., Erdmann, M., Fensel, D., & Studer, R. (1999). Ontobroker: Ontology based access to distributed and semi-structured information. In *Database Semantics* (pp. 351–369). Boston, MA: Springer. doi:10.1007/978-0-387-35561-0_20

Demsar, J., Curk, T., Erjavec, A., Gorup, C., Hocevar, T., Milutinovic, M., ... Zupan, B. (2013). Orange: Data Mining Toolbox in Python. *Journal of Machine Learning Research*, *14*(Aug), 2349–2353.

Deng, L., & Yu, D. (2014). Deep Learning: Methods and Applications. *Foundations and Trends in Signal Processing*, *7*(3–4), 197–387. doi:10.1561/2000000039

Deshmukh, J. S., & Tripathy, A. K. (2018). Entropy based classifier for cross-domain opinion mining. *Applied Computing and Informatics*, *14*(1), 55–64. doi:10.1016/j.aci.2017.03.001

Drake. (n.d.). *Open Source project*. Retrieved from https://github.com/Factual/drake/wiki

Drias, H., Khennak, I., & Boukhedra, A. (2009, November). A hybrid genetic algorithm for large scale information retrieval. In *Intelligent Computing and Intelligent Systems, 2009. ICIS 2009. IEEE International Conference on* (Vol. 1, pp. 842-846). IEEE. 10.1109/ICICISYS.2009.5358038

Duo, Z., Juan-Zi, L., & Bin, X. (2005). *Web service annotation using ontology mapping.* Paper presented at the Service-Oriented System Engineering, SOSE 2005, IEEE International Workshop.

Du, T. C., Li, F., & King, I. (2009). Managing knowledge on the Web–Extracting ontology from HTML Web. *Decision Support Systems*, *47*(4), 319–331. doi:10.1016/j.dss.2009.02.011

ECAI-02. (2002). *Ontology Learning Tools Workshop*. Retrieved from http://www-sop.inria.fr/acacia/WORKSHOPS/ ECAI2002-OLT /accepted-papers.html

ECAI-02. (2002). *Workshop on Machine Learning and Natural Language Processing for Ontology Engineering*. Retrieved from http://www-sop.inria.fr/acacia/WORKSHOPS/ECAI2002-OLT/

El-Din, D. M., Mokhtar, H. M., & Ismael, O. (2015). Online paper review analysis. *International Journal of Advanced Computer Science and Applications*, *6*(9).

Fajszi, B., Cser, L., & Fehér, T. (2013). *Business Value in an Ocean of Data: Data Mining From a User Perspective*. Alinea Press.

Fan, J., Luo, H., Gao, Y., & Jain, R. (2007). Incorporating concept ontology for hierarchical video classification, annotation, and visualization. *IEEE Transactions on Multimedia*, *9*(5), 939–957. doi:10.1109/TMM.2007.900143

Farias, D., Mendes, T., Roxin, A., & Nicolle, C. (2015). SWRL rule-selection methodology for on-tology interoperability. *Data & Knowledge Engineering*.

Farooq, U., Mansoor, H., Nongaillard, A., Ouzrout, Y., & Qadir, M. A. (2017). Negation Handling in Sentiment Analysis at Sentence Level. *JCP*, *12*(5), 470–478. PMID:28097676

Faure, D., & Nédellec, C. (1998, May). A corpus-based conceptual clustering method for verb frames and ontology acquisition. In LREC workshop on adapting lexical and corpus resources to sublanguages and applications (Vol. 707, No. 728, p. 30). Academic Press.

Fellbaum, C. (1998). *WordNet: An Electronic Lexical Database (Language, Speech, and Communication)*. Academic Press.

Fensel, D. (2002). Ontology-based knowledge management. *Computer*, *35*(11), 56–59. doi:10.1109/MC.2002.1046975

Fernández, M., Cantador, I., López, V., Vallet, D., Castells, P., & Motta, E. (2011). Semantically enhanced information retrieval: An ontology-based approach. *Journal of Web Semantics*, *9*(4), 434–452. doi:10.1016/j.websem.2010.11.003

Ferraresi, A., Zanchetta, E., Baroni, M., & Bernardini, S. (2008). Introducing and evaluating ukwac, a very large web-derived corpus of english. *Proceedings of the 4th Web as Corpus Workshop (WAC-4)*.

Filatova, E. (2012, May). Irony and Sarcasm: Corpus Generation and Analysis Using Crowdsourcing. In LREC (pp. 392-398). Academic Press.

Flekova, L., Preoţiuc-Pietro, D., & Ruppert, E. (2015). Analysing domain suitability of a sentiment lexicon by identifying distributionally bipolar words. In *Proceedings of the 6th Workshop on Computational Approaches to Subjectivity, Sentiment and Social Media Analysis* (pp. 77-84). Academic Press. 10.18653/v1/W15-2911

Fong, S., Deb, S., Chan, I. W., & Vijayakumar, P. (2014). An event driven neural network system for evaluating public moods from online users' comments. *Fifth International Conference on the Applications of Digital Information and Web Technologies (ICADIWT)*, 239-243. 10.1109/ICADIWT.2014.6814688

Freitas, L. A., & Vieira, R. (2013). Ontology based feature level opinion mining for portuguese reviews. *Proceedings of the 22nd international conference on World Wide Web companion*. 10.1145/2487788.2487944

Fu, Jones, & Abdelmoty. (2005). Ontology-based spatial query expansion in information retrieval. *OTM Confederated International Conferences on the Move to Meaningful Internet Systems*, 1466-1482.

Furht, B. (Ed). (2010). Handbook of Social Network Technologies and Applications. Springer. doi: . doi:10.1007/978-1-4419-7142-5

Gacitua, R., Sawyer, P., & Rayson, P. (2008). A flexible framework to experiment with ontology learning techniques. *Knowledge-Based Systems*, *21*(3), 192–199. doi:10.1016/j.knosys.2007.11.009

Gal, A., Modica, G., & Jamil, H. (2004, March). Ontobuilder: Fully automatic extraction and consolidation of ontologies from web sources. In *Data Engineering, 2004. Proceedings. 20th International Conference on* (p. 853). IEEE.

Gamon, M., Aue, A., Corston-Oliver, S., & Ringger, E. (2005). Pulse: Mining customer opinions from free text. *Lecture Notes in Computer Science*, *36*(6), 121–1324. doi:10.1007/11552253_12

García, M. D. M. R., García-Nieto, J., & Aldana-Montes, J. F. (2016). An ontology-based data integration approach for web analytics in e-commerce. *Expert Systems with Applications*, *63*, 20–34. doi:10.1016/j.eswa.2016.06.034

Gašević, D., Zouaq, A., Torniai, C., Jovanović, J., & Hatala, M. (2011). An approach to folksonomy-based ontology maintenance for learning environments. *IEEE Transactions on Learning Technologies*, *4*(4), 301–314. doi:10.1109/TLT.2011.21

Gasse, F., & Haarslev, V. (2008, April). DLRule: A Rule Editor plug-in for Protege. OWLED (Spring).

GATE. (n.d.). *GATE User Guide*. Retrieved from http://gate.ac.uk/sale/tao/split.html

Ghasemi, F., Mehridehnavi, A. R., Fassihi, A., & Perez-Sanchez, H. (2017). Deep Neural Network in Biological Activity Prediction using Deep Belief Network. *Applied Soft Computing*.

Go, A., Bhayani, R., & Huang, L. (2009). Twitter sentiment classification using distant supervision. CS224 Project Report, Stanford.

Golbreich, C. (2004, November). Combining rule and ontology reasoners for the semantic web. In *International Workshop on Rules and Rule Markup Languages for the Semantic Web* (pp. 6-22). Springer. 10.1007/978-3-540-30504-0_2

González-Ibáñez, R., Muresan, S., & Wacholder, N. (2011, June). Identifying sarcasm in Twitter: a closer look. In *Proceedings of the 49th Annual Meeting of the Association for Computational Linguistics: Human Language Technologies: Short Papers-Volume 2* (pp. 581-586). Association for Computational Linguistics.

Goodfellow, I., Bengio, Y., & Courville, A. (2016). *Deep Learning*. Cambridge, MA: MIT Press.

Griewank, A. (2012). Who Invented the Reverse Mode of Differentiation? *Documenta Matematica*, 389–400.

Groh, G., & Hauffa, J. (2011). Characterizing Social Relations Via NLP-based Sentiment Analysis. *Proceedings of the Fifth International AAAI Conference on Weblogs and Social Media (ICWSM-2011)*.

Gruber, T. R. (1993). A Translation Approach to Portable Ontology Specifications Acquisition. *Current Issues in Knowledge Modeling, 5*(2), 199-220.

Gruber, T. R. (1993). A Translation Approach to Portable Ontologies. *Knowledge Acquisition, 5*(2), 199–220. doi:10.1006/knac.1993.1008

Gruber, T. R. (1995). Toward principles for the design of ontologies used for knowledge sharing? *International Journal of Human-Computer Studies, 43*(5-6), 907–928. doi:10.1006/ijhc.1995.1081

Gu, S., Lillicrap, T., Sutskever, I., & Levine, S. (2016). Continuous deep q-learning with model-based acceleration. *The 33rd International Conference on International Conference on Machine Learning, 48*, 2829–2838. Retrieved from https://arxiv.org/abs/1603.00748

Guarino, N. (1995). Formal ontology, conceptual analysis and knowledge representation. *International Journal of Human-Computer Studies, 43*(5), 1–15.

Guo. (2016, April). Deep learning for visual understanding. *Neurocomputing, 187*(26), 27–48.

Guo, Y. W., Tang, Y. T., & Kao, H. Y. (2014). Genealogical-Based Method for Multiple Ontology Self-Extension in MeSH. *IEEE Transactions on Nanobioscience, 13*(2), 124–130. doi:10.1109/TNB.2014.2320413 PMID:24893362

Gupta & Kumar. (n.d.). Reusable Software Component Retrieval System. *International Journal of Application or Innovation in Engineering and Management, 2*(1), 187–194.

Guzman, E., & Maalej, W. (2014, August). How do users like this feature? a fine grained sentiment analysis of app reviews. In *Requirements Engineering Conference (RE), 2014 IEEE 22nd International* (pp. 153-162). IEEE. 10.1109/RE.2014.6912257

Hakeem, A., & Shah, M. (2004, August). Ontology and taxonomy collaborated framework for meeting classification. In *Pattern Recognition, 2004. ICPR 2004. Proceedings of the 17th International Conference on* (*Vol. 4*, pp. 219-222). IEEE. 10.1109/ICPR.2004.1333743

Hamad, M. M., & Jihad, A. A. (2011). *An Enhanced Technique to Clean Data in the Data Warehouse* (pp. 306–311). Dubai, UAE: Developments in E-systems Engineering. doi:10.1109/DeSE.2011.32

Han, J., Kamber, M., & Pei, J. (2006). *Data preprocessing. Data mining: concepts and techniques* (pp. 47–97). San Francisco: Morgan Kaufmann.

Hao, Y., & Zhang, Y. F. (2010, October). Research on knowledge retrieval by leveraging data mining techniques. In *Future Information Technology and Management Engineering (FITME), 2010 International Conference on* (Vol. 1, pp. 479-484). IEEE.

Hassan, A., Abbasi, A., & Zeng, D. (2013). Twitter Sentiment Analysis: A Bootstrap Ensemble Framework. *International Conference on Social Computing*, 357-364. 10.1109/SocialCom.2013.56

Hatzivassiloglou, V., & McKeown, K. R. (1997). Predicting the semantic orientation of adjectives. *Proceedings of Annual Meeting of the Association for Computational Linguistics (ACL-1997).*

HealeyC. (2016). Retrieved from https://www.csc2.ncsu.edu/faculty/healey/tweet_viz/

Hearst, M. (1992). Direction-based text interpretation as an information access refinement. In P. Jacobs (Ed.), *Text-Based Intelligent Systems* (pp. 257–274). Lawrence Erlbaum Associates.

Heerschop, B., van Iterson, P., Hogenboom, A., Frasincar, F., & Kaymak, U. (2011). Accounting for negation in sentiment analysis. In *11th Dutch-Belgian Information Retrieval Workshop (DIR 2011)* (pp. 38-39). Academic Press.

He, Y., Chenghua, L., & Harith, A. (2011). Automatically extracting polarity-bearing topics for cross-domain sentiment classification. *Proceedings of the Annual Meeting of the Association for Computational Linguistics.*

Hilario, M., Nguyen, P., Do, H., Woznica, A., & Kalousis, A. (2011). Ontology-based meta-mining of knowledge discovery workflows. In *Meta-learning in computational intelligence* (pp. 273–315). Berlin: Springer. doi:10.1007/978-3-642-20980-2_9

Hinton, G. E., Osindero, S., & Teh, Y.-W. (2006). A Fast Learning Algorithm for Deep Belief Nets. *Neural Computation*, *18*(7), 1527–1554. doi:10.1162/neco.2006.18.7.1527 PMID:16764513

Hochreiter, S., & Schmidhuber, J. (1996). LSTM can solve hard longtime lag problems. *10th Annual Conference on Neural Information Processing Systems. NIPS*, *1996*, 473–479.

Holte, R. C. (1993). Very simple classification rules perform well on most commonly used datasets. *Machine Learning*, *11*(1), 1–27. doi:10.1023/A:1022631118932

Hoxha, J., Jiang, G., & Weng, C. (2016). Automated learning of domain taxonomies from text using background knowledge. *Journal of Biomedical Informatics*, *63*, 295–306. doi:10.1016/j.jbi.2016.09.002 PMID:27597572

Hu, X., & Liu, H. (2012). Text analytics in social media. *Mining text data*, 385-414.

Huang, E. H., Socher, R., Manning, C. D., & Ng, A. Y. (2012). MaxMax: A Graph-based Soft Clustering Algorithm Applied to Word Sense Induction. In *Proceedings of the 14th International Conference on Computational Linguistics and Intelligent Text Processing* (pp. 368–381). Samos, Greece: Springer Verlag.

Huang, E. H., Socher, R., Manning, C. D., & Ng, A. Y. (2012).MaxMax: A Graph-based Soft Clustering Algorithm Applied to Word Sense Induction. *Proceedings of the 14th International Conference on Computational Linguistics and Intelligent Text Processing*, 368–381.

Huang, C. J., & Cheng, M. Y. (2008). Similarity Measurement of Rule-based Knowledge Using Conditional Probability. *Journal of Information Science and Engineering*, *24*(3).

Huang, H. D., Lee, C. S., Wang, M. H., & Kao, H. Y. (2014). IT2FS-based ontology with soft-computing mechanism for malware behavior analysis. *Soft Computing*, *18*(2), 267–284. doi:10.100700500-013-1056-0

Hu, M., & Liu, B. (2004). Mining and summarizing customer reviews. In *Proceedings of the Tenth ACM SIGKDD International conference on Knowledge discovery and Data mining* (pp. 168-177), ACM.

Hu, W., Qu, Y., & Cheng, G. (2008). Matching large ontologies: A divide-and-conquer approach. *Data & Knowledge Engineering*, *67*(1), 140–160. doi:10.1016/j.datak.2008.06.003

Indurkhya, N., & Damerau, F. J. (Eds.). (2010). *Handbook of natural language processing* (Vol. 2). CRC Press.

Irfan, R., King, C. K., Grages, D., Ewen, S., Khan, S. U., Madani, S. A., & Tziritas, N. (2015). A survey on text mining in social networks. *The Knowledge Engineering Review*, *30*(2), 157–170. doi:10.1017/S0269888914000277

Ittoo, A., Nguyen, L. M., & van den Bosch, A. (2016). Text analytics in industry: Challenges, desiderata and trends. *Computers in Industry*, *78*, 96–107. doi:10.1016/j.compind.2015.12.001

Ivakhnenko, A. G. (1973). *Cybernetic Predicting Devices*. CCM Information Corporation.

Jakoband & Gurevych (n.d.). *Extracting Opinion Targets from User-Generated Discourse with an Application to Recommendation Systems* (Doctor of Philosophy). Darmstadt University of Technology, Darmstadt, Germany.

Jiajia, W., Yezheng, L., Yuanchun, J., Chunhua, S., Jianshan, S., & Yanan, D. (2016, June). Clustering Product Features of Online Reviews Based on Nonnegative Matrix Tri-factorizations. In *Data Science in Cyberspace (DSC), IEEE International Conference on* (pp. 199-208). IEEE. 10.1109/DSC.2016.32

Jiang, X., & Tan, A. H. (2005, November). Mining ontological knowledge from domain-specific text documents. In *Data Mining, Fifth IEEE International Conference on* (pp. 4-pp). IEEE. 10.1109/ICDM.2005.97

Jindal, N., & Liu, B. (2007, May). Review spam detection. In *Proceedings of the 16th international conference on World Wide Web* (pp. 1189-1190). ACM. 10.1145/1242572.1242759

Jindal, N., & Liu, B. (2008, February). Opinion spam and analysis. In *Proceedings of the 2008 International Conference on Web Search and Data Mining* (pp. 219-230). ACM.

Jin, X., & Long, Y. (2007). *Research on ontology based representation and retrieval of components. In Software Engineering, Artificial Intelligence, Networking and Parallel/Distributed Computing* (Vol. 1, pp. 494–499). IEEE.

Joshi, M., Das, D., Gimpel, K., & Smith, N. A. (2010). *Movie reviews and revenues: An experiment in text regression. Proceedings of the North American Chapter of the Association for Computational Linguistics Human Language Technologies Conference (NAACL 2010).*

Jun-shan, T., Wei, H., & Yan, Q. (2009, March). Application of genetic algorithm in data mining. In *Education Technology and Computer Science, 2009. ETCS'09. First International Workshop on* (Vol. 2, pp. 353-356). IEEE. 10.1109/ETCS.2009.340

Kaisler, S., Armour, F., Espinosa, J. A., & Money, W. (2013, January). Big data: Issues and challenges moving forward. In *System Sciences (HICSS), 2013 46th Hawaii International Conference on* (pp. 995-1004). IEEE.

Kalra, V., & Agrawal, R. (2017). Importance of Text Data Preprocessing & its implementation using RapidMiner. Academic Press.

Karpov, A. V., Sysoev, A. A., Poteshin, S. S., Chernyshev, D. M., & Sysoev, A. A. (2015). Genetic algorithm for voltage optimization of gridless ion mirror. *Physics Procedia, 72*, 236–240. doi:10.1016/j.phpro.2015.09.070

Kasper, W., & Vela, M. (2011, October). Sentiment analysis for hotel reviews. In Computational linguistics-applications conference (Vol. 231527, pp. 45-52). Academic Press.

Kaur, N., & Budwal, J. S. (2014, May). Intelligent Web search optimization with reference to mutation operator of Genetic and Cultural Algorithms framework. In *Advanced Communication Control and Computing Technologies (ICACCCT), 2014 International Conference on* (pp. 619-623). IEEE. 10.1109/ICACCCT.2014.7019162

K-CAP. (2003, October 26). *Knowledge mark-up and Semantic Annotation workshop.* Retrieved from http://km.aifb.kit.edu/ws/semannot2003/

Keshtkar, F. (2011). *A Computational Approach to the Analysis and Generation of Emotion in Text* (Doctor of Philosophy). University of Ottawa, Canada.

Khairnar, J., & Kinikar, M. (2013). Machine Learning Algorithms for Opinion Mining and Sentiment Classification. *International Journal of Scientific and Research Publications, 3*(6). Retrieved from www.ijsrp.org

Khan, K., Baharudin, B., Khan, A., Ullah, A. (2014). Mining opinion from text documents with the help of Machine learning methods based on Opinion Mining (OM). *Journal of King Saud University-Computer and Information Sciences, 26*(3), 258-275.

Khan, L., McLeod, D., & Hovy, E. (2004). *Retrieval effectiveness of an ontology-based model for information selection. The VLDB Journal—The International Journal on Very Large Data Bases, 13(1),* 71–85.

Khobreh, Ansari, Fathi, Vas, Mol, Berkers, & Varga. (2013). *An Ontology-based Approach for the Semantic Representation of Job Knowledge.* Academic Press.

Kiritchenko, S., Zhu, X., & Mohammad, S. M. (2014). Sentiment analysis of short informal texts. *Journal of Artificial Intelligence Research, 50,* 723–762.

Kiwelekar, A. W., & Joshi, R. K. (2014). An ontological framework for architecture model integration. *4th International Workshop on Twin Peaks of Requirements and Architecture,* 24-27.

Knoblock, C., Lopresti, D., Roy, S., & Subramaniam, L. V. (2007). Special issue on noisy text analytics. *International Journal on Document Analysis and Recognition, 10*(3), 127–128. doi:10.100710032-007-0058-9

Kober, J., Bagnell, J. A., & Peters, J. (2013). Reinforcement learning in robotics: A survey. *The International Journal of Robotics Research, 32*(11), 1238–1274. doi:10.1177/0278364913495721

Köhler, J., Philippi, S., Specht, M., & Rüegg, A. (2006). Ontology based text indexing and querying for the semantic web. *Knowledge-Based Systems, 19*(8), 744–754. doi:10.1016/j.knosys.2006.04.015

Krizhevsky, A., & Hinton, G. E. (2011). *Using very deep auto encoders for content-based image retrieval.* 19th European Symposium on Artificial Neural Networks (ESANN'11), Bruges, Belgium.

Kshirsagar, A. A., & Deshkar, P. A. (2015). Review analyzer analysis of product reviews on WEKA classifiers. *International Conference on Innovations in Information, Embedded and Communication Systems (ICIIECS),* 1-5. 10.1109/ICIIECS.2015.7193034

Kuptabut, S., & Netisopakul, P. (2016). Event Extraction using Ontology Directed Semantic Grammar. *Journal of Information Science and Engineering, 32*(1), 79–96.

Kusumasari & Fitria. (2016). Data profiling for data quality improvement with OpenRefine. *International Conference on Information Technology Systems and Innovation (ICITSI),* 1-6. 10.1109/ICITSI.2016.7858197

Kweon, S. C., Sawng, Y. W., & Kim, S. H. (2006, May). An Integrated Approach Using Data Mining & Genetic Algorithm in Customer Credit Risk Prediction of Installment Purchase Financing. In *Collaborative Technologies and Systems, 2006. CTS 2006. International Symposium on* (pp. 125-131). IEEE.

Lacity, M. C., & Janson, M. A. (1994). Understanding qualitative data: A framework of text analysis methods. *Journal of Management Information Systems*, *11*(2), 137–155. doi:10.1080/07421222.1994.11518043

Lahl, D. (2011). Better Decisions by Analyzing Structured and Unstructured Data Together. *Business Intelligence Journal*, *16*(1), 9–1.

Lau, R. Y., Lai, C. C., Ma, J., & Li, Y. (2009). Automatic domain ontology extraction for context-sensitive opinion mining. *ICIS 2009 Proceedings*, 1-18.

Lau, R. Y., Li, C., & Liao, S. S. (2014). Social analytics: Learning fuzzy product ontologies for aspect-oriented sentiment analysis. *Decision Support Systems*, *65*, 80–94. doi:10.1016/j.dss.2014.05.005

Lazhar, F., & Yamina, T. G. (2012). Identification of Opinions in Arabic Texts using Ontologies. *J Inform Tech Soft Engg*, *2*(2), 1–4. doi:10.4172/2165-7866.1000108

Lenat, D. B., & Guha, R. V. (1989). *Building large knowledge-based systems; representation and inference in the Cyc project*. Academic Press.

Lexalytics. (n.d.). Received from https://www.lexalytics.com

LightSIDE. (n.d.). Retrieved from http://www.cs.cmu.edu/~cprose/LightSIDE.html

Li, J., & Jurafsky, D. (2015). Improving word representations via global context and multiple word prototypes. *Proceedings of the ACL*, 873– 882.

Lillicrap, T. P., Hunt, J. J., & Pritzel, A. (n.d.). *Continuous control with deep reinforcement learning*. Cornel University Library. Retrieved from https://arxiv.org/abs/1509.02971

Li, M., Du, X., & Wang, S. (2005, October). A semi-automatic ontology acquisition method for the semantic web. In *International Conference on Web-Age Information Management* (pp. 209-220). Springer. 10.1007/11563952_19

Lin, D., & Pantel, P. (2001, August). DIRT@ SBT@ discovery of inference rules from text. In *Proceedings of the seventh ACM SIGKDD international conference on Knowledge discovery and data mining* (pp. 323-328). ACM. 10.1145/502512.502559

Lindberg, C. (1990). The Unified Medical Language System (UMLS) of the National Library of Medicine. *Journal of the American Medical Record Association*, *61*(5), 40–42. PMID:10104531

Li, Q., Jina, Z., Can, W., & Zenga, D. D. (2016). Mining opinion summarizations using convolutional neural networks in Chinese microblogging systems. *Knowledge-Based Systems*, *107*, 289–300. doi:10.1016/j.knosys.2016.06.017

Li, S., Wang, Z., Lee, S. Y. M., & Huang, C. R. (2013). Sentiment Classification with Polarity Shifting Detection. *International Conference on Asian Language Processing (IALP)*, 129-132.

Liu, B. (2012). Sentiment analysis and opinion mining. *Synthesis Lectures on Human Language Technologies, 5*(1), 1-167.

Liu, C. H., Lee, C. S., Wang, M. H., Tseng, Y. Y., Kuo, Y. L., & Lin, Y. C. (2013). Apply fuzzy ontology and FML to knowledge extraction for university governance and management. *Journal of Ambient Intelligence and Humanized Computing, 4*(4), 493–513. doi:10.100712652-012-0139-6

Li, X., Dai, L., & Shi, H. (2010). Opinion mining of camera reviews based on semantic role labeling. *Proceedings of the Seventh International Conference on Fuzzy Systems and Knowledge Discovery*, 5, 2372–2375. 10.1109/FSKD.2010.5569525

Li, X., Martínez, J. F., & Rubio, G. (2016). A new fuzzy ontology development methodology (FODM) proposal. *IEEE Access: Practical Innovations, Open Solutions, 4*, 7111–7124. doi:10.1109/ACCESS.2016.2621756

López, M. F., Gómez-Pérez, A., Sierra, J. P., & Sierra, A. P. (1999). Building a chemical ontology using methontology and the ontology design environment. *IEEE Intelligent Systems & their Applications, 14*(1), 37–46. doi:10.1109/5254.747904

Lo, S. L., Cambria, E., Chiong, R., & Cornforth, D. (2017). Multilingual sentiment analysis: From formal to informal and scarce resource languages. *Artificial Intelligence Review, 48*(4), 499–527. doi:10.100710462-016-9508-4

Luo, N., Deng, H., Zhao, L., Liu, Y., Wang, X., & Tan, Z. (2017, July). Multi-aspect Feature based Neural Network Model in Detecting Fake Reviews. In *2017 4th International Conference on Information Science and Control Engineering (ICISCE)* (pp. 475-479). IEEE. 10.1109/ICISCE.2017.106

Ma, B., Zhang, D., Yan, Z., & Kim, T. (2013). An LDA and synonym lexicon based approach to product feature extraction from online consumer product reviews. *Journal of Electronic Commerce Research, 14*(4), 304–314.

Maedche, A. D. (2002). *Ontology learning for the semantic Web.* Kluwer Academic Publishers.

Maedche, A., & Staab, S. (2000). Mining ontologies from text. *Knowledge Engineering and Knowledge Management Methods, Models, and Tools,* 169-189.

Maedche, A., & Staab, S. (2000, August). The text-to-onto ontology learning environment. In *Software Demonstration at ICCS-2000-Eight International Conference on Conceptual Structures* (Vol. 38). Academic Press.

Maedche, A., Staab, S., Hovy, E., & Nedellec, C. (2001). The IJCAI-2001 Workshop on Ontology Learning. *Proceedings of the Second Workshop on Ontology Learning-OL'2001.*

Mahesh, K., & Nirenburg, S. (1996). Meaning representation for knowledge sharing in practical machine translation. *Proceedings of the FLAIRS Track on Information Interchange.*

Ma, J., Xu, W., Sun, Y. H., Turban, E., Wang, S., & Liu, O. (2012). An ontology-based text-mining method to cluster proposals for research project selection. *IEEE Transactions on Systems, Man, and Cybernetics. Part A, Systems and Humans, 42*(3), 784–790. doi:10.1109/TSMCA.2011.2172205

Malviya, N., Mishra, N., & Sahu, S. (2011). Developing University Ontology using protégé OWL Tool: Process and Reasoning. *International Journal of Scientific & Engineering Research, 2*(9), 1–8.

Marrero, M., Urbano, J., Sánchez-Cuadrado, S., Morato, J., & Gómez-Berbís, J. M. (2013). Named entity recognition: Fallacies, challenges and opportunities. *Computer Standards & Interfaces, 35*(5), 482–489. doi:10.1016/j.csi.2012.09.004

Maynard, D., Bontcheva, K., & Rout, D. (2012). Challenges in developing opinion mining tools for social media. *Proceedings of the @ NLP can u tag# user-generated content,* 15-22.

Maynard, D., Bontcheva, K., & Rout, D. (2012). Challenges in developing opinion mining tools for social media. *Proceedings of the @ NLP can u tag# usergeneratedcontent,* 15-22.

McCallum. (2002). *MALLET: A Machine Learning for Language Toolkit.* Retrieved from http://mallet.cs.umass.edu

McGlohon, M., Natalie, G., & Zach, R. (2010). Star quality: Aggregating reviews to rank products and merchants. *Proceedings of the International Conference on Weblogs and Social Media (ICWSM-2010).*

McGuinness, D. L., Fikes, R., Rice, J., & Wilder, S. (2000, April). *An environment for merging and testing large ontologies.* Academic Press.

Meersman, M. (2005). The use of lexicons and other computer-linguistic tools in semantics, design and cooperation of database systems. *Star Lab Technical Report.* Available at: http://www.starlab.vub.ac.be/website/files/STAR-1999-02_0.pdf

Mikolov, Chen, Corrado, & Dean. (2013). An information-theoretic definition of similarity. *Proceedings of ICML, 98,* 296–304.

Minanovic, A., Gabelica, H., & Krstić, Ž. (2014). Big data and sentiment analysis using KNIME: Online reviews vs. social media. *37th International Convention on Information and Communication Technology, Electronics and Microelectronics (MIPRO),* 1464-1468. 10.1109/MIPRO.2014.6859797

Mishra, N., & Jha, C. K. (2012). Classification of opinion mining techniques. *International Journal of Computers and Applications, 56*(13).

Mohammad, S., & Tony, Y. (2011). Tracking Sentiment in Mail: How Genders Differ on Emotional Axes. *Proceedings of the ACL Workshop on ACL 2011: Workshop on Computational Approaches to Subjectivity and Sentiment Analysis.*

Mohandas, N., & Nair, J. P. S. (2012). Domain Specific Sentence Level Mood Extraction from Malayalam Text. *International Conference on Advances in Computing and Communications (ICACC),* 78-81. 10.1109/ICACC.2012.16

Morinaga, S., Yamanishi, K., Tateishi, K., & Fukushima, T. (2002). Mining product reputations on the web. In Proceedings of the eighth ACM SIGKDD international conference on Knowledge discovery and data mining, Edmonton, Canada (pp. 341-349). ACM.

Moro, A., Raganato, A., & Navigli, R. (2014). Efficient estimation of word representations in vector space. *Workshop at International Conference on Learning Representations (ICLR), 1310–1318.*

Mukherjee, S., & Joshi, S. (2013). *Sentiment aggregation using conceptnet ontology.* Paper presented at the 6th International Joint Conference on Natural Language Processing.

Mukherjee, A., & Liu, B. (2012, August). Mining contentions from discussions and debates. In *Proceedings of the 18th ACM SIGKDD international conference on Knowledge discovery and data mining* (pp. 841-849). ACM.

Nasukawa, T., & Yi, J. (2003). *Sentiment analysis: Capturing favorability using natural language processing. Proceedings of the K-CAP-03, 2nd Intl. Conf. on Knowledge Capture.* 10.1145/945645.945658

Navigli, R. (2009). Entity linking meets word sense disambiguation: a unified approach. *ACM Computing Surveys, 41*(2), 10.

Navigli, R. (2009). Entity linking meets word sense disambiguation: A unified approach. *Transactions of the Association for Computational LinGUIstics, 2,* 231–244.

Navigli, R., & Velardi, P. (2004). Learning domain ontologies from document warehouses and dedicated web sites. *Computational Linguistics, 30*(2), 151–179. doi:10.1162/089120104323093276

Negash, S., & Gray, P. (2008). Business intelligence. In F. Burstein & C. Holsapple (Eds.), Handbook of decision support systems. Springer Link.

Netowl. (n.d). *Software package.* Retrieved from https://www.netowl.com/

Niu, J., & Issa, R. R. (2015). Developing taxonomy for the domain ontology of construction contractual semantics: A case study on the AIA A201 document. *Advanced Engineering Informatics, 29*(3), 472–482. doi:10.1016/j.aei.2015.03.009

Noy, N. F., & Musen, M. A. (1999, October). SMART: Automated support for ontology merging and alignment. *Proc. of the 12th Workshop on Knowledge Acquisition, Modelling, and Management (KAW'99).*

Noy, N. F., & Musen, M. A. (2000, August). Algorithm and tool for automated ontology merging and alignment. *Proceedings of the 17th National Conference on Artificial Intelligence (AAAI-00). Available as SMI technical report SMI-2000-0831.*

O'Connor, B., Balasubramanyan, R., Routledge, B. R., & Smith, N. A. (2010). From Tweets to Polls: Linking Text Sentiment to Public Opinion Time Series. *Proceedings of the International AAAI Conference on Weblogs and Social Media (ICWSM 2010).*

Ojokoh, B. A., & Kayode, O. (2012). A feature-opinion extraction approach to opinion mining. *Journal of Web Engineering, 11*(1), 51–63.

Ott, M., Choi, Y., Cardie, C., & Hancock, J. T. (2011, June). Finding deceptive opinion spam by any stretch of the imagination. In *Proceedings of the 49th Annual Meeting of the Association for Computational Linguistics: Human Language Technologies-Volume 1* (pp. 309-319). Association for Computational Linguistics.

Ozzie, R. E., Gates, W. H., III, Flake, G. W., Bergstraesser, T. F., Blinn, A. N., Brumme, C. W., . . . Glasser, D. S. (2011). *U.S. Patent No. 7,930,197*. Washington, DC: U.S. Patent and Trademark Office.

Padhy, N., Mishra, D., & Panigrahi, R. (2012). *The survey of data mining applications and feature scope.* arXiv preprint arXiv:1211.5723

Pang, B., & Lee, L. (2008). Opinion mining and sentiment analysis. *Foundations and Trends® in Information Retrieval, 2*(1–2), 1-135.

Pang, B., Lee, L., & Vaithyanathan, S. (2002). Thumbs up? Sentiment Classification Using Machine Learning Techniques. *Proceedings of the conference on Empirical Methods in Natural Language Processing (EMNLP)*, 79-86. 10.3115/1118693.1118704

Pang, B., & Lee, L. (2008). Opinion mining and sentiment analysis. *Foundations and Trends in Information Retrieval, 2*(1-2), 1–135. doi:10.1561/1500000011

Park, S., & Kang, J. (2012). Using rule ontology in repeated rule acquisition from similar web sites. *IEEE Transactions on Knowledge and Data Engineering, 24*(6), 1106–1119. doi:10.1109/TKDE.2011.72

Park, S., Kang, J., & Kim, W. (2007, June). A framework for ontology based rule acquisition from web documents. In *International Conference on Web Reasoning and Rule Systems* (pp. 229-238). Springer. 10.1007/978-3-540-72982-2_17

Park, S., & Lee, J. K. (2007). Rule identification using ontology while acquiring rules from Web pages. *International Journal of Human-Computer Studies, 65*(7), 659–673. doi:10.1016/j.ijhcs.2007.02.004

Pawlak, Z. (1982). Rough sets. *International Journal of Computer & Information Sciences, 11*(5), 341-356.

Pearl, J. (1984). *Heuristics: intelligent search strategies for computer problem solving.* Academic Press.

Penalver-Martinez, I., Garcia-Sanchez, F., Valencia-Garcia, R., Rodriguez-Garcia, M. A., Moreno, V., Fraga, A., & Sanchez-Cervantes, J. L. (2014). Feature-based opinion mining through ontologies. *Expert Systems with Applications, 41*(13), 5995-6008.

Peng, Y., Peng, C., Huang, J., & Huang, K. (2009). An Ontology-Driven Paradigm for Component Representation and Retrieval. *IEEE Ninth International Conference on Computer and Information Technology.* 10.1109/CIT.2009.26

Peng, Q., & Zhong, M. (2014). Detecting Spam Review through Sentiment Analysis. *JSW, 9*(8), 2065–2072. doi:10.4304/jsw.9.8.2065-2072

Pennebaker, J. W., Booth, R. J., Boyd, R. L., & Francis, M. E. (2015). Linguistic Inquiry and WorCount. LIWC2015, Austin, TX.

Pereira, Á. R., & Baeza-Yates, R. (2005, August). Applications of a web information mining model to data mining and information retrieval tasks. In *Database and Expert Systems Applications, 2005. Proceedings. Sixteenth International Workshop on* (pp. 1031-1035). IEEE.

Pham, H. T., Vu, T. T., Tran, M. V., & Ha, Q. T. (2011, December). A solution for grouping Vietnamese synonym feature words in product reviews. In *Services Computing Conference (APSCC), 2011 IEEE Asia-Pacific* (pp. 503-508). IEEE. 10.1109/APSCC.2011.48

Poria, S., Cambria, E., & Gelbukh, A. (2016). Aspect extraction for opinion mining with a deep convolutional neural network. *Knowledge-Based Systems, 108*, 42–49. doi:10.1016/j.knosys.2016.06.009

Prabowo, R., & Thelwall, M. (2009). Sentiment Analysis: A Combined Approach. *Journal of Informetrics, 3*(2), 143–157. doi:10.1016/j.joi.2009.01.003

Princeton University. (2010). *WordNet Software.* Retrieved February 1, 2016 from: http://wordnet.princeton.edu/wordnet/license/

Prusa, J. D., & Khoshgoftaar, T. M. (2017). Improving deep neural network design with new text data representations. *Big Data, 4*(1), 7. doi:10.118640537-017-0065-8

R language. (n.d.). Retrieved from https://www.r-project.org/about.html

R Studio. (n.d.). *Software package.* Retrieved from https://www.rstudio.com/

Rahmath, H. (2014). Opinion mining and sentiment analysis-challenges and applications. *International Journal of Application or Innovation in Engineering & Management, 3*(5).

Rajeev, P. V., & Rekha, V. S. (2016). Opinion Mining of User Reviews Using Machine Learning Techniques and Ranking of Products Based on Features. *Advances in Intelligent Systems and Computing., 39*(8), 78–85.

Razmerita, L. (2011). An ontology-based framework for modeling user behavior—A case study in knowledge management. *IEEE Transactions on Systems, Man, and Cybernetics. Part A, Systems and Humans, 41*(4), 772–783. doi:10.1109/TSMCA.2011.2132712

Remi, S., & Varghese, S. C. (2015). Domain Ontology Driven Fuzzy Semantic Information Retrieval. *Procedia Computer Science, 46*, 676–681. doi:10.1016/j.procs.2015.02.122

Reyes, A., Rosso, P., & Veale, T. (2013). A multidimensional approach for detecting irony in Twitter. *Language Resources and Evaluation, 47*(1), 239–268. doi:10.100710579-012-9196-x

Reynolds, D. (2004). *Jena 2 inference support.* Retrieved from http://jena. sourceforge. net/ inference/index. html

Rob Speer, L. F. (2016). *ConceptNet Database.* Retrieved February 1, 2016 from: http:// conceptnet5.media.mit.edu/

Roberts, C. W. (2000). A conceptual framework for quantitative text analysis. *Quality & Quantity, 34*(3), 259–274. doi:10.1023/A:1004780007748

Sadikov, E., Parameswaran, A., & Venetis, P. (2009). Blogs as predictors of movie success. *Proceedings of the Third International Conference on Weblogs and Social Media (ICWSM-2009).*

Sakunkoo, P., & Sakunkoo, N. (2009). Analysis of Social Influence in Online Book Reviews. *Proceedings of third International AAAI Conference on Weblogs and Social Media (ICWSM-2009).*

Samal, B., Behera, A. K., & Panda, M. (2017). Performance analysis of supervised machine learning techniques for sentiment analysis. *Third International Conference on Sensing, Signal Processing and Security (ICSSS)*, 128-133. 10.1109/SSPS.2017.8071579

Sanchez-Pi, N., Martí, L., & Garcia, A. C. B. (2016). Improving ontology-based text classification: An occupational health and security application. *Journal of Applied Logic, 17*, 48–58. doi:10.1016/j. jal.2015.09.008

Sarin, R. K., Sicherman, A., & Nair, K. (1978). Evaluating proposals using decision analysis. IEEE Transaction on Systems, Man, and Cybernetic, 8(2), 128-131.

Schmidhuber, J. (2015). Deep learning in neural networks: An overview. *Neural Networks, 61*, 85–117. doi:10.1016/j.neunet.2014.09.003 PMID:25462637

Schmidhuber, J. (2015). Deep Learning. *Scholarpedia, 10*(11), 32832. doi:10.4249cholarpedia.32832 PMID:25462637

Sentiment140. (n.d.). Retrieved from http://help.sentiment140.com/

Seth Grimes. (2010, February 8). *Text Analytics Opportunities and Challenges for 2010, BeyeNETWORK.* Retrieved from http://www.b-eye-network.com/view/12638

Shaefer, C. G. (1993). *U.S. Patent No. 5,255,345.* Washington, DC: U.S. Patent and Trademark Office.

Sharma, A., Gupta, S., Motlani, R., Bansal, P., Srivastava, M., Mamidi, R., & Sharma, D. M. (2016). *Shallow Parsing Pipeline for Hindi-English Code-Mixed Social Media Text.* arXiv preprint arXiv:1604.03136

Sharma, R., Nigam, S., & Jain, R. (2013). Supervised Opinion Mining Techniques: A Survey. *International Journal of Information and Computation Technology, 3*(8), 737–742.

Shehnepoor, S., Salehi, M., Farahbakhsh, R., & Crespi, N. (2017). NetSpam: A network-based spam detection framework for reviews in online social media. *IEEE Transactions on Information Forensics and Security, 12*(7), 1585–1595. doi:10.1109/TIFS.2017.2675361

Shein, K. P. P., & Nyunt, T. T. S. (2010). Sentiment Classification Based on Ontology and SVM Classifier. *Second International Conference on Communication Software and Networks (ICCSN '10),* 169-172. 10.1109/ICCSN.2010.35

Shi, L., & Setchi, R. (2012). User-oriented ontology-based clustering of stored memories. *Expert Systems with Applications, 39*(10), 9730–9742. doi:10.1016/j.eswa.2012.02.087

Shirani-Mehr, H. (2014). *Applications of deep learning to sentiment analysis of movie reviews. Technical report.* Stanford University.

Silva, F., & Girardi, R. (2014). An Approach to Join Ontologies and Their Reuse in the Con-struction of Application Ontologies. *2014 IEEE/WIC/ACM International Joint Conferences, 1,* 424-431.

Simpson, M. S., & Demner-Fushman, D. (2012). Biomedical text mining: A survey of recent progress. In Mining text data (pp. 465-517). Springer US.

Singh & Jain. (2014). *Information Retrieval (IR) through Semantic Web (SW): An Over-view.* Academic Press.

Singhal & Bhattacharyya. (2016). *Sentiment Analysis and Deep Learning: A Survey.* Dept. of Computer Science and Engineering Indian Institute of Technology, Powai Mumbai, Maharashtra, India.

Singh, M., Kumar, L., & Sinha, S. (2018). Model for Detecting Fake or Spam Reviews. In *ICT Based Innovations* (pp. 213–217). Singapore: Springer. doi:10.1007/978-981-10-6602-3_21

Sklyarov, V., Skliarova, I., Silva, J., Sudnitson, A., & Rjabov, A. (2015, May). Hardware accelerators for information retrieval and data mining. In *Information and Communication Technology Research (ICTRC), 2015 International Conference on* (pp. 202-205). IEEE.

Slimani, T. (2015). Ontology development: A comparing study on tools, languages and formal-isms. *Indian Journal of Science and Technology, 8*(24). doi:10.17485/ijst/2015/v8i1/54249

Song, H., Fan, Y., Liu, X., & Tao, D. (2011). Extracting product features from online reviews for sentimental analysis. *6th International Conference on Computer Sciences and Convergence Information Technology (ICCIT),* 745-750.

Staab, S., Maedche, A., Nedellec, C., & Wiemer-Hastings, P. (2000). ECAI'2000 Workshop on Ontology Learning. *Proceedings of the First Workshop on Ontology Learning-OL'2000.*

Stafylopatis, A., & Likas, A. (1992). Pictorial information retrieval using the random neural network. Software Engineering. *Transfer: European Review of Labour and Research, 18*(7), 590–600.

Stavrianou & Chauchat.(2008). *Opinion Mining Issues and Agreement Identification in Forum Texts.* Academic Press.

Stumme, G., & Maedche, A. (2001, August). FCA-Merge: Bottom-up merging of ontologies. *IJCAI (United States)*, *1*, 225–230.

Suárez-Figueroa, M. C., de Cea, G. A., Buil, C., Dellschaft, K., Fernández-López, M., Garcia, A., ... Villazon-Terrazas, B. (2008). NeOn methodology for building contextualized ontology networks. *NeOn Deliverable D*, *5*, 4–1.

Su, J. H., Yeh, H. H., Philip, S. Y., & Tseng, V. S. (2010). Music recommendation using content and context information mining. *IEEE Intelligent Systems*, *25*(1), 16–26. doi:10.1109/MIS.2010.23

Sukumaran, S., & Sureka, A. (2006). Integrating Structured and Unstructured Data Using Text Tagging and Annotation. *Business Intelligence Journal*, *11*(2), 8–16.

Sulthana, A. R., & Subburaj, R. (2016). An improvised ontology based K-means clustering approach for classification of customer reviews. *Indian Journal of Science and Technology*, *9*(15).

Sulthana, R., & Ramasamy, S. (2017). Context Based Classification of Reviews Using Association Rule Mining, Fuzzy Logics and Ontology. *Bulletin of Electrical Engineering and Informatics*, *6*(3), 250–255.

Sun, J., Long, C., Zhu X. & Huang M. (2009). Mining Reviews for Product Comparison and Recommendation. *Research Journal on Computer Science and Computer Engineering With Applications, 3*(9), 33- 409.

Sun, X. (2014). Structure regularization for structured prediction. In Advances in Neural Information Processing Systems (pp. 2402-2410). Academic Press.

Sun, S., Luo, C., & Chen, J. (2017). A review of natural language processing techniques for opinion mining systems. *Information Fusion*, *36*, 10–25. doi:10.1016/j.inffus.2016.10.004

Sureka, A. (2010). *U.S. Patent No. 7,801,836*. Washington, DC: U.S. Patent and Trademark Office.

Szpektor, I., Tanev, H., Dagan, I., & Coppola, B. (2004). Scaling web-based acquisition of entailment relations. *Proceedings of the 2004 Conference on Empirical Methods in Natural Language Processing*.

Takenouchi, H., & Tokumaru, M. (2015, September). Applying a hybrid IGA-SimE algorithm to a multimedia retrieval system. In *Awareness Science and Technology (iCAST), 2015 IEEE 7th International Conference on* (pp. 60-65). IEEE.

Tang, D., Qin, B., & Liu, T. (2015). Learning for sentiment analysis: Successful approaches and future challenges. *WIREs Data Mining Knowledge Discovery*, *5*, 292–303. doi:10.1002/widm.1171

Tated Aggarwal, C. C., & Zhai, C. (Eds.). (2012). *Mining text data*. Springer Science & Business Media. doi:10.1007/978-1-4614-3223-4

Tated, R. R., & Ghonge, M. M. (2015). A survey on text mining-techniques and application. *International Journal of Research in Advent Technology*, *1*, 380–385.

Thelwall, M., Buckley, K., Paltoglou, G., Cai, D., & Kappas, A. (2010). Sentiment strength detection in short informal text. *Journal of the American Society for Information Science and Technology*, *61*(12), 2544–2558. doi:10.1002/asi.21416

Thomas, E. H., & Galambos, N. (2004). What Satisfies Students? Mining Student-Opinion Data with Regression and Decision Tree Analysis. *Research in Higher Education*, *45*(3), 251–269. doi:10.1023/B:RIHE.0000019589.79439.6e

Tong, R. (2001). An Operational System for Detecting and Tracking Opinions in on-line discussion. *Proceedings of SIGR Workshop on operational Text Classification.*

Trappey, C. V., Wang, T. M., Hoang, S., & Trappey, A. J. (2013). Constructing a dental implant ontology for domain specific clustering and life span analysis. *Advanced Engineering Informatics*, *27*(3), 346–357. doi:10.1016/j.aei.2013.04.003

Tripadvisor. (2016). *Hotel reviews*. Retrieved January 1, 2016 from: https://www.tripadvisor.com/

Tumasjan, A., Sprenger, T. O., Sandner, P. G., & Welpe, I. (2010). Predicting elections with twitter: What 140 characters reveal about political sentiment. *Proceedings of the International Conference on Weblogs and Social Media (ICWSM-2010).*

Turney, P. (2002). Thumbs Up or Thumbs Down? Semantic Orientation Applied to Unsupervised Classification of Reviews. *Proceedings of the 40th Annual Meeting of the Association for Computational Linguistics (ACL)*, 417-424.

Turney, P. D. (2002). Thumbs up or thumbs down? Semantic orientation applied to unsupervised classification of reviews. In *Proceedings of the Association for Computational Linguistics (ACL)* (pp. 417–424).

Tweet. (n.d.). Retrieved from https://www.csc2.ncsu.edu/faculty/healey/tweet_viz/

Twitter. (n.d.). Retrieved from https://about.twitter.com/

Van Rees, R. (2003). Clarity in the usage of the terms ontology, taxonomy and classification. *CIB REPORT*, *284*(432), 1–8.

Velardi, P., Navigli, R., Cuchiarelli, A., & Neri, R. (2005). Evaluation of OntoLearn, a methodology for automatic learning of domain ontologies. *Ontology Learning from Text: Methods, evaluation and applications, 123*(92).

Verbert, K., Gašević, D., Jovanović, J., & Duval, E. (2005). Ontology-based learn-ing content repurposing. Special interest tracks and posters of the 14th international conference on World Wide Web, 1140-1141.

Vincent, P., Larochelle, H., Lajoie, I., & Manzagol, P. (2010). Stacked de noising auto encoders: Learning useful representations in adeep network with a local de noising criterion. *Journal of Machine Learning Research*, *11*, 3371–3408.

Volz, R., Oberle, D., Staab, S., & Motik, B. (2003, May). KAON SERVER-A Semantic Web Management System. *WWW (Alternate Paper Tracks)*.

Vyas, Y., Gella, S., Sharma, J., Bali, K., & Choudhury, M. (2014, October). *POS Tagging of English-Hindi Code-Mixed Social Media Content* (Vol. 14). EMNLP. doi:10.3115/v1/D14-1105

Web Scraper. (n.d.). *Software package*. Retrieved from http://webscraper.io/

Wen, B., Fan, P., Dai, W., & Ding, L. (2013). Research on analyzing sentiment of texts based on semantic comprehension. *3rd International Conference on Consumer Electronics, Communications and Networks*, 529-532. 10.1109/CECNet.2013.6703386

Weng, S. S., Tsai, H. J., Liu, S. C., & Hsu, C. H. (2006). Ontology construction for information classification. *Expert Systems with Applications*, *31*(1), 1–12. doi:10.1016/j.eswa.2005.09.007

Wenyun, L., & Lingyun, B. (2010). Application of Web Mining in E-Commerce Enterprises Knowledge Management. *International Conference on E-Business and E-Government*, 1769-1772. 10.1109/ICEE.2010.447

Wiebe, J. (1990). Identifying subjective characters in narrative. *Proceedings of the International Conference on Computational Linguistics (COLING-1990)*.

Wiebe, J. (1994). Tracking point of view in narrative. *Computational Linguistics*, *20*, 233–287.

Wiebe, J. (2000). Learning subjective adjectives from corpora. In *Proceedings of National Conf. on Artificial Intelligence* (pp. 735-740). AAAI Press.

Wiebe, J., Rebecca, F. B., & Thomas, P. O. (1999). Development and use of a gold-standard data set for subjectivity classifications. *Proceedings of the Association for Computational Linguistics (ACL-1999)*. 10.3115/1034678.1034721

Wilson, T., Hoffmann, P., Somasundaran, S., Kessler, J., Wiebe, J., Choi, Y., . . . Patwardhan, S. (2005, October). OpinionFinder: A system for subjectivity analysis. In Proceedings of hlt/emnlp on interactive demonstrations (pp. 34-35). Association for Computational Linguistics.

Wimalasuriya, D. C., & Dou, D. (2010). Components for information extraction: ontology-based information extractors and generic platforms. *19th ACM international conference on Information and knowledge management*, 9-18. 10.1145/1871437.1871444

Witten, I. H., & Frank, E. (2005). *Data mining: Practical machine learning tools and techniques*. San Francisco: Morgan Kaufmann.

Wives, L. K., & Loh, S. (1998, September). Hyperdictionary: a knowledge discovery tool to help information retrieval. In *String Processing and Information Retrieval: A South American Symposium, 1998. Proceedings* (pp. 103-109). IEEE.

Xia, F., Wang, W., Bekele, T. M., & Liu, H. (2017). Big scholarly data: A survey. *IEEE Transactions on Big Data*, *3*(1), 18–35. doi:10.1109/TBDATA.2016.2641460

Yaakub, Li, & Feng. (2011). Integration of Opinion into Customer Analysis Model. *Proceedings of Eighth IEEE International Conference on e-Business Engineering,* 90-95.

Yaakub, M.R., Li, Y., & Zhang, Y. (2013). *Integration of Sentiment Analysis into Customer Relational Model: The Importance of Feature Ontology and Synonym.* Academic Press.

Yadav, U. (2016). Development and Visual-ization of Domain Specific Ontology using Protégé. *Indian Journal of Science and Technology, 9*(16). doi:10.17485/ijst/2016/v9i16/88524

Yaguinuma, Marilde, & Vieira. (2005). Ontology-based meta-model for storage and retrieval of software components. *31st VLDB Conference.*

Yamaguchi, T. (2001, August). Acquiring Conceptual Relationships from Domain-Specific Texts. In *Workshop on Ontology Learning (Vol. 38,* pp. 69-113). Academic Press.

Yang, C. C., & Wong, Y. C. (2008, May). Mining Consumer Opinions from the Web. In WEBSITE (2) (pp. 187-192). Academic Press.

Yang, J., & Hou, M. (2010). Using Topic Sentiment Sentences to Recognize Sentiment Polarity in Chinese Reviews. *CIPS-SIGHAN Joint Conference on Chinese Language Processing.*

Yao, J. T., & Yao, Y. Y. (2003, October). Web-based information retrieval support systems: building research tools for scientists in the new information age. In *Web Intelligence, 2003. WI 2003. Proceedings. IEEE/WIC International Conference on* (pp. 570-573). IEEE.

Younga, T., Hazarikab, D., Poriac, S., & Cambria, E. (2016). *Recent Trends in Deep Learning Based Natural Language Processing.* Retrieved from https://arxiv.org/pdf/1708.02709.pdf

Yue, L., Zuo, W., Peng, T., Wang, Y., & Han, X. (2015). A fuzzy document clustering approach based on domain-specified ontology. *Data & Knowledge Engineering, 100,* 148–166. doi:10.1016/j.datak.2015.04.008

Záková, M., Kremen, P., Zelezny, F., & Lavrac, N. (2011). Automating knowledge discovery workflow composition through ontology-based planning. *IEEE Transactions on Automation Science and Engineering, 8*(2), 253–264. doi:10.1109/TASE.2010.2070838

Zanjani, M., Dastjerdi, A. B., Asgarian, E., Shahriyari, A., & Kharazian, A. A. (2015). Short Paper_. *Journal of Information Science and Engineering, 31,* 315–330.

Zhai, Z., Liu, B., Xu, H., & Jia, P. (2010, August). Grouping product features using semi-supervised learning with soft-constraints. In *Proceedings of the 23rd International Conference on Computational Linguistics* (pp. 1272-1280). Association for Computational Linguistics.

Zhang, L., & Liu, B. (2011, June). Identifying noun product features that imply opinions. In *Proceedings of the 49th Annual Meeting of the Association for Computational Linguistics: Human Language Technologies: short papers-Volume 2* (pp. 575-580). Association for Computational Linguistics.

Zhang, W., Yoshida, T., & Tang, X. (2008). Text classification based on multi-word with support vector machine. *Knowledge-Based Systems*, *21*(8), 879–886. doi:10.1016/j.knosys.2008.03.044

Zhao, W. X., Jing, J., Hongfei, Y., & Xiaoming, L. (2010). Jointly modeling aspects and opinions with a MaxEnt-LDA hybrid. *Proceedings of Conference on Empirical Methods in Natural Language Processing*, 56-65.

Zhou, L., & Chaovali, P. (2008). Ontology-Supported Polarity Mining. *Journal of the American Society for Information Science and Technology*, *59*(1), 98–110. doi:10.1002/asi.20735

Zhuang, L., Jing, F., & Zhu, X.-Y. (2006). Movie review mining and summarization. *Proc. CIKM Conf.*, 43–50.

Zou, Y., Finin, T., & Chen, H. (2004, April). F-owl: An inference engine for semantic web. In *International Workshop on Formal Approaches to Agent-Based Systems* (pp. 238-248). Springer. 10.1007/978-3-540-30960-4_16

About the Contributors

Neha Gupta is currently working as an Associate professor, Faculty of Computer Applications at Manav Rachna International Institute of Research and Studies, Faridabad campus. She has completed her PhD from Manav Rachna International University and has done R&D Project in CDAC-Noida. She has total of 12+ year of experience in teaching and research. She is a Life Member of ACM CSTA, Tech Republic and Professional Member of IEEE. She has authored and coauthored 30 research papers in SCI/SCOPUS/Peer Reviewed Journals (Scopus indexed) and IEEE/IET Conference proceedings in areas of Web Content Mining, Mobile Computing, and Web Content Adaptation. She is a technical programme committee (TPC) member in various conferences across globe. She is an active reviewer for International Journal of Computer and Information Technology and in various IEEE Conferences around the world. She is one of the Editorial and review board members in International Journal of Research in Engineering and Technology.

* * *

Parul Agarwal is working as Assistant Professor in Jamia Hamdard since 2002. Her area of specialization include Fuzzy Data Mining, Cloud Computing, Sustainable Development and Soft Computing. She has published several papers in Springer and Scopus indexed journals. She is a member of Technical programme Committee of IEEE sponsored and Elsevier Indexed Conferences and has also chaired several sessions of several reputed International Conferences. Member of several committees at university level and is also a member of ISTE.

Morteza Amirhosseini is currently a PhD student in IT management, Faculty of management at Allame Tabab'e University, Tehran, IRAN. He has completed his Master from Shiraz University in Artificial intelligence and has done several projects in data science. He has total of 10+ year of experience in teaching and research in university of applied science and technology (UAST) in Tehran, IRAN. He has been working as a project manager for over 15 years in business intelligence, data warehousing and data mining. He has some research in machine learning and deep learning issues.

Mridula Batra is currently working as an Assistant professor, Faculty of Computer Applications at Manav Rachna International Institute of Research and Studies, Faridabad campus. She has completed her Masters in Computer Applications from Maharishi Dayanand University, Rohtak. She has total of 12+ year of experience in teaching and research. She has authored and coauthored 4 research papers in various National and International Journals.

Rajesh Kumar Bawa is working as Professor in the department of Computer Science, Punjabi University Patiala. His areas of expertise are Parallel Scientific Computing and Digital Image Processing. He has guided many M.Tech and PhD students. He has published more than 70+ papers in reputed international journals.

Nguyen Cuong obtained his doctorate in Computer Science / Resource Allocation Cloud Computing in 2017 from the University of Da Nang. He has published over 30 research papers. His main research interests include the resource allocation, detection, prevention, and avoidance of cloud computing and distributed systems. He serves as a technical committee program member, track chair, session chair and reviewer of many international conferences and journals. He is a guest editor journal "International Journal of Information Technology Project Management (IJITPM)" with Special Issue On: Recent Works on Management and Technological Advancement.

Chitra Jalota is currently working as an Assistant professor, Faculty of Computer Applications at Manav Rachna International Institute of Research and Studies, Faridabad campus. She has completed her Masters in Computer Applications from Maharishi Dayanand University, Rohtak. She has total of 12+ year of experience in teaching and research. She has authored and coauthored 6 research papers in various National and International Journals.

Simran Jolly is working as an assistant professor at Faculty of Computer Applications, Manav Rachna International Institute of Research and Studies, Faridabad. She has done her M.Tech From CITM, Faridabad. Her research interest lies in the area of natural language processing (NLP) where she has worked on statistical approaches and computational models to extract semantic information from text. Currently she is pursuing PhD from MRIIRS.

Iqbaldeep Kaur is a research student pursuing PhD at Punjabi University, Patiala. She has worked as a professional teacher for Fifteen years. She is a researcher dedicated to serve community and society at large. She has to her credit a number of publications in reputed international journals, twenty five patents and five copyrights.

Joan Lu is Professor in the Department of Computing Science and is the research group leader of Information and System Engineering (ISE) in the Centre of High Intelligent Computing (CHIC). Her extensive research covers XML technology, data mining, information retrieval/extraction and visualization, mobile learning, technology enhanced learning. She was an invited speaker for XML World, an industrial event to present XML and ontology in science and technology in USA, 2003. She has published seven academic books and more than 200 peer reviewed academic papers. Professor Lu has acted as the founder and a program chair for the International XML Technology Workshop for 11 years and serves as Chair of various international conferences. She is the founder and Editor in Chief of International Journal of Information Retrieval Research and served as a BCS examiner of Database and Advanced Database Management Systems. She has been the UOH principle investigator for four recent EU interdisciplinary (computer science, engineering, Law and psychology) projects.

Sunil M. E. is currently working as an Assistant Professor, Faculty of Computer Science and Engineering at PES Institute of Technology and Management, Shivamogga, Karnataka. He is perusing PhD under the Guidance of Dr. Vinay S at PES College of Engineering, Mandya. He has total of 5+ year of experience in teaching. He is a Life Member of ISTE, ISRD. His research area includes Data Mining, Sentimental Analysis, and Big Data. He has published papers in peer reviewed journals.

Iman Raeesi Vanani is a PhD Graduate in Systems Management, School of Management, University of Tehran. He is currently an assistant professor in Allameh Tabataba'i University. He received his MSc in Information Technology Management from School of Management, University of Tehran and his BA in Public Administration from Allameh Tabataba'i University. His research interests include Data Science, Advanced Analytics, Business Intelligence, Data Mining, Enterprise Resource Planning, and Big Data Management. He has published many conceptual and practical research papers in various international journals, conference proceedings, and books including International Journal of Hospitality Management, Neural Computing and Applications, The IUP Journal of Knowledge Management, Intelligent Engineering Informatics, Iranian Management Vision Journal, Iranian Journal of Science and Technology Policy, Journal of Information Technology and Sciences, Information Science Reference Publications, and other international and Iranian journals, Books and conferences.

Subburaj Ramasamy is currently Professor and Consultant in the Department of Information Technology, School of Computing, SRM University, Kattankulathur, TamilNadu, India - 603203. His specialization areas include Software Engineering / Testing / Reliability, Programming Languages, Machine Learning & Big Data Analytics. He is Author of 7 books and 57 papers published in International/National Journals and presented in International Conferences. He served as Senior Director and Head of the Government of India Institutions under Ministry of Electronics and Information Technology/STQC for 19 years.

Vishaw Rathee is currently working as an Assistant professor, Faculty of Computer Applications at Manav Rachna International Institute of Research and Studies, Faridabad campus. She has completed her Masters in Computer Applications from Maharishi Dayanand University, Rohtak. She has total of 16+ year of experience in teaching and research. She has authored and coauthored 6 research papers in various National and International Journals.

Vinay S. is currently working as Professor in the Department of Computer Science and Engineering at PES College of Engineering, Mandya, Karnataka. He completed his Ph.D from Manipal University in the area of Decision Support System in Requirements Engineering. He has 15+ years of experience in teaching. He has authored and co-authored 30 papers in various journals, IEEE and Springer conferences. His current research area includes Machine Learning, Internet of Things and Big Data Analytics. He has received grants from Nokia to set up Mobile Innovation lab and received Certificate of Appreciation from Nokia University relations. He is also convener of PES College of Engineering Business Incubator approved by Ministry of Micro, Small and Medium Enterprises (MSME), Government of India.

Ashish Seth is a Consultant, Researcher and Teacher. He is presently working as an Associate Professor in the Department of Computer Science & Engineering, INHA University Tashkent. He has more than 15 years of research and teaching experience and worked at various universities in India and abroad holding different positions and responsibilities. He has organized and participated very actively in various conferences, workshops and seminars. He has published research papers in journals like ACM, ISTE, WSEAS, Inderscience, IEEE, Springer, etc. and also authored 2 Books and several book Chapters. He is an active member of International societies like IEEE, CSI, IACSIT, IAENG, etc. He holds Technical Review committee and Editorial Review Board for many International Journal of Computer Science and Information Technology. His youtube channel provides many video lectures on various areas of computer science. His online forum provides guidance to student on various subjects and helps them to discuss their problems. He is the recipient of many awards including Best Faculty Award, Young Researcher Award-Computer Science, Most Promising Educationist Award. He finds interest in reading and writing articles on emerging technologies.

Dolly Sharma graduated in Computer Science & Engineering from Kurukshetra University in 2004 and received Masters in Information Technology with honours from Panjab University, Chandigarh in 2007. She was the second University topper. She is pursuing PhD from PEC University of Technology, Chandigarh. She is currently working as Associate Professor in Department of Computer Science in Chandigarh Group of Colleges, Landran, Mohali. Her area of interests includes Bioinformatics, Grid Computing and Data Mining. She has published a number of research papers and chapters indexed in SCI and SCOPUS. She has a rich teaching experience of around 14+ years. She has contributed as a reviewer in important conferences and Journals. She is a member of ISTE and AIENG.

Farheen Siddiqui is currently Assistant Professor in Department of Computer Science, Jamia Hamdard, New Delhi. She has teaching computer science since 15 years. She has been involved in developing the course content for several courses related to programming language. Her professional interest includes application of ontology in software engineering and cloud computing. She has contributed several research papers to various national and international conferences and journals and is reviewer of several international journals. She has published over 25 research papers in various international journals.

Inderjeet Singh is associated with Chandigarh Group of Colleges since two years. He is a Research Scholar in Computer Science Department. His area of Research is Data Mining. He has published a number of research papers in this area.

Vijender Kumar Solanki, Ph.D., is an Associate Professor in the department of Computer Science & Engineering, CMR Institute of Technology (Autonomous), Hyderabad, TS, India. He has more than 10 years of academic experience in network security, IoT, Big Data, Smart City and IT. He has authored or co-authored more than 25 research articles that are published in journals, books and conference proceedings. He has edited or co-edited 4 books in the area of Information Technology. He teaches graduate & post graduate level courses. He received Ph.D in Computer Science and Engineering from Anna University, Chennai, India. He is Editor in International Journal of Machine Learning and Networked Collaborative Engineering (IJMLNCE) ISSN 2581-3242, Associate Editor in International Journal of Information Retrieval Research (IJIRR), IGI-GLOBAL, USA, ISSN: 2155-6377 I E-ISSN: 2155-6385 . He is guest editor with IGI-Global, USA, InderScience & Many more publishers. He can be contacted at spesinfo@yahoo.com .

Razia Sulthana Sulthana is currently working as assistant professor in School of Computing, SRM Institute of Science and Technology, Kattankulathur, TamilNadu, India - 603203. She has done her Masters and Bachelor's degree under Anna University. Her current area of interest is machine learning, big data analytics, recommender systems and ontology. She has published notable papers in indexed journals in the above areas. She was adjudged as first rank in Anna University in her Masters course in M.Tech, Computer Science.

Kirti Tyagi is presently working as an Associate Professor in School of Computer and Information Engineering, INHA University, Tashkent. She is PhD (Computer Science and Engineering) in the area of "Component Based Systems" from Department of Computer Sciences and Engineering, Dr. APJ Abdul Kalam Technical University, Lucknow (Uttar Pradesh), India in 2016. M.Tech (Computer Science), from Banasthali Vidyapeeth, Banasthali, Rajasthan, India, 2009. She also holds MSc (CS) degree and has been into research and academics for last fourteen years. She has published more than 40 research papers in reputed journals like ACM, Springer and Elsevier and authored four books. She is a member of Technical Review Committee for IJCSI, Malaysia. Computing Reviews, ACM, Columbus, ESASD, JCT, USA. She has been participating and organizing seminar, conferences, workshops, expert lecturers and technical events to share knowledge among academicians, researchers and to promote opportunities for new researchers.

Uma V. received the M.Tech, and PhD degrees in computer science from Pondicherry University in 2007 and 2014 respectively. She was awarded the Pondicherry University gold medal for M.Tech. degree in Distributed Computing Systems. She has more than 10 years of teaching experience at PG level. Her research interest includes Data mining, knowledge representation and reasoning (spatial and temporal knowledge) and sentiment analysis. She has authored and co-authored more than 20 peer-reviewed journal papers, which includes publications in Springer, Elsevier and Inderscience. She received the Best Paper Award in International Conference on Digital Factory in the year 2008. She has authored a book on Knowledge Representation and Reasoning and has written 3 chapters.

Amit Verma is a young and innovative academician and researcher. He is presently working as Professor and Head Computer Science Engineering Dept at Chandigarh Engineering College, Landran (Mohali)Punjab Dr. Verma has graduated from Kurukshetra University, Kurukshetra, Haryana. He has done doctorate degree in the field of Image Processing. He has a decade long experience of teaching with two years of experience in Industry as well. He has got the exposure of working with a telecommunication industry at Canada also. He has guided around 60 students for their M.Tech and two Phd Students. Thesis. He has been attending various national and international conferences as chairperson. He has always been actively involved in research and development. He has to his credit around 100+ research papers with a number of research publications in coveted and referred journals. He also has filed 30 patents and six copyrights. He is a reviewer of various research journals. His expertise and areas of interest are Image processing, Simulation and modeling, face detection and recognition and Biometric security.

Siddharth Verma is working as Assistant Professor at Faculty of Computer Applications, Manav Rachna International Institute of Research and Studies, Faridabad. He has total of 8 years of experience and is working on various real time projects.

Vishal Vyas is a PhD research scholar in the department of computer science at Pondicherry University. He completed his Masters in IT from Central university of Himachal Pradesh in 2015. He has 2 year of Industry experience. His research interests lie in natural language processing, Deep learning, Sentiment analysis etc. His work has primarily been on innovative sentiment analysis approaches. He has authored papers in SCOPUS/Peer reviewed journals and book chapters contributed to edited volumes published by International Publishers in the area of natural language processing.

Index

A

ambiguous 97-98, 165, 265
Applications of Opinion Mining 33, 36, 100

C

clustering 33, 68, 149, 154, 156, 159, 163-164, 170, 182, 192, 268-269, 287, 293, 300
CNN 45, 52-53, 57-59, 62
collocation 183-184, 232, 247-248
ConceptNet 91-96, 123, 125, 128, 131, 134, 137, 141, 144
context free grammar 253, 263
corpus 84, 93, 133, 139, 157, 186, 206-207, 232, 240, 242, 248, 253, 257, 265, 269, 283-284, 292

D

database 15, 21, 27, 33-34, 73, 93, 108, 126, 128, 134, 141, 155, 193, 299-301, 305, 307-308
datasets 52, 58-59, 86, 129, 140, 144, 193-194, 203
Decision Tree 66-67, 73-74, 129, 140
deep learning 40-41, 44-47, 49-62, 193, 265
disambiguation 93, 253-254, 269, 272, 288

F

feature based opinion mining 20-23, 25-28, 31, 37, 89, 91, 128
feature extraction 23, 33, 37, 43, 45, 52, 86, 125, 133, 210, 261, 288

G

genetic algorithm 299-301, 303-304, 306-308

I

information extraction 86, 99, 123, 131, 265, 271, 300
information retrieval 34, 55, 139, 162-163, 167, 182, 299-300, 306-307
issues 34, 47, 79, 124, 132, 149, 154, 156, 169, 269, 283-290, 293-294

K

knowledge base 92, 95

L

learning algorithms 40-41, 44, 46-47, 50, 52-53, 61, 86, 192-193, 279
lexical analysis 271-272, 274

M

machine learning 40-47, 50, 52, 60-61, 66-68, 72-74, 76-77, 79-80, 85-86, 129-130, 139, 149-150, 163-164, 166-167, 169, 182, 192-193, 206, 210, 271, 279, 287, 289, 293

N

natural language 9, 14, 33, 41, 43, 46, 50, 52-54, 60, 62, 85, 91, 93, 99-101, 125, 164, 182, 206-207, 210, 232, 239, 242, 254, 257, 260, 265, 269, 271, 283-285
natural language processing 14, 33, 41, 43, 46, 50, 52-54, 62, 85, 93, 99-101, 125, 207, 239, 242, 265, 269, 271, 283-284
neural networks 42, 45-53, 57, 62, 69, 206
NLP 41, 43, 52-54, 60, 68, 182, 207, 233, 239, 242, 253-254, 265, 270-271, 274, 283-285, 288-290, 293
NLTK 182-184, 186-187, 192, 203, 210, 232-233, 240-241, 244, 254-255, 257, 260, 263, 265

O

ontologies 85, 89-91, 94-95, 104-106, 108-109, 111, 113, 116, 125, 131, 151-152, 157, 159, 162-163
ontology 84-85, 89-91, 94-96, 104-109, 111-112, 116-120, 123, 125-128, 131-144, 149-157, 159-161, 163-167, 169-170, 206, 208
ontology learning 154, 156-157, 159, 163, 170
ontology tools 111, 156, 163

P

parser 136, 251, 264, 273
parsing 33, 50, 97, 182, 232, 251-253, 273, 288

polarity 21, 25, 37, 58-59, 62, 84, 86, 88, 91, 93, 97-99, 127-128, 131-133, 137-138, 143-144, 189, 206, 278, 292-293
Python 76, 91, 93, 182, 184-185, 210, 232-235, 237, 239-241, 255

R

RNN 45-48, 52-53, 62
rule mining 149, 159

S

semantic 15, 50, 52-53, 58-60, 86, 89, 91, 93-95, 105-109, 116-117, 120, 127, 130-131, 150, 152, 155-156, 162, 164, 169, 179, 182, 257, 260, 265, 269-271, 273-274
semantic analysis 179, 269, 271, 273-274
semantic web 105-106, 108, 117, 120, 150, 152, 155-156, 162, 169
sentiment 1-3, 6-7, 13-14, 21-22, 34, 36, 41, 52-53, 58-60, 66-67, 84-89, 91, 96-101, 124-126, 150, 166, 179-180, 182, 189, 192, 194, 203-208, 210, 224, 271, 278, 280, 283-286, 291, 293
sentiment analysis 1-3, 7, 13-14, 21-22, 34, 36, 41, 52-53, 58-60, 66-67, 84-89, 91, 98-101, 124-126, 150, 166, 179, 182, 189, 203, 271, 278, 280, 283, 286, 291, 293
social media 1, 3, 6-7, 11, 124-125, 166, 204, 207, 228, 270, 285, 287, 290, 292-294
stemming 123, 125, 127, 144, 182-183, 209, 245-246, 260-261
subjective reviews 37
supervised learning 2, 45-47, 50, 52, 61, 165
Support Vector Machines 45, 51, 69, 74, 77-78, 165
syntactic analysis 264, 271-272, 274

T

tagging 41, 52-53, 127, 182, 187, 192, 209, 232, 265, 272, 274
task of opinion mining 3-4, 14, 31
text mining 33-34, 36, 46, 52-53, 56, 87-88, 91, 109, 164, 207, 254, 269, 275, 283-285, 290
tokenization 125, 182, 209, 244, 265, 270
tools of opinion mining 179, 182

U

unambiguous 97-98
unsupervised learning 2, 46, 48, 50, 60-61

V

visualize 269

W

web service description language 108
WEKA 182, 192-194, 203, 212-213, 216
WordNet 15, 93-94, 128-129, 131, 134, 144, 182, 274

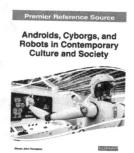

Ensure Quality Research is Introduced to the Academic Community

Become an IGI Global Reviewer for Authored Book Projects

Premier Reference Source
Emerging GIS Applications for Emergency and Disaster Management

Premier Reference Source
Managerial Strategies and Green Solutions for Project Sustainability

Premier Reference Source
Comparative Approaches to Using R and Python for Statistical Data Analysis

Premier Reference Source
Solutions for High-Touch Communications in a High-Tech World

The overall success of an authored book project is dependent on quality and timely reviews.

In this competitive age of scholarly publishing, constructive and timely feedback significantly expedites the turnaround time of manuscripts from submission to acceptance, allowing the publication and discovery of forward-thinking research at a much more expeditious rate. Several IGI Global authored book projects are currently seeking highly qualified experts in the field to fill vacancies on their respective editorial review boards:

Applications may be sent to:
development@igi-global.com

Applicants must have a doctorate (or an equivalent degree) as well as publishing and reviewing experience. Reviewers are asked to write reviews in a timely, collegial, and constructive manner. All reviewers will begin their role on an ad-hoc basis for a period of one year, and upon successful completion of this term can be considered for full editorial review board status, with the potential for a subsequent promotion to Associate Editor.

If you have a colleague that may be interested in this opportunity, we encourage you to share this information with them.

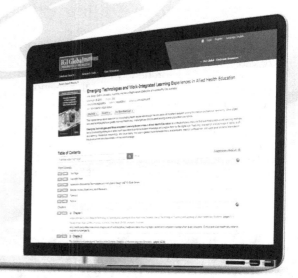